ONE DAY IN HISTORY

The Days That Changed the World

SEPTEMBER 11, 2001

ONE DAY IN HISTORY

The Days That Changed the World

REMEMBER NOT THE HORROR BUT THE HEROISM

SEPTEMBER 11, 2001

Rodney P. Carlisle, Ph.D., General Editor

Collins

An Imprint of HarperCollinsPublishers

ONE DAY IN HISTORY: SEPTEMBER 11, 2001. Copyright © 2007 by HarperCollins Publishers. All rights reserved. Printed in China. No part of this book may be used or reproduced in any manner whatsoever without written permission except in the case of brief quotations embodied in critical articles and reviews. For information, address HarperCollins Publishers, 10 East 53rd Street , New York , NY 10022.

HarperCollins books may be purchased for educational, business, or sales promotional use. For information please write: Special Markets Department, HarperCollins Publishers, 10 East 53rd Street , New York , NY 10022 .

FIRST EDITION

Library of Congress Cataloging-in-Publication Data is available upon request.

ISBN: 978-0-06-112038-1
ISBN-10: 0-06-112038-3

07 08 09 10 11 TP 9 8 7 6 5 4 3 2 1

Golson Books, Ltd.

President and Editor	J. Geoffrey Golson
General Editor	Rodney P. Carlisle
Creative Director	Mary Jo Scibetta
Managing Editor, Authors	Susan Moskowitz
Copy Editors	Barbara Paris, Kenneth Heller, Linda Angér
Proofreader	Janelle Schiecke
Indexer	J S Editorial, LLC

Photo Credits

©Loretta Carlisle Photography: Pages ii-iii, iv left, 210 top right; ©Gabrielsen Photography: Pages 44 top right, 128, 204, 217; ©Wernher Krutein/Photo-vault.com: Page 13; ©Mary Jo Scibetta: Page 148 center; ©Steve Spak/911 Pictures: Page 170; ©United in Memory™ Inc., The 9/11 Victims Memorial Quilt™: Pages 21, 26, 27, 83, 144, 158, 160; Getty Images: Pages 3, 5, 6 left, 12, 16, 18, 25, 29, 44 top left, 46, 56, 61, 68, 76, 78, 81, 84, 97, 102, 104, 119, 120, 125 top left, 133, 166, 168, 171, 174, 179, 192, 206, 208, 221, 222, 232; Associated Press Photos: Pages 10, 109, 125 top left and lower right, 201; U.S. Navy Photos: Pages xii center, 15, 35, 37, 48, 50, 58, 60, 63 left, top right, 72, 74, 90, 110, 134, 157, 181; U.S. Air Force Photos: Pages ii, xiii. 39, 43, 112, 127, 165, 165; U.S. Coast Guard Photos: Pages xii left, 6, 38, 44 lower right, 63 top right, 129 left; U.S. Army Photos: Pages 130, 177, 212; Department of Defense Photos: Pages v left, 30, 31, 40, 42, 64, 93, 149 left, 151, 152, 176, 180, 181 right, 198, 214; Defense Intelligence Agency Photos: Pages 99, 100; National Commission on Terrorist Attacks Upon the United States Photo: Page 137; NATO Photo: Page 139; Federal Bureau of Investigation: Page 94, NASA Photo: Page 162; U.S. Dept. of Justice Evidence: Pages 23, 107, 131, 182–191, 194, 197; American Red Cross Photos: Pages 53, 148 center; Library of Congress: Pages 9, 24, 34, 71, 73, 82, 86, 114 (photo by David Finn), 140 (photo by Don Halasy), 143, 203 (photos by Don Halasy), 210 left; Silverstein Properties Inc./dbox: Pages xiii, 66 courtesy of the Lower Manhattan Development Corp., 223, 225, 226; ©Flickr.com: Pages v right, 101, 196; ©Morguefile.com/ Christy Nyberg: Page 130; ©iStock International: Pages xvi, 2, 20, 32, 54, 123, 146, 148 left, 149 right, 210 lower right, 215, 229, 230, 234; National Archives and Records Administration: Page 228.

CONTENTS

Articles are presented in alphabetical order. Cross-references to other articles are in SMALL CAPS within the text.

PREFACE

BY ALAN BRINKLEY

As of this writing, it has been slightly over five years since the attacks on New York City and the Pentagon of September 11, 2001—the first foreign attacks on U.S. soil since the Japanese bombing of Pearl Harbor in 1941. In many ways, both America and the world are already significantly different as a result of that day. Many people now refer to events in their own lives, and in those of others, as occurring "before" or "after" September 11, as if to mark a turning point not only for the nation and the world but also for themselves. Most Americans, I suspect, continue to live with an unspoken but strongly felt sense that the world—and thus their own lives—are more fragile than they had once believed; that the dangers facing them are greater, the future less certain. Outside the United States, of course, the impact of September 11 has also been tangible: a protracted and increasingly frustrating war in Iraq; an even more protracted and still uncertain war in Afghanistan; turbulence throughout the Middle East; anxiety in much of the rest of the world—about terrorism and about the United States itself as a source of instability and aggression.

And yet, what is in many ways equally striking about the period since 2001 is how many ways America, and much of the rest of the world, appear not to have changed at all. In the United States, most people continue to move through their lives more or less as they would have had the attacks not occurred. American culture, after a brief period of intense patriotism and grim seriousness (accompanied by portentous announcements that the nation's culture had reached the "end of irony"), has returned to frivolousness perhaps even greater than the highly frivolous culture of September 10, 2001, despite the undercurrents of anxiety that continue to underlay it. Despite nearly 3,000 deaths on September 11 and more than 3,000 American deaths so far in Iraq, despite serious assaults on civil liberties, and despite the continuing anxiety of the American Muslim community about their own security, the shining, commercial surface of American life remains largely unchanged. For a nation at war, the American people—and the media on which they rely for their knowledge of the world—have seemed to a large degree to be in denial, as if to acknowledge the dangers the nation faces would somehow increase them.

"Everything has changed, nothing has changed," an eminent journalist wrote not long after September 11, in a statement that seems as apt today as it was five years ago. So how do we measure the significance of September 11 at this early point in its history? Is the world we have known slowly unraveling, largely unseen, just as the European world was in the months before the beginning of World War II? Or is September 11 simply a symptom of a slowly changing world—a world that had been rocked by terrorism for decades before 2001 and continues to be rocked by it still; a world that was already destabilizing in the aftermath of the Cold War, when regional conflicts and ethnic passions began replacing the ideological rigidity of the age of the Soviet Union?

For almost everyone old enough to recall the autumn of 1963, the assassination of John Kennedy remains among the most vivid public memories of their lives. Many historians would now argue that the Kennedy assassination, tragic as it was, did not have a significant impact on history. The liberal initiatives Kennedy had championed were enacted by Lyndon Johnson after his death. The Vietnam War continued on its inexorable course toward catastrophe, arguably unaffected by the death of a president. In retrospect, the Kennedy assassination appears to have been less a cause than a symbol of change. And yet, symbols—particularly powerful symbols embedded in a society's collective memory—are themselves forces in history. The Kennedy assassination was and remains such an event—a catalytic moment continues to represent an extinguishing of youthful idealism and the launching a period of upheaval and division.

September 11 will almost certainly retain a similar iconic place in our collective memory, whether or not it eventually proves to have been a substantive cause of national and global change. The attacks on New York City may come to be seen as a turning point in American foreign and domestic policy, in the nation's international role and image, and in the fragile equilibrium of the Middle East. But even if they do not, the cultural weight of this extraordinary event—which so powerfully unsettled our sense of the character of our world—will almost certainly continue to be seen as an important moment in American history.

INTRODUCTION

Putting the events of our own time in historical perspective is never easy. When we look back at the events of a prior century, good historical work often reflects an effort to stand back from the passions and politics of the era to take a balanced and objective viewpoint. But when looking at our own time, that same objectivity often eludes us. As we look at the events of September 11, 2001, most observers remember where we were when we heard the news. We vividly recall the shock and horror of the unfolding events as they happened through the medium of live television broadcasts. For those with friends or relatives who perished or were injured during those attacks, the pain is even more immediate.

The skies were clear over New York that morning, and it was one of those rare fall days that are not too warm, not too cold to enjoy. In the space of less than two hours, that image was destroyed forever. In a confused tumble of crises, those watching from the ground or their television screens saw four civilian aircraft, commandeered by nineteen hijackers, turned into weapons aimed at the symbols of American wealth and power.

The events of that day not only had great emotional impact, they changed the political landscape in profound ways. Soon the United States sought allies in pursuing the leadership of al-Qaeda in Afghanistan. Announcing a War on Terror, President George W. Bush took his search for those connected with the terror attacks further afield. Linking the American public's dismay at the attacks on New York and Washington to concerns that the rogue regime of Saddam Hussein might supply weapons of mass destruction to terrorists, the United States launched a war on the Iraqi regime.

Although Hussein's army was soon defeated, U.S. and coalition forces from a few allied nations found themselves trapped in a growing insurgency, compounded by internal sectarian warfare, insurgency against the occupying forces, and an influx of foreign fighters, many so devoted to international jihad that they were willing volunteers for suicide attacks. No evidence of weapons of mass destruction was uncovered. Within the United States, the administration's policies in Iraq began to be questioned, although President George W. Bush won reelection in the fall of 2004. Nevertheless, as the conflict continued, support for the administration began to decline; in the next two years polls showed Bush's approval rating falling from more than 50 percent approval to close to 30 percent. As the conflicts in Afghanistan and Iraq continued, they produced heated political debates and recriminations.

For these reasons, both emotional and political, it has become extremely difficult to review the facts of the September 11 attacks with the sense of detachment expected in balanced historical writing. However, if one puts aside the effort to place blame, to criticize policy, and to engage in recrimination, it is possible to limit reporting to the facts that can be determined with certainty. While retaining a sense of anger and horror at the events, a researcher may be able to look at those events without attempting to make political points, and by reporting with some precision what is known as fact.

Hundreds of books cover the events of September 11. Some are authoritative; many are simply works of opinion, and others are outright conspiracy theorists spinning together scraps of information to support unlikely or impossible explanations. This book does not attempt to turn the facts of that day into arguments for a political stand, or into a form of commemoration or eulogy for those who died. It is our intention to compile in one volume a reference tool that presents facts that can be verified.

Moreover, in researching the events of September 11, different authoritative sources provide conflicting information—even the specific timing of the attack on the World Trade Center North Tower is slightly disputed and the exact tally of all victims do not necessarily add up from different sources. We have used the figures and information from the National Commission on Terrorist Attacks report and national news organizations so that readers will find the statistics, the names and known information about many of those involved, both as attackers and as victims, and the moment-by-moment schedule or timeline of the event.

The articles include biographical sketches and analyses of the planning and activities that lay behind the attacks, details regarding the first responders in New York and Washington, close accounts of some survivors, information about the organizations supporting the terrorists, the story of related attacks of a similar nature before and after the September 11 events, analyses of the media coverage, and much more. In all of these analyses and narratives, our effort has been to uncover and present factual information, rather than conjecture or opinion.

In presenting some of the stories about the victims of September 11, we have included personal biographical information. Rather than attempting to describe the lives of all those who perished, the stories included here serve as examples of the humanity involved; the narratives are typical. In some cases, the information was available because these people's last minutes are part of the official record: they had made phone calls during the attacks. To complete the scope of all victims, we have included an extensive index listing the names, ages, hometown, and state or country of each person killed on September 11.

The date "Nine-Eleven" has entered the vocabulary of public discourse in the United States, representing a watershed between the era before and the era after that date. The events of that day did in fact represent a shock much like that of December 7, 1941, becoming another date that will live in infamy. The similarities between the two days and the American popular reaction to them are profound. On December 7, some 2,400 Americans died, mostly members of the U.S. military forces in Hawaii. On September 11, over 2,900 Americans and foreign citizens resident in the United States died, most of them civilians. The shock of the surprise attack in both cases had immediate effects.

The attack on Pearl Harbor in 1941 was both symbolic and strategic. That is, Pearl Harbor represented the naval power of the United States in the Pacific and it was assaulted both as a representation of that power and as the physical embodiment of that power in the form of battleships and auxiliary ships. In 2001, the World Trade Center and the Pentagon represented the power of the United States as an economic force in the world and as a military power.

Before December 7, 1941, it was possible for Americans to believe that the crises of Europe that had turned into World War II would avoid them. On December 6, 1941, many Americans were still proud to call themselves isolationist. The bombing of Pearl Harbor converted most isolationists overnight into interventionists. Before September 11,

2001, it was possible for most Americans to believe that the growing jihadist movement in the Muslim and Arab world was a faraway issue, remote from the daily concerns of the average U.S. citizen. On September 11, that perception changed. Although radical Islamic jihad continued to seem strange and almost incomprehensible to Americans raised in a climate of religious toleration and relatively easy-going moral standards, it was no longer possible for Americans to believe that the ideas of radical Islam did not matter.

The immediate reaction to both events was a wave of emotional patriotic fervor, followed by a commitment to take military action to avenge the attack and to destroy its planners and perpetrators. Yet the two events, despite their surface similarities and their similar consequences, were profoundly different in important ways. The attack of December 7, 1941, was a military attack by a sovereign nation on American military facilities, caused by a failure to resolve differences through diplomacy. The attack of September 11, 2001, was an attack by individual civilian conspirators, representing not a national entity, but a loosely-organized international group, held together by a commitment to a radical version of a religion. While December 7, 1941, united Americans in their commitment to war, the unity that sprang from September 11, 2001, was quite temporary, and the target of revenge remained both physically elusive and more diverse.

Despite the clear differences between the two events, September 11, 2001, represents a profound turning point in American history as significant as December 7, 1941. The new watershed date will probably be remembered as such for decades to come.

As in 1941, the United States now finds itself engaged in a world struggle that it did not ask for, but that it cannot avoid. If Americans know the facts that led up to September 11, know the details of the date uncolored by any attempt to score political points, and understand the consequences of that date, we believe they will enter the new international environment better informed and better prepared.

—RODNEY P. CARLISLE
GENERAL EDITOR

READER'S GUIDE TO ARTICLES

This list is provided to assist readers in finding related articles by topic.

SEPTEMBER 11, 2001: *TIMELINE*

5:45 Terrorists Mohamed Atta and Abdulaziz Alomari clear Portland, Maine, airport security.

7:59 Takeoff: American Airlines Flight 11, Boston to LA, with 81 passengers and 11 crew.

8:14 Takeoff: United Airlines Flight 175, Boston to LA, with 56 passengers and 9 crew.

8:19 Flight Attendant Betty Ong calls: American Airlines Flight 11 hijacked.

8:20 Takeoff: American Airlines Flight 77, from Washington, D.C., to LA, with 58 passengers, 6 crew.

8:25 Control tower notifies air traffic control centers of American Airlines Flight 11 hijacking.

8:35 FAA (Federal Aviation Administration) alerts NORAD (North American Aerospace Defense Command), American Airlines Flight 11 hijacked.

8:42 Takeoff: United Airlines Flight 93, Newark, NJ, to San Francisco.

8:44 The elevator doors close on the last people to leave Windows on the World restaurant.

8:45 American Airlines Flight 11 hits WTC North tower. NORAD scrambles two F-15s from Falmouth, MA, Otis Air National Guard Base.

8:53 Controller announces possible hijacking of United Airlines Flight 175.

8:59 Emergency trauma unit set up at Chelsea Pier, NY.

9:00 200 firefighters converge on WTC North Tower, some already climbing the stairs of the building.

9:03 United Airlines Flight 175 hits WTC South Tower. NORAD notified of United Airlines Flight 175 hijacking.

9:09 Mayor Rudy Giuliani rushes to the disaster site.

9:21 Port Authority closes metropolitan area bridges and tunnels.

9:24 Two F-16s scramble from Langley, VA.

9:29 First casualty report made.

9:30 President Bush makes first official statement, orders perpetrators hunted down.

9:30 NY Stock Exchange evacuated, trading suspended.

9:32 All U.S. financial markets close.

9:40 Historical first: FAA grounds all civilian flights in the United States.

9:43 American Airlines Flight 77 hits Pentagon. First claim of responsibility broadcast on Abu Dhabi TV by the Democratic Front for the Liberation of Palestine, later denied.

9:45 White House evacuated.

9:48 U.S. Capitol evacuated due to bomb threats. Other federal buildings closed.

9:57 Passenger resistance begins on United Airlines Flight 93.

10:00 From aboard Air Force One, Bush puts United States on highest alert.

10:03 WTC South Tower collapses.

10:08 Secret Service deploys around White House with automatic weapons.

10:10 United Airlines Flight 93 crashes near Shanksville, PA.

10:13 UN evacuated in New York City.

10:22 In Washington, D.C., State and Justice Departments, World Bank evacuated.

10:24 FAA reports all inbound transatlantic flights are diverted to Canada.

10:28 WTC North Tower collapses.

10:29 People flee the collapse down Broadway, Greenwich, West, and Liberty Streets.

10:30 NY Governor George Pataki declares state of emergency.

10:50 Rumor: Second attack on Pentagon.

10:53 New York primary elections postponed.

10:54 Israel evacuates all diplomatic missions.

11:00 Giuliani orders lower Manhattan evacuated, requests others stay home.

11:16 CDC states emergency response teams are assembling.

11:18 American Airlines confirms 2 planes hijacked, presumed crashed.

11:45 U.S. military on nuclear alert. The afternoon and evening:

THE AFTERNOON

12:04 Los Angeles airport evacuated.

12:15 U.S. closes borders with Mexico and Canada. San Francisco airport evacuated and closed.

12:55 Taliban spokesman denies responsibility for attacks.

1:27 Washington, D.C., declares state of emergency.

2:30 FAA announces commercial air traffic suspended until at least noon on September 12.

2:49 Giuliani news conference: subway and bus services to be partially restored.

4:00 U.S. officials: Osama bin Laden involvement suspected.

4:25 American Stock Exchange, NASDAQ, NY Stock Exchange announce they will stay closed through September 12.

4:36 President Bush calls wife, tells her he is returning to White House.

5:20 Building 7 WTC, damaged and burning from the fall of the towers, collapses.

5:30 First official speculation on United Airlines Flight 93 destination: Camp David, White House, or U.S. Capitol.

THE EVENING

6:00 Hospitals find few new victims to treat. Explosions in Kabul, Afghanistan, credited to the Northern Alliance. U.S. denies involvement.

6:40 Pentagon declared operational.

6:54 Bush returns to White House. Wife Laura, also returns.

7:45 NYPD reports 78 officers missing, and 200 firefighters presumed dead.

8:30 Bush addresses the nation, says that no distinction will be made between terrorists and those who harbor them.

8:35 Bush attends security meeting.

9:57 Giuliani closes NYC schools for September 12. Says no more volunteers necessary. Power is out on Manhattan's West Side. The Health Department finds no evidence of airborne chemical agents.

10:21 Bush ends meeting, goes to bed.

10:49 Reported: Between three and five hijackers per plane armed only with knives.

10:56 Reported: NYPD believes there are survivors in buildings around the World Trade Center.

— ELIZABETH A. KRAMER

A

Abdel-Rahman, Sheikh Omar (1938–)

Omar Abdel-Rahman, known as the "Blind Sheikh," has inspired Islamists around the world, particularly in the United States. He is currently serving a life sentence for conspiring to destroy the World Trade Center and several other landmarks in the New York City area. Abdel-Rahman is one of the influential clerics whose writings are cited by AL-QAEDA in justifying martyrdom and the mass murder of nonbelievers.

Born in Egypt in 1938, Abdel-Rahman was blinded by diabetes as a child, and developed an obsessive interest in studying the Koran in braille. He graduated from the Al-Azhar University in Cairo and had ties with Islamist groups, including Islamic Jihad (see YEMEN ISLAMIC JIHAD) and Al-Gama'a al-Islamiyya. He spent three years in prison awaiting trial after the 1981 assassination of Egyptian president Anwar Sadat. Though treated harshly, the "Blind Sheikh" was acquitted and expelled from Egypt. Making his way to AFGHANISTAN, he developed close relationships with the MUJAHIDEEN leadership battling against the Soviet occupation, and became a spiritual leader and a well-traveled recruiter for the cause.

In the 1990s, with the Soviet war in Afghanistan over, Abdel-Rahman traveled to the United States under a visa provided by the Central Intelligence Agency, grateful for his contributions in the defeat of the Soviet army. President Hosni Mubarak of Egypt warned the United States that it would rue the day it allowed Abdel-Rahman into

FORMER GLORY *The Twin Towers of the World Trade Center were not only a trademark of the New York City skyline, they were also a target. Omar Abdel-Rahman was convicted in conjunction with the 1993 bombing of the World Trade Center, and had plotted to bomb the UN building, the George Washington Bridge, the Holland and Lincoln tunnels, and an FBI office concurrently.*

the country. The "Blind Sheikh" became a fixture in New York City mosques, preaching a virulent brand of Islam and strident anti-Americanism.

The investigation of the 1993 bombing of the World Trade Center (see WORLD TRADE CENTER 1993) demonstrated the influence the "Blind Sheikh" wielded over his followers in metropolitan New York. The investigation also uncovered an advanced plot to execute concurrent bombings of the United Nations building, the George Washington Bridge, the Holland and Lincoln tunnels, and a Federal Bureau of Investigation office. Abdel-Rahman was convicted of seditious conspiracy in 1995.

Imprisonment has not ended the "Blind Sheikh's" influence. The day after his conviction, al-Islamiyya followers gunned down western tourists in Luxor, Egypt, killing 56 and wounding 28. Bodies were mutilated and stuffed with pamphlets demanding Abdel-Rahman's release. While in prison, the "Blind Sheikh" has issued fatwas, smuggled out by his lawyer Lynne Stewart. Stewart has been convicted of aiding a conspiracy to kill American citizens.

Further Reading: Jason Burke, *Al-Qaeda: The True Story of Radical Islam* (I.B.Tauris, 2004); Steve Emerson, *American Jihad: The Terrorists Living Among Us* (Simon & Schuster, 2003); Rohan Gunaratna, *Inside al-Qaeda* (Penguin, 2003).

— **RAY BROWN**

Aden, Islamic Army of

The Islamic Army of Aden (IAA), also known as the Islamic Army of Aden Abyan, was founded by Abu al-Hassan in 1992 after his return from the guerrilla war against the Soviet Union in Afghanistan. Initially, the group was formed to shut down U.S. bases in Yemen used to support the peacekeep-

Muslim Law

SHARIA IS a system of law inspired by the *Sunna*, the *Koran*, older Arabic systems of law, and the work of Muslim scholars over the first 200 years of Islam. It is believed to be the "will of God," and the regulations of Sharia divided

ABOVE *A detail from the* Koran, *the holy book of Islam.*

into laws for worship and laws for judicial and political issues. Although the Sharia is frequently referred to as Islamic law, only a small part is undeniably based on the *Koran*. The correct designation is "Muslim" law, or Islam-inspired law. Sharia represents the entirety of religious, political, social, domestic, and private-life issues. Primarily meant for Muslims, Sharia can also apply to other individuals living in a Muslim society.

ing mission in Somalia in the 1990s. Today, the group is extremist, wanting to establish an Islamist government that adheres strictly to Sharia (Muslim) law, and remove all Western interests and influence from Yemen and the Middle East.

The Islamic Army of Aden Abyan is best known for participation in the bombing of the USS *Cole* in October 2000. The attack killed 17 American soldiers and 39 were injured. This group has also been linked with the kidnapping of 16 tourists in December 1998, and various other bombings and kidnappings in Yemen.

Intelligence sources indicate the group is a loose guerilla network of a few dozen men who may receive funding and support from Osama bin Laden, the al-Qaeda leader. The group primarily operates in the southern Yemeni provinces. Although the Yemeni government has cracked down on terrorist activities, it is unclear whether the Islamic Army of Aden Abyan is trying to regain power in the area, in addition to planning operations to advance their agenda.

The Islamic Army of Aden Abyan was designated a terrorist financier by President George W. Bush in 2001. The U.S. Treasury Department froze assets of the organization's chief legal officer in 2002. To help the Yemen government fight terrorist groups, the United States provides training and equipment to Yemen's Coast Guard, border patrol, and military.

Further reading: Center for Defense Information, "In the Spotlight: The Islamic Army of Aden (IAA)," www.cdi.org (November 23, 2004); U.S. Department of State, "Al-Qaida" *Terrorist Group Profiles: Country Reports on Terrorism,* http://nps.navy.mil (April 2005); Sheila Carapico, "Yemen and the Aden-Abyan Islamic Army," Middle East Report Online, www.merip.org (October 18, 2000).

— **DR. MARGARET H. WILLIAMSON**

Afghanistan

Even as the Twin Towers were burning and collapsing, the question of who was responsible burned in the minds of the American public and government. The question was made more troubling by the astonishing lack of communication from any groups claiming responsibility; the usual suspects in the terrorist world (see TERRORISM) were most notable in the loudness with which they deplored the attacks.

Among the leaders condemning the attacks was Mullah Mohammad Omar, leader of the TALIBAN, the religious government of Afghanistan. In the days that followed, evidence mounted that the attacks were the work of AL-QAEDA. This organization, whose Arabic name means "the base" or "the foundation," was created by OSAMA BIN LADEN as an umbrella uniting fundamentalist Islamic terrorist organizations around the world. Its center of operations was Afghanistan, whose religious government followed a similar extremist interpretation of Islam and which allowed them to maintain extensive facilities, including training camps for terrorists. Although bin Laden had been living in primitive conditions since coming to Afghanistan in the 1980s to help the MUJAHIDEEN fight the Soviet occupation, he was in fact highly educated and sophisticated in dealing with the Western world, the son of a wealthy construction company owner in Saudi Arabia.

It was bin Laden's knowledge of international finance that funded al-Qaeda. Although the Taliban

LEFT *Unidentified Taliban soldiers ride a tank outside Kabul, Afghanistan. The Taliban took over most of the country in 1996 and imposed strict Muslim law.*

controlled the opium poppy fields, it was bin Laden and his Saudis who had the technical knowledge to refine heroin, and the connections to the Turkish drug dealers and Sicilian mafiosi to ship and distribute it to the West. Ironically, because of this network, heroin users in the United States helped fund the attacks on America.

Although the Taliban might be inexperienced in worldly matters, they held firm to the tribal tradition of hospitality in which one's obligations to a guest are sacred. When the United States demanded the extradition of bin Laden to stand trial for the September 11 attacks, they refused to hand him over. Furthermore, they refused to close the terrorist camps that al-Qaeda had been running in the country since 1996 and that had been bombed by the Clinton administration in 1998 in retaliation for the bombings of U.S. embassies in Africa (see EMBASSY BOMBINGS).

Although the Taliban's initial reaction to the ultimatum delivered by U.S. president GEORGE W. BUSH was resolute, as it became clear that the United States was willing to go to war, they offered to let bin Laden be tried in an Islamic court or to be extradited to a neutral country. The United States considered both options unacceptable, largely because it believed it unlikely that either option would result in bin Laden facing genuine justice for his actions. On October 7, 2001, an American-led coalition began military operations directed at toppling the Taliban and capturing bin Laden. For the first time in its history, the mutual defense provisions of the North Atlantic Treaty Organization (NATO) were invoked, calling upon member nations to respond to the attack on the United States as if it were upon them. Seven NATO members—the United Kingdom, Canada, France, Italy, Spain, Portugal, and Germany—contributed forces to Operation Enduring Freedom, as did nonmembers Australia, New Zealand, and Pakistan. A substantial reward was offered for bin Laden's capture, in hopes that his less dedicated followers might betray him.

Further Reading: Kelly Barth, ed., *The Rise and Fall of the Taliban* (Gale, 2005); Peter L. Bergen, *The Osama bin Laden I Know* (Free Press, 2006); Douglas Farah, *Blood from Stone: The Secret Financial Network of Terror* (Broadway Books: 2004); Walter Laqueur, *No End to War: Terrorism in the Twenty-First Century* (Continuum, 2003).

— LEIGH KIMMEL

Air Force One

A secretly configured Boeing 747-200B jet, Air Force One served as President GEORGE W. BUSH's command post on September 11. Visiting an elementary school in Florida when the attack occurred, Bush was quickly put aboard Air Force One. He wanted to head back to Washington, D.C., but as his safety in the capital was uncertain, the plane flew to Barksdale Air Force Base in Louisiana, then Offutt Air Force Base, home of the U.S. Strategic Command Center in Nebraska, and finally back to Washington, D.C. Throughout the day, Bush was in contact with Vice President Dick Cheney (see RICHARD B. CHENEY), his staff, and advisors. Air Force One proved to be an effective office for the president during a crisis.

Bush had flown to Florida on September 10, spending the night with his brother, Governor Jeb Bush. The next morning he prepared for his visit to Emma E. Booker Elementary School in Sarasota, Florida, to talk about his ideas on education reform. His motorcade was en route to the school when AMERICAN AIRLINES FLIGHT 11 struck the first tower at 8:45. It is unclear as to who told Bush of the crash. One account states that Captain Deborah Loewer informed him when the motorcade arrived at the school (8:55).

ABOVE *President Bush aboard Air Force One on September 11, 2001. In the first few hours after the attacks, Air Force One served as the presidential command post as officials decided where it should land.*

of Defense DONALD RUMSFELD reviewed the procedures air force pilots would use if faced with having to shoot down a civilian airliner, and the president gave permission for pilots to fire on civilian U.S. planes exhibiting hostile intent.

Air Force One landed at Barksdale at 11:45 and departed for Offutt Air Force Base, Nebraska at 1:30 P.M. While at Barksdale, Bush recorded a short statement to be televised. Bush arrived at Offutt at 2:50, and at 3:00 he met with the National Security Council via a secure videoconferencing facility. At 4:00, Bush decided to return to Washington, D.C. Air Force One arrived in Washington at 6:42 P.M.

Passengers on board Air Force One on September 11 were U.S. Representatives Adam Putnam and Dan Miller from Florida, chief political strategist Karl Rove, chief of staff Andrew Card, White House communications director Dan Bartlett, White House press secretary Ari Fleischer, assistant press secretary Gordon Johndroe, chief White House photographer Eric Draper, education advisor Sandy Kress, Blake Gottesman who was standing in for the president's personal assistant, Colonel Mark Tillman (pilot of Air Force One), several reporters, Secret Service agents, and members of Bush's military and civilian staff.

Another states that Karl Rove told Bush inside the school. Either way, Bush continued with his visit. At 9:06, Chief of Staff Andrew Card notified Bush that another plane had struck the World Trade Center and that the United States was under attack. Bush stayed in the classroom until 9:16 and then moved to an empty classroom where his staff briefed him. There he prepared the short speech delivered at 9:30, telling the students and teachers that terrorists had attacked the country.

There was some concern that Bush and Air Force One might also be a terrorist target. Air Force One took off at 9:55 without a destination; Cheney and the Secret Service advised against returning to Washington, D.C. In the meantime, Air Force One circled Sarasota. At 10:35 the decision was made to head toward Barksdale Air Force Base. Bush and Secretary

Further Reading: Cooperative Research, "Complete 911 Timeline: Bush's Actions on 9/11," www.cooperativeresearch.org (cited September, 2006); Von Hardesty, *Air Force One: The Aircraft that Shaped the Modern Presidency* (Creative Publishing, 2003); Kenneth T. Walsh, *Air Force One: A History of the Presidents and Their Planes* (Hyperion, 2003).

— DALLACE W. UNGER, JR.

Airport Security

Although airplane HIJACKING in the United States dates back to 1961, the 1970s marked the beginning of airport security in which passengers were subjected to inspection of person and baggage. Checked luggage was removed from the plane if the passenger who checked it failed to board.

Particularly after the bombing of Pan Am Flight 103 in 1988, security measures were tightened, with requirements to show photo identification matching the name on the ticket and resultant restrictions on switching a ticket to a different passenger if the original purchaser were unable to fly. Passengers were also required to demonstrate that electronic devices such as portable music players and laptop computers actually functioned, since it was believed that the explosives that destroyed the plane were hidden in a portable stereo.

Many critics claimed that the restrictions did little to protect against future attacks, while imposing unreasonable burdens on passengers and violating their privacy. Some civil libertarians argued that requiring photo identification effectively created a domestic passport and discriminated against those who object to having their lives documented at every turn.

After September 11, security increased exponentially. Because the hijackers had carried out their attacks using box cutters, strict new rules were decreed regarding items allowed in carry-on luggage. With the realization that the terrorists were inventive with their weapons, security personnel began confiscating even such items as nail clippers. Steel knives were no longer included in the utensils for first-class meal service.

Because of questions about the effectiveness of private security companies such as Argenbrite, which had staffed the security scanners at the airports from which the hijackers flew, there were calls to nation-

AT LEFT *Massachusetts State Police guard Boston's Logan Airport on September 15, 2001. Mohamed Atta and his team boarded American Airlines Flight 11 at Logan Airport and hijacked the plane.* **ABOVE** *A Customs Border Patrol canine officer screens passengers' luggage for prohibited items.*

alize airport security in the belief that civil service employees would provide a higher caliber of work. The sky marshal program was revived, putting plainclothes agents on many international and major domestic flights. A government "no-fly" list was created, listing persons considered potential terrorists.

Complaints began pouring in that the new rules were enforced in an arbitrary and heavy-handed fashion. A Medal of Honor winner had his medal confiscated by a security screener who mistook it for a *shiruken*, or Japanese throwing star. People were detained and prevented from boarding flights solely because their names resembled those of unrelated persons on the no-fly list. In an incident that attracted particular ire, a young mother was ordered to drink from several bottles of breast milk she carried for her infant, to prove that it was not a toxic substance. Pointing out that drinking directly from the bottles would contaminate the milk, she asked politely if she could drip a few drops onto her forearm and lick it up, she was told to either drink directly from the bottles or discard them.

Security increased further after the "shoe bomber," Richard Reid, tried to ignite explosives hidden in his shoes while aboard a transatlantic flight. Passengers were subsequently required to remove their shoes for inspection before boarding, and often were required to stand on one foot during the process. When a man physically incapable of doing so because of knee surgery asked for an alternative means of inspection, he was arrested for refusing to comply with a lawful direction.

Criticism of the new rules was harsh and unsparing, pointing out that the only two foiled terrorist attempts—UNITED AIRLINES FLIGHT 93 and Richard Reid—were disrupted not by government agents but by ordinary passengers. Some critics even suggested that the manner in which airport security had been implemented was actually making air travel more vulnerable to TERRORISM by simultaneously creating a false sense of security and driving away the very people who would be most likely to take action against an actual terrorist. In a foiled terrorist plot in the summer of 2006, authorities apprehended suspects in England allegedly planning to blow up transcontinental airliners with liquid or gel explosives that could evade security in shampoo and perfume bottles. Immediately, security at airports was stepped up, and passengers were restricted from having bubble bath, gel deodorants, mouthwash and toothpaste in their carry-on luggage.

Further Reading: Walter Laqueur, *No End to War: Terrorism in the Twenty-First Century* (Continuum, 2003); Michael A. Ledeen, *The War Against the Terror Masters: Why It Happened. Where We Are Now. How We'll Win* (St. Martin's, 2002).

— LEIGH KIMMEL

Al-Muhajiroun

Even before September 11, the transnational Salafi Sunni group al-Muhajiroun had a reputation for religious activism and the radical, outlandish statements of its leader, the Syrian-born Sunni Muslim preacher Omar Bakri Muhammad. The group emerged in early 1996 after he left Hizb ut-Tahrir (HTT), another transnational Islamic group dedicated to the reestablishment of Islamic states and eventually the caliphate, the Islamic empire. Under Bakri Muhammad's leadership, al-Muhajiroun publicly expressed its desire to create an Islamic state in the United Kingdom and was suspected of supporting radical Muslim groups in places as far away as Kashmir.

Unlike HTT, which limits its activities to regions where the establishment of an Islamic state is considered possible, al-Muhajiroun believed that the establishment of such a state was the duty of every Muslim regardless of location. Bakri Muhammad argued that Muslims in the United Kingdom should seek to establish an Islamic state there. At its height, the group had branches in 30 British cities with 160 members and at least 700 associates who were students of Bakri Muhammad.

Al-Muhajiroun ran an advanced network with units assigned to missionary work, religious education, and public demonstrations for the establishment of an Islamic state in the United Kingdom. After September 11, al-Muhajiroun distributed provocative flyers with titles such as "The Magnificent 19," a reference to the hijackers.

Bakri Muhammad disbanded al-Muhajiroun in the United Kingdom in October 2004. In the summer of 2005, after the July suicide bombings in London, he was refused reentry into the country after a vacation in Syria and Lebanon.

Further Reading: Peter Mandaville, "Towards a Critical Islam: European Muslims and the Changing Boundaries of Transnational Religious Discourse," in *Muslim Networks and Transnational Communities in and across Europe*, Stefano Allievi and Jorgen Nielsen, eds. (Brill, 2003); Quintan Wiktorowicz, *Radical Islam Rising: Muslim Extremism in the West* (Rowman & Littlefield, 2005).

— CHRISTOPHER ANZALONE

Al-Qaeda

Terrorism expert Michael Scheuer has described al-Qaeda as "more ethnically diverse, more geographically dispersed, younger, richer, better educated, better led, and more militarily trained and combat experienced" than any other terrorist organization in world history. Nevertheless, prior to September 11, 2001, the U.S. government did not fully recognize al-Qaeda as a potent enemy capable of launching devastating attacks on U.S. soil.

OSAMA BIN LADEN and a coterie of Arab militants who had fought in the JIHAD against the Soviet Union formed Al-Qaeda in 1988, in Afghanistan. They called the organization *al-Qaeda*, which means "the base" or "the foundation" because they saw themselves as leaders inciting jihad across the Muslim world. The group chose to target pro-Western Muslim governments, which they condemn as corrupt and overly secular, and the United States, which they believe exerts hegemonic control in the Middle East. Bin Laden's stated goal is to "awaken the Muslims" so that they will "fight [the West] to the last breath."

POLITICAL RESENTMENT

Al-Qaeda's ideology mixes political resentment with extremist religious convictions, including a desire to destroy the U.S.-backed Jewish nation of Israel; the belief that an "infidel" U.S. military presence in places sacred to Islam is intolerable; and the sense that Muslim nations have been humiliated by imperialist Western powers, deliberately kept militarily and politically weak. Although the Koran expressly forbids suicide and the intentional harming of noncombatants in wartime, al-Qaeda justifies "martyrdom" operations and the mass murder of unbelievers by citing the writings of a few militant religious scholars, such as SHEIKH OMAR ABDEL-RAHMAN.

The organization has been successful in part because of its pragmatism. The group is nonhierarchical, governed by few rules, and quick to adapt to changing circumstances. While radical Islam (see ISLAMIC FUNDAMENTALISM) is driven by factionalism, often stemming from theological disputes or ethnic tensions, al-Qaeda attempts to downplay differences. Bin Laden, a Sunni Muslim who believes that Shia

Muslims are heretics, has nevertheless made common cause with the Shia terrorist group Lebanese Hizbullah. Al-Qaeda is a diffuse, worldwide network composed of core participants, satellite cells, and affiliated independent terrorist groups.

The membership includes perhaps 3,000 elite operatives. They are typically well-educated young men from middle-class families, handpicked from an estimated 10,000 to 110,000 fighters who trained in camps in AFGHANISTAN before September 11. The camps, which made rigorous demands on participants, offered courses such as close-range combat and shooting from a motorcycle. Al-Qaeda members have included a physician from a prominent Cairo family, a microelectronics specialist educated in Wales, and a U.S. army sergeant who taught seminars at the Special Warfare Center at Fort Bragg, North Carolina. Terrorism experts note al-Qaeda's facility with new technologies, its "virtuality," which makes the group elusive: "With their Macintosh laptops and encrypted communications, stolen credit cards, access to Internet cafes and disposable cell phones, and false passports, jihadists can be everywhere and anywhere," conclude terrorism experts Daniel Benjamin and Steven Simon.

FIRST ATTACKS

Al-Qaeda may have carried out its first attacks in 1992, when three hotels in Yemen frequented by U.S. troops were bombed. Operatives are also alleged to have taken part in the "Black Hawk Down" incident in Mogadishu, Somalia, in 1993, when several U.S. servicemen were killed. The 9/11 Commission has determined that other significant terrorist attacks during the mid-1990s, such as the 1993 bombing of the World Trade Center (see WORLD TRADE CENTER 1993) and the 1996 bombing of the KHOBAR TOWERS in Saudi Arabia, may be distantly linked to al-Qaeda.

AT RIGHT *In a poster in Arabic, titled "Soldier of Islam—Osama bin Laden," a portrait of the terrorist is shown with him holding a rifle, with tanks behind him, and with an American aircraft carrier in the foreground.*

In 1998 bin Laden publicly announced the establishment of the World Islamic Front for Jihad against Jews and Crusaders, formalizing ties between al-Qaeda and other terrorist groups such as the Egyptian Islamic Jihad. At the same time, the World Islamic Front issued a fatwa calling on Muslims to kill Americans. Per the 9/11 Commission Report, bin Laden told an American interviewer, "We believe that the worst thieves in the world today and the worst terrorists are the Americans. Nothing could stop you except perhaps retaliation in kind. We do not have to differentiate between military or civilian. As far as we are concerned, they are all targets." The fatwa was the prelude for the first terrorist attack definitively ascribed to al-Qaeda: the bombing of U.S. embassies in Kenya and Tanzania in August 1998.

EMBASSY BOMBINGS became the template for al-Qaeda's terrorist activities. The group began surveillance of the embassy in Kenya as early as 1993. Terrorists married local women and opened businesses to provide cover as they gathered intelligence. The suicide attacks were precise, carried out in different locations simultaneously. In 2000 al-Qaeda used a small boat laden with explosives to attack the U.S.

Encyclopedia of Jihad

IN 1997, the Central Intelligence Agency became aware of a comprehensive, 7,000-page al-Qaeda training manual, the *Encyclopedia of Jihad*. Terrorists fluent in English compiled this multivolume work, available in print and on a CD-ROM; some of the information was taken from U.S. and British military field manuals. The manual provides how-to guidance for, among other things how to booby-trap a tube of toothpaste; how to conduct surveillance, brainwashing, and assassinations; and how to use weapons ranging from knives to Stinger antiaircraft missiles. The cover of each volume shows a machine gun alongside the Koran, linking warfare and religious obligation.

ABOVE *Initially there were only 30 copies of the Encyclopedia of Jihad. Until 2003, trainees had to write out dictated text to have their own copies. Then the entire set of manuals was made available on the internet.*

Navy destroyer USS *Cole*. Bin Laden created a media committee to capitalize on the attack's success, producing a short film that lionized the operation's suicidal "martyrs," circulated among young Muslims for recruiting purposes.

Planning for the September 11 hijackings began in late 1998 or early 1999, masterminded by KHALID SHEIKH MOHAMMED, a mechanical engineer from Kuwait who had been educated in the United States. The 9/11 Commission has identified Mohammed as a "terrorist entrepreneur" who retained his independence from al-Qaeda. Bin Laden recognized him as a creative thinker and a talented administrator. Mohammed, who had been tangentially involved in planning the 1993 World Trade Center bombing with his nephew, RAMZI AHMED YOUSEF, scrutinized that failed attack to learn from mistakes.

GUIDED AIRBORNE EXPLOSIVES

Mohammed came up with the idea of using hijacked commercial aircraft as guided airborne explosives. His initial plan was to commandeer 10 airplanes and fly them into targets on both U.S. Coasts, including nuclear power plants. Bin Laden convinced him that this scale was impractical. Bin Laden, Mohammed, and al-Qaeda military commander Mohammad Atef eventually developed the list of targets, chosen for their symbolic value: the World Trade Center, a centerpiece of Western economies; the Pentagon; and the U.S. Capitol.

Bin Laden originally intended to use veteran al-Qaeda members to carry out the operation, but in late 1999 he asked four new recruits to become the central actors. Mohamed Atta, RAMZI BIN AL SHIBH, Marwan Alshehri, and Ziad Jarrah were aspiring jihadists who had formed their own extremist cell in Hamburg, GERMANY. The men were technologically adept, relatively fluent in English, and knowledgeable about Western living. They readily agreed to carry out the suicide missions, subscribing to al-Qaeda's belief that martyrdom in the name of Islam was a supreme honor for which they would reach the highest level of paradise. Khalid Sheikh

Mohammed assembled materials such as western aviation magazines, airline timetables, flight simulator software, and Hollywood movies depicting HIJACKINGS to training the men to hijack and fly commercial aircraft.

Mohammed eventually determined that the operatives would be best prepared by attending flight schools in the United States. Atta, Alshehri, and Jarrah successfully applied for visas and enrolled in schools in Florida in July 2000. Bin al Shibh was denied a visa because he was suspected of possibly overstaying his visa for economic reasons.

The terrorists (see TERRORISTS OF SEPTEMBER 11) made efforts to blend in with their surroundings in the United States. Several opened bank accounts in their own names and received Virginia state driver's licenses. They lived in efficiency apartments, and did most of their shopping at Wal-Mart, keeping in frequent contact with Mohammed and Bin al Shibh, who functioned as administrators. Using cell phones and e-mail, they assumed the role of university students and spoke in a coded language—for example, when they discussed their study of "architecture," they meant the World Trade Center.

Atta and Alshehri earned commercial pilot licenses. Jarrah failed to complete his certification. In December 2000, a fourth pilot, Hani Hamjour, arrived in the United States. Fifteen "muscle hijackers"—those who would control the passengers and flight crew so that the hijacker pilots could fly the aircraft—followed between April and July 2001. During the summer of 2001, the pilot hijackers made several surveillance flights as passengers on commercial airlines, seeking out airline routes that typically carried relatively few passengers, because these flights would be easier to overpower. Their experience with U.S. airport security assured them that they could carry knives and box cutters onto

Financing Terror

DURING THE 1990s, American intelligence experts believed that al-Qaeda's primary source of funding was OSAMA BIN LADEN's personal fortune. After September 11 the INTELLIGENCE community realized that a highly creative financial network supported the organization. Bin Laden—whose personal assets were frozen by the Saudi government in 1994—can provide only a small portion of his organization's operational costs, which are estimated at around $30 million annually.

Before 2001, the bulk of this amount was funded by charities. Charitable giving, known as *zakat*, is an important tenet of Islam. The Central Intelligence Agency has identified more than 50 Islamic charitable organizations channeling funds to al-Qaeda, most headquartered in the Gulf nations. Some were bogus "fronts" for the terrorist group. Others were unknowingly infiltrated by terrorist sympathizers, who misdirected funds. For example, the Kuwait-based Mercy International, which helps to run orphanages and hospitals in Africa, was infiltrated by al-Qaeda supporters who agreed to fund a malaria research clinic. Experts also believe that al-Qaeda has supported itself by conducting widespread credit card fraud, particularly in Europe, where the group was able to make as much as $1 million per month during the 1990s. One of the training camps in AFGHANISTAN was devoted to teaching schemes for conducting financial crimes.

Al-Qaeda also used mainstream Islamic and Western banks in preparing for September 11, evidently with little fear of detection. The September 11 operation, which cost $500,000, relied on dozens of wire transfers between the United Arab Emirates and the United States. Hijacker Mohamed Atta received $70,000 in a single transfer to his bank account in Florida. Shortly before the attacks, he dutifully wired back $2,000 in unused funds from a Mailboxes, Etc. store.

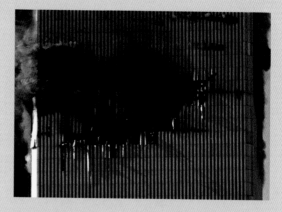

ABOVE *A close up of the damage inflicted by American Airlines Flight 11.* **AT LEFT** *The North Tower of the World Trade Center, moments after Flight 11 cut through the steel and glass. The hijackers intended to topple one of the world's tallest buldings.*

the airplanes unimpeded. They bought first-class tickets, which would seat them close to the cockpit. In keeping with al-Qaeda's organizational philosophy, the cell leader was given considerable latitude in making decisions. Atta, not bin Laden, fixed the date for the attacks.

Further Reading: Daniel Benjamin and Steven Simon, *The Age of Sacred Terror* (Random House, 2002); Peter L. Bergen, *The Osama bin Laden I Know: An Oral History of al Qaeda's Leader* (Free Press, 2006); Rohan Gunaratna, *Inside al-Qaeda: Global Network of Terror* (Columbia University Press, 2002); Terry McDermott, *Perfect Soldiers: The Hijackers: Who They Were, Why They Did It* (HarperCollins, 2005); National Commission on Terrorist Attacks Upon the United States, *The 9/11 Commission Report* (W.W. Norton, 2004); Marc Sageman, *Understanding Terror Networks* (University of Pennsylvania Press, 2004); Michael Scheuer, *Through Our Enemies' Eyes: Osama Bin Laden, Radical Islam, and the Future of America* (Potomac Books, 2003).

— **TOM COLLINS**

American Airlines Flight 11

At 5:45 A.M. on Tuesday, September 11, 2001, Mohamed Atta and Abdulaziz Alomari cleared security at the Portland International Jetport in Portland, Maine, and boarded a 6 A.M. flight to Logan International Airport in Boston. Both held $2,500 first-class, one-way tickets on Flight 11 to Los Angeles via Boston, which Atta had purchased online on August 29, 2001. Although the flight was late in departing Portland, Atta and Alomari arrived in Boston well in advance of the 7:45 connection to Los Angeles.

Because the flight from Portland had been delayed, Atta's baggage was not aboard the flight to Los Angeles. A four-page jihadist manifesto was later discovered in these bags by federal agents, a declaration imploring fellow conspirators to "make an oath to die and make your knife sharp [so as] not [to] discomfort your animal during the slaughter."

By 7:45 most of the 92 passengers and crew had passed through security at Logan and boarded a Boeing 767. Captain John Ogonowski, 50, was an experienced 767 pilot from Dracut, Massachusetts, who regularly made the flight to Los Angeles. First Officer and copilot Thomas McGuinness, 42, was a former navy pilot from Portsmouth, New Hampshire, who had also made the transcontinental journey to Los Angeles many times.

PASSENGERS

The passengers were a diverse group (see APPENDIX for complete list of crew and passengers). A few were in the entertainment industry, including David Angell, 54, executive producer of the situation comedy *Frasier*; actress and photographer Berinthia Berenson Perkins, 53; filmmaker and video producer Carolyn Mayer Beug, 48; Thomas Nicholas Pecorelli, 30, cameraman for Fox Sports and E! Entertainment Television; and Daniel John Lee, 34, a member of the road crew for the musical group Backstreet Boys. Those traveling to Los Angeles on business included Daniel C. Lewin, 31, of Charlestown, Massachusetts, cofounder of Akamai Technologies, an internet company, and a veteran of the Israeli Defense Forces; a group of seven executives from the retailer TJX Company; and three engineers and executives from Raytheon.

Two retired couples on vacation were among the passengers: Robert Norton, 85, and his wife Jacqueline, 61, of Lubec, Maine; and retired teacher and assistant principal James Trentini, 65, and his wife Mary Barbara, 67, of Everett, Massachusetts. Other passengers included Cora Hidalgo Holland, 52, of the Sudbury Food Pantry at Our Lady of Fatima Church in Sudbury, Massachusetts; Paige Farley-

ABOVE *An American Airlines Boeing 767-223ER, the same model as the plane that was commandeered and piloted into the North Tower of the World Trade Center.*

Hackel, 46, of Newton, Massachusetts, a spiritual counselor; and 20-year-old Candace Lee Williams, a student at Northeastern University.

The Boeing 767 is a wide-bodied jumbo jet, a workhorse of the commercial airline industry since its introduction in 1982. With a wingspan of 156 feet and a fuselage of 155 feet, the 767 could accommodate up to 255 passengers and 2,875 cubic feet of cargo. For transcontinental flights, such as Flight 11, American Airlines employed a 767-223ER, with a range of 6,600 miles. Fully loaded with passengers, crew, cargo, and fuel, Flight 11 weighed over 395,000 pounds and was loaded with approximately 10,000 gallons of jet fuel.

HIJACK

Heading due west after takeoff, the cabin crew aboard American Airlines Flight 11 began serving breakfast. Approximately 15 minutes into the flight, at 8:15, Atta and his four accomplices made their way toward the cockpit. The five hijackers either forced their way in using knives or boxcutters, or possibly killed passengers or crew to lure the flight crew out of the locked cockpit. Two flight attendants reported that three people—two flight attendants and a passenger—were stabbed or had their throats slashed by the hijackers. The passenger, Daniel Lewin, a former special forces officer in the elite Israeli Sayeret

Matkal, was killed by hijacker Safam Al Sugami when he attempted to stop the hijacking.

Flight attendant Betty Ong said that the hijackers used mace or pepper spray against passengers and crew. The hijackers claimed to have a bomb, although there is no evidence to support their claims. At 8:15, Boston air traffic control began unsuccessful attempts to contact the pilots of American Airlines Flight 11 after they failed to respond to an order to climb to 35,000 feet. At 8:20, the transponder signal ceased and the plane veered northward, departing dramatically from its planned route. Although air traffic controllers suspected that the plane had been hijacked, neither of the pilots pressed the distress call button.

PHONE CALLS

At 8:21 A.M. flight attendant Madeline Sweeney, a mother of two, called American Airlines ground manager Michael Woodward at Logan and said, "Listen, and listen to me very carefully. I'm on Flight 11. The airplane has been hijacked." Sweeney said she saw only four of the five hijackers whom she described as Middle Eastern, and said they had stabbed two flight attendants and that "a hijacker cut the throat of a business-class passenger, and he appears to be dead." Sweeney added that the hijackers stormed the front of the plane and "had just gained access to the cockpit." Almost immediately, the plane changed direction and began to descend.

At 8:24, air traffic controllers in Boston heard a heavily accented voice, believed to be Atta's, declare, "We have some planes. Just stay quiet, and you'll be ok. We are returning to the airport." Seconds later, the same unknown voice warned, "Nobody move, everything will be ok. If you try to make any moves, you'll endanger yourself and the airplane. Just stay quiet." Apparently, one of the hijackers confused the aircraft's radio with its public-address system.

Flight attendant Betty Ong got through to an American reservations agent in Fort Worth at 8:27 A.M., saying two flight attendants had been stabbed and one was on oxygen. "A passenger had his throat slashed and looked dead," Ong reported, "and [the hijackers] had gotten into the cockpit." At 8:28 A.M., controllers saw Flight 11 execute a 100-degree turn south from Albany, New York, and the Catskill Mountains toward the Hudson River valley and New York City. At 8:45 A.M., just before the crash, Flight attendant Madeline Sweeney said, "I see the water…I see buildings—Oh my God!"

Atta is believed to have been piloting the plane when it crashed into the North Tower of the World Trade Center. American Airlines Flight 11 hit the North Tower between the 94th and the 98th floors at an estimated 470 to 500 miles per hour, instantly killing all 92 passengers and crew on board. At 10:28 A.M., after burning intensely for over an hour, the 110-story North Tower collapsed.

Further Reading: "American's Flight 11 Victims at a Glance," www.usatoday.com/ news/nation/2001/09/12/victim-capsule-flight11.htm (September 12, 2001); National Commission on Terrorist Attacks upon the United States, *The 9/11 Commission Report* (W.W. Norton, 2004); *New York Times*, "Transcript American Airlines Flight 11," http://911research.wtc7.net/cache/planes/attack/nyt_f11transcript.html (October 16, 2001).

— **BRIAN REFFORD, PH.D.**

American Airlines Flight 77

Tuesday, September 11, 2001, seemed an ordinary day for the 58 passengers, four flight attendants, and two pilots aboard American Airlines Flight 77, a Boeing 757-223 jet departing Dulles International Airport on a scheduled flight to Los Angeles. The jetliner had been scheduled to depart at

8:10 A.M., but did not leave until 8:20. Later, investigators discovered that three of the hijackers had been stopped before they boarded the flight because they failed the metal detector screening. Inexplicably, after a slight delay, they were allowed to board.

The passengers of Flight 77 seemed safe with the excellent flying skills of pilot Charles "Chic" Frank Burlingame III. Growing up in England, he attended the U.S. Naval Academy in Annapolis, flying F-4 Phantom jets as a navy pilot and eventually worked in the Pentagon. A graduate of the navy's "Top Gun" fighter-pilot school in Miramar, California, Captain Burlingame accepted a position in 1988 with American Airlines where his wife, Shari, was a flight attendant. The next day, September 12, was his 51st birthday.

Copilot David Charlebois, 39, was the first officer on American Airlines Flight 77. Marching in uniform, David helped carry the banner for the National Gay Pilots Association in the Millennium March on Washington in 2000. He walked the parade again with the Gay and Lesbian Employees of American Airlines. He also helped raise money for the Sexual Minority Youth Assistance League. The most important people in his life were his parents and his life partner of fourteen years, Tom Hay.

There were four flight attendants on American Airlines Flight 77. Michelle M. Heidenberger, 57, had been with American for 30 years. Her husband Tom was a pilot for U.S. Airways, and her father, the late Richard McDonald, had been general manager of American Airlines operations at Bradley in Windsor Locks, Connecticut, for 36 years. About five years earlier, Heidenberger had successfully completed training in how to deal with a HIJACKING.

Friends thought that Jennifer and Kenneth Lewis were such a good match that they called them "Kennifer." The husband-and-wife team from Culpep-per, Virginia, often worked separate flights, but they were together on American Airlines Flight 77, flying to a Los Angeles vacation. Flight attendant Renee Ann May, a graduate of San Diego State University, also worked as a docent for the Walters Art Museum in Baltimore. She and David Spivock Jr. of Rockville, Maryland, were engaged.

The passenger list of American Flight 77 (see APPENDIX for a complete list of passengers and crew) included National Geographic Society personnel, several teachers, and three students on an educational trip to the Channel Islands National Marine Sanctuary near Santa Barbara, California. Joe Ferguson, who accompanied the group, directed the National Geographic Society's Geography Education Outreach Program in Washington, D.C. Ann Judge, 49, of Virginia, was the travel office manager for the Society.

ABOVE *The only photo made available to the public showing an airplane part on the grounds of the Pentagon. Conspiracy theorists have speculated that a plane of that size would have left larger debris.*

From All Walks of Life

DIANE SIMMONS and her husband George were on a trip to Hawaii to place her father's ashes beside those of her mother.

NORMA LANG STEUERLE, 54, a clinical psychologist, was on a trip to Japan to meet her family. From there she planned to visit Thailand.

LEONARD TAYLOR, 44, was a technical manager at Xon-Tech, a research and development firm specializing in sensor technologies for defense and industry.

Australia was SANDRA TEAGUE's dream vacation. The 31-year-old physical therapist was heading overseas to raft, trek, and rock climb. She worked at Georgetown University Hospital and lived in Fairfax, Virginia.

JOHN D. YAMNICKY SR., 71, had retired from naval aviation in 1979, but worked as a defense contractor for Veridian Corporation. He would sometimes tell stories about his navy service in Korea and Vietnam. A friend of the family said, "He crash landed five times and walked away from each of them, but not this last one."

BRYAN JACK, 48, of Alexandria, Virginia, was a budget analyst/director of the programming and fiscal economics division of the Defense Department.

STEVEN "JAKE" JACOBY, 43, was vice president and chief operating officer of Metrocall wireless communications company. He was on his way to a wireless communications conference in Los Angeles.

CHANDLER "CHAD" RAYMOND KELLER, 29, was a lead propulsion engineer and project manager with Boeing Satellite Systems. He and his wife Lisa were married on July 22, 2001.

YVONNE KENNEDY, 62, of Sydney, New South Wales, Australia, had been an employee of the Australian Red Cross before her retirement.

NORMA KHAN, 45, of Reston, Virginia, was manager of member services with Plumbing-Heating-Cooling Contractors-National Association.

KAREN A. KINCAID, a 40-year-old partner in a Washington, D.C., law firm, was traveling to a conference in Los Angeles where she was doing pro bono work for people in need of organ transplants.

DONG LEE, 48, of Leesburg, Virginia, was an engineer with Boeing.

DORA MENCHACA, 45, of Santa Monica, California, was associate director of clinical research at Amgen.

LISA J. RAINES, one of the earliest and most prominent lobbyists for the biotechnology industry, was senior vice president for government relations at the Genzyme Corporation.

ROBERT SPEISMAN, 48, executive vice president at Lazare Kaplan International in New York, a worldwide diamond manufacturer, was traveling from Washington to Los Angeles on business. (See APPENDIX for a complete list of victims of Flight 77.)

Local coordinators of the National Geographic Alliance had chosen three teachers and three students for the trip: Bernard Curtis Brown, 11, of Leckie Elementary School in Washington, D.C. and his teacher Hilda Taylor; Rodney Dickens, 11, of Ketcham Elementary School, and teacher James Debeuneure, 58, of Upper Marlboro, Maryland; and Asia Cottom, 11, a student at Backus Middle School in Washington, D.C., and his teacher, Sarah Clark, 65, of Columbia, Maryland.

Other teachers included Barbara Edwards, 58, who had taught French and German for five years at Palo Verde High School in Las Vegas. As a student in the 1980s, Mari-Rae Sopper had led her girls' gymnastics team to perennial state power. She was leaving a Washington, D.C., law career to take the head coaching job at the University of California, Santa Barbara.

Georgetown University economics professor Leslie A. Whittington, 45, her husband Charles S.

Falkenberg, 45, and their two daughters Zoe, 8, and Dana, 3, were moving to Australia. Professor Whittington had been awarded a fellowship at the University at Canberra.

Other passengers included Barbara K. Olson, conservative writer and commentator; Dr. Paul Ambrose, 32, a senior clinical advisor with the Office of the Surgeon General; and Yenenuh Betru, 35, of Burbank, California, director of medical affairs with IPC. Businessmen on Flight 77 included Ian J. Gray, 55, who helped create McBee Associates, a national healthcare finance and management consulting firm based in Columbia, Maryland, and Stanley Hall, 68, director of program management at the Washington, D.C., facility of Raytheon.

Mary Jane Booth, 64, secretary to the American Airlines general manager at Dulles International Airport, was a 45-year employee of the airline. Suzanne Calley worked for Cisco Systems; William E. Caswell was a physicist working on secret programs for the government; Eddie Dillard was a retired marketing manager with Philip Morris; Charles Droz was vice president of software development for EM Solutions; and Richard P. Gabriel Sr. was managing partner of Stratin Consulting.

Investigators estimate that Flight 77 was probably hijacked between 8:51 and 8:54 by Khalid Almindar, Majed Moged, Nawaf Alhazmi, Salem Alhazmi, and the suicide pilot Hani Hamjour (see TERRORISTS OF SEPTEMBER 11). By 8:56, the pilots had broadcast their last communication to air traffic control, the flight had turned around, and the transponder had been disabled. At this point, the Federal Aviation Administration (FAA) realized that there was an emergency. In New York, AMERICAN AIRLINES FLIGHT 11 had already crashed into the World Trade Center, and the FAA knew that UNITED AIRLINES FLIGHT 175 had been hijacked.

Flight attendant Renee May called her mother in Las Vegas at 9:12. She said that six individuals were hijacking her flight and passengers had been moved to the rear of the plane. Passenger Barbara K. Olson called her husband, U.S. Solicitor General Theodore Olson, at the Justice Department twice to tell him about the hijacking.

Hurtling at over 400 miles an hour, the hijacker-pilot of Flight 77 was forced to dive low enough, according to multiple eyewitness accounts, to glance off the ground before hitting the PENTAGON, reducing some of the impact of the crash. The plane slammed into the west side of the Pentagon at 9:43 A.M. The Pentagon is constructed in five concentric rings. The jetliner hit a section of the Pentagon consisting mainly of recently renovated, unoccupied offices. The impact penetrated three outer-ring sections of the western side, largely destroying the outermost ring section. A large portion collapsed, killing 125 people working in the building.

Because of the thick limestone walls and sturdy materials used in the renovation of the Pentagon, Flight 77 fully penetrated only the outer three rings, although it damaged all five rings. Most of the plane disintegrated in the massive explosion and subsequent fire, but investigators found some wreckage from the airliner within the impact zone and inside the building. A day after the crash, pieces of the fuselage were discovered as far as 90 feet away from the crash site.

Further Reading: Carolyn Gard, *The Attack on the Pentagon on September 11, 2001* (Rosen Publishing Group, 2003); David Ray Griffin, *The 9/11 Commission Report: Omissions and Distortions* (Interlink Publishing Group, 2005); "Hell on Earth," *UU World* (Jan/Feb, 2002); Eric Hufschmid, *Painful Questions: An Analysis of the September 11 Attacks* (Endpoint Software, 2002-2009); *One Nation: America Remembers September 11, 2001* (Little, Brown, 2001).

— KATHY WARNES

B

Bali

On October 12, 2002, two bombs exploded in the Kuta tourist area on the Indonesian resort island of Bali: one in Paddy's Irish Bar, and the other outside the Sari Club. The bombs killed 202 Indonesians and foreign tourists. A third bomb was detonated near the U.S. consulate in Bali, but caused no injuries or deaths.

Although not planned by individuals directly involved in al-Qaeda, the Bali attack demonstrated that September 11 was part of a worldwide campaign by radical jihadists. Jemaah Islamiyah (or Islamic Group) launched the Bali attack. Based in Southeast Asia and particularly strong in Indonesia, Jemaah Islamiyah has been supportive of al-Qaeda's goals, and its members follow a similar ideology. Within a month of the bombings, OSAMA BIN LADEN gave his approval with a taped message praising the bombers as "zealous sons of Islam."

Planning for the Bali bombings reportedly began about 10 months before the operation. Riduan Isamuddin, a Jemaah Islamiyah leader known as Hambali and reportedly the operations chief, was said to have instructed members of the organization to strike soft targets such as nightclubs instead of more difficult targets such as embassies and government sites.

The attacks reportedly were originally timed for the first anniversary of September 11, but were postponed because the explosives were not ready. The Paddy's bombing was conducted by a suicide bomber; the other bomb was in a van outside the Sari Club. Although the

TERROR AFTERMATH *A Balinese woman pays respect to the victims of the terrorist bombing in the Kuta tourist area of Bali, Indonesia. The attack was originally planned for the first anniversary of September 11 but was postponed until October 12 when the explosives could not be prepared in time. The bombing killed more than 180 people and injured 132.*

Indonesia has a predominantly Muslim culture. The organization Jemaah Islamiyah seeks to establish an Islamic state in the country, and began operations in the 1950s toward that goal.

Jemaah Islamiyah

JEMAAH ISLAMIYAH (JI), meaning Islamic group or community, is the principal terrorist group in Southeast Asia. Its antecedents began in the 1950s, when a group called Darul Islam (the Abode of Islam) fought to establish an Islamic state in West Java in Indonesia. Darul Islam also was active in the Indonesian war for independence from the Dutch.

Two radical Muslim clerics, Abu Bakar Ba'asyir and Abdullah Sungkar, were the founders. Both fought in the war in AFGHANISTAN against the Soviet occupation, then moved to Malaysia and founded JI in about 1993. The organization's stated goal is to establish an Islamic state encompassing all of Southeast Asia—including Indonesia, Malaysia, and the southern Philippines—that would be ruled by Sharia, or Islamic law.

Jemaah Islamiyah initially conducted nonviolent activities, primarily disseminating propaganda calling for Islamic rule. This changed when Ba'asyir met Riduan Isamuddin, better known as Hambali. After some talks about strategy, Hambali formed JI's military wing while Ba'asyir became the group's spiritual leader.

Prior to 2001, JI had a very formal structure headed by an emir, or leader, supported and advised by a leadership council and a consultative council, and divided into four functional areas that also had geographic responsibilities.

Mantiqi (brigade) One was responsible for fund-raising and covered Malaysia and Singapore. Mantiqi Two was responsible for leadership and recruiting and covered Indonesia. Mantiqi Three, covering the southern Philippines and Sabah and Sulawesi, oversaw training. Mantiqi Four was responsible for Australia and Papua New Guinea, an area into which JI wanted to expand its activities. JI was further subdivided into tactical battalions and companies to conduct operations.

Much of this structure seems to have crumbled in recent years. In part, this has been because of law enforcement and intelligence operations by regional governments against the JI organization. It is also probable that JI leaders have learned the lessons provided by al-Qaeda, and have recognized that a more networked, less hierarchical structure provides more security and operational flexibility.

Besides the 2002 Bali bombing, JI has been implicated in other significant attacks. It struck the Indonesian Stock Exchange on August 1, 2000, killing 15 and wounding 20. On August 5, 2003, a suicide bomber struck the Marriott Hotel in Jakarta, Indonesia, killing 12 and injuring about 150. On September 9, 2004, JI bombed the Australian embassy in Jakarta, killing 10 people and wounding 182. JI hit Bali again on October 1, 2005, with three suicide bombers in a resort area. This attack killed 19 and injured about 132.

plotters focused on killing Americans, most of the casualties came from other nations: 88 Australians, 38 Indonesians, 26 Britons, nine Swedes, seven Americans, six Germans, and four Dutch.

Indonesian security officials launched a massive investigation, greatly aided by Australian police and intelligence officials. In total, more than 30 persons were detained. The most important figures implicated in the bombings included Amrozi bin Nurhasyim, Imam Samudra, Muklas, Ali Imron, Azahari Husin, Idris, and Dulmatin. Two were Malaysian and the others Indonesian. They included a mechanic, a university lecturer, a technician, an Islamic teacher, and a computer expert. Three were brothers.

Despite confessions and testimony by some members against the others, the trials had only mixed results. Several defendants later recanted their confessions, claiming that they had been tortured.

Further Reading: Zachary Abuza, *Militant Islam in Southeast Asia: Crucible of Terror* (Lynne Rienner, 2003); Ralph Peters, *Beyond Terror* (Stackpole Books, 2004); Kumar Ramakrishna and See Seng Tan, eds., *After Bali: The Threat of Terrorism in Southeast Asia* (World Scientific, 2003).

— **LAWRENCE E. CLINE, PH.D.**

Beamer, Todd (1969–2001)

United Airlines Flight 93 was prevented from reaching its target by the courageous actions of passengers who had been told that hijacked planes had hit the World Trade Center and the Pentagon. Todd Beamer, a 32-year-old top sales representative for Oracle software, participated in an attempt to overpower the hijackers and prevent the plane from attacking the White House or the Capitol Building.

Todd and his wife Lisa had returned from Italy on the afternoon of September 10. He was due in San Francisco the following day and had considered flying straight out from the Newark airport but wanted to see his sons, David and Drew. Even if he had tried to leave New Jersey on the 10th, Beamer would not have been able to—outgoing flights had been canceled due to a fire at the Newark airport. The next plane to San Francisco was the 8:00 A.M. flight on September 11, UNITED AIRLINES FLIGHT 93.

Todd spent the evening playing with his sons. He rose at 5:45 A.M, leaving his wife of seven years and his sons asleep in their home in Cranbury, New Jersey. The day before, Todd had seemed reluctant to make the trip to San Francisco and told his wife that he would be glad when the coming week was over. He planned to return home that night on a red-eye flight.

After taking control of Flight 93, one hijacker was assigned to guard the passengers and remaining

ABOVE *Quilt tile created in memory of Todd Beamer for the United In Memory 9/11 Victims Memorial Quilt.*

crewmembers. It is believed that the pilot and copi-lot were killed early in the HIJACKING. The guard did not prevent anyone from using the telephone, and most of the passengers and crew used cell phones to contact family and friends. Rather than scaring his wife Lisa who was five months pregnant, Beamer used an Airfone to call for help. Beamer was connected with GTC Airfone operator Lisa Jefferson in Cleveland, Ohio. Through her meticulous notes and later through the plane's voice recorder, officials were able to get a partial picture of the events.

Beamer was a golfer, skier, and baseball player. He was also used to being in charge and not the type to submit to threats without taking action. Beamer told Jefferson that he and some of the other passengers were planning to attack the hijackers and seize control of the plane, asked her to call his family if he didn't survive, and to say the Lord's Prayer with him, which she did. They also recited the 23rd Psalm together, and Jefferson could hear other voices joining in the recitation.

Immediately before the passengers rushed the cockpit, Jefferson heard Beamer say, "Are you ready? OK, let's roll!"—a favorite expression in Beamer's household. Jefferson heard screams, followed by silence. She remained on the line for 15 minutes after Beamer's rallying cry. Finally, her supervisor told her to end the call.

Lisa Beamer first learned that a plane had crashed into the the World Trade Center when a friend called her at 9 A.M. Concerned about her husband, she left a message on his cell phone, then tried calling Continental Airlines, which Todd generally flew, but representatives refused to confirm whether Todd had been on a flight. Lisa knew Todd sometimes flew United, but her calls to United did not go through. Twice around 10 A.M., Lisa's phone rang, but no one was on the line when she answered. The

The Todd M. Beamer Foundation

AFTER THE tragedy of September 11, with the donations that poured in from around the world, Lisa Beamer started the Todd M. Beamer Foundation (www.thebeamerfoundation.org) to work with children who have experienced trauma. Lisa Beamer serves as chair of the foundation's board. Heroic Choices, the signature program of the foundation, works with but is not exclusive to children who lost parents and other loved ones on September 11. The program also works with children in the northeast and mid-Atlantic regions who have experienced traumas that range from death of a loved one to sexual abuse. Plans are under way to extend the program throughout the United States. The year-long program allots $5,000 per child to cover such activities as a retreat for the child, a family member, and a mentor; training and counseling; and special events. In addition to working directly with children, the foundation conducts research on the effects of childhood trauma.

calls were never explained. She learned later that United Airlines Flight 93 had crashed at 10:10. Lisa later said that when she saw televised images of an airliner driven into the ground, she knew that it was Todd's plane and that he was gone.

The families and friends of the passengers and crew of United Airlines Flight 93 were invited to a memorial in Shanksville on September 17. At the site, a makeshift altar had been made from bales of hay. Todd Beamer's family left personal notes, a Chicago

Bulls baseball hat, M&Ms candy, an Oracle pen, and *A Life of Integrity* by Howard Hendricks, which Todd had been reading in his Friday-morning breakfast group. Todd's daughter Megan was born January 11, 2002, exactly four months after his death.

With the donations that poured in from around the world, Lisa Beamer started the Todd M. Beamer Foundation (www.thebeamerfoundation.org) to work with children who have experienced trauma.

Further Reading: Lisa Beamer, *Let's Roll: Ordinary People, Extraordinary Courage* (Tyndale House, 2002); Steven Brill, *After: How America Confronted the September 12 Era* (Simon and Schuster, 2003); Lisa Jefferson, *Called* (Northfield, 2006); Jerre Longman, *Among the Heroes: United Flight 93 and the Passengers and Crew Who Fought Back* (HarperCollins, 2002).

— **ELIZABETH PURDY, PH.D.**

AT RIGHT *Ramzi Bin al Shibh was assigned a leadership role for what was called the "plane operation." He was a go-between for Mohamed Atta and Khalid Sheikh Mohammed.*

Bin al Shibh, Ramzi (1972–)

Delegated the role of plot supervisor after failing to obtain a U.S. visa, Ramzi Bin al Shibh coordinated final plans, pay, and targets for the terrorists. He first attempted to leave Yemen in 1995, by applying for a U.S. visa. After his application was rejected, he went to GERMANY and applied for asylum under the name Ramzi Omar, claiming to be a Sudanese citizen.

In Hamburg, Bin al Shibh met the other terrorists at al-Quds Mosque. In 1998, Bin al Shibh shared an apartment in Hamburg with Mohamed Atta and a young student from the United Arab Emirates named Marwan Alshehri. Like the other, he went to Chechnya to fight the Russians in 1999 and emergd in AFGHANISTAN, trained to be a martyr.

In Afghanistan, Bin al Shibh met and pledged obedience to OSAMA BIN LADEN and went on to Ka-

rachi, Pakistan, where he and Atta were introduced to KHALID SHEIKH MOHAMMED and assigned their leadership roles for the "planes operation." Since Bin al Shibh could not accompany the other Hamburg cell members (see SLEEPER CELLS) to the United States, he was assigned the role of go-between for Atta and Sheikh Mohammed.

One year after September 11, Bin al Shibh was captured in a raid by Pakistani forces in Karachi and turned over to the United States three days later. At the end of 2006, he remained in U.S. custody at an undisclosed location.

Further Reading: Rohan Gunaratna, *Inside Al Qaeda: Global Network of Terror* (Penguin Group, 2003); National Commission on Terrorist Attacks Upon the United States, *The 9/11 Commission Report: Final Report of the National Commission on Terrorist Attacks Upon the United States* (W.W. Norton, 2004).

— **WADE K. EWING**

Bin Laden, Osama (1957–)

In a videotape released to the Al-Jazeera Arabic television network in October 2001, Osama bin Laden, the wealthy Saudi Arabian leader of the AL-QAEDA terrorist organization, exulted over the

Bin Laden on September 11

ON SEPTEMBER 11, all AL-QAEDA camps in AFGHANI-STAN were placed on high alert, and Osama bin Laden tuned in his radio to await the news reports. Sulayman Abu Ghaith, the official spokesperson for al-Qaeda, later recalled the atmosphere "Do you know when there is a soccer game and your team wins, it was the same expression of joy," according to Peter Bergen. After the first plane hit the World Trade Center, the 50 or 60 people in the room, unaware that there were more attacks impendent, erupted with shouts. Bin Laden calmly advised them to be patient. In another room, RAMZI BIN AL SHIBH, one of the principal organizers of the attacks, was watching on television when the second plane appeared, headed for the South Tower. He remembered praying, "God.. aim...aim...aim." Abu Ghaith, also watching on television, became so excited that he went to bin Laden to inform him of what was happening. "I tried to tell him about what I saw, but he made a gesture with his hands, meaning: 'I know, I know.'"

AT LEFT *A poster depicting Osama bin Laden entitled "A drop of my blood will give birth to hundreds of Osamas."*

September 11 attacks. "There is America," he proclaimed, "full of fear from its north to its south, from its west to its east. Thank God for that. What America tastes now, is something insignificant compared to what we [the Islamic world] have tasted for scores of years." By implicitly admitting his responsibility for the attacks, bin Laden positioned himself as the world's most lethal terrorist and—in the eyes of his followers—a champion defender of Islam.

Bin Laden's formative experience was the Islamic JIHAD in Afghanistan after the Soviet Union's invasion in 1979. The following year the 23-year-old left his elite life in Saudi Arabia—his family became billionaires in the construction industry and had close ties to the Saudi royal family—to help drive out the Soviets from a traditionally Muslim nation. He became an important financier for the Afghan resistance fighters (see MUJAHIDEEN), and by 1987 had gained a reputation as a war hero in the Arab press, although he played a negligible military role.

In AFGHANISTAN, bin Laden was involved in a significant ideological quarrel among jihadists. His mentor, the popular radical Palestinian cleric Abdullah Azzam, preached a jihad of resistance. He called for Muslim unity and opposed the use of terrorist tactics. But bin Laden was also swayed by members from the Egyptian Islamic Jihad, who insisted jihad should be expansive, international, and relentlessly violent.

The Egyptians sought the revolutionary overthrow of "apostate" Muslim governments, which they regarded as corrupt and insufficiently Islamic. Bin Laden eventually sided with the Egyptians and may have been involved in Azzam's assassination in 1989. He took their ideas a step further: rather than concentrate on apostate Middle Eastern regimes, he would attack the United States, which often provided their bulwark. He reasoned that he must kill "the head of the snake."

Bin Laden founded al-Qaeda in 1988, shortly before the Soviet Union withdrew from Afghanistan. He returned to Saudi Arabia in 1989, becoming an outspoken critic of the Saudi regime, particularly after the royal family permitted the United States to deploy troops on Saudi land during the PERSIAN GULF WAR in 1991. For bin Laden, this was an act of apostasy, enabling infidels to occupy the sacred Muslim cities of Mecca and Medina. He later cited the permanent U.S. military presence after the war as confirmation of the Saudi regime's illegitimacy, and one of the principal justifications for the September 11 attacks.

Bin Laden left SAUDI ARABIA in 1991, and was harbored for a few years by the Islamist government in Sudan. He returned to Afghanistan in 1996 and issued his first fatwa, a declaration of war against "the Zionist-Crusaders alliance"—Israel and the United States—that addressed, among other issues, the treatment of Palestinians and the United Nations sanctions against IRAQ. In an American television interview in 1997 on CNN, a soft-voiced bin Laden warned the audience that he would carry out jihad against them. U.S. INTELLIGENCE officials, who had regarded him as simply an "extremist financier," began to pay serious attention to bin Laden as a possible terrorist organizer.

Bin Laden has been described by TERRORISM expert Peter Bergen as "the chairman of the company," a charismatic figure who draws jihadists to al-Qaeda's cause. He leaves the planning of operations to subordinates such as KHALID SHEIKH MOHAMMED, who masterminded the September 11 attacks, but retains ultimate authority. The 9/11 Commission found that he sometimes took a hands-on approach—while also making compromises—as planning progressed. He scaled back Mohammed's original idea to hijack ten planes simultaneously and hit targets that included a nuclear power plant. He personally chose the first two terrorists assigned to the operation, Nawaf Alhazmi and Khalid Almindhar, and interviewed and approved all of the "muscle hijackers." Bin Laden chose Mohamed Atta as the leader of the sleeper cell (see SLEEPER CELLS) in the United States. At the same time, he deferred to Atta's opinion that the White House—bin Laden's own choice—was too difficult a target, and allowed Atta to set the attack date.

Further Reading: Peter L. Bergen, *The Osama bin Laden I Know: An Oral History of al Qaeda's Leader* (Free Press, 2006); Rohan Gunaratna, *Inside Al Qaeda: Global Network of Terror* (Columbia University Press, 2002); National Commission on Terrorist Attacks Upon the United States, *The 9/11 Commission Report* (W.W. Norton, 2004); Jonathan Randal, *Osama: The Making of a Terrorist* (Alfred A. Knopf, 2004).

— TOM COLLINS

ABOVE *Osama bin Laden founded al-Qaeda in 1988, and trained guerrilla fighters at his al-Farooq camp in Afghanistan. A video grab above from June 19, 2001, shows members of "The Base" organization, training with AK-47 (Kalashnikov) sub-machine-guns in a videotape said to have been prepared and released by bin Laden himself.*

Bingham, Mark (1970–2001)

The head of his own bicoastal public relations firm, Mark Bingham, 31, frequently flew between New York and California. When UNITED AIRLINES FLIGHT 93 left Newark on September 11, Bingham was in seat 4-D in the rear of the first-class compartment. Standing 6'4" and 220 pounds, Bingham played on the Fog, a gay rugby team. He had also played rugby at the University of California, Berkeley, and was on his college baseball team in Wheaton, Illinois. The previous summer, he had ridden the horns of a bull in Pamplona, Spain. Several years before, Bingham had taken a gun away from a mugger and thrashed him and his accomplice.

Bingham spent the night of September 10 at the home of his partner Matt Hall, discussing Bingham's moving to the east coast and the couple making their relationship permanent. The two men left for the Newark airport just before 7 A.M. on September 11. From the plane, Bingham made one quick call to Hall, thanking him for the lift to the airport.

Bingham was particularly close to his mother, Alice Hoglan, who had raised him alone. They had been through hard times together, at one time living in the back of a pickup truck. When Bingham called Alice around 6:54 A.M. (9:54 A.M. on the east coast) he was so rattled that he said, "Mom, this is Mark Bingham." He told her that three men had taken control of the plane and were claiming to have a bomb. It was not until after they ended the conversation that Hoglan learned of the hijackings of the planes that had already found targets in New York City and Washington, D.C.

As a flight attendant for United Airlines, Hoglan was trained to deal with hijackers, and she believed that the HIJACKING of Flight 93 was likely connected to the earlier attacks. Hoglan left two messages on her son's phone telling him the hijackers were on a suicide mission and urging him to do anything he could to prevent them from hitting another target. She did not learn until later that Bingham and his fellow passengers had rammed the cockpit door with a food cart.

At 10:10 A.M., Flight 93 crashed into an isolated field near Shanksville, PENNSYLVANIA, some 20 flight-minutes from the nation's capital. At Bingham's memorial service on September 22, 2001, his friend Todd Sarner stated that he believed Mark, despite any fear, would have been involved in any attempt to take back the plane.

ABOVE *Mark Bingham's quilt tile from the United In Memory 9/11 Victims Memorial Quilt. To keep the memory of Bingham and those of Flight 93 alive, friends and family created the Mark Bingham Leadership Fund Scholarship, and also raise charitable funds through events such as the annual Beer-Bust Fundraiser held at Finnegans Wake, a favorite bar of Bingham's.*

In *Hero of Flight 93: Mark Bingham: A Man Who Fought Back on September 11*, released on the first anniversary of the September 11 attacks, Jon Barrett relates the story of Bingham and the other heroes of Flight 93. Barrett presents Bingham as a man who lived his life to the fullest and one who did not hesitate to unite with the other passengers to foil the terrorists' plot. Family and friends of Mark Bingham have created the Mark Bingham Leadership Fund Scholarship, awarding $3,000 to $5,000 each year to cover tuition, room and board, and other academic expenses for a student at the University of California, Berkeley.

Further Reading: Jon Barrett, *Hero of Flight 93: Mark Bingham: A Man Who Fought Back on September 11* (Alyson Publications, 2002); Lisa Beamer, *Let's Roll: Ordinary People, Extraordinary Courage* (Tyndale House, 2002); Jerre Longman, *Among the Heroes: United Flight 93 and the Passengers and Crew Who Fought Back* (HarperCollins, 2002).

— **ELIZABETH PURDY, PH.D.**

ABOVE *Detail of the quilt tile in memory of Thomas E. Burnett from the United In Memory 9/11 Victims Memorial Quilt. Burnett's family raises money for the Tom Burnett Family Foundation, the Moyer Foundation, and provides a scholarship at Burnett's alma mater, Pepperdine University.*

Burnett, Thomas E. (1963–2001)

Thomas E. (Tom) Burnett, Jr., 38, of San Ramon, California, was seated in the fourth row of the first class section of UNITED AIRLINES FLIGHT 93 on September 11. He was one of four men who organized a plan to prevent the hijackers from reaching a possible target in Washington, D.C. Burnett, the senior vice president and chief executive officer of Thoretec, a manufacturer of medical devices, was the father of five-year-old twins Madison and Haley and three-year-old Anna, and had been married to his wife Deena for ten years. Burnett had spent much of the last six days on airplanes, arriving home in the afternoon on September 5 and leaving the same night on a hunting trip to Minnesota. On September 11, he was returning home.

Burnett's call to his wife at 9:27 A.M. (6:27 on the West Coast) was one of the first made from United Airlines Flight 93. Burnett told Deena that a passenger had been knifed and asked her to report the HIJACKING to authorities. She did so at 6:31. After several transfers, Deena talked to an agent at the Federal Bureau of Investigation. Seven minutes after the first call, Burnett called again. He told her that the passenger who had been stabbed was dead, and she related news of the attacks that had occurred in New York City and Washington, D.C.

Burnett called Deena again at 9:45 A.M. and told her that a group of passengers were planning to "do something" when they got to a rural area in order to "take back the airplane." The final call came a few minutes later. Burnett asked about his daughters, who were eating breakfast, and told Deena he would talk to them later. He again mentioned that they were watching for a rural area before making their move. As a former flight attendant, Deena advised Burnett not to call attention to himself. He asked her to pray. When Deena told him she loved him, he said not to worry and hung up.

Shortly after 10 A.M., the passengers of United Airlines Flight 93 rushed the cockpit, using a food cart as a battering ram. They wielded forks, knives, and boiling water as weapons. It is assumed that when it became obvious that the passengers could not be deterred, the hijackers flew the plane into the ground.

The crash occurred at 10:10 in a deserted field near the small town of Shanksville, Pennsylvania (see PENNSYLVANIA, SHANKSVILLE). Armed with knowledge about the other hijackings, the passengers and crew of United Airlines Flight 93 had managed what no others had been able to do on September 11. No one on the ground was involved in the crash. The plane was only seconds away from the local elementary school and less than 20 minutes from the nation's capital.

Tom Burnett's family has created the Tom Burnett Family Foundation (www.tomburnettfoundation.org) to work with local communities in providing leadership, citizenship, and scholarship programs nationwide.

Further Reading: Lisa Beamer, *Let's Roll: Ordinary People, Extraordinary Courage* (Tynydale House, 2002); Tonya Buell, *The Crash of United Flight 93 on September 11, 2001* (Rosen, 2005); Jerre Longman, *Among the Heroes: United Flight 93 and the Passengers and Crew Who Fought Back* (HarperCollins, 2002).

— ELIZABETH PURDY, PH.D.

Bush, George W. (1946–)

September 11, 2001, was an exciting day at the Emma E. Booker Elementary School in Sarasota, Florida: President George W. Bush was coming to visit. Booker students had shown remarkable improvement in reading test scores, and the Bush administration had chosen the school as a photo opportunity for the president to tout his proposed education reform bill.

Bush arrived at the school at 8:55 A.M., ten minutes after AMERICAN AIRLINES FLIGHT 11 crashed into the World Trade Center, about seven minutes after the first news reports. The president most likely learned about it from his press secretary, Ari Fleischer, who was alerted through a call on his cell phone during the short drive through Sarasota.

Bush said in an October 2001 interview that "... I thought it was pilot error and I was amazed that anybody could make such a terrible mistake. And something was wrong with the plane..."

Bush was escorted to Sandra Kay Daniels' second-grade classroom, where her 16 pupils were waiting. After introductions and photos, Daniels said, "Are you ready, my butterflies?" and led her children through some reading exercises. Then she asked them to open their books and turn to Lesson 60 on page 153, a story entitled "The Pet Goat."

AL-QAEDA ATTACKS

Suddenly, White House Chief of Staff Andrew Card whispered into Bush's ear. Tyler Radkey, a student sitting close to the president, saw him sag back into his chair. "His face just sort of turned red," Radkey said in 2006. As they would learn later, Card had told Bush that a second plane had struck the World Trade Center and that "America is under attack."

The Secret Service did not immediately escort the president from the room. Card stepped back; Bush asked no questions. Later he described his thoughts and feelings: "I am very aware of the cameras. I'm trying to absorb that knowledge. I have nobody to talk to. I'm sitting in the midst of a classroom with little kids, listening to a children's story and I realize I'm the commander in chief and the country has just come under attack."

The children began to read in unison. In the back of the room, Fleischer held up a note written in big block letters so the president could see it: DON'T SAY ANYTHING YET.

When the children finished reading at around 9:16, Bush thanked them and told them to study hard and be good citizens. A presidential aide hustled everyone out of the classroom. Bush has come under repeated criticism for not leaving the classroom immediately.

Bush met with his staff in an empty classroom and watched news coverage on television. He made brief phone calls to National Security Advisor Condoleezza Rice and Vice President Dick Cheney (see RICHARD B. CHENEY) in Washington, D.C., and to New York Governor George Pataki. His aides handed him some prepared remarks.

At 9:30, he stepped in front of the cameras. "Today we've had a national tragedy. Two airplanes have crashed into the World Trade Center in an apparent terrorist attack on our country." Bush wanted to go straight back to Washington, D.C., but his advisors and security staffs were unsure. On the way to the Sarasota airport, they learned that AMERICAN AIRLINES FLIGHT 77 had struck the Pentagon.

At 9:45, the White House was evacuated. Rumors were that at least 11 planes still in the air might have been hijacked. There were also rumors that terrorists were planning to attack AIR FORCE ONE. The president's jet left Sarasota at 9:55 without waiting for a fighter escort.

During the hour or so he was in the air, the president called First Lady Laura Bush, who had been at the Capitol for a Senate education committee hearing. Her security detail had taken her and their daughters, Jenna and Barbara, to a secure location. "She couldn't have been more calm, resolved—almost placid," Bush said later. "It was very reassuring for me. I told her: 'I'll be home soon.'"

SAFE HAVEN

At 11:45 A.M., the plane put down at Barksdale Air Force Base in Louisiana, where the president taped a brief statement for the media and discussed where he should go next with Cheney and advisor Karl Rove. The media was asking why the president had not returned to the White House, but there were still reports that he might be the target of an attack. The president was taken to Offutt Air Force Base in Nebraska, home of the U.S. Strategic Command center. "As much as anything, he didn't want to use up any more time talking about it," Card told the media later. "He knew he'd be criticized, whatever. But it was the right thing to do."

Air Force One took off from Barksdale at about 1:30 P.M., and during the flight, Bush called New York City Mayor RUDOLPH GIULIANI. "He sounded very calm, very purposeful. He said: 'We're going to rebuild the city. And we're going to get whoever did this,'" Giuliani later recalled. "The last bit didn't sound like an afterthought."

Landing at Offutt around 2:50 P.M. local time, Bush was escorted into a hardened underground bunker where he met with Cheney, Rice, Secretary of Defense DONALD RUMSFELD and the National Security Council via teleconference. Rice remembered him saying: "This is an attack on freedom, and we're going to treat it as such. We have to minister to the country, and deal with the horrors, but we're not going to lose focus. We have to mobilize the world and rid it of this scourge." She told him that early reports indicated the attack was the work of OSAMA BIN LADEN and his AL-QAEDA network.

His Secret Service detail wanted Bush to stay at Offutt indefinitely or at the very least overnight. But with political and media pressure mounting, U.S.

AT LEFT *President George W. Bush (L), and Secretary of Defense Donald Rumsfeld (R) view the disaster scene at the Pentagon on September 12, 2001. The Pentagon was struck by American Airlines Flight 77 the day before.*

airspace clear of all traffic, and more than six hours having passed since the last attack, it was time to return to Washington, D.C. Bush arrived at the White House around 7:00 P.M., and went into planning sessions with his national security staff.

The next days would offer a number of iconic images of Bush standing atop the rubble with a bullhorn on September 15, and vowing to bring bin Laden to justice "dead or alive" on September 17. But the strategy and tactics of the War on Terror were in gear: the narrative, rhetoric, and philosophy that would dominate the remaining years of the Bush presidency were set within hours of the attacks.

Bush's response to the attacks was based on his personality and his worldview. Raised in an Episcopalian family, Bush joined the Methodist Church after marrying Laura and becoming a father. In the mid-1980s, he become a born-again Christian under the guidance of evangelist Billy Graham. This gave a religious underpinning to his belief that the world was divided between good and evil.

The United States was good and the terrorists were evil, and since good would always prevail over evil, it was his job to to destroy the terrorists at all costs. "We will make no distinction between the terrorists who committed these acts and those who harbor them," he said at 8:30 P.M. on September 11. Within days, the United States was at war with AFGHANISTAN, where Osama bin Laden was believed to be hiding.

Further Reading: Ivo H. Daalder and James M. Lindsay, *America Unbound: The Bush Revolution in Foreign Policy* (John Wiley and Sons, 2005); Paul Kengor, *God and George W. Bush: A Spiritual Life* (HarperCollins, 2005); Bill Sammon, *Fighting Back: The War on Terrorism from Inside the Bush White House* (National Book Network, 2002); Bob Woodward, *Bush at War* (Simon and Schuster, 2003).

— **HEATHER K. MICHON**

"Terrible Sadness"

PRESIDENT BUSH addressed the nation from the Oval Office on the night of September 11, 2001. The following is an excerpt:

"Today, our fellow citizens, our way of life, our very freedom came under attack in a series of deliberate and deadly terrorist acts. The victims were in airplanes or in their offices: secretaries, business men and women, military and federal workers, moms and dads, friends and neighbors. Thousands of lives were suddenly ended by evil, despicable acts of terror. The pictures of airplanes flying into buildings, fires burning, huge structures collapsing have filled us with disbelief, terrible sadness, and a quiet, unyielding anger. These acts of mass murder were intended to frighten our nation into chaos and retreat. But they have failed. Our country is strong.

A great people has been moved to defend a great nation. Terrorist attacks can shake the foundations of our biggest buildings, but they cannot touch the foundation of America. These acts shatter steel, but they cannot dent the steel of American resolve. America was targeted for attack because we're the brightest beacon for freedom and opportunity in the world. And no one will keep that light from shining. Today, our nation saw evil—the very worst of human nature—and we responded with the best of America."

ABOVE *Defense Department poster with the inscription "A terrorist attack designed to tear us apart has instead bound us together as a nation." — President George W. Bush.*

C

Cantor Fitzgerald

Normally, Cantor Fitzgerald chief executive officer Howard Lutnick was in his office on the 105th floor of World Trade Center One by 8 A.M., but September 11 was a special day: it was his 5-year-old son Kyle's first day of kindergarten.

Lutnick had just left the Horace Mann School when he learned that a plane had struck the North Tower. Cantor Fitzgerald, a brokerage firm specializing in trading government bonds between banks and other financial institutions, was one of the World Trade Center's largest tenants, occupying most of floors 101 through 105. He raced to the scene. "The people, they're all wet because of the sprinklers. They're zombies, walking straight. They have no idea what's going on," he said later. As they went by, he asked their floor numbers. They stopped at 91—ten floors below his offices.

AMERICAN AIRLINES FLIGHT 11 struck the North Tower between the 94th and 98th floors with a power equivalent to 480,000 pounds of dynamite. Of the 1,360 people killed above the 98th floor, 658—nearly half—worked for Cantor Fitzgerald.

Most of the brokers were young men in their 30s, just starting their careers and families. Cantor Fitzgerald lost about a quarter of its workforce, and at least 1,350 children lost a parent. The company employed more than 20 sets of brothers. Among them was Lutnick's younger brother Gary, who, trapped in his office on the 103rd floor, called their sister Edie. His was among dozens of calls made from

ABOVE *Workers on the upper floors of the World Trade Centers had few viable escape routes from the burning wreckage.*

Cantor Fitzgerald workers reaching out in their final moments.

Lutnick ran for his life as the South Tower thundered down at 10:03. The North Tower followed 25 minutes later. Lutnick spent the next four hours wandering around the city. "I—I was—I'm a pretty together person, and I—four hours I walked," he said in an interview two days later. "I just walked—walked. I just kept walking."

Lutnick was a familiar face on television the next few days, often in tears – a departure from his reputation as one of the financial world's more ruthless operators. In 1996, Lutnick wrested control of the company as his mentor Bernie Cantor, the company's founder, lay dying. Many people had difficulty accepting his emotional pledges to care for the families of those lost in the attacks.

Early events seemed to confirm suspicions. On September 15, Cantor Fitzgerald stopped payroll for the employees presumed dead in the attacks. Executives explained the move was necessary to stop the outflow of cash that threatened to bankrupt the company. With many of its top brokers gone and its principal markets closed, the company was losing millions every day. Some of the families were outraged by what they perceived as a cold-hearted corporate response to their personal tragedies.

Surviving staff members moved to office space donated by UBS Warburg in Connecticut. Changes in data storage methods after the WORLD TRADE CENTER 1993 bombings meant that the company did not lose critical information, but the majority of its brokers were killed, and it took time to get back into operation.

Most of Cantor Fitzgerald's clients stayed with the company during the transition. As the company revived, Lutnick began to make good on his promises to victims' families. In October and November 2001, Cantor Fitzgerald paid out $45 million in bonuses. Lutnick also pledged 25 percent of the company's profits through September 2006 to a special relief fund, and to pay full healthcare benefits for survivors and their children for 10 years.

The Cantor Fitzgerald Relief Fund was created to collect and distribute money to affected families. By September 2006, the fund had given out $175 million to more than 800 families. It continues to offer financial, legal, and emotional counseling and support to all survivors who need assistance.

Five years after the tragedy, Cantor Fitzgerald was financially on track and established in new offices about five miles from Ground Zero.

Further Reading: Tom Barbash, *On Top of the World: Cantor Fitzgerald, Howard Lutnick, and 9/11* (HarperCollins, 2003); Greg Manning, *Love, Greg & Lauren: A Powerful True Story of Courage, Hope, and Survival* (Bantam Books, 2002).

— **HEATHER K. MICHON**

Casualty Figures

Americans could not turn away from their televisions as they witnessed the devastation at the World Trade Center (WTC) and the Pentagon on September 11. Millions knew someone who worked in Manhattan, and more widespread attacks were feared. In the first hours and days after the attack, little information was available beyond the images of crashing planes, collapsing buildings, and the knowledge that thousands were certainly dead.

There were fewer injured than thought because so many died. Still, more than 1,000 were treated at area hospitals on September 11, 200 of them in critical condition. Another 1,600 still ambulatory were treated at Liberty State Park in New Jersey. By September 20, 6,291 people, including rescue and recovery workers, had been treated for injuries. Only five were found alive in the post-collapse rubble: Port Authority police David Lim, Will Jimeno, and John MacLaughlin; Port Authority clerk Genelle Guzman; and Armando Reno of the FIRE DEPARTMENT OF NEW YORK (FDNY).

By September 16, Mayor RUDOLPH GIULIANI reported 180 confirmed dead from WTC, with 115 identified. He called losses "staggering," but asked that people not bow to TERRORISM, and continue life as normally as possible.

There are empty spaces in collapsed buildings called "triangles of life." They adjoin areas like cars, drink machines, and large, sturdy furnishings. Due to the weight of the WTC, it was already known that finding such spaces was unlikely. Salvage operations were made more difficult by mud from heavy rains.

As duplicate names were removed from lists and loved ones located, the death count actually dropped. A final total may never be known.

At first, casualty reports for Washington, D.C., were between one and 800. It was later determined that 189 died there, including the 64 on AMERICAN AIRLINES FLIGHT 77. In New York, 300 firefighters were feared dead, and dozens of police officers were missing; 265 people were known killed in the four airliners. On September 16, 5,097 were reported missing from the Twin Towers. Fifty thousand people worked in the WTC.

PLANES HIJACKED

AMERICAN AIRLINES FLIGHT 11 carried 81 passengers, nine flight attendants, and two pilots. "Oh my God," said flight attendant Madeline Sweeney, very calmly, as she gave information on the HIJACKING

ABOVE *A lone firefighter stands amid the rubble and smoke in New York City. Fires burned for days at Ground Zero.*

World Casualties

ON SEPTEMBER 12, 2001, countries from around the world were reporting dozens missing and feared dead. Initial reports showed 700 Germans, 500 Mexicans, 300 from the United Kingdom, and 50 Bangladeshi as missing.

In the end, the attack was not just on the United States but on many nations, including: Antigua and Barbuda, Argentina, Australia, Austria, Bangladesh, Barbados, Belgium, Belarus, Belize, Bolivia, Brazil, Canada, Chile, China, Colombia, Congo, Czech Republic, Dominica, Dominican Republic, Ecuador, Egypt, El Salvador, Ethiopia, France, Gambia, Germany, Ghana, Greece, Grenada, Guatemala, Guyana, Haiti, Honduras, Hong Kong, India, Indonesia, Iran, Ireland, Israel, Italy, Jamaica, Japan, Jordan, Kazakhstan, Kenya, Lebanon, Liberia, Luxembourg, Malaysia, Mexico, Netherlands, New Zealand, Nicaragua, Nigeria, Pakistan, Panama, Paraguay, Peru, Philippines, Poland, Portugal, Romania, Russia, Slovakia, South Africa, South Korea, Spain, Sri Lanka, St. Kitts–Nevis, St. Lucia, St. Vincent and the Grenadines, Sweden, Switzerland, Taiwan, Thailand, Togo, Trinidad and Tobago, Turkey, Ukraine, United Kingdom, Uruguay, Uzbekistan, Venezuela, Yemen, and Zimbabwe.

September 11 Casualties

VICTIMS	NUMBER
American Airlines Flight 11	92
American Airlines Flight 77	64
United Airlines Flight 175	65
United Airlines Flight 93	44
Pentagon	125
World Trade Center	2,152
Fire Department of New York	343
New York Police Department	23
Port Authority Police Department	37
TOTAL CONFIRMED DEAD	2,948

to ground supervisor Michael Woodward at Logan Airport in Boston, just before Flight 11 crashed into the North Tower. It was 8:45 A.M.

UNITED AIRLINES FLIGHT 175 had 56 passengers and nine crew. It crashed into the South Tower between floors 78 and 84 at 9:03. Portions of the jet, traveling 590 miles per hour at impact, went out the north side, crashing to earth six blocks away. Passenger Peter Burton Hanson had reported to his father in a phone call that the terrorists were stabbing flight attendants to force crew to open the cockpit doors.

AMERICAN AIRLINES FLIGHT 77, which crashed into the PENTAGON, carried 58 passengers and six crew. Barbara Olson, former Congressional staffer, Republican activist, and Fox News commentator, was among the victims. She managed two phone calls to her husband, reporting the use of "knife-like" weapons by hijackers. Two National Geographic Society staff members, three teachers, and three children were among the dead. In the Pentagon, 125 people were dead or missing. Lieutenant General Timothy Maude was the highest-ranking officer to die, along with Max Bielke, the last official U.S. combat soldier to leave Vietnam.

Earliest reports had UNITED AIRLINES FLIGHT 93 headed for Camp David. There were 37 passengers and seven crew aboard. Several phone calls were made from aboard the plane, and passengers were apparently aware of the attacks on the WTC and Pentagon.

"I know we are going to die. Some of us are going to do something about it," said Tom Burnett Jr. (see THOMAS E. BURNETT) in a call to his wife. JEREMY GLICK said to his wife, Lyzbeth, in another call, "We're going to rush the hijackers." Voice box recordings show passengers successfully entered the cockpit. All died when the plane crashed into a Shanksville, PENNSYLVANIA, field at 10:10 A.M.

WORLD TRADE CENTER HIT

The greatest loss of life occurred at the World Trade Center (see WORLD TRADE TOWERS). The only escape from the heat and smoke on upper floors for many was to jump. It is estimated that 50 people did just that. FDNY's Daniel Thomas Suhr died when a falling body hit him. Other attempts at escape involved heading to the roof for helicopter rescue. There were no plans for rooftop rescue, and some accounts state roof doors were locked. Some who tried to reach the roof were among the 67 fatalities at Keefe and Bruyette. Many had gathered in offices and conference rooms on the 88th and 89th floors. The 9/11 Commission found that the city's 9-1-1 operators had not known that the police had ruled out helicopter rescues, nor that an evacuation order had been issued.

Evacuations started in the North Tower. Those in the South Tower were told they were safe, and to return to their offices. Some evacuated anyway. Evacuation drills had been ongoing since before the bombing in 1993, when six were killed. These drills, which enabled all but six of Morgan Stanley's 2,700 employees to survive, were directly attributable to Rick Rescorla, head of security of Morgan Stanley, who had predicted that there would be another attack on the WTC and that it would come by air. As the public-address announcements told people in the South Tower to stay put, Rescorla was marching people two-by-two down the stairs to safety. He feared that the first tower might topple onto the second.

Up to 1,366 people were trapped on or above the floors of impact in the North Tower. None survived; as many as 600 were trapped on or above the floors of impact in the South Tower. About 18 managed to escape.

According to information released in 2006, 130 calls were made to 9-1-1 from inside the towers; 27 callers were identified, and next of kin were notified and allowed to listen. Fifteen thousand people were

ABOVE *Billowing smoke fills the Manhattan skyline after the collapse of the Twin Towers.*

at the towers that day, but large groups rather than individuals made many of the calls. One such group was on the 105th floor of the South Tower, where people had come together after trying to reach the roof. Kevin Cosgrove, a worker on the 100th floor, had earlier called his family to tell them he was going downstairs, but turned back with breathing trouble.

Those on the highest floors suffered from rising heat and smoke. In the Cantor Fitzgerald offices on the 104th floor of the North Tower, 25 to 50 people gathered in a conference room. Andrew Rosenblum called his wife and gave her names and home phone numbers of those with him. He also called and told a friend that they had smashed windows for air. Cantor Fitzgerald had occupied most of floors 101 to 105, and all there perished.

THE TOWERS TUMBLE

Just prior to the South Tower collapse, several calls came in to 9-1-1, including one from Shimmy Biegelei-

sen of Fiduciary Trust on the 97th floor. He had called his wife and a friend, who prayed with him. He spent his last minutes telling a police operator and fire dispatcher his location, and that he was with six others. Seconds later, the South Tower collapsed.

Others were too badly injured to go far, even when evacuation may have been possible. One survivor of the North Tower, Donald Burns, reported passing four severely burned people in a stairwell on the 82nd floor. He said that their burns were so deep they could not be touched.

At 10:03 A.M., the South Tower collapsed. At 10:28 A.M., the North Tower followed suit. Its longer survival has been attributed to three factors: higher region of impact, lower air speed of the impacting plane, and fireproofing upgrades on the affected floors. The Saint Nicholas Greek Orthodox Church, evacuated, was destroyed by debris from the North Tower.

Problems in evacuating included loss of elevators, poor communications, and the construction of the towers themselves. Lack of communication between police and firefighters, and faulty firefighter equipment led to a greater loss of life for the FDNY than for the police. Minutes before the collapse of the South Tower, dozens of firefighters were in the lobby, awaiting orders.

As of 2002, according to the Associated Press, 1,600 of the dead had been identified; approximately 1,100 were yet unidentified. The report cited about 10,000 unidentified bone and tissue fragments. The passport of a suspected hijacker was found, but actual identification of any hijackers' remains was deemed unlikely because of the vaporizing heat of the impacts. As of September 11, 2005, the official count was 2,948 confirmed dead.

In October 2006, more than 100 pieces of human remains or bone fragments were discovered during new construction at the World Trade Center site.

Underground spaces—such as manholes that had been not fully searched and paved over in 2002—were opened, yielding a continuing legacy of the victims of September 11, 2001.

Further Reading: Jim Dwyer and Kevin Flynn, *102 Minutes: The Untold Story of the Fight to Survive Inside the Twin Towers* (Times Books, 2005); "Number of People Killed on September 11, 2001," www.night-lightfund.org/people.html (cited April 2006); Robert Sullivan, ed., *One Nation, America Remembers September 11, 2001* (Little, Brown, 2001).

— **ELIZABETH A. KRAMER**

Cheney, Richard B. (1941–)

When radar showed a rogue airplane heading toward the White House on the morning of September 11, Vice President Richard Bruce "Dick" Cheney was in his West Wing office. According to the *Washington Post*, Secret Service agents "...propelled him down the steps into the White House basement... to the underground bunker," the Presidential Emergency Operating Center. There, along with National Security Advisor Condoleezza Rice, and other senior officials, Cheney watched the initial news coverage and began directing the country's immediate response to the attack. According to some accounts of the day, Cheney ran the country while President GEORGE W. BUSH flew in AIR FORCE ONE looking for a secure base in the confused aftermath of the attacks.

After the third hijacked plane hit the PENTAGON, Cheney called Bush, airborne in Air Force One, suggesting that Bush authorize military planes to shoot down civilian planes that might have been hijacked. Fighters were dispatched nearly in time to engage UNITED AIRLINES FLIGHT 93, the plane that civilian passengers forced down in Shanksville, PENNSYLVANIA.

Because the vice president had a history of cardiac-related health problems, rumors quickly surfaced that he had suffered another heart attack. However, Cheney had been fitted with a "super pacemaker" in June 2001. He suffered no cardiac-related difficulties despite the stress of the day, and was fully conscious as the Secret Service agents carried him to the bunker.

Cheney has been one of the most powerful and most talked about vice presidents in American history. He has played a key role in shaping military, foreign, and energy policy. Advocates see him as a powerful figure that has done much to keep the country secure after the tragedy of September 11. His opponents see him as a Machiavellian figure that controls the presidency from behind a curtain of secrecy.

Born in 1941 in Lincoln, Nebraska, Cheney attended Yale in 1959, but dropped out due to poor grades. He transferred to the University of Wyoming, where he flourished. He was a doctoral candidate in

ABOVE *Vice President Richard Cheney giving a speech at Robins Air Force Base, Georgia.*

political science when he left in 1966 after completing all required work except his dissertation. He also sought and received four deferments from the draft for service in the Vietnam War, claiming he had "other interests" at the time. The deferments became another biographical fact that political foes would recall for decades.

In 1967, he went to work for Illinois Representative DONALD RUMSFELD. Rumsfeld and Michigan Representative Gerald Ford were political allies. When Ford became president, Rumsfeld later became secretary of defense and Cheney became chief of staff in 1975. Cheney returned to Wyoming in 1978 and became the state's Republican representative. In 1988, President George H. W. Bush named Cheney secretary of defense.

As secretary of defense, Cheney helped lead Operation Desert Storm during the PERSIAN GULF WAR. His visits to Saudi Arabia are cited as one of the prime reasons King Fahd allowed U.S. troops on Islamic soil —a major rationale used by some Islamic terrorists for their declaration of JIHAD against the West.

In 1995, Cheney became chairman and chief executive officer (CEO) at Halliburton, an oil services firm and a major U.S. military contractor. In 2000, before George W. Bush won the presidential election, he initially asked Cheney to advise him, but ended up selecting Cheney as vice president.

Further Reading: Richard B. Cheney, *Public Statements of Richard B. Cheney, Secretary of Defense* (Office of the Secretary of Defense, 1993); Richard B. Cheney and Lynne V. Cheney, *Kings of the Hill: Power and Personality in the House of Representatives* (Continuum, 1983); John Nichols, *Dick: The Man Who Is President (Dick Cheney)* (New Press, 2004).

— **B. KEITH MURPHY, PH.D.**

Conspiracy Theories

Within hours of the attacks, alternative theories—many posing conspiracies—appeared on the internet and in the alternative press, challenging the official interpretation. Some even put forth the idea that September 11 was orchestrated by the U.S. government as either an attempted coup against the United States by forces of the New World Order or an attempt by the U.S. government to justify invasions into Muslim lands. The theories gained attention from filmmaker Michael Moore's 2004 movie *Fahrenheit 9/11*. According to a 2004 poll conducted by Zogby International, over one half of New Yorkers believed that American governmental leaders "knew in advance that attacks were planned on or around September 11, 2001, and that they consciously failed to act."

A quick search of the internet turns up hundreds of conspiracy websites evangelizing theories or debunking a position. The theorists vary widely in political orientation, and in the degree of their understanding of the events.

Many theorists believe discrepancies in published information, or the absence of specific pieces of information, serve as proof that the government has intentionally withheld the "true" story. The theories may be categorized in five broad groups: false flag operations, foreknowledge and motives, destruction of the towers, the PENTAGON, and UNITED AIRLINES FLIGHT 93.

"False flag operations" refers to maritime warfare when ships would fly the flag of another nation, pretending to be an ally of an unfriendly ship in an attempt to get close enough to attack. In reference to September 11, the charge is that the attacks were orchestrated by U.S. forces operating under the false flag of Arab Muslims so that Muslims would be blamed.

Foreknowledge theories claim not only that the U.S. government was warned of the attack in advance, but that the government arranged for it and that the terrorists were, at best, simply tools of the government conspiracy. There are also claims that many of the hijackers are still alive. The supposed

Organized Conspiracy

THE 9/11 Truth Movement is a group of researchers, groups, and individuals, including Georgia Representative Cynthia Mckinney, at the forefront of questioning the "official" version of events. They are demanding a new Congressional investigation into September 11. They, along with the 9/11 Visibility Project, whose activists have distributed more than 6 million "deception dollars," continue to gain high-visibility support including such voices as Brigham Young University physics professor Steven Jones in 2005 and actor Charlie Sheen in 2006. Another well-organized group is the Citizen's Commission on 9-11, which is launching its own investigation of the events of September 11. Barry Zelman, who lost his brother in the attacks, leads this group.

motive for perpetrating such an attack on the symbols of the United States was to get the American people angry enough to fight a second crusade against Islamic states with the ultimate goal of creating a new American empire.

Some theories center on the destruction of the World Trade Center itself, and are based on the concept that the destruction could not have been accomplished by the two jetliners. They claim that the buildings were pre-wired with explosives, and further assert that the burning jet fuel was not hot enough to cause the structural failure evident on September 11. Their evidence is the collapse of SEVEN WORLD TRADE CENTER (7 WTC) as an obvious example of

ABOVE *The hole from the inside of the Pentagon's C Ring, where the aircraft's mass stopped its forward movement. One of the objections raised by conspiracy theorists entails not seeing pieces of the aircraft wings or damage inflicted by them.*

were scrambled to intercept the jetliners, the U.S. Air Force must have been ordered to stand down on September 11. Those who suspect that the damage was not caused entirely or at all by aircraft, point to the lack of wreckage and windows that remained intact near the impact site as proof. The lack of plane wreckage at the Pentagon site, which can be explained by the nature of the crash, has fed the claims of another whole group of theorists.

A variety of claims revolve around Flight 93, which crashed near Shanksville, PENNSYLVANIA. One claim suggests that a missile fired by a North Dakota Air National Guard jet brought down Flight 93. Others have claimed that Flight 93—and perhaps others—landed safely in Ohio, where passengers were taken into federal custody. The aircraft wreckage, one such claim suggests, was that of a military cargo plane intentionally crashed as part of the conspiracy.

The purpose of conspiracy theory in modern society is complex. To some, government has become large, impersonal, and frightening, and the government is as threatening and evil as the outside terrorists. Conspiracy theories allow the individual to create a rhetorical vision of a world where the evil forces come from within rather than without and the individual—rather than the anonymous, oppressive government—can be the hero of the narrative.

Further Reading: David Dunbar and Brad Reagan, eds., *Debunking 9/11 Myths: Why Paranoid Conspiracy Theories Can't Stand Up to the Facts* (Hearst, 2006); David Ray Griffin, *The 9/11 Commission Report: Omissions And Distortions* (Olive Branch Press, 2004); Jim Marrs, *Inside Job: Unmasking the 9/11 Conspiracies* (Origin Press, 2004); Thierry Meyssan, *9/11: The Big Lie* (Carnot USA, 2003); Eric D. Williams, *9/11 101: 101 Key Points that Everyone Should Know and Consider that Prove 9/11 was an Inside Job* (Book Surge Publishing, 2006).

— **B. KEITH MURPHY, PH.D.**

collapse due to a controlled demolition. In fact, Larry Silverstein, the leaseholder for 7 WTC, was quoted as saying, "And they made that decision to pull and we watched the building collapse," which is claimed to be evidence that the building had been rigged with demolition devices.

Some of the theorists claim that the planes were military drones or missiles, proving the attacks were an "inside job." Others argue that since no fighters

Contamination

After the attacks, lower Manhattan was covered by thousands of tons of asbestos and heavy metals. Two meters of dust covered 16 acres, and smaller particles from thousands of computers, copy machines, and fluorescent lights remained airborne for months. The dust included 560,000 square meters of masonry, 464,500 square meters of painted surfaces, 56,000 square meters of windows, and 650,000 square meters of flooring. The cleanup has subsequently involved charges of mishandling, ineptitude, and inadequate adherence to correct procedures.

Charges were made of gross mishandling by the Environmental Protection Agency (EPA), including that the U.S. government endangered some 50,000 lower Manhattan residents and 400,000 workers within a mile of Ground Zero. The EPA agreed to test and decontaminate some buildings. Asbestos was a major concern: 5,000 tons coated the first 40 floors of just one high-rise. The EPA assured safety, but up to four percent asbestos was found in some independent samplings. The U.S. Geological Survey found dust containing aluminum, inorganic and carbonate carbon, copper, lead, magnesium, silicon in glass fibers, sulphur, titanium, zinc, and other contaminants.

The core temperature of Ground Zero was 1,200 degrees Centigrade on September 11 and stayed at 800 Centigrade for weeks–the ruins were, essentially, a high-temperature chemical reactor. As of June 2002, the EPA had yet to give HEALTH guidelines on exposure to such metallic particles as copper, iron, nickel, titanium, vanadium, and zinc.

The National Contingency Plan procedures were not followed; instead indoor cleanups were delegated to the New York City Department of Health, which passed the responsibility to apartment residents and landlords. Professional cleaning of a single apartment could run $20,000 to $36,000. Insurance companies often refused claims because of the EPA's lack of clarity on dangers. The EPA was criticized for not declaring a health alert and failure to warn of the hazards of cleanup. Many buildings were still not clean as of 2006.

For the first 25 days, 800 police officers were given only paper masks labeled "Warning, this mask does not protect your lungs." Within six months, 332 firefighters and a paramedic needed treatment. Only about half could return to full duty. Smoke inhalation typically has a 90-percent recovery rate.

From September 11 on, asthma, sinus infections, and headaches were reported. Of 79 firefighters in one group, 70 percent had symptoms and half had chronic coughs. Workers called it "Ground Zero Syndrome." The EPA, which had failed to test for the finest particles—those most deeply inhaled, and

ABOVE *Tech. Sgt. Nick Marchisello, an Air Force Reservist and New Jersey firefighter, awaits the order to enter the rubble of the North Tower during recovery efforts.*

TOP LEFT *The streets of New York were filled with smoke and debris for days following the attacks.* **TOP RIGHT** *Dust and particles in the area led to reports of asthma, sinus infections, headaches, and chronic coughs from rescue workers.* **BOTTOM RIGHT** *Officials from the U.S. Coast Guard and the EPA tested air quality to determine whether or not the air was safe for office workers to return for their belongings.*

most damaging—finally assumed limited responsibility in 2002.

In 2004, half of the 9,000 monitored first responders and Ground Zero workers were sick; many lacked health coverage, or lost their jobs and health coverage because they were sick. Representative Carolyn Maloney introduced the Remember 9-11 Health Act, legislation meant to correct aspects of contamination. The Center for Disease Control and Prevention finally released $81 million for health monitoring, after Senators Hillary Rodham Clinton and Charles Schumer spearheaded an effort including the entire New York Congressional delegation. By 2006, class-action lawsuits were launched against the EPA and Christine Todd Whitman, then administrator of the EPA. Half of the more than 16,000 cleanup workers showed physical symptoms, including rare cancers. At least 23 deaths have been claimed.

Five years after the attacks, the largest study of the long-term HEALTH effects showed that "the impact... on [workers'] health has been more widespread and persistent than previously thought, and is likely to linger far into the future," according to the *New York Times*. The newspaper also reported: "The study, released by doctors at Mount Sinai Medical Center, is expected to erase any lingering doubts about the connection between dust from the trade center and numerous diseases that the workers have reported suffering. It is also expected to increase pressure on the federal government to provide health care for sick workers who do not have health insurance. Roughly 70 percent of nearly 10,000 workers tested at Mount Sinai from 2002 to 2004 reported that they had new or substantially worsened respiratory problems while or after working at Ground Zero."

Further Reading: "Cough, Stress Hinder Emergency Workers," www.sptimes.com/2002/09/10/911/Cough_stress_hinder_.shtml (Associated Press, 2002); Juan Gonzalez, *Fallout: The Environmental Con-* *sequences of the World Trade Center Collapse* (New Press, 2002); Anthony DePalma, "Illness Persisting in 9/11 Workers, Big Study Finds," *New York Times* (September 6, 2006).

— **ELIZABETH A. KRAMER**

Counterterrorism

There are essentially two approaches to counterterrorism: One focuses on law enforcement, the other primarily on military tools. The approach used depends on a number of factors, but probably the major consideration is governmental perception of threat. Countries typically have relied on their law enforcement system to stem TERRORISM, until that system becomes overwhelmed.

The choice is influenced by a country's legal system and background. Many countries, including some European democracies, have either a tradition or a formal legal structure that enables better internal control. Many countries have found that building and maintaining a focus on counterterrorism is not easy; it will always necessitate political leadership that can retain legitimacy in its goals and methods. A country's political leaders must identify the specific threats from terrorist groups, establish effective policies and strategies, and articulate these policies to both the bureaucracy and the public.

Another critical tool is an effective INTELLIGENCE system. Unless intelligence agencies effectively track and analyze terrorist groups, any counterterrorism strategy is certain to fail. Most countries have developed specialized counterterrorism intelligence centers or other organizational means that focus on terrorism threats. These agencies are crucial: with good intelligence, counterterrorism efforts will be long and costly. With bad intelligence, the effort is doomed.

ABOVE *President George W. Bush receives a guided tour of the National Counterterrorism Center from Interim Director John Brennan on June 10, 2005.*

Public opinion is crucial: Unless a government retains public support for its counterterrorism efforts—likely to be long-term and difficult—policies cannot be sustained. The public must believe that the government can protect them. Although journalism as a profession demands independence, unless the media is enlisted in the public information effort, government can have significant problems in retaining legitimacy in its efforts. Most countries have developed specialized police or counterterrorism military units. Some of the best known are the British Special Air Service, the German GSG-9, and Delta Force and Naval Special Warfare Development Group (formerly known as SEAL Team Six) in the United States.

Successful counterterrorism strategies must focus on attacking what the military calls centers of gravity, those factors that have the greatest impact on the opposing side. For terrorist groups, these include legitimacy and recruitment; finances; logistic support; training and training camps; command and control systems; terrorist group leaders; group cohesion; and sanctuary.

Even with these tools in place, success is not assured. Unless a country and the international community has managed to create a system that ensures coordination and cooperation among its various services and agencies, even the best crafted strategies may fail. The major focus for improving coordination has been to better integrate intelligence into the counterterrorism decision-making process.

The National Counterterrorism Center (NCTC) was founded in the United States in August 2004,

Building Counterterrorism Coalitions

COALITION BUILDING will be a key tool in defeating transnational terrorist groups. The reality, however, is that there are many political constraints in crafting coalitions. The first problem is the most basic: defining "terrorists." Political, diplomatic, and historical factors all play a role in who is labeled a terrorist rather than a freedom fighter. There is still no commonly accepted single definition of TERRORISM—but progress has been made in at least agreeing on basic concepts within the United Nations and other international and multinational bodies.

The second political constraint is that of differing perceptions of the threats to particular countries. Countries that do not consider terrorism as a significant threat to their national interests have little incentive to join coalitions. While terrorist groups have exponentially increased their areas of operations, more countries are focused on the threat they face, motivating most governments to increase cooperation with others.

The final political constraint is that of unrelated policy disagreements limiting or precluding cooperation on terrorism issues. The most obvious example of this in 2006 was the international diplomatic response to U.S. operations in Iraq. Experience has shown, however, that even countries that have major disagreements can put them aside to cooperate in the larger arena of counterterrorism.

with the mission "to serve as the primary organization in the United States Government (USG) for integrating and analyzing all intelligence pertaining to terrorism and counterterrorism and to conduct strategic operational planning by integrating all instruments of national power." The center, in the Office of the Director of National Intelligence, includes representatives from all federal agencies involved in counterterrorism.

The U.S. government has placed more emphasis on improving coordination with other countries and at lower working levels within the United States. Joint centers at the national level have been created or strengthened in an effort to remove bureaucratic barriers. The United States also has established intelligence-sharing mechanisms, and in some cases formal centers, to improve joint efforts with other countries and multilateral groupings.

The final issue in counterterrorism is to identify the ultimate goal. It is almost certainly impossible to completely eradicate terrorism as a tactic. Perhaps the best that can be achieved is to reduce the number of terrorist groups and—in the long term—reduce their ideological appeal. In that way terrorist groups can be limited to being a local problem handled by the usual law enforcement mechanisms. Attainment of even these more limited goals requires many improvements in national and international counterterrorism strategies and efforts.

Further Reading: Yonah Alexander, ed., *Counterterrorism Strategies: Success and Failures of Six Nations* (Potomac Books, 2006); Audrey Kurth Cronin and James M. Ludes, eds., *Attacking Terrorism: Elements of a Grand Strategy* (Georgetown University Press, 2004); Michael Jacobson, *The West at War: U.S. and European Counterterrorism Efforts Post-September 11* (Washington Institute for Near East Policy, 2006); Paul R. Pillar, *Terrorism and U.S. Foreign Policy* (Brookings Institution Press, 2004).

— **LAWRENCE E. CLINE, PH.D.**

D

Department of Homeland Security

At the end of the day on September 11, nearly 3,000 lives had been lost to terrorism, and the security that Americans enjoyed had been lost. The government responded by passing the Emergency Supplement Act (PL-107-38), which appropriated $40 billion for recovery from the attacks, and by enacting the USA PATRIOT ACT, which gave the national government unprecedented powers to fight terrorism. By the following year, Congress had created the Department of Homeland Security (DHS) and charged it with overseeing the interior defense of the United States and coordinating intelligence information and response capabilities among other government agencies, private industry, and state, local, and regional governments.

CREATING DHS

Early in 2001, former Democratic senator and presidential candidate Gary Hart and former Republican senator Warren Rudman issued the final report of a presidential commission they had cochaired, predicting that a terrorist attack was likely to take place on American soil in the near future. The Hart-Rudman Commission contended that homeland security should be the focus of new national security initiatives and suggested that government agencies such as Customs, the Immigration and Naturalization Service, and the Federal Emergency Management Agency (FEMA) should be brought under one umbrella to coordinate security measures. An interim commission report to

KEEPING WATCH *The U.S. Coast Guard patrols near the Brooklyn Bridge in New York City. Watchmen were deployed by the U.S. Coast Guard to support President Bush's Homeland Security initiatives.*

the Clinton administration in 1999 received little support. The government changed hands in January 2001, and President GEORGE W. BUSH asked Vice President Dick Cheney (see RICHARD B. CHENEY) to conduct a study on TERRORISM in response to the suggestions made by the Hart-Rudman Commission and by other groups studying national security. Admiral Steven Abbot launched a task force on Labor Day, September 3, 2001.

President Bush wanted to use an executive order to create a homeland security department that would serve only as an advisory body on security issues, but Congress preferred creating the new department by statute and giving it substantial authority to implement policy and coordinate security programs and policies. In the absence of a consensus, the issue was shelved. By the summer of 2002, however, under heavy criticism for his failure to resolve the issue, Bush responded to public pressure and began supporting the creation of the Department of Homeland Security.

Congress subsequently passed the Homeland Security Act of 2002 (PL 107-296), vesting the Department of Homeland Security with considerable power. The reorganization of the executive branch that followed the founding of DHS was the most extensive reorganization of the federal government since 1947 when the Department of Defense, the National Security Council, and the Central Intelligence Agency (CIA) were established. The 2002 reorganization under DHS involved 22 agencies and 170,000 government employees.

When UNITED AIRLINES FLIGHT 93 crashed in the rural area of Shanksville, PENNSYLVANIA, Governor Tom Ridge—a military hero and a former congressman—was drawn into the national arena. On September 19, Ridge received an invitation to the White House, where he was asked to take charge as the first director of the newly created Department of Homeland Security. In 2002, Bush asked Congress to appropriate about $38 billion to fund homeland security programs for DHS, the Department of Defense, and the Federal Bureau of Investigation (FBI), earmarking a substantial portion of the funds for improving security technologies.

OPERATING DHS

The Department of Homeland Security was initially charged with three primary objectives: preventing terrorist attacks within the United States, enhancing the ability of the United States to thwart terrorist acts before they occur, and providing a coordinated response to terrorist attacks and natural disasters. In December 2003, President Bush supplemented its statutory functions with Presidential Directive HSPD-8, which assigned the responsibility for identifying, prioritizing, and protecting critical infrastructure to the new department.

Billions of DHS dollars have been allotted to the Office of Domestic Preparedness for grants to assist states and territories in enhancing homeland security by hiring additional police officers, purchas-

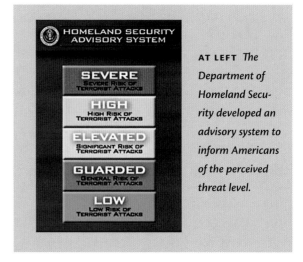

AT LEFT *The Department of Homeland Security developed an advisory system to inform Americans of the perceived threat level.*

ing security equipment, and training key personnel. Emergency Management Performance Grants provide similar funding for firefighters.

The DHS Homeland Security Information Network (HSIN) connects Washington, D.C., with all 50 states and with the nation's 50 largest cities. Counties will eventually be connected to the network, which provides for the immediate exchange of information and response strategies in case of another terrorist attack. Some DHS funds go to private companies to support security-related research. For example, in 2004 funds were used to promote research into creating more effective antibiotics, antidotes, and vaccines and for strengthening the capability of the public health system to respond to terrorist attacks and natural disasters. DHS also finances programs such as BioWatch, which is designed to detect the use of biological and chemical weapons.

ASSESSING DHS

Critics have charged that DHS has essentially become irrelevant because of "turf wars" within the national government. With the support of the president, in early 2003 the Terrorist Threat Integration Center (TTIC) took over much of the responsibility for domestic security by coordinating the efforts of DHS, the FBI's Counterterrorism Division, and the Director of Central Intelligence's (DCI) Counterterrorism Center, in addition to similar operations at the Department of Defense and other agencies. By executive order in December 2004, the TTIC was replaced by the National Counterterrorism Center (NCTC), which is specifically charged with strengthening intelligence analysis and strategic policy and supporting counterterrorism efforts.

Much fault has also been found with the fact that funding for DHS research has been relatively small. In the 2003 budget, for instance, only one-half bil-lion was allocated for research out of an overall budget of $37.5 billion. The Bush administration has further been criticized for underfunding essential DHS programs such as the Coast Guard's Deepwater Program that provides protection from potential attacks on the United States via waterways and for inadequate support of the Customs Service's need to improve its capacity to prevent contraband material such as nuclear weapons and explosives from entering the United States.

Two years after the September 11 attacks, the Washington, D.C.-based Pew Research Center for the People and the Press found that 75 percent of American respondents believed the world had become more dangerous, and nearly as many expected another major attack on the United States. The London-based World Markets Research Center ranked the United States fourth out of 186 countries at risk for terrorist attacks. Only Colombia, Israel, and Pakistan were ranked higher.

DHS ORGANIZATION

The Department of Homeland Security is organized into eight secondary departments: Management, responsible for finances and procurement; Science and Technology, which oversees research and development; Policy, responsible for planning and strategy; Preparedness, which works with the telecommunications industries and state and local governments; Intelligence and Analysis; Operations Coordination; Nuclear Detection; and Transportation Security.

By 2006, the process of bringing other relevant agencies under the umbrella of the department had been completed. Major departments that are now coordinated by the secretary of DHS include:

- Customs and Border Protection
- U.S. Secret Service
- Citizenship and Immigration Services

- Immigration and Customs Enforcement
- Federal Emergency Management Agency
- U.S. Coast Guard

DHS ADVISORY SYSTEM

The Department of Homeland Security has developed an advisory system designed to alert Americans to potential threats. The most urgent advisory is red, signaling a severe possibility that a terrorist attack is imminent. Orange indicates a terrorist attack is highly possible, and yellow denotes an elevated possibility of an attack. A blue advisory means that conditions are guarded, and green suggests only a low possibility of an attack. The color-coding may be used to signal threats to specific regions or cities or to the entire country.

In the summer of 2005, the government reduced the threat of a possible attack on the mass transit system from orange to yellow. Current threats against the United States are displayed daily on the DHS Web site (www.dhs.gov), and links to the Homeland Security Advisory System are included on other government Web sites. Additionally, DHS issues Homeland Security Information Bulletins to federal, state, and local governments and to private organizations and foreign governments to keep them advised of security issues and reports that may require their attention.

Further Reading: Steven Brill, *After: How America Confronted the September 12 Era* (Simon and Schuster, 2003); Department of Homeland Security, www.dhs.gov/dhspublic (cited May, 2006); Bob Graham, *Intelligence Matters: The CIA, the FBI, and the Failure of America's War on Terror* (Random House, 2004); Russell D. Howard, et al., *Homeland Security and Terrorism: Readings and Interpretations* (McGraw-Hill, 2006); David G. Kamien, ed., *The Homeland Security Handbook* (McGraw-Hill, 2005); The 9/11 Commission, *The 9/11 Commission Report* (W.W. Norton, 2005); Jeffrey Rosen, *The Naked Crowd: Reclaiming Security and Freedom in an Anxious Age* (Random House, 2004).

— **ELIZABETH PURDY, PH.D.**

Disaster Relief and Recovery

Police, firefighters, and ambulance crews rushed to the scene immediately after the first plane crashed into the North Tower (see FILMS OF SEPTEMBER 11). The logs of the city's 9-1-1 system have proven invaluable to historians studying the disaster, from the first calls through the collapse of the towers and after.

The NEW YORK CITY Office of Emergency Management, headed by Richard Sheirer, had to flee its office in SEVEN WORLD TRADE CENTER and set up temporary headquarters in the police academy, where it coordinated more than 90 city, state, and federal agencies throughout the recovery period. Mayor RUDOLPH GIULIANI also had to run for safety from a nearby building, where he had been holding a press conference.

Thousands of ordinary people helped one another escape from the doomed buildings. In the subsequent days and weeks, stories of courage abounded. Not all of them ended happily, and more than a few people doomed themselves by staying behind with a disabled coworker or total stranger.

As the day progressed, workers streamed into the area to help rescue survivors trapped in the wreckage. Almost all were skilled in building trades employed in constructing high-rises: welders, steamfitters and craftsmen. They came in response to an inner prompting, knowing that their skills would be useful and feeling that they could not stand by when needed. They had hard hats and union cards to back their claims to vital skills, and more than a few of them had worked on the construction of the Twin Towers in the 1960s. By Friday, September 14, they had removed 9,000 tons of debris; and by the following Monday 40,000 tons had been delivered to the Fresh Kills Landfill on Staten Island.

With so many of the city's own police and fire-fighters dead in the collapse of the Twin Towers (see FIRE DEPARTMENT OF NEW YORK: NEW YORK POLICE DEPARTMENT), police and firefighters from the suburbs and communities across the country streamed into the city to fill the breach. At least one unit was subsequently disciplined by a local government agency for having taken off without official approval, but such was the public reaction that punishment was soon rescinded. When people learned how many fire engines, police cars, and ambulances had been destroyed, they began taking up collections to buy new ones. New Orleans shipped a brand new fire engine to New York, an act of generosity that would become particularly poignant four years later when the city on the Gulf coast was battered and partially destroyed by Hurricane Katrina—New York firefighters reciprocated with disaster relief.

HELP POURS IN

Disaster relief agencies such as the Red Cross and the Salvation Army swung into action, setting up first-aid stations, feeding centers, and other support services. Shopkeepers and street vendors opened their doors to rescue workers, feeding them for free and providing places to catch a brief nap before returning to the grim labors of sifting through the wreckage.

In total, the Red Cross served more than 11 million meals to the 50,000 disaster workers who swarmed over the giant mass of wreckage at Ground Zero. It made nearly 200,000 referrals to mental health clinics, and issued more than 3,000 checks totaling over $50 million to the families of people slain in the attack.

All over the country, the Red Cross and local blood banks experienced an upsurge in blood donations. However, the destruction of the Twin Towers had been so total that there were few survivors

ABOVE *American Red Cross volunteers head toward Ground Zero. The organization served more than 11 million meals to disaster workers.*

needing transfusions, and much of the donated blood had to be sent to hospitals across the country so that it would not be wasted.

In Washington, D.C., supermarket chain Giant Foods offered to match the value of contributions made in its stores and raised nearly $1 million. Celebrities made special musical recordings for charity, with all proceeds from sales going to the victims and their families.

The Windows of Hope Family Relief Fund was created to help survivors of the workers at the WINDOWS ON THE WORLD restaurant, none of who escaped. Other specialized funds were administered by groups such as police and firefighters' organizations.

Not all donations were welcome. When Saudi Prince Alwaleed bin Talal insinuated that the September 11 attacks were the result of U.S. policies regarding Israel and the Palestinians, his $10 million donation for recovery and reconstruction was returned to him by Mayor Giuliani, a symbolic gesture that was widely supported by angry Americans.

Firefighters poured water on the wreckage in an effort to quell the inferno. Rescue workers struggled to find survivors, not realizing that almost all of the victims had died within moments after the Twin Towers' collapse.

AT LEFT *A perfect Latin cross was discovered among the beams and wreckage and became the first memorial to victims of the attack.*

Beyond the perimeter, people posted photographs of their loved ones, asking if anyone knew anything about them. The long walls of photographs soon became a grim reminder of how many people had been killed in the attacks. Due to the fragmentary nature of many of the remains, DNA scans were generally the only means of identification, leading family members to bring in razors and hairbrushes that might contain DNA traces.

FROM RESCUE TO RECOVERY

As the realization took hold that there would be few, if any, survivors, the operations began to shift from rescue to recovery. Heavy equipment was brought in to move the broken slabs of concrete and steel beams. For the next nine months, thousands of workers would "unbuild" the wreckage, piling it onto trucks to be taken to the Fresh Kills Landfill on Staten Island, where it was studied by engineers and other experts in order to better understand the nature and cause of the collapse of the Twin Towers. Periodically human remains were found and carefully disinterred and removed. When the body clearly belonged to a police officer or firefighter, all work halted while the body was removed, recognizing the special status these men and women had earned through their courage.

Beams were discovered that had been severed in such a way as to form a perfect Latin cross. The cross became the first informal memorial (see MEMORIALS), and many workers placed items at its foot in tribute to those who had died. The cross was not removed until the end of the recovery period, with the understanding that it would become part of a permanent memorial included in whatever was later built on the site.

There was concern that the "Bathtub," the giant construction that kept the Hudson River from flooding the basement levels, might have been damaged and at risk of collapse. As the rubble was removed from the basement levels, the exposed slurry wall had to be propped to ensure that it would not crumble. Worse, there were concerns that the Freon contained in the giant chillers on the B-6 level, which had once provided air conditioning for both towers, might be released as a result of a rupture in one of the tanks or lines. If that were to occur, the entire area would be flooded with a gas that would drive out oxygen and lead to the suffocation of the workers. As it turned out, the chillers had been destroyed in the initial collapse, and the Freon had vaporized during the subsequent fires. That particular danger had never been a threat, but there was plenty of risk from precariously tilted slabs of concrete and from the ever-present asbestos dust in the air (see HEALTH).

Further Reading: Mitchell Fink and Lois Mathias, *Never Forget: An Oral History of September 11, 2001* (HarperCollins, 2002); William Langewiesche, *American Ground: Unbuilding the World Trade Center* (North Point, 2002); Dean E. Murphy, *September 11: An Oral History* (Doubleday, 2002); The Reporters, Writers and Editors of *Der Spiegel* Magazine, *Inside 9-11: What Really Happened*, Trans. Paul de Angelis and Elisabeth Kaestner (St. Martin's, 2001).

— **LEIGH KIMMEL**

E

Embassy Bombings

On August 7, 1998, two truck bombs exploded four minutes apart at U. S. embassies in Nairobi, Kenya, and Dar es Salaam, Tanzania. In Nairobi, the bombing killed 213, almost all Kenyan and 12 Americans, and wounded about 5,000. In Dar es Salaam, 11 were killed, none of them American, and about 85 were injured.

Planning for the bombings began as early as December 1993, with a team of AL-QAEDA members casing targets in Nairobi. The leader of the team was Ali Mohamed, once an Egyptian army officer. He moved to the United States in the 1980s, joined the U.S. Army, and became an instructor at the Special Warfare Center at Fort Bragg, North Carolina. He later reportedly provided training to some members of the cell involved in the WORLD TRADE CENTER 1993 attack.

The al-Qaeda team quartered in a Nairobi apartment, processing surveillance photos and reviewing targeting options. Khaled al Fawwaz was appointed to head the team, which submitted surveillance reports to OSAMA BIN LADEN and other al-Qaeda leaders in January 1994. Their reports suggested that the U.S. embassy in Nairobi was an ideal target since a car or truck bomb could be parked close to it for maximum impact.

Over the next few years, bin Laden was forced to move from Sudan to Afghanistan. The al-Qaeda chief military planner accidentally drowned, and—most significantly—U.S. and Kenyan agents searched the apartment of Wadi al Hage, the new leader of the cell (see SLEEPER

CELLS) in Nairobi in August 1997. His role had to be assumed by Harun Fazul, a Kenyan. Despite these setbacks, by 1998 the cells had reconstituted and preparations for the attacks intensified.

The operational teams in Nairobi and Dar es Salaam rented apartments, obtained bomb-making materials, and bought the trucks necessary to move the bombs. Explosives experts were brought in to supervise bomb assembly. Expecting retaliation from the attacks, the al-Qaeda leadership, including bin Laden, moved out of Kandahar, Afghanistan. Communiqués taking credit for the attacks were faxed to the al-Qaeda Egyptian Islamic Jihad office in Azerbaijan with instructions to hold them until directed.

The truck bomb in Nairobi detonated at 10:35 A.M. and the bomb in Dar es Salaam at 10:39 A.M.

Quickly afterward, the declarations of responsibility were faxed to London. The bombings cost al-Qaeda approximately $50,000.

The carnage and damage in Nairobi were particularly severe. The embassy was located in the center of the city in a busy area. It did not have the recommended 100-foot security zone from the street to the embassy building itself. Training of the Marine guards and local perimeter security forces was inadequate for dealing with vehicular bombs, and the security gates reportedly were not working at the time of the attack. Conditions at the Dar es Salaam embassy were better than in Nairobi. The U.S. ambassador in Kenya, Prudence Bushnell, had been warning of the poor security conditions at the embassy since her arrival in 1996. General Anthony Zinni of

The U.S. Response

THE AMERICAN government responded to the bombings economically and militarily. President Bill Clinton signed Executive Order 13099 on August 20, 1998, declaring that OSAMA BIN LADEN and al-Qaeda were responsible for the bombings and froze their assets in the United States. The order also forbade U.S. citizens and companies from doing business with AL-QAEDA.

Clinton also ordered Operation Infinite Reach, a military operation focused on two sets of targets. The first was al-Qaeda training camps in AFGHANISTAN. The United States launched cruise missiles against these camps in hope of killing senior al-Qaeda leaders. The results were disappointing; the missiles destroyed buildings and killed a few probable terrorists, but had virtually no impact on al-Qaeda itself.

The second prong of the operation became mired in controversy. The target was the al Shifa pharmaceutical plant in Sudan. In December 1997, U.S. INTELLIGENCE services claimed that a soil sample from nearby the plant contained trace amounts of a chemical that can be used to make VX nerve gas. The United States claimed that the al Shifa plant's owner had direct ties to the Sudanese military-industrial complex, and through those ties had links to al-Qaeda. The administration also claimed that the factory had links to IRAQ's chemical weapons program.

U.S. Central Command visited the embassy in early 1998 and warned of significant security shortfalls, but the State Department concluded that it could not afford further security upgrades.

After the bombing, the United States and Kenya conducted massive joint law enforcement operations to track the perpetrators. Four members of the Nairobi cell were captured and tried in New York in 2001. Mohamed Rashed Daoud al Owhali, Mohammed Odeh, Wadi al Hage, and Kalfan Khamis Mohamed were found guilty and sentenced to life in prison without parole. Two other defendants later were arrested in Britain, extradited to the United States, and sentenced to prison. Several of the suspects still remain active; the Kenyan government believes that some of them are operating out of Somalia.

Further Reading: Jane Corbin, *Al-Qaeda: In Search of the Terror Network that Threatens the World* (Avalon, 2003); Amanda Ferguson, *Attack against the U.S. Embassies in Kenya and Tanzania* (Rosen, 2003); Lawrence Wright, *The Looming Tower: Al-Qaeda and the Road to 9/11* (Knopf, 2006).

— LAWRENCE E. CLINE, PH.D.

Emergency Workers

High-rise fires had occurred in the United States in the past, but nothing involving 220 football-field-sized floors collapsing into giant, superheated piles of rubble.

According to official records, more than 400 rescue workers died on September 11 (see APPENDIX for a complete list of victims). While others fled the area, emergency workers continued to hurry to the scene. The FIRE DEPARTMENT OF NEW YORK (FDNY) response began within five seconds of the first impact. Witnesses cite the NEW YORK POLICE DEPARTMENT (NYPD) responding immediately. The Port Authority Police Department (PAPD) response began within moments of dodging the fireball that came roaring down the elevator shafts near its executive offices in the North Tower.

Firefighter Maureen McArdle-Schulman heard someone cry out that there was something falling from the tower. It was people, jumping to escape the heat and flames. "I was getting sick. I felt like I was intruding on a sacrament. They were choosing to die, and I was watching them and shouldn't have been. So me and another guy turned away and looked at a wall and we could still hear them hit."

Radio calls became more frantic as the situation progressed. The first, at 8:46 A.M. had been calm. After that, as equipment malfunctioned or did not work within the buildings, rescuers cried out one to another.

ABOVE *A lone FDNY fire engine is surrounded by damage and destruction at the World Trade Center.*

Evacuation orders for the North Tower, after the collapse of the South Tower, may have gone unheard. Some personnel received the calls clearly. From the 35th floor, at least one emergency worker escaped. Yet others were heading in. Some personnel were certain that they never received the message by radio. Some received the evacuation order and continued with their work.

Mayor RUDOLPH GIULIANI said that the approximately 121 firefighters who died in the collapse of the North Tower did so because they were still saving civilian lives. Firefighters, weighed down by their gear, were making their way up between the 19th and 37th floors when the tower fell. Most of the police got out, aware of what was going on from the helicopter broadcasts. A handful of the firefighters were assisting workers who could not escape on their own. The rest were mostly resting in the corridors of the 19th floor, as other firefighters who were leaving attested.

Rivalries and misuse of technology may explain why police and fire department radios did not mutually communicate. Giuliani explained it as the departments having "different missions." He also suggested that technology was not adequate, though it did exist, but had stalled in part due to politics. Fire chiefs used a frequency at 800 MHz for major emergencies, and though it was supposed to be shared, the police did not use it.

Since the 1996 fire department takeover of the city's emergency medical response, medical technicians and firefighters lacked the ability to listen to police bands. The city spent thousands of dollars during 1997 and 1998 on new radios to allow police to communicate with fire commanders. The equipment remained on shelves and in car trunks, and the two departments, except for once after the WORLD TRADE CENTER 1993 attack, never returned to drill together.

Operators and Dispatchers

OPERATORS AND dispatchers did their best to contend with the chaos and to bring order, even when training ran counter to the unprecedented circumstances. Fire department and police operators did, apparently, communicate at some points, relaying information back and forth as they knew it at the time. In tapes released to the public, operators can be heard speaking to the edited-out voices of the victims, relaying the standard recommendations to stay put (which would normally be correct), attempting to calm the panicky, advising the trapped to stay low and to place wet towels over their heads, and even praying with the workers.

Due to failures in the communication systems, emergency operators did not know to advise against the possibility of roof rescues, which may have led some to go up to the roof. Some callers were told not to break windows where there was no other option for fresh air. Police Commissioner Raymond Kelly praised the 9-1-1 operators' efforts in a public statement.

Call tapes released in August 2006 captured the intensity of the moment: A 9-1-1 operator, speaking to a woman trapped on the 83rd floor of the World Trade Center, offered hope of a rescue team that never appeared.

"Listen to me, ma'am," the operator told a panicked Melissa Doi during a 20-minute phone call. "You're not dying. You're in a bad situation, ma'am."

"I'm going to die, aren't I?" Doi asked the dispatcher. "Please God, it's so hot. I'm burning up."

The operator encouraged Doi to keep her composure: "Ma'am, just stay calm for me, OK?"

The conversation was one of 1,613 previously undisclosed calls. They include the voices of at least 19 firefighters and two emergency medical technicians killed when the Twin Towers collapsed. Most of the calls were from firefighters asking dispatchers where they should report for duty, the fire department said, adding the calls "reveal extraordinary professionalism and bravery."

The police command center had been located at the corner of Church and Vesey Streets. Initially in the North Tower, interior fire-command centers were in the lobbies of the building. Just west of there, top officials at the exterior fire command center pulled back from the median on West Street to avoid falling debris. The fire-vehicle staging area was south of the South Tower, and in line with SEVEN WORLD TRADE CENTER on West Street. The ambulance staging area was located just west of another, more northern fire-vehicle staging area.

According to a tape found in the wreckage, two firefighters made it as far as the 78th floor of the South Tower before it collapsed. *New York Times* sources stated that a fire commander was heard summoning reinforcements, but those reinforcements were delayed by traffic and by confusion about where they were to report.

Assistant Fire Chief Joseph Callan admitted to deficiencies in emergency planning. They had never trained for or experienced a high-rise fire that spanned more than two floors, and they had never trained for an operation that would run into months instead of days.

As the dust clouds settled, the rescuers regrouped once more at West and Vesey streets. One building, Six World Trade Center, stood burning, smoke rising 6,500 feet high. Fire trucks littered the area like smashed toys.

John McLoughlin of the PAPD was the last survivor to be pulled from the wreckage. McLoughlin was passed along a makeshift plywood ramp, going

ABOVE *A rescue dog is carried out after searching the debris of the World Trade Center. Fake rescues were staged to keep up the morale of the dogs, who became distressed not to find survivors.*

Further Reading: Associated Press, "9/11 Emergency Call Tapes Released" (August 16, 2006); Jim Dwyer and Kevin Flynn, *102 Minutes, The Untold Story of the Fight to Survive Inside the Twin Towers* (Times Books, 2006); Thomas H. Kean and Lee H. Hamilton, *The 9/11 Report* (St. Martin's Press, 2004); Christopher Sweet, *Above Hallowed Ground, A Photographic Record of 9/11/01* (Penguin Books, 2002).

— **ELIZABETH A. KRAMER**

Evacuation, Buildings

At 8:45 A.M. on the morning of September 11, there were 16,400 to 18,800 people in the World Trade Center complex. The casualty count indicated most were at or above the impact zones.

Below impact in the North Tower three stairways were open, but no elevators. At companies like Marsh & McClellan on floors 93 to 100, all 295 workers present died, as did the 35 employees present at Fred Alger Management on the 93rd floor. Because of toxic smoke and extreme heat, it is believed no one above the 91st floor survived.

During the WORLD TRADE CENTER 1993 attack, 28 people were evacuated from the roof by helicopter. In 2001, roof doors had been locked for security reasons.

At 9:03 A.M. the South Tower was hit at the 78th floor. All but nine of 1,900 Empire Blue Cross Blue Shield employees from floors 17 to 31 survived. The earliness of the hour helped; by lunchtime, there would have been 50,000 in the towers.

Port Authority improvements after the 1993 attack saved lives. Then, evacuation took six hours. Where there had been smoke and darkness in 1993, upgraded ventilation systems, batteries in every other light fixture, handrails painted to glow in the dark, stripes down the center of stairways, and a public address system had been added by 2001.

through dozens of rescue worker's hands. As he passed, the men in their black coats with yellow fluorescent bands applauded.

By September 21, West and Church streets had been cleared, and a massive crane brought in to South Bridge. The wreckage went by tons to the Fresh Kills Landfill on Staten Island. It was searched for bodies, personal effects, and evidence. Some of the missing were never found.

Emergency workers dealt with hazardous conditions from the rubble itself and airborne contaminants in the dust (see HEALTH, LONG-TERM EFFECTS) during the eight months required to clear the site. The last steel beam to be removed from Ground Zero, about 60 feet long, was stood upright with a flag placed atop it, and marked PAPD 37, NYPD 23, FDNY 343 for the emergency workers lost on September 11. (See APPENDIX for a complete list of victims of the September 11 attacks.)

Special evacuation chairs were purchased, saving several people, including John Abruzzo, a quadriplegic and associate accountant for the Port Authority. Ten people helped four at a time to maneuver the special chair. What took six hours in a regular wheelchair and by stretcher now took 90 minutes.

Some companies, such as the architectural firm Mancini Duffy on South Tower's 22nd floor, had trained employees to evacuate immediately and ask questions later, which they did.

Morgan Stanley, the largest WTC tenant, occupied 21 floors between the 43rd and 74th in the South Tower. Of its 2,500 employees, only six died, mostly security officials like Rick Rescorla, who stayed to evacuate others.

Once the South Tower was hit, only stairway A was clear from the top, but few used it. Announcements were made by the Port Authority that the South Tower was safe and to stay put because falling debris outside was too dangerous. Those who had survived the 1993 bombing either rushed to get out, or thought the towers would survive and heeded announcements to wait.

Tom Sullivan, one of the survivors from Fiduciary Trust on the 97th floor of the South Tower, saw the first jet coming and hit the floor, yelling for people to get away from the windows. Forty yards away, it rammed the North Tower. On the other side of the South Tower the explosion was muffled, and fewer people were aware of what had happened. Of 50 people in an interior conference room meeting at Aon Insurance on the 105th floor, only six survived.

The 99-passenger Otis elevators in the South Tower saved thousands. Higher floors disembarked at the 78th floor lobby for a 45-second trip down in elevators carrying up to 55 people. The elevators could move 500 people every two minutes. One of UNITED AIRLINES FLIGHT 175's wings went through the 78th floor lobby, exploding, and killing or wounding over 100 people. Fires in the South Tower stayed within the impact zone. The floor's fire marshal, Richard Blood, had earlier told coworkers there had been an explosion in the North Tower and to leave. Elizabeth Parisi, there to give a presentation, bolted. Blood insisted all leave before he would. Survivor Andrecia Douglin-Traill, an Aon employee, evacuated immediately upon realizing that the falling objects next door were people. Joe Dittmar at the 105th floor Aon meeting did the same.

Executives stayed at Sandler O'Neil on the 104th floor, where 66 of 83 died. Keefe Bruyette Woods

ABOVE *Crowds flee the enormous cloud of smoke, dust and falling objects in the area surrounding the World Trade Center.*

on the 89th floor lost 67 of 81 employees. Nearly half of all South Tower deaths involved financial traders; 54 of 59 on the trading floor did not leave in time.

In the 87th floor's New York State Tax Department, all 60 Corporation Services workers lived. Executives gave orders and left. No one gave orders in the Tax Department, and nine of 20 died.

Tamitha Freeman delayed to retrieve pictures of her toddler and died. Brian Moran continued with three others down the building. Mike Dunn escaped death twice, first leaving the Aon conference room where others perished, then taking an elevator down from the 78th floor lobby to see what was going on, reaching safety as the second plane hit. (See APPENDIX for a complete list of victims of the September 11 attacks.)

Further Reading: Jim Dwyer, "In Operators' Voices, Echoes of Calls for Help," *New York Times* (March 31, 2006); Sara Kugler, "Evacuation Plans Saved Thousands at WTC," Associated Press (December 7, 2001); Martha T. Moore and Dennis Cauchon, "Delay Meant Death on 9/11," *USA Today* (September 11, 2002); National Commission on Terrorist Attacks, *The 9/11 Commission Report* (W.W. Norton, 2004).

— **ELIZABETH A. KRAMER**

Evacuation, Lower Manhattan

At 11:00 A.M. Mayor Rudy Giuliani (see RUDOLPH GIULIANI) told Manhattan residents to stay home and ordered an evacuation south of Canal Street. At 2:49 P.M. he announced partial restoration of bus and subway service. Bridges and tunnels remained closed, as did access to lower Manhattan, except for emergency vehicles. Later in the day, some bridges reopened for pedestrian traffic only, allowing office workers and others to flee the island en masse.

New York University (NYU) had to evacuate thousands of students from six of its residence halls within 20 blocks of the World Trade Center (WTC). No one was hurt, but the police ordered Broome Street, Lafayette Street, Water Street, Cliff Street, John Street, and The Ocean residence halls evacuated. Water Street, just eight blocks away, offered a perfect view of the North Tower's fall, and then began to fill with smoke.

NYU Downtown Hospital was an evacuation site. Next closest was St Vincent's Catholic Medical Center, which provided emergency care and medical trauma treatment. Cabrini Medical Center provided triage and screening for emergency room patients. Beth Israel Medical Center of Lower Manhattan gave inpatient psychiatric care to some evacuees. The medical centers provided physical and mental support to survivors and workers in coming days, often free of charge.

Those fleeing the north side of the WTC headed uptown, overland. The rest headed for the water, trying to escape choking smoke and then massive clouds of debris, wading through as much as six inches of dust and ash. Some had no shoes; others wore no shirts, using them instead as masks to breathe.

About 2.2 million commuters were in Manhattan that day. Streets were barricaded and nearest Ground Zero they were choked with debris and clouds of smoky polluted dust.

Many fled south, some to the sea walls at Manhattan's tip. Here, and down by the docks, by 11 A.M., a massive flotilla had arrived. Private craft, high-speed ferries, Circle Line tour boats, dinner boats, pilot boats, tugs, towboats, outboard runabouts, oil-spill response vessels, a Coast Guard cutter, other Coast Guard vessels, New York City Harbor Patrol, sightseeing craft, and a retired fireboat all came. Meant for passengers or not, if it floated, it came.

TOP LEFT *Belongings left behind in the hurried evacuation of the World Trade Center.* **TOP RIGHT** *New Yorkers waiting to be evacuated by ferries and tugboats in lower Manhattan.* **BOTTOM RIGHT** *Strollers abandoned in the rush to leave Battery Park. Behind them, a U.S. Coast Guard cutter patrols the waters of Manhattan.*

Navigation was difficult due to the thick smoke. Some had to use radar. Radio communication with other boats was vital.

The local Coast Guard broadcast for assistance, made via a VHF 13-frequency announcement, asked all area vessels to go to the shore of lower Manhattan. The Coast Guard established a security cordon around lower Manhattan, notifying ferries and others with whom they held regular contact that accident and safety regulations would not be strictly enforced. Many craft that came had very little contact if any with the Coast Guard.

Thousands of civilians patiently waited in line, helping each other into boats. No one was in charge. Boat operators decided who went to New Jersey or to Staten Island. Most vessels were privately owned, and simply worked alongside the more official ones.

When sea traffic at one point became too heavy, a port captain from a major private shipping company simply took over, working to coordinate boat traffic in that area of the bay.

There were no accidents or casualties. Some 300,000 to 500,000 people were evacuated in seven hours. One ferry company alone carried out 158,502. Estimates by the Coast Guard have gone as high as 1 million total evacuees, but no exact records exist.

Oddly, this massive rescue effort goes mostly unknown, and for all the media coverage, unacknowledged.

Further Reading: Jean Holabird, *Out of the Ruins a New York Record: Lower Manhattan, Autumn 2001* (Gingko Press, 2002); Mike Magee, *All Available Boats: The Evacuation of Manhattan Island on September 11, 2001* (Spencer Books, 2002).

— **ELIZABETH A. KRAMER**

F

Families of September 11

When it was clear there would be no more survivors at the World Trade Center or the Pentagon, officials requested that families provide DNA samples and dental records for identification. The media requested comments and interviews. There were public MEMORIALS and private funerals.

Within weeks of the attacks, the federal government set up the framework for a VICTIM COMPENSATION FUND. The goal was to make it unnecessary for families to enter into costly and time-consuming litigation with governments or companies that might be seen to have some liability. Under the fund, there would be no LAWSUITS, no trials, and once the compensation was decided and agreed upon, there would be no appeal.

Probably no other aspect of the post–September 11 recovery was more contentious. The bill was hastily written, its flaws and limitations quickly apparent. Washington, D.C., lawyer Kenneth Feinberg was appointed Special Master of the fund, and for the next 33 months, he worked to evaluate the financial worth of thousands of human lives. "It's a brutal, sort of cold, thing to do. Anybody who looks at this program and expects that by cutting a U.S. Treasury check, you are going to make 9/11 families happy, is vastly misunderstanding what's going on with this program," Feinberg told ABC News in 2003.

Early on, Feinberg was described as aloof, even cold. "I underestimated the emotion of this at the beginning," he later said. "I didn't fully appreciate how soon this program had been established after

WORST NIGHTMARE *Family members at the Pentagon on September 15, 2001, view the scene where their loved ones died.*

65

9/11, so there was a certain degree of unanticipated anger directed at me that I should have been more attuned to."

Because compensation was based on potential lifetime earnings, the widow of a stockbroker, for example, received a higher payout than the widow of a janitor. "It was very divisive," Feinberg said in September 2005. "One fireman's widow would say, 'I'm getting $825,000, and my next door neighbor, a widow of a fireman, is getting $1.2 million. You're denigrating the memory of my husband. Why?' I'd try and explain that under the statute, I was required to deduct from an award life insurance, pension, 401(k)s, but it didn't sit well with victims."

Feinberg announced early in the process that while he had no statutory authority to give compensation to unmarried or same-sex partners of those who died, he would hear their claims, while trying to figure out compensation amounts. If a victim had a will naming a significant other as his or her executor, the money would be distributed to the estate; otherwise, it went to the closest blood relative. Only about 25 percent of those who died in the attacks left wills.

At least 22 same-sex partners filed suits against families. There were also fights between families and spouses who were in the process of divorce, between stepchildren and widows, and over whether the families of illegal immigrants were eligible at all.

In 33 months, the fund paid out over $7 billion. The average payout was more than $1.6 million, up to about $7 million for some of the highest paid victims. This lead to resentment between families and eroded some of the goodwill that had poured out from Americans all over the country. It also raised some uncomfortable questions: why did American servicemen dying in the WAR ON TERROR receive only $25,000 if they died in combat? Why did September 11 victims receive federal compensation

ABOVE *A rendering of the planned World Trade Center memorial site. Many families object to aspects of the memorial, which features reflecting pools on the footprints of the fallen towers, an underground museum, and the possibility of their loved ones names being memorialized below ground level.*

when victims in the 1995 Oklahoma City bombings did not?

September 11 families began to enter the political and legal squabbles surrounding the attacks. Many families remained strong supporters of the GEORGE W. BUSH administration. Others became openly critical.

Five years after the attacks, many families say not knowing when they will be reminded of their grief is the hardest part. "There's absolutely no escape," said Mary Fetchet, founding director of VOICES of September 11th, whose son Brad died at the World Trade Center. "There's really no forewarning about when we're going to be confronted about some 9/11 issue connected to the horrific deaths our family members suffered."

In the spring of 2006, federal prosecutors tried to have ZACARIAS MOUSSAOUI, the only man tried for plotting the attacks, put to death. About four dozen victims' family members testified for the prosecution, speaking about their personal loss. But about a dozen victims testified for the defense, saying they did not want Moussaoui put to death, stating they did not want him to become a martyr or that they did not want to perpetuate the cycle of violence. Other families criticized them for their stance, especially when Moussaoui was spared the death penalty by the jury. Marilynn Rosenthall, whose son John died at the World Trade Center, had a simple response to the criticism: "Nobody speaks for all the 9/11 families."

FAMILIES UNITE

A major point of contention for many families is how to properly memorialize their loved ones, particularly at the World Trade Center site. The design calls for a tree-lined memorial plaza with reflecting pools on the "footprints" of the collapsed buildings and an underground museum. Many family members object to the plan that the names of those killed in the attacks will be scattered all over the memorial and museum; some do not want the names below ground, and some firefighters' families want their loved ones names listed at their stations or precincts. Others argue that the underground area is unsafe, calling it a potential "death trap" should there be another terrorist attack at the site.

At least 3,000 children lost a parent on September 11. Americans have reached out to support these young victims, donating millions of dollars

New Jersey Widows

KRISTEN BREITWEISER, Patty Casazza, Lorie Van Auken, and Mindy Kleinberg did not know each other on September 11. That morning, each had sent a husband off to work from the New Jersey suburbs to the World Trade Center. None of the husbands returned.

Now young widows with seven children between them, Breitweiser, Casazza, Van Auken, and Kleinberg were drawn together by the need to have their government answer just one question: why?

They were among the earliest advocates of a government commission to look into the September 11 attacks, but as early as the spring of 2002, it looked like a commission might not happen. Kleinberg had become friends with the father of a victim of the 1988 bombing of Pan Am Flight 103 over Lockerbie, Scotland. "He said, 'The bill is languishing. If you want it to go anywhere, you have to make it happen.'"

None of the widows was politically savvy. "I remember saying to Patty: 'Which one is the one with more people, the Senate or the House?'" Van Auken recalled. They quickly educated themselves in the fundamentals of grassroots political organizing and working with the media. They staged events at the Capitol and worked the phones, calling anyone in power that might help them. Formally, they were the Family Steering Committee; informally, they were the Jersey Girls.

"They call me all the time," said commission chairman Thomas H. Kean, "They monitor us, they follow our progress, they've supplied us with some of the best questions we've asked. I doubt very much if we would be in existence without them."

Vilified by the political right as tools of the Democratic Party and media celebrities, the Jersey Girls have been careful to keep their goals clear and to stay above the partisan fray. "A victory implies that this is a game," said Breitweiser in 2004. "And this is not a game."

as seed money for college funds, advocacy groups, and counseling centers to assure that September 11 families will get the material and emotional support that they need.

Several groups have set up support groups, camps and away-programs for the children. In the summer of 2002, the Twin Towers Fund established America's Camp, a weeklong, co-ed, summer camp program for children in grades 2 through 10, held at Camp Mah-Kee-Nac in the Berkshire Mountains near Lennox, Massachusetts. The Center for Grieving Children in Portland, Maine, has staff living on-site for the duration of the camp, and counselors receive sensitivity training, but the goal of America's Camp is to allow grieving kids to have some time to just be regular kids. The Twin Towers Fund has raised $216 million for the camp.

Further Reading: Kristen Breitweiser, *Wake-Up Call: The Political Education of a 9/11 Widow* (Warner Books, 2006); Marian Fontana, *A Wid-*

ow's Walk: A Memoir of 9/11 (Simon and Schuster, 2006); Thomas H. Kean and Lee H. Hamilton, *Without Precedent: The Inside Story of the 9/11 Commission* (Knopf, 2006).

— **HEATHER K. MICHON**

Films of September 11

Films about September 11 appeared almost immediately. Evan Fairbanks was filming Trinity Church when the planes hit the towers right before his camera. His video appeared in part on the ABC evening news that day, on two televison shows the next morning, and two months later in its entirety at the New York Historical Society. Mexican film student Fernando Zamora made two short documentaries, *Steps* and *Dust*, which aired on network television on September 12 and 13.

AT RIGHT *Nicolas Cage on a press junket for Oliver Stone's film* **World Trade Center.** *Cage stars as a Port Authority Police officer, one of the last two rescue workers found alive.*

Jules and Gedeon Naudet's *9/11* came about when the brothers were filming a rookie fireman at the time of the attacks. They caught on film the first plane hitting the tower. One brother followed the firemen into the towers, filming the destruction and getting out just before the collapse.

Six months after September 11, some of the families indicated concerns about exploitation of the events in the broadcast of two documentaries about firefighters, including the Naudet brothers' *9/11*. The other, *New York Firefighters: the Brotherhood of September 11*, drew a television audience of 39 million, the most watched non-sport broadcast of the season.

Etienne Sauret's documentary, *WTC: The First 24 Hours*, was released in February 2002, showing the destruction and the initial rescue efforts. Eleven minutes long at first, it was expanded to half an hour. The film has no music or narration and minimal dialogue.

The Guys dealt with a firefighter who had trouble writing eulogies for his dead comrades. *11/09/01— September 11* was a collection of 11 stories by 11 directors from around the world. Each story was 11 minutes, 9 seconds, and 1 frame long. Not all segments were sympathetic and some focused on the invasions of AFGHANISTAN and IRAQ, as well as memories of the United States in Vietnam or other negative aspects of U.S. foreign policy.

Other movies, some as short as four minutes, appearing in the first year after September 11, include: *In Memoriam: New York City, 9/11/01; America Rebuilds; Artist Response to 9.11; The Bridge Back; Brief Encounter with Tibetan Monks; Brothers on Holy Ground; Carefully Taught; China Diary; The End of Summer; From the Ashes; Isaiah's Rap; Last Night in New York; Loss; Morning: September 11; NYC: 9/11; Prayer; September 10th (Uno Nunca Muere la Vispera); Site; Stranded Yanks; A Strange Mourning; Tales from Ground Zero; Telling Nicholas; The Voice of the Prophet; Turning Tragedy into War; Voices for Peace; WTC Uncut; WTC: The First 24 Hours;* and *Yesterday and Today.*

Movies released between 2002 and 2005 include: *Stairwell, 25th Hour, Yasmin, Crash,* and *The Great New Wonderful.*

Works in Progress

THE FIRST reaction by filmmakers was to remove images of and references to September 11 in works in progress. *Zoolander* and *Serendipity* digitally eliminated images of the World Trade Center. *Men in Black 2* reshot its climax to relocate the setting away from the World Trade Center, and *The Time Machine* cut a scene of meteors destroying New York City. A trailer for *Spider-Man* was pulled because it showed the towers. Some films delayed their release, including *Collateral Damage, Big Trouble, Heist,* and *Sidewalks of New York.* Jackie Chan's *Nosebleed* was cancelled entirely; the story centered on a window washer who thwarted a plot to blow up the World Trade Center.

The Simpsons reedited an episode set in New York. *Lilo & Stitch,* an animated movie, changed a scene of the main character stealing a 747 and joyriding through the skyscrapers of Honolulu to one of the character on a spaceship flying through clouds and a valley. Even the PlayStation2 game *Metal Gear Solid 2: Sons of Liberty* removed a scene in which military hardware destroyed much of Manhattan Island.

Films about UNITED AIRLINES FLIGHT 93, the plane taken down in Pennsylvania by its passengers, include *United 93*, *Flight 93* (made for television), and *The Flight That Fought Back*.

The most noted movie was *Fahrenheit 9/11*, Michael Moore's 2004 examination of how the GEORGE W. BUSH administration responded to the attacks. Moore focused on the reactions of the eyewitnesses rather than on the destruction of the towers. His film had the highest gross sales of any documentary ever produced. But Moore's film also bore a political message critical of the Bush administration, the WAR ON TERRORISM, and the war in Iraq. Although he contended that it was factually accurate, Moore himself described the film as an "op-ed piece" and stated that his goal was to prevent the reelection of George W. Bush in 2004. Moore's critics pointed to numerous factual errors and highly partisan selectivity in collection and presentation of evidence.

Two years later, in the run-up to the 2006 Congressional elections, partisan rhetoric turned to controversy over another September 11 feature, this one the docudrama *The Road to 9/11*. This miniseries aired on ABC on the fifth anniversary of the September 11 attacks. Created by avowed conservative Cyrus Nowrasteh, better known for his fiction, and produced/directed by Christian evangelical conservative David Cunningham, the fictional piece provoked liberal and Democratic outrage even before its screening because it purportedly portrayed the Bill Clinton administration in a bad light and the Bush administration in a favorable one. The educational publisher Scholastic, which had intended to use the film in American classrooms, dropped its support. ABC rewrote and edited some of the offensive scenes. When the first of the two parts aired, almost twice as many people watched football as watched the documentary.

The much less controversial *World Trade Center*, Oliver Stone's contribution, appeared in August 2006. It dealt with the stories of the last two rescue workers found alive at Ground Zero. Critics objected to the implied link between September 11 and the war in Iraq.

Further Reading: Wheeler Winston Dixon, ed., *Film and Television after 9/11* (Southern Illinois University Press, 2004); David I. Grossvogel, *Scenes in the City: Film Visions of Manhattan before 9/11* (Peter Lang Publishing, 2003); Michael Moore, *The Official Fahrenheit 9/11 Reader* (Simon and Schuster, 2004); Robert Brent Toplin, *Michael Moore's Fahrenheit 9/11: How One Film Divided a Nation* (University Press of Kansas, 2006).

— JOHN H. BARNHILL

Fire Department of New York

When the first plane hit the North Tower at 8:45 A.M., the morning was sunny and clear, and no one could see how such an accident might occur. A fire department officer from Squad 18 announced over the department radio that this was a terrorist attack. Any doubts about the crash being unintentional ended at 9:03 A.M. when the second plane hit the South Tower.

After assessing the scene, Fire Department of New York (FDNY) officials concluded that it was impossible to fight fires of such scale, and the focus shifted to rescuing as many people as possible from the burning towers.

The FDNY emerged from September 11 as heroes celebrated around the globe, but the honor came at a loss of 343 firefighters who left behind 244 widows and 606 children. Despite this price, firefighters were instrumental in saving the lives of tens of thousands of people.

According to protocol, emergency dispatchers told all callers from the upper floors of the towers to stay put, stating that rescuers were coming to lead them out of the buildings. The dispatchers lacked sufficient information to tell workers whether to go up or down and did not know that FDNY had agreed with Twin Towers security personnel, according to some reports, that doors to the roof should be locked at all times for security reasons. Many office workers began evacuating the North Tower even before FDNY officials ordered them to do so. By 8:57 A.M., the word had gone out to evacuate the South Tower. However, these instructions were not fully conveyed to either the 9-1-1 operators or the FDNY dispatchers. There is also the question of how many people were killed in the

South Tower because they obeyed instructions to return to their desks after being told the building was in no danger from the first crash into the North Tower. Shortly after the announcement to return to work was made, the second plane crashed into the South Tower.

CASUALTIES

As office workers filed down the stairs, hundreds of firefighters were climbing upward. Many climbed as high as the 78th floor carrying 60 pounds of equipment. Some carried additional items such as fire extinguishers, axes, and ropes. At 10:03 A.M., the South Tower collapsed, burying the FDNY command center set up in the lobby. Unaware that the South Tower had collapsed, firefighters did not evacuate

the North Tower. At 10:28 A.M., the North Tower also collapsed.

Approximately half of the firefighters who responded to the World Trade Center attack were off duty when the alarm was given. The 343 firefighters lost that day were more than the combined fatalities for the department for several decades. Seventy-five FDNY companies lost at least one member; some lost as many as 11.

The casualty list included 23 fire chiefs—among them were Peter Ganci Jr., the chief of department; William Feehan, the first deputy commissioner; and citywide assistant chiefs Gerard Barbara and Donald Burns. The collapse of the South Tower thus wiped out the upper echelons of the FDNY command structure. FDNY also lost Chaplain MYCHAL JUDGE, Fire Marshall Ronald Bucca, 19 battalion chiefs, 22 captains, 46 lieutenants, two paramedics, and 253 firefighters.

INSIDE THE TOWER

When the first alarms were transmitted, fire department duty rosters were changing, and firefighters who were going off duty were still present at many stations. They responded to the alarm along with on-duty personnel. Other off-duty firefighters also reported for duty after hearing the news about the World Trade Center on television or radio. Even retired firefighters rushed to Manhattan to help deal with the emergency. By 9 A.M., FDNY's highest-ranking officials were on the scene and had called up 235 firefighters in 21 engine companies, nine ladder companies, and four elite rescue teams. Additional units were subsequently called, and other firefighters came on their own.

Firefighters inside the World Trade Center soon realized that their radios were working no better than they had during the 1993 bombing (see WORLD

TRADE CENTER 1993). Some messages were garbled; others were never received. This lack of adequate communication between firefighters on the upper levels of the towers and their commanders, and between the police and fire departments, has been cited by many, including the 9/11 Commission Report, as a contributing factor to the deaths of so many EMERGENCY WORKERS.

Needing only minimal power to communicate with commanders at on-site communication posts and with colleagues during firefighting activities, firefighters had only a few boosters in the city to enhance radio signals, and were not equipped to handle communication within a high-rise. A few months before September 11, the department had issued new handheld Motorola radios to firefighters but recalled them when they proved ineffective. Consequently, the department had reissued the Motorola Saber radios that had proved inadequate at the World Trade Center in 1993. Furthermore, the Office of Emergency Management that Mayor RUDOLPH GIULIANI had created to facilitate communication between the fire and police departments had been forced to evacuate its offices located at SEVEN WORLD TRADE CENTER.

When firefighters inside the North Tower heard the South Tower collapse, some believed that a bomb had exploded. Up to that time, firefighters had been able to safely lead evacuees out of the North Tower, but the building lost power when the South Tower collapsed, trapping hundreds of people inside elevators and stairwells. They were still in the building when the North Tower collapsed.

ASSIGNING RESPONSIBILITY

In the months and years that followed the attacks, numerous individuals, groups, and governmental bodies have attempted to explain why the FDNY paid such a heavy price. The 9/11 Commission,

ABOVE *Covered with dust and debris, a Fire Department of New York fire truck stands ready in the ruins at Ground Zero.*

which served as the official investigatory body of the national government (see NATIONAL COMMISSION ON TERRORIST ATTACKS UPON THE UNITED STATES), upheld earlier findings that determined the two major causes of deaths among firefighters: the inability of firefighters to communicate with their own command centers and the lack of cooperation with the NEW YORK POLICE DEPARTMENT (NYPD).

According to the 9/11 Commission's Final Report, "each [department] considered itself operationally autonomous. Consequently, neither department was "prepared to comprehensively coordinate their efforts in responding to a major incident." The Commission determined that the lack of communication from NYPD aviation units were of most consequence for FDNY, noting that that Fire Department officials had knowledge of a possible collapse just as early as Police Department officials did, but were unable to transfer that information to their own personnel because of poor internal communication.

The 9/11 Commission announced after two years of investigation that the fire department's radios were simply too weak to handle the burden placed on them by an event of such magnitude. After the 1993 bombing of the World Trade Center, the Port Authority (see PORT AUTHORITY OF NEW YORK AND NEW JERSEY) had spent its own funds to place a repeater system designed to boost FDNY radio power within the towers, intending to have it on at all times. However, fire department officials demanded that the repeater be used only when it was needed and only at the discretion of the FDNY. In the spring of 2000, a console had been placed in the lobby of each building, but these were not correctly activated on September 11.

Protocol called for FDNY personnel to be aboard the police helicopters flying overhead, but FDNY officials had not assigned anyone to report to the helicopters that morning. Even if NYPD members aboard the helicopters had tried to communicate with FDNY officials, they would have been unable to do so because the radios did not communicate with one another. Some police officers say they told firefighters of the orders to evacuate but were ignored, while some firefighters say they never received such

information. There were also documented incidents when firefighters and police officers worked together inside the towers.

"MORE THAN WE CAN BEAR"

Even before the number of firefighter casualties was known, Mayor Giuliani said in a press conference that the tally would "be more than we can bear." The loss of 343 members of New York's "bravest" impacted 75 companies in the New York area. Some entire companies were wiped out. Thirty firefighters were lost from various battalions, including five from Battalion 9. According to published sources, six deaths occurred among Divisions 1, 11, and 15. Together, 32 engine companies lost 81 members.

Overall, the hardest-hit were the ladder companies, rescue units, and special squads. All five rescue units were wiped out, suffering 40 losses, with six to 11 members on each team. Special Operations experienced four fatalities. Five squads lost a total of 35 members, ranging from Squad 252's loss of five members to Squad 1's loss of 11 members. 79 firefighters left Staten Island to answer the call at the Twin Towers. Only one returned. (See APPENDIX for a complete list of victims of September 11.)

The federal government provided a tax-free death benefit of $250,000 to each firefighter's widow. The City of New York paid one year's salary to each family, plus an additional $25,000 death benefit. Widows receive lifetime pensions equal to the firefighter's average salary for the five years before death, for an average of $60,000. Children of all firefighters killed on September 11 are eligible to receive free college tuition in New York. Additional funds were received from the Twin Towers Fund established by Giuliani, which allotted approximately $355,000 to each family. Families also received $418,000 from the International Association of Firefighters and

$293,000 from the New York Police and Fire Widows and Children's Benefit Fund. Other programs set up by the national government provided $1 to $2 million tax free to each family (see VICTIM COMPENSATION FUND). Payments were also received from group and private insurance companies, pension funds, and private and corporate donors.

GROUND ZERO

All the hospitals in the New York area prepared for a spate of injuries from the World Trade Center; but after the initial flurry of injuries, few people arrived. Teams of firefighters and other workers dug through the debris, hoping to find survivors among the wreckage. In the beginning, workers had to evacuate every time a bomb threat was received. On one occasion, this may have cost a life because workers had to abandon Ground Zero as they were frantically digging toward the sound of a human voice. When they returned 20 minutes later, no sounds were heard.

For the eight months following the attacks, firefighters from all over the country came to New York City to assist in recovery efforts. By this time, the only hope was that something identifiable could be found to give the families and offer them a chance to bury their loved ones. Debris removal was carried out by hand to avoid damage to fragile remains buried underneath. Rescue dogs played a vital role and often worked until their paws bled. Each time a firefighter was found, the remains were wrapped in an American flag and carried from the site with traditional observances.

Firefighters were allowed to work at Ground Zero no longer than 30 days at a stretch, after which they received stress debriefings. In addition to the psychological trauma, hundreds of firefighters began to experience lung damage that occurred from working at the debris-laden site without adequate respiratory protection. At least 500 firefighters have left FDNY with respiratory problems, as of September 2006 (see HEALTH, LONG-TERM EFFECTS).

Further Reading: Steven Brill, *After: How America Confronted the September 12 Era* (Simon and Schuster, 2003); Jim Dwyer and Kevin Flynn, *102 Minutes: The Untold Story of the Flight to Survive Inside the Twin Towers* (Times Books, 2005); Terry Golway, *So Others Might Live: A History of New York's Bravest* (Basic Books, 2002); "The Heroes: Helping Hands," *Newsweek, Commemorative Issue: The Spirit of America* (Fall, 2001); Dean E. Murphy, *September 11: An Oral History* (Doubleday, 2005); New York City Fire Department, http://nyc.gov/html/fdny/html/home2.shtml (cited August, 2006).

ELIZABETH PURDY, PH.D.

Fire Codes

AFTER THE attack on the World Trade Center in 1993, FDNY officials had discussed a possible collapse of the towers if they took a direct hit that could cause the steel supports to melt. However, officials determined that an evacuation could be carried out before such a collapse occurred. The 1938 fire code had required that steel columns of all high-rise buildings be able to stand for at least four hours after fire broke out. But in 1968, the new fire code that applied to the towers cut back on the number of evacuation and exit areas required by law and removed the required "fire tower" designed to capture smoke and allow evacuees to escape down smoke-free stairs. The number of stairways required in high-rise buildings was reduced from six to three by the new code, and the minimum amount of time that surrounding walls were required to maintain fire resistance was decreased from three to two hours. Stairwells at the Twin Towers were located near each other, making mass exits extremely difficult.

G

Gander, Newfoundland

At 9:26 A.M. on September 11, 2001, the Federal Aviation Administration ordered all international flights en route to the United States to divert to Canada. This order affected nearly 240 flights in the air at that time, and nearly 1,500 over the course of the day. Of this number, 38 landed in Gander, Newfoundland.

Gander, a town of 9,600 near the northeast coast of the island, is perched on the very edge of the North American continent. Its airport had become a key refueling station for warplanes crossing the Atlantic during World War II. The advent of long-range aircraft had diminished Gander's importance, but the town still boasted an important international airport. An estimated 6,700 air travelers were stranded in Gander for almost three days, waiting for U.S. airspace to reopen. The town opened its homes and hearts to the displaced, donating food and clothing, toothbrushes and soap, and generally working to make people feel safe and welcome.

In May 2002, Lufthansa Airlines named its newest Airbus A340 plane the "Gander Halifax" as a tribute to the residents of two towns who had done so much to help their passengers and crews in their time of need. Many who had been diverted to Gander later spoke of the town's kindness. Following are excerpts from letters to the editor that appeared in newspapers in the fall of 2001:

"Everyone was extraordinarily thoughtful of each other. One woman must have put her life on hold and was constantly checking

AVIATION HISTORY *Smoke continued to billow from the remains of the World Trade Center as aircrafts sat at the closed Newark Airport in Newark, New Jersey.*

on us. She even came to the airport when we finally left to make sure we all were fine. I never saw her without a smile. The lady who ran the cafeteria along with many neighbors made hot meals and brought in casseroles each day. Students helped us to use e-mail, and we were able to use the phone to call our families. No organization with financial backing was behind this—this was a call to neighbors and friends to come and help those of us in need." (Cleveland *Plain-Dealer*)

"During that time when all of us were frantic to find out what had happened, make sure our loved ones were safe and contact those who would be missing us in the next few days, our hosts were endlessly cheerful, giving and kind. They dropped everything to cook for us and make us feel less isolated and abandoned during those five days of uncertainty....When we finally received word of the plane's clearance for leaving, we said goodbye with bittersweet memories of a group of people of unlim-

ited generosity. This experience will stay with us during this time and continue to remind us that we have more friends than enemies in this world, and we are grateful for the proximity to our country of some of them." (Pittsburgh *Post-Gazette*)

Further Reading: Jim DeFede, *The Day the World Came To Town: 9/11 and Gander, Newfoundland* (Regan Books, 2003).

— HEATHER K. MICHON

Germany

After the full investigation by the 9/11 Commission and the FBI, the connections between the plotters of the September 11 attacks and the city of Hamburg, Germany, proved irrefutable. According to court documents, in 1998 Ramzi Bin al Shibh, Mohamed Atta, Marwan Alshehri, Samir Ziad Jarrah, and others maintained an AL-QAEDA

LEFT *Muslims pray at a mosque in October 2001 in Berlin, Germany. According to investigators, three of the September 11 terrorists lived in Germany for years and took advantage of the country's large Muslim population as well as the country's open society to plan and coordinate their attacks. Germany is home to 3.3 million Muslims.*

terrorist cell in Hamburg. It was in the apartment at 54 Marienstrasse that cell members (see SLEEPER CELLS) joined together in prayer and indoctrination to support the belief that the West was to blame for the loss of Muslim lands to entities such as Israel, and it was the United States and its Western allies that were responsible for atrocities carried out against Muslims since the 16th century.

Hamburg served as the logistical hub, and eventually the spiritual home of the September 11 plot. It was in Hamburg that Mamoun Darkanzali recruited each of the 20 hijackers and sent them first to AFGHANISTAN and later to the United States at the behest of Khalid Sheikh Mohammed and OSAMA BIN LADEN. Even though men like Darkanzali and Mohammad Aydar Zammar were under surveillance by German authorities, they were not detained until after the attacks because they led what was described by a senior intelligence official as "inconspicuous lives."

The surveillance of Atta and others in Hamburg did not produce any significant information in the eyes of the German investigators. According to then attorney general John Ashcroft, "It is clear that Hamburg served as a central base of operations for these six individuals and their part in the planning of the September 11 attack." The cell members held to the mindset of soldiers. They prayed and talked politics, listened to the preaching of favored imams, and watched videos made and distributed by radical Islamic groups (see ISLAMIC FUNDAMENTALISM), showing atrocities committed against Muslims in Bosnia, Chechnya, and Palestine. In 1999, they decided to commit their lives to JIHAD and join up to fight in Chechnya. Ramzi Bin al Shibh, the only surviving cell member, claimed that during 1999, he and Alshehri were referred to Mohamedou Ould Slahi—an al-Qaeda member living in Germany. He advised

54 Marienstrasse

THE APARTMENT at 54 Marienstrasse was known as *Beit-al Ansar,* the house of the followers. According to the author John Miller, the apartment functioned as the principal war room, billet, and research center for the cadre of AL-QAEDA officers who carried out the September 11 attacks. Not only was it an important logistical base for the cell members of this attack, but other members were to pass through in the months leading up to their departure to the United States.

During the 28 months that Mohamed Atta's name appeared on the lease, 29 men of Middle Eastern or North African descent who were registered with the German authorities cited this apartment as their home address. In the aftermath of the attacks, it would be discovered that only three of the original roommates died in the event. Many more would be hunted down as conspirators through this connection or sought by intelligence operatives for their involvement in al-Qaeda.

them that it was difficult to get to Chechnya and they should go to Afghanistan first. Following Slahi's advice, between November and December 1999, Atta, Jarrah, Alshehri, and Bin al Shibh traveled separately to Afghanistan.

By early March 2000, all four were back in Germany. They began researching flight schools in Europe, but quickly found that training in the United States would be cheaper and faster. Atta, Alshehri, and Jarrah obtained U.S. visas, but Bin al Shibh—the sole Yemeni in the group—was rejected repeatedly. In the spring of 2000, Atta, Alshehri, and Jarrah prepared to travel to the United States to begin flight training (see HUFFMAN AVIATION; SIMCENTER INC.; SORBI'S FLYING CLUB).

Further Reading: Richard Bernstein, *Out of the Blue* (Times Books, 2002); "Inside the Mind of a Terrorist," *The Observer* (August 22, 2004); Global Security, "World Trade Center and Pentagon Attacks: Recruitment," www.globalsecurity.org/security/ops/911-recr.htm (cited July, 2006); John C. Miller, Chris Mitchell, and Michael Stone, *The Cell: Inside the 9/11 Plot, and Why the FBI and CIA Failed to Stop It* (Hyperion Books, 2003).

— WADE K. EWING

Giuliani, Rudolph (1944–)

On the morning of September 11, 2001, Rudy Giuliani was a controversial mayor whose second term was drawing to a close. Three months earlier, Giuliani had moved out of Gracie Mansion in the middle of a scandal over an extramarital affair. The mayor had been forced to withdraw from a Senate race against First Lady Hillary Rodham Clinton to deal with his prostate cancer. By day's end on September 11, Giuliani had emerged as a take-charge mayor capable of leading NEW YORK CITY and the nation through the crisis. His ability to lead was particularly important since both the president and vice president had been secluded after the attacks, and Governor George Pataki was keeping a low profile. Over the coming weeks, the nation embraced Giuliani as, in the words of television journalist Barbara Walters, "America's mayor." The *Washington Post* called Giuliani "Churchill in a Yankees cap."

In the aftermath of September 11, Giuliani was highly visible, especially at funerals and memorial services. Many New Yorkers were reluctant for the mayor to leave office, despite a two-term mandate.

Time magazine named Giuliani 2001's Person of the Year, and he received an honorary knighthood from Britain's Queen Elizabeth. Giuliani received a standing ovation from a joint session of Congress. David Granger of *Esquire* magazine called Giuliani the most well-known crisis-management expert in the world.

September 11 was primary election day in New York City. Giuliani awoke at the apartment of his friend Howard Koeppel and shared the day's newspapers over breakfast, then left for a breakfast meeting at the Peninsula Hotel on 55th Street. During the meeting, Giuliani and his colleagues discussed possible impacts of the trial of one of OSAMA BIN LADEN's associates who was scheduled to be sentenced the next day, convicted of murdering 213 people at the U. S. embassy in Kenya in 1998 (see EMBASSY BOMBINGS). To be prepared in case of reprisal, officials had scheduled an antiterrorism exercise for the next day. Giuliani received the news of the attack on the World Trade Center from Deputy Mayor Joe Lhota. At this time, none of the officials were sure whether the first crash was an accident or a terrorist attack.

Doubt was erased when the second plane hit the South Tower at 9:03 A.M. Thirty-three minutes after receiving news of the first crash, the mayor and his aides arrived at the temporary command center that had been set up in front of the towers. Giuliani consulted with Police Commissioner Bernie Kerik, Fire Commissioner Tom Von Essen, and Pete Ganci of the FIRE DEPARTMENT OF NEW YORK (FDNY), who was in charge of the rescue operations. Ganci believed everyone below the point of impact could be successfully evacuated from the North Tower. The rescue workers wanted the mayor to go on television and radio and inform everyone inside the towers to head for the stairways, where rescuers would be waiting. Before he left the scene, Giuliani said "God bless you" to Ganci. Running into Father Mychal

ABOVE *New York City Mayor Rudolph Giuliani consoles the mother of a missing Cantor Fitzgerald employee on September 12, 2001. In the days following the attack, the previously controversial mayor reassured and comforted many New Yorkers and gained a reputation as a crisis-management expert.*

locked. However, two janitors led the group to the basement where a passage connected the building to an adjacent structure. It had been only one hour and 40 minutes since the first plane hit the North Tower.

Giuliani was focused on getting on television to relay evacuation plans for lower Manhattan and to reassure New Yorkers that the city would survive. He feared that fatalities might number as high as 12,000 to 15,000, and was concerned about attacks on innocent Arabs who had nothing to do with TERRORISM. Giuliani did not learn until later that rescuers had successfully evacuated 25,000 people from the towers. Most of the 2,800 fatalities of the WTC attacks were people located above the points of impact, firefighters, and rescue workers. Approximately 100 fatalities were people on the street, killed by falling debris.

Meanwhile, Deputy Mayor Rudy Washington followed established emergency procedures and contacted the PENTAGON to request air cover for New York City. Plans were under way to bring in the navy to protect the city from an approach by sea. All bridges and tunnels were closed, and heavy machinery and medical supplies were dispatched to the scene. At Police Plaza, the phones were not working, and few cell phones could get signals. The electricity was out. No subways or taxicabs were operating— the only way out of the area was on foot (see EVACUATION, LOWER MANHATTAN). Giuliani's group eventually ended up at the Engine Company 24 Firehouse off Houston Street. Since all the firefighters were at the World Trade Center, they had to force the lock.

As mayor of the country's most populous city, Giuliani was well aware that New York was a target

Judge, the FDNY chaplain, Giuliani asked him to "pray for us." Within 15 minutes of Giuliani's departure from the command center, Ganci and Judge were killed when the South Tower collapsed.

The mayor's staff had set up temporary headquarters on Barclay Street when the South Tower came down, creating an avalanche that registered 2.4 on the Richter Scale. Giuliani was in the process of putting together an impromptu press conference when the tower collapsed, and again was forced to flee for his life. At first, the group appeared to be trapped because doors leading to the street were

ABOVE *A car burns in the darkened and deserted landscape left by the fallen towers. The mayor initially closed all bridges and tunnels, and everyone in the vicinity of the World Trade Center evacuated by foot.*

to the diet of stewed tomatoes and fruit that had been prescribed after his cancer was diagnosed. Giuliani's need for "comfort food" was not surprising. His city had suffered devastating losses; he had been close to many who perished at the World Trade Center. Giuliani admitted that visiting Ground Zero during that period frequently made him cry. He continued to visit the site at least once a day.

Further Reading: Jonathan Alter, "Grits, Guts, and Rudy Giuliani," *Newsweek* (September 24, 2001); David Granger, "The Good That Men Do," *Esquire* (May 2003); Andrew Kurtzman, *Rudy Giuliani: Emperor of the City* (Perennial, 2001); Jack Newfield, *The Full Rudy: The Man, The Myth, The Mania* (Thunder's Mouth Press, 2002); Robert Polner, ed., *America's Mayor: The Hidden History of Rudy Giuliani's New York* (Soft Skull Press, 2005).

— **ELIZABETH PURDY, PH.D.**

for international terrorism. Observers say that Giuliani began mapping out a response to a possible terrorist attack from the day he entered office on January 2, 1994. Consequently, he already had some idea of what needed to be done to mobilize the city's emergency resources. Within a few days, a more permanent command center was established at Pier 42 on the Hudson River, the site of the antiterrorism exercise planned for September 12.

On Sunday, September 23, a citywide memorial service (see MEMORIALS) was held to honor those who had perished in the attacks. Many of the 20,000 people attending still hoped to discover that their loved ones had somehow survived the attack. As Giuliani stepped up to the microphone, the crowd cheered. Flanked by Fire Commissioner Tom Von Essen, Police Commissioner Kerik, and Emergency Operations Chief Richard Scheirer, Giuliani assured his listeners that New York would rise again.

Onlookers continued to remark about Giuliani's apparent calm in the weeks following the crisis. However, one of his aides discovered him "wolfing down" a greasy sandwich despite his usually close adherence

Glick, Jeremy (1970–2001)

When the passengers of UNITED AIRLINES FLIGHT 93 set out to overpower their hijackers, 31-year-old Jeremy Glick of Hewlett, New Jersey, was one of the chief architects of the plan. Glick was a sales manager for Vividence, a California internet firm. Glick had been scheduled to fly out of Newark, New Jersey on Monday, September 10, but a fire at the airport had grounded planes. He was not looking forward to the trip, and Glick was pleased to have Monday night at home with his family. Since his wife Lyz had been up all night with their 3-month-old daughter Emerson, Glick slipped away on Tuesday morning without waking her. He left a message on the answering machine before boarding Flight 93.

At 9:45 A.M., Glick called his wife from aboard Flight 93 and told her that there were "bad Arab-looking men" on the plane and that one passenger had been killed. After informing Lyz that the men had at least one knife and were claiming to have a bomb, Glick asked about the crashes at the World Trade Center. Choosing to play the disaster down to keep from making Jeremy's situation seem hopeless, Lyz did not go into the horrific details of the burning towers. Glick told his wife that some passengers were planning to overpower the hijackers and seize control of the plane and asked if she thought they should proceed with the plan. Lyz told him to be brave and do what he had to do. After telling Lyz how much he loved her and Emerson and that she should go on with her life if he did not come home, Glick left her with a final "I love you" and a promise to come right back. He then joined his fellow passengers in rushing the hijackers.

Like a number of others on United Airlines Flight 93, Glick was athletic. He was over six feet tall, a college judo champion, and had played football in high school. The tape from the plane's voice recorder later revealed that using silverware from the galley, boiling water, and anything else they could lay their hands on, the passengers of Flight 93 lined up single file behind a food cart and rushed the hijackers. The silent phone was more than she could bear, and Lyz Glick passed the phone to her father who heard a whishing sound followed by silence. He hung up the phone more than an hour later. Law enforcement officers who were also on the line heard silence and then screams, which gave way to final silence. At 10:10 A.M., Flight 93 crashed into an empty field near rural Shanksville, PENNSYLVANIA, some 20 flight-minutes away from Washington, D.C.

In her grief, Lyz Glick joined a group of September 11 widows and met Lisa Beamer, the widow of TODD BEAMER, who had sat near Glick on Flight 93 and helped devise the plan to rush the hijackers. Lyz Glick and Lisa Beamer became instant friends. Lyz Glick draws comfort from the fact that her husband helped to foil the hijackers' plans to target either the White House or the Capitol Building. She believes that Jeremy was destined to be on Flight 93 so that he could be a force against the evil unleashed on September 11. In 2005, Lyz Glick published *Your Father's Voice: Letters for Emmy about Life with Jeremy—And without him after 9/11* so that their daughter could come to know the father who had loved and wanted her so much. Jeremy's Heroes (www.jeremysheroes.com) was founded as a memorial to Jeremy Glick to promote childhood participation in sports and build confidence and self-esteem in children.

Further Reading: Lisa Beamer, *Let's Roll: Ordinary People, Extraordinary Courage* (Tyndale House, 2002); Lyz Glick and Dan Zegart, *Your Father's Voice: Letters for Emmy about Life with Jeremy—And without him after 9/11* (St. Martin's Press, 2005); Jerre Longman, *Among the Heroes: United Flight 93 and the Passengers and Crew Who Fought Back* (HarperCollins, 2002).

— **ELIZABETH PURDY, PH.D.**

ABOVE *Detail of the quilt tile in memory of Jeremy Glick from the United In Memory 9/11 Victims Memorial Quilt.*

H

Health, Long-Term Effects

In the years following the attacks, it has become evident that the heroes of the cleanup efforts paid a heavy price for their valor, both physically and psychologically. Many firefighters, police officers, emergency personnel, and construction workers labored 12 to 16 hours a day for weeks, sifting through debris by hand. Other workers dealt with millions of tons of debris taken to the city's Fresh Kills Landfill. Many workers today suffer to some degree from post-traumatic stress disorder, an emotional disorder that may render them unable to work or to go about their daily lives. Public attention, however, has generally centered on the long-term physical ailments of post–September 11 workers.

The debris at Ground Zero was made up of 200,000 tons of steel, 600,000 square feet of window glass, 5,000 tons of asbestos, 12,000 miles of electric cables, and 425,000 cubic yards of concrete mixed with 24,000 gallons of jet fuel, human remains, and other paraphernalia. A heavy wind the night of September 11 spread the toxic dust for blocks, depositing the dust in homes and businesses. The fusion of burning jet fuel and plastic also released a number of known carcinogens into the debris and air, including dioxins, polycyclic aromatic hydrocarbons, polychlorinated biphenyls, and polychlorinated furans.

Health problems among the most severely stricken include chronic sinus infections and inflammations, lung diseases that have robbed workers of up to one-third of their lung capacity, a chronic cough that has come to be known as "World Trade Center Cough," shortness of

A MOUNTAIN OF DEBRIS *Two days after the attacks, rescue workers search the wreckage of the World Trade Center. At the time, hope still remained that survivors could be found. Many workers suffered physical effects as well as post-traumatic stress disorder symptoms after sifting through the remains of Ground Zero.*

ABOVE *Less than half of the rescue workers had more than paper or medical masks to protect them from the dust made up of steel, glass, asbestos, powdered concrete, human remains, and other unknown substances.*

breath that prevents individuals such as firefighters from performing their jobs, skin lesions, stomach and intestinal diseases, and various forms of cancer. These problems have not cleared up over time, and the real impact will not be known for years since many cancers, such as those from asbestos, may not appear for 10 to 20 years. Medical personnel are also concerned about workers who have not yet been diagnosed but who may be suffering from various conditions.

At least seven workers have died from health problems believed to be associated with WTC rescue efforts. On January 5, 2006, Detective James Zadroga became the first victim whose death was officially tied to the cleanup activities at Ground Zero. In April 2006, doctors at Mount Sinai released results of an autopsy on Zadroga, who had spent 470 hours working at Ground Zero, revealing that his lungs were filled with debris from the WTC that caused asphyxiation. An autopsy performed on New York police officer James Godbee, who died in December 2004 after spending 850 hours at the WTC site, revealed that

Godbee's lungs were pocked with blisters and marked by sarcoidosis, a lung-scarring disease. The FIRE DEPARTMENT OF NEW YORK (FDNY), which lost two firefighters from post–September 11 disorders, has reported high incidence of sarcoidosis among its personnel. By the end of 2006, the number of firefighters forced to retire in response to aftereffects of September 11 approached 700.

On September 5, 2006, Mount Sinai Medical Center in New York City released the results of a landmark study of 9,442 September 11 first responders and volunteers. The study, published on September 8 in *Environmental Health Perspectives*, the journal of the National Institute of Environmental and Health Sciences, provided solid evidence linking current illnesses with post–September 11 work at the WTC: 60 percent have persistent coughs; 50 percent have sinus or nasal problems; 85 percent suffer from upper respiratory problems; over one-half experience lower respiratory problems; 75 percent have been diagnosed with acid reflux disease; 40 percent experience shortness of breath and/or wheezing; and nearly half suffer from psychological disorders.

Only about 40 percent of the workers wore any protective gear other than paper or medical masks or goggles. Within minutes of arriving at the site, they began suffering from burning eyes, coughing, and skin lesions. Firefighters department-issued breathing packs supplied only 18 minutes of oxygen and were woefully inadequate during long hours in the rubble. Even when thousands of respirators were made available, there was no central distribution point, no training on usage, and no one to require workers to use the equipment. Most workers chose to ignore the bulky equipment that made breathing and working in escalating temperatures virtually unbearable, and erroneously believed symptoms would disappear within days. In direct contrast to workers at Ground

Post-Traumatic Stress Disorder

MANY OF the rescue workers and the volunteers who cared for them during cleanup efforts are suffering mental anguish. The most commonly diagnosed disorder is post-traumatic stress disorder (PTSD), which is frequently identified among survivors of major disasters and other traumatic experiences. In some cases, PTSD has led to violence. A firefighter, for instance, offered PTSD as a defense after pleading guilty to second-degree assault against a colleague who was left with a broken jaw and nose and with brain and spinal injuries. In other cases, PTSD has led to a dependence on drugs and alcohol. In 2004, the FIRE DEPARTMENT OF NEW YORK reported that it was treating 723 firefighters for substance abuse.

More commonly, rescue workers experience depression, headaches, insomnia, nightmares, appetite loss, anger, and other symptoms typical of PTSD. The problem is so severe among workers, volunteers, survivors, and survivors' families that the September 11 Fund set aside up to $3,000 a person to provide psychotherapy for eligible individuals. Through a special program, the Red Cross agreed to finance up to 24 sessions of psychotherapy, pay up to $500 for psychiatric medications, and cover up to a month of psychiatric inpatient care. Private charities such as the Robin Hood Foundation have also set aside funds to aid individuals needing physiological assistance. A number of studies currently monitoring long-term psychological effects of September 11 on those closely associated with the disaster will provide much-needed information to help those suffering trauma.

Zero, over 90 percent of workers at Fresh Kills and all of the workers at the PENTAGON wore respirators. Some 75,000 Tyvek suits were also issued to the city, but they were never distributed at Ground Zero.

When workers expressed concern about possible levels of toxicity at Ground Zero, they were assured by Environmental Protection Agency administrator Christine Todd Whitman that all tests suggested that toxic levels were in acceptable ranges.

Although many believe it is too little too late, bowing to pressure from New York's congressional delegation and in response to the plethora of information published by advocacy groups such as the Sierra Club, the Bush administration released additional federal funds and appointed a federal WTC coordinator. At the state level, New York governor George Pataki sponsored three bills extending benefits for affected workers. New York City mayor Michael Bloomberg responded to protracted criticism by appropriating additional funding, establishing several new programs, creating a coordinating team, and expanding tracking capabilities of the WTC Health Registers, which monitor long-term health problems among 71,000 workers and residents affected by the events of September 11. A special clinic for post-emergency workers was scheduled to open in early 2007 at the Belleview Hospital/New York University Medical Center, where workers would be able to receive free treatment and long-term medical assistance.

Further Reading: Anthony DePalma, "Illness Persisting in 9/11 Workers, Big Study Finds," *New York Times* (September 6, 2006); Anthony De-Palma, "Survey Finds That Grief Is a Constant Companion for Those at the Scene of the 9/11 Attacks," *New York Times* (May 26, 2006); Juan Gonzalez, *Fallout: The Environmental Consequences of the World Trade Center Collapse* (The New Press, 2002); Graham Rayman, "Early on, Dissent over Air Quality," *Newsday* (August 27, 2006); "September 11, 2002 Ground Zero," *Journal of Environmental Health* (December, 2003).

— ELIZABETH PURDY, PH.D.

Hijacking

Coined in the 1920s, the word *hijacking* initially referred to organized crime operatives seizing trucks off the streets. A decade later the word became associated with the seizure of aircraft.

One of the first recorded aircraft hijackings took place in 1931 in Arequipa, Peru, when insurgents seized a small plane and ordered its American pilot to fly them over the city of Lima so that they could drop political leaflets. The pilot refused and the rebels held the plane for several days before the incident ended without bloodshed or damage to the aircraft. In the summer of 1948 one of the first attempts to hijack a commercial airliner ended after three armed men tried to gain control of the *Miss Macao*, a Cathay Pacific seaplane traveling from Macao to Hong Kong. During a struggle with the pilot the plane nose-dived into the sea, killing 25 on board. Over the next 10 years almost two dozen reported hijackings took place worldwide, most of which involved political refugees trying to escape from Eastern European countries.

After Fidel Castro came to power in Cuba, a number of individuals seeking political asylum hijacked airplanes from Cuba to the United States. In the Cold War era the American government welcomed those fleeing Castro's communist regime and the American news media commended their actions. Soon American attitudes changed as pro-Castro nationals began hijacking airplanes from the United States to Cuba. In the United States the first recorded aircraft hijacking took place on May 1, 1961, when Puerto Rican–born Antulio Ramirez Ortiz drew a large knife and forced the pilots of a National Airlines Convair 440 bound for Miami to detour to Havana. Claiming that he knew of an assassination plot against Castro, Ortiz arrived in Havana to a hero's welcome and Castro's government gave him asylum.

Over the next months similar hijackings to Cuba took place. On September 5, 1961, President John F. Kennedy signed new legislation making air piracy a felony punishable by 20 years in prison or by death, depending on the circumstances. Despite this new law, hijackings to Cuba continued through the 1960s with such frequency that "take me to Havana" became a national catch phrase. Finally, in 1973 the United States and Cuba reached an agreement by which hijackers would be extradited and tried for their crimes.

AT LEFT *On December 26, 1994, an Air France flight was held hostage by Islamic extremists at the airport in Marseilles, France. Passengers are seen using the emergency slides to escape from the plane. The jet was stormed by French police, and two of the four presumed hijackers were killed.*

During the 1970s the federal government and the aviation industry took steps to discourage hijackings in the United States. The Federal Aviation Administration (FAA) began a profiling program designed to identify potential hijackers through behavior patterns, and installed metal detectors at airports. Airlines also began scanning checked luggage with X-rays and searching carry-on bags by hand. In 1970 President Richard Nixon announced a comprehensive antihijacking campaign that included the use of armed air marshals on some domestic flights. Although hijackings increased worldwide, precautionary measures taken in the United States dramatically decreased the number of domestic aircraft seizures. Between 1968 and 1972 there were an average of 29 hijacking attempts per year in the United States, compared to less than 10 per year during the following decade. By the 1980s the fear of hijackings had subsided in the United States, though isolated incidents of domestic terrorism involving aircraft still took place.

Further Reading: Cindy C. Combs, *Terrorism in the 21st Century* (Prentice Hall, 2002); Terry McDermott, *Perfect Soldiers: The Hijackers: Who They Were, Why They Did It* (HarperCollins, 2005); Peter St. John, *Air Piracy, Airport Security, and Internal Terrorism: Winning the War Against Hijackers* (Quorum Books, 1991).

— BEN WYNNE, PH.D.

Huffman Aviation

Huffman Aviation, a flight school located in Venice, Florida, became central to the September 11 story because terrorists Mohamed Atta and Marwan Alshehri attended the school from July 2000 through December 2000.

The details of their enrollment are muddled by conflicting testimony on the part of owner Rudi Dekkers, who claims to have heard of their general intentoions in attending flight school. What is known is that Atta and Alshehri arrived in Florida in June 2000, first enrolling in Jones Aviation in Sarasota, Florida.

When they failed their instrumentation test at Jones Aviation, they enrolled in Huffman Aviation. Co-owner Wally Hilliard helped change Atta's and Alshehri's visa status from tourist to student, allowing a longer stay. After passing their commercial pilot's test in December 2000, the two terrorists trained at SIMCENTER INC. in Miami, Florida, on a simulation Boeing 727.

As of 2001, there were just over 100 aviation programs in Florida, with many of them offering tuition rates as low as $4,000. The temperate environment in Florida allows for more days in the air, and the state has few high elevations, which ensures beginning pilots a safe opportunity to learn. Programs at Embry-Riddle University and Flight Safety Academy offered the terrorists the opportunity to learn on smaller single-engine aircraft, while the flight simulators at SimCenter gave Atta and Alshehri experience at the standardized controls of larger Boeing aircraft. The schools have come under scrutiny for their handling of foreign-national applications and for not performing thorough background checks. Many still resist changing their application policies.

Further Reading: Damion Dimarco, *Tower Stories: The Autobiography of September 11, 2001* (Revolution Publishing, 2004); National Commission on Terrorist Attacks, *The 9/11 Commission Report: Final Report on the National Commission on Terrorist Attacks Upon the United States* (W.W. Norton, 2004); Steve Strasser, ed., *The 9/11 Investigations* (Perseus Publishing, 2004).

— NICHOLAS KATERS

I

Intelligence

The universal question among the American public and government following September 11 was "how could this have happened?"

The U.S. intelligence community is large and complex. The "big four" agencies—Central Intelligence Agency (CIA), National Security Agency (NSA), Federal Bureau of Investigation (FBI), and Defense Intelligence Agency (DIA)—are the best known. Other major intelligence operations include the military services, National Reconnaissance Office, National Geospatial Intelligence Agency, Department of State, Department of Energy, and Department of the Treasury. On paper, the Director of Central Intelligence coordinated the activities of all agencies and managed the U.S. intelligence community. In practice, however, differing corporate cultures, missions, and bureaucratic competition led to severe problems in coordination and cooperation.

PEACE DIVIDEND

After the Cold War and the sharp reduction in perceived threats to the United States, voices both within and outside government argued that since the existential threat of the Cold War had ended, the large and expensive intelligence establishment designed to support the decades-long conflict could be cut, along with the military forces. Many cuts were in fact carried out, with most of the major intelligence agencies shrinking by the late 1990s. During the Cold War, priorities were clear and organizations concentrated their efforts on relatively defined targets. In the 1990s, such focus was nearly impossible. Threats and opportunities became much more amorphous, and policymakers demanded a broader set of collection requirements from the intelligence services.

Experts point to two key questions regarding the U.S. intelligence community and COUNTERTERRORISM that ask what actually needs to be known by the intelligence community, and how should the intelligence system adapt to answer these requirements.

What in the historic context would be considered at the tactical level–tracking 19 individuals–became strategically importance since 19 terrorists had international impact. Ultimately, counterterrorism intelligence must succeed at the traditional strategic level in which broad trends and future possibilities are identified, and at the tactical level—including a particularly strong and detailed indications and warning system—in which individual operations are detected and deterred before they are launched.

Intelligence Indicators

THE FOLLOWING excerpt from the 9/11 Commission Report provides a useful summary of some specific intelligence indicators that were missed before the September 11 attacks:

OPERATIONAL OPPORTUNITIES

1) JANUARY 2000: the CIA does not watch list Khalid Almindar or notify the FBI when it learned Almindar possessed a valid U.S. visa.

2) JANUARY 2000: the CIA does not develop a transnational plan for tracking Almindar and his associates so that they could be followed to Bangkok and onward, including the United States.

3) MARCH 2000: the CIA does not watchlist Nawaf Alhazmi or notify the FBI when it learned that he possessed a U.S. visa and had flown to Los Angeles on January 15, 2000.

4) JANUARY 2001: the CIA does not inform the FBI that a source had identified Khallad, or Tawfiq bin Attash, a major figure in the October 2000 bombing of the USS Cole, as having attended the meeting in Kuala Lumpur with Khalid Almindar.

5) MAY 2001: a CIA official does not notify the FBI about Almindar's U.S. visa, Alhazmi's U.S. travel, or Khallad's having attended the Kuala Lumpur meeting.

6) JUNE 2001: FBI and CIA officials do not ensure that all relevant information regarding the Kuala Lumpur meeting was shared with the Cole investigators at the June 11 meeting.

7) AUGUST 2001: the FBI does not recognize the significance of the information regarding Almindar and Alhazmi's possible arrival in the United States and thus does not take adequate action to share information, assign resources, and give sufficient priority to the search.

8) AUGUST 2001: FBI headquarters does not recognize the significance of the information regarding Zacarais Moussaoui's training and beliefs and thus does not take adequate action to share information, involve higher-level officials across agencies, obtain information regarding Moussaoui's ties to al-Qaeda, and give sufficient priority to determining what Moussaoui might be planning.

9) AUGUST 2001: the CIA does not focus on information that Khalid Sheikh Mohammed is a key al-Qaeda lieutenant or connect information identifying him as the "Mukhtar" mentioned in other reports to the analysis that could have linked "Mukhtar" with Ramzi Bin al Shibh and Moussaoui.

10) AUGUST 2001: the CIA and FBI do not connect the presence of Almindar, Alhazmi, and Moussaoui to the general threat reporting about imminent attacks.

INCREASED RESOURCES

The CIA had established a Counterterrorism Center in the 1980s. The FBI also increased resources but continued to focus on investigating crimes rather than preventing attacks.

After the American EMBASSY BOMBINGS in Africa in 1998, the FBI increased its focus on counterterrorism, but reports suggested that major changes were difficult to implement. There reportedly was also an internal disincentive to produce and share background intelligence analyses on suspected terrorists for fear that such documents might have to be provided during trials and the possibility that they might taint a case.

The "office of origin" structure within the FBI, which puts a single office in charge of an investigation to avoid duplication of efforts, may have complicated its COUNTERTERRORISM efforts. The New York Field Office had been in charge of the investigation of OSAMA BIN LADEN before the bombings in Africa, and was put in charge of the bin Laden case. Since other field offices would neither control nor receive credit for investigations involving bin Laden, there was little incentive for them to devote resources to him or to AL-QAEDA.

HUMAN INTELLIGENCE

The collection of human intelligence (HUMINT), particularly critical in counterterrorism operations, has been a special area of concern. Although the CIA's Clandestine Service logically would be the principal source for foreign information on terrorists, it has faced difficulties in collection efforts. One former Director of Central Intelligence noted a number of issues with CIA case officers in the 1990s. These issues included poor morale, frequent transfers, insufficient training, and a general sense that supervisors "just didn't get it." Field

ABOVE *The Pentagon burns during the night of September 11, 2001, with the U.S. Capitol building visible in the distance. The Pentagon is home to the American military—a desirable target, both logistically and symbolically.*

human intelligence officers and the signal intelligence personnel of the NSA also note the lack of linguists capable in languages such as Arabic, Pushtu, and Dari.

The bureaucratic and legal structures for collecting, sharing, and disseminating foreign and domestic intelligence have been difficult to resolve. There has been considerable confusion over which agency should have responsibility over the "watch list" for identified or suspected foreign terrorists, and significant breakdowns in sharing watch list information with key agencies such as the Immigration and Naturalization Service. There has been little evidence to suggest that this issue has been resolved, even after September 11.

Another issue deals with the legal barriers against sharing foreign intelligence for law enforcement purposes. The Foreign Intelligence Surveillance Court, designed to reduce or eliminate these barriers, has not operated as efficiently as intended. Moreover, the Department of Justice actually required more justification for obtaining wiretap warrants than was statutorily required. Additionally, an executive order restricted mingling foreign intelligence with domestic law enforcement information. The National Security Agency also reportedly put restrictions on sharing its reports on al-Qaeda with law enforcement agencies. Many of these firewalls may have played a role in the lead-up to September 11.

WARNINGS BEFORE SEPTEMBER 11

In his testimony to the 9/11 Commission (see NATIONAL COMMISSION ON TERRORIST ATTACKS UPON THE UNITED STATES), Director of Central Intelligence George Tenet stated that "the [warning] system was blinking red" during the summer of 2001. The intelligence community identified numerous terrorist threats. Many of these reports actually dated back to the late 1990s.

A series of reports suggested the prospect of aircraft HIJACKINGS. In late 1998, the U.S. intelligence community received reports of a possible al-Qaeda plot to hijack aircraft in an effort to free Omar Abdel-Rahman, in prison for the 1993 World Trade Center attack. In August 1998, it was reported that a Libyan group wanted to crash an aircraft into the World Trade Center. There also was a report in September 1998 about a possible plot to fly an aircraft filled with explosives into an unspecified U.S. city. This information had been received from a "walk-in" to a U.S. consulate in East Asia. There was no corroboration for either report, and intelligence officers apparently discounted the information. These reports followed a foiled incident in which a group of Algerians hijacked an airliner in 1994, intending to either to blow it up over Paris or fly it into the Eiffel Tower.

Throughout 1999, the warnings regarding al-Qaeda intensified, including a threat to blow up the FBI Building and a possible threat to a flight out of

Los Angeles or New York City. Threat reports were high in 2000, and even more intense in 2001. At the end of March, intelligence reports argued that "Sunni extremists" might attack U.S. interests. In May, separate reports indicated an increased threat specifically from bin Laden. An informant reported

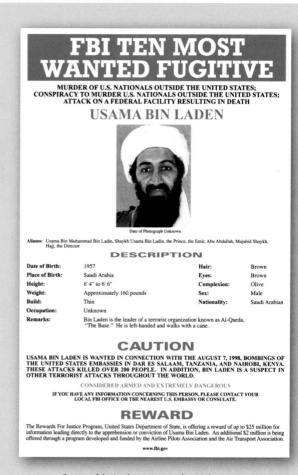

ABOVE *Osama bin Laden was on the FBI's Ten Most Wanted list as early as 1999, shown in this fugitive poster that was revised in November 2001. There was confusion over which of the government intelligence agencies was responsible for the "watch list" for suspected terrorists.*

the possibility of attacks in New York, Boston, and London, with another telephone call to a U.S. embassy warning that al-Qaeda was planning an attack in the United States using high explosives. As with earlier reports, however, none of these were verified with other sources.

Other reports suggested that there might be a plot to seize Americans abroad to force the release of jihadists (see JIHAD) held prisoner in the United States, with the possibility of embassy seizures or aircraft hijackings. Some reports pointed to the possibility of plots in Yemen and Italy, or a Canadian cell (see SLEEPER CELLS) plotting an operation in the United States. In June and July, more intelligence indicated the prospects of attacks in the Middle East or in Italy. Other countries' intelligence services also reportedly passed along attack warnings but their specificity and credibility apparently were not sufficient for specific responses. On June 22, the CIA warned of possible al-Qaeda suicide operations against unspecified U.S. targets over the next few days.

Based on the types and volume of the reports, on July 2 the FBI Counterterrorism Division sent a message to law enforcement agencies noting the increased threat assessment. It emphasized the potential for attacks against U.S. interests overseas and stated that it had "no information indicating a credible threat of terrorist attack in the United States." It did note, however, that such an attack could not be ruled out.

The 9/11 Commission summarized the shortfall of the intelligence system in predicting the September 11 attacks: "The September 11 attacks fell into the void between the foreign and domestic threats. The foreign intelligence agencies were watching overseas, alert to foreign threats to U.S. interests there. The domestic agencies were waiting for evidence of a domestic threat from sleeper cells within the United

States. No one was looking for a foreign threat to domestic targets. The threat that was coming was not from sleeper cells. It was foreign—but from foreigners who had infiltrated into the United States." National Security Advisor Condoleezza Rice at the time noted the essential problem with the intelligence reporting. The intelligence system worked in that it did in fact report on general strategic threats; it clearly identified a major increase in terrorist planning and intentions to attack U.S. interests. At the same time, however, in Rice's words, it failed to identify the "who, what, when, where, and how" of the attacks.

Further Reading: Roger Z. George and Robert D. Kline, eds., *Intelligence and the National Security Strategist: Enduring Issues and Challenges* (Rowman & Littlefield, 2005); Bill Gertz, *Breakdown: How America's Intelligence Failure Led to September 11* (Plume, 2003); William E. Odom, *Fixing Intelligence: For a More Secure America* (Yale University Press, 2003); Richard A. Posner, *Uncertain Shield: The U.S. Intelligence System in the Throes of Reform* (Rowman & Littlefield, 2006); Jennifer E. Sims and Burton Gerber, eds., *Transforming U.S. Intelligence* (Georgetown University Press, 2005).

— **LAWRENCE E. CLINE, PH.D.**

International Reaction

On September 11, the international media generally ignored sensationalism and stuck to the grisly details of the hijackings and attacks on the World Trade Center and the Pentagon. Most accounts used official government press releases, and sources generally refrained from speculation. Citizens from more than 80 nations were employed at the World Trade Center, or were passengers on the planes that crashed. Most countries saw the attacks as global, not just against the United States.

Immediately after the attacks, the U.S.-Canada border was closed for several hours. Canadian Prime Minister Jean Chretien placed his country on full alert and agreed to accept planes that were diverted from the United States after the Federal Aviation Administration (FAA) closed American airspace for 24 hours. Even before the FAA banned all except military air traffic, a number of European airlines canceled flights to the United States and recalled or rerouted flights already in transit. Prayer vigils and memorial services for the victims of September 11 and their families were held in many countries and televised around the world.

The New York Stock Exchange, the American Stock Exchange, and NASDAQ closed from September 11 to September 17. Stocks fell, partially in response to the fact that some countries had been directly affected by the attacks. The Deutsche Bank Building in New York City, for example, suffered major damage from the World Trade Center attacks.

PERSONAL AND MEDIA RESPONSES

The attack on the United States increased feelings of personal and national vulnerability in many countries, particularly in the West and in nations such as Israel and India where TERRORISM was already a fact of life. In countries such as Singapore, where racial and ethnic divisions had created deep cleavages, a heightened sense of vulnerability was also expressed. Television around the globe switched to live coverage of the developing story; newspapers in many nations carried interviews with locals discussing their increased sense of vulnerability. In the West, the media tended to draw a distinct line between Good– the United States–and Evil–the terrorists.

Less than a third of foreign newspapers attempted to explain why the hijackers engaged in suicide missions, and not even a quarter of international news coverage considered the notion that the terrorists had any justification for their actions. In the United States, sales of the *New York Times* climbed by 130,000 copies throughout the month of September. In Australia, sales of the *Sydney Morning Herald* rose by 44 percent on September 12 and by 35 percent on September 13. In Norway, street sales of newspapers climbed 40 percent. In Singapore, the *Straits Times* devoted its entire front page to the terrorist attacks for two days. In the United Kingdom, media coverage was particularly comprehensive, with residents buying close to 13 million newspapers every day in September.

Flowers, flags, and tokens were left outside American embassies and public locations in Australia, Israel, Russia, Japan, Lebanon, Jordan, and India. Flags on government buildings were lowered to half-mast in countries that included Israel and Turkey; marches were organized in Canada and Germany; OSAMA BIN LADEN was burned in effigy in India and other countries; moments of silence were observed in nations as diverse as Britain and Palestine. *Le Monde*, a Parisian newspaper, summed up much of the international reaction by insisting that at such a time "We Are All Americans."

GOVERNMENT AND ORGANIZATION RESPONSES

Statements of support for the United States poured in from governments and international organizations around the world. The staunchest support came from Canada, which immediately stepped in to offer direct assistance, and from Great Britain, where Prime Minister Tony Blair insisted that those responsible for the attacks would be shamed for all eternity and promised that Britain stood "shoulder-to-shoulder with the United States government."

President Jacques Chirac of France condemned the attacks and expressed solidarity with the United

the government, and the American people despite the fact that images of jubilant Palestinians had been broadcast around the world. General Pervez Musharraf of Pakistan declared that the entire world must unite against all forms of terrorism and subsequently handed over several hundred suspected AL-QAEDA terrorists to the United States. When President Bush made plans to invade AFGHANISTAN, the Pakistani government granted use of its airports and military bases. Hosni Mubarak, president of Egypt, condemned the attacks and expressed particular horror that the attacks had been against innocent victims.

States. Prime Minister Goran Perssan of Sweden called for all democratic nations to present a united front against terrorism. Prime Minister Ariel Sharon of Israel pledged assistance at any time and proclaimed that the terrorists would be unable to find refuge anywhere in the world. In Israel, the day after the attacks was declared a national day of mourning. Vicente Fox, president of Mexico, declared that his country was opposed to all forms of violence and terrorism. From Singapore, Prime Minister Goh Chok Tong and the Ministry of Foreign Affairs sent messages to President GEORGE W. BUSH condemning all acts of terrorism.

Russian President Vladamir Putin described the attacks as an affront to all mankind and insisted that they should not go unpunished by the international community. Palestinian leader Yasser Arafat dispatched condolences to the president,

Chinese President Jiang Zemin sent condolences to the families of the victims and expressed concern for all Chinese who were currently in the United States. Mahathir Mohamad Mahathir, prime minister of Malaysia, cautioned against avenging the deaths by methods that would lead to more violence and death. North Korea announced that it was opposed to such overt acts of terrorism. In Libya, Moammar Gadhafi called on Muslims to show sympathy and support for the American people despite existing differences with the United States. The TALIBAN condemned the September 11 attacks and insisted that Osama bin Laden was not responsible. Bin Laden did not actually claim responsibility for the attacks until 2004. Many Arab countries, though, celebrated the attacks with fanfare, rejoicing in the loss of American lives. On the first anniversary of September 11, the Iraqi state-owned newspaper, *Al Iktisadi*, ran a photograph of the burning World Trade Center with the blood-red caption, "God's Punishment."

Chris Patten of the European Union mirrored the words of German Chancellor Gerhard Schroeder in calling the attacks declarations of war and pledging support for the United States. The foreign ministers of the European Union called for three minutes of silence to honor the victims of September 11. Silvio Berlusconi, prime minister of Italy, suggested that the Group of Eight, which includes the seven most industrialized nations and Russia, hold a summit to formulate an organized response to the terrorist attacks.

The Secretary-General of the North Atlantic Treaty Organization (NATO) invoked Article 5 of the NATO charter for the first time in its history, honoring the pledge that members "agree that an armed attack against one or more of them in Europe or North America shall be considered an attack against them all and consequently they agree that, if such an armed attack occurs, each of them, in exercise of the right of individual or collective self-defence" [would employ] "such action as it deems necessary, including the use of armed force, to restore and maintain the security of the North Atlantic area."

SECURITY ISSUES

As the urgency receded, those critical of the Bush administration rushed to assign blame for the fact that the United States was unprepared for the attacks despite INTELLIGENCE that might have prevented them. Scholars accused a number of governments of failing to alert their citizens to the rising threat of international terrorism. Over the ensuing months, intelligence operations were enhanced and national security funding was increased dramatically. Countries around the world created COUNTERTERRORISM units and tightened their own security mechanisms, particularly those related to air travel. A number of countries also froze the financial assets of groups suspected of having connections to al-Qaeda; and countries such as Italy, Malaysia, Indonesia, and the Philippines launched a concentrated campaign to round up suspected terrorists. In India, where thousands of people have died in terrorist attacks since the 1990s, the armed forces were mobilized and placed near national borders for nine months.

The United Nations also condemned the attacks and enacted anti-terrorism measures that built on resolutions SC 1269 of October 19, 1999, and SC 1368 of September 12, 2001. Security Council Resolution 1373 of February 28, 2001, promoted the prevention and suppression of terrorism and endorsed the enhancement of intelligence sharing and cooperation among member states. The Counter Terrorism Committee was charged with monitoring compliance with all anti-terrorism measures. The United Nations also provided member states with assistance in drafting counterterrorism legislation and in enacting and implementing supplementary laws in the related fields of finance, customs, immigration, extradition, law enforcement, and illegal arms trafficking. In 2002, the United Nations passed Security Council Resolution 1390, designed to develop retaliatory policies aimed at curtailing support for Osama bin Laden, al-Qaeda, the Taliban, and other terrorist groups.

Further Reading: CNN, "Anti-Americanism in Europe Deepens," www.cnn.com/2003/WORLD/meast/02/14/sprj.irq.protests.rodgers. otsc (cited May, 2006); William Crotty, ed., *The Politics of Terror: The United States Response to 9/11* (Northeastern University Press, 2004); Peter Vander Veer and Shoma Munsh, *Media, War, And Terrorism: Responses from the Middle East and Asia* (Routledge, 2004); S. Venkatraman, *Media in a Terrorized World: Reflections in the Wake of 9/11* (Eastern University Press, 2004).

— **ELIZABETH PURDY, PH.D.**

Iraq

Prior to September 11, 2001, many Americans identified Saddam Hussein, president of Iraq, as the worst threat in the Middle East. The Iraqi dictator remained in power after the 1991 PERSIAN GULF WAR. Severe trade sanctions were imposed to prevent him from purchasing weapons to rebuild military forces devastated in the conflict. No-fly zones were enforced by the U.S. Air Force, preventing Hussein from using his air force against the Kurds in the north and the marsh Arabs in the south.

Even with these measures, Hussein was contained, not deposed. He repeatedly obstructed the work of international inspection teams tasked with ensuring compliance with the terms of the 1991 ceasefire, and there were widespread complaints of abuses and corruption in the United Nations (UN) Oil For Food program.

Even after evidence mounted in favor of OSAMA BIN LADEN and his AL-QAEDA terrorist network as the primary instigators of the September 11 attack, the American intelligence community continued to suspect a contributory role by Hussein.

Smoking Gun or Desert Mirage?

THE 2003 Iraq War ended with Saddam Hussein deposed and American forces in possession of the country. It was assumed that it was only a matter of time before hard evidence surfaced of Hussein's involvement with international terrorists, and particularly AL-QAEDA. However, finding such connections proved to be just as frustrating as finding the weapons of mass destruction (WMD) that were supposedly hidden all over the nation. Although several notorious terrorists were apprehended on Iraqi soil, they had all been given asylum by Hussein long before September 11 and had played no role in masterminding the attacks. As concern mounted over whether the invasion of Iraq was justified, critics of the administration charged that intelligence regarding Iraqi WMDs was flawed, and that there was no known connection between the Iraqi regime and al-Qaeda.

The 9/11 Commission carefully reviewed administrative decisions made during the week following the attacks, noting that some in the administration immediately suspected that Hussein was behind the attacks, including Deputy Secretary of Defense Paul Wolfowitz and Central Command chief Tommy Franks. As evidence was collected and analyzed in mid-September 2001, the president and other advisers decided that the blame clearly lay with al-Qaeda and with Osama bin Laden, and that the target for military action in response to September 11 should be Afghanistan. The administration worked out a four-phase plan, originally entitled Infinite Justice, which included operations against Afghanistan, but not Iraq. Thus, although there was some popular conception that the 2003 attack on Iraq was in retaliation for the September 11 attacks, the commission concluded that the administration had officially discounted that connection well before launching the first military strikes on Afghanistan in 2001.

AT RIGHT *A book entitled* Iraq: A Year of Progress *is among the government papers littering the floor of the destroyed Iraqi Foreign Ministry building in Baghdad.*

Evidence of connections with various terrorist organizations began to appear. An Iraqi defector told of an installation at Salman Pak, south of Baghdad, where terrorists trained in a mockup of a Boeing 707. His testimony was later corroborated by Charles Duelfer, a UN weapons-inspection team leader, who had visited the site and seen the airliner mockup. At the time, the inspectors were reassured that it was used by police counterterrorist teams to practice the rescue of hostages from a grounded airliner in terrorist hands. Critics argued that none of this evidence necessarily proved a connection and offered several strong arguments against such a link. Most importantly, Hussein's Ba'athist regime was secular, with policies opposite to the religious fundamentalism of Osama bin Laden and his supporters (see ISLAMIC FUNDAMENTALISM).

Furthermore, critics argued, there was suspicion that President GEORGE W. BUSH had Hussein on a "hit list" from the moment he was elected, and found the September 11 attacks a convenient way to create support for an attack on the Iraqi dictator. They suggested that the president felt Hussein had embarrassed his father, President George H.W. Bush, by clinging to power after the end of the 1991 war, and that the embarrassment led to the elder Bush's defeat in the 1992 election. Some critics claimed that George W. Bush told his advisors on the afternoon of September 11 to find a link between Hussein and the attacks.

Further Reading: Peter L. Bergen, *The Osama bin Laden I Know* (Free Press, 2006); Lawrence Freedman and Efraim Karsh, *The Gulf Conflict 1990-1991: Diplomacy and War in the New World Order* (Princeton University Press, 1993); Michael A. Ledeen, *The War Against the Terror Masters: Why It Happened. Where We Are Now. How We'll Win* (St. Martin's, 2002); National Commission on Terrorist Attacks, *The 9/11 Commission Report: Final Report of the National Commission on Terrorist Attacks Upon the United States* (W.W. Norton, 2004).

— **LEIGH KIMMEL**

ABOVE *Signage from the Baghdad International Airport Building with word "Saddam" removed.* **AT RIGHT** *An Army soldier keeps his eye on an Iraqi woman as other members of his squad search a shed on her farm in Samarra, Iraq. Coalition forces raided the farm after an informant tipped off authorities to the location of a weapons dealer and possible weapons cache.*

Islamic Fundamentalism

Following September 11, American attention focused on AFGHANISTAN, a nation controlled in many areas by an Islamic fundamentalist group known to be harboring OSAMA BIN LADEN. The Taliban had come to power in 1996 by imposing an extremely strict interpretation of Sharia on the Afghan people. Pictures and portraits were abolished as "idolatry." Computers, televisions, movies, and recorded music were banned. Men were required to wear beards at least a fist-length below their chin or be imprisoned until they grew. Women were forbidden to work or attend school, and not permitted to leave their home unless accompanied by a male relative. The country's religious police force–the Ministry for the Promotion of Virtue and the Prevention of Vice–enforced the law with whips and automatic weapons. The TALIBAN instituted weekly public executions, amputations, and floggings as punishments.

Western news reporters in 2001 found that, while Afghans chafed at some of the rules, they also respected the Taliban for their efforts to found a "pure" Islamic state and bring the Sharia to a chronically chaotic, war-torn country. The greater majority of Muslims found the Taliban's extremist version of Sharia abhorrent, yet three countries—Saudi Arabia, Pakistan, and the United Arab Emirates—granted them diplomatic recognition because they shared their ultimate aspirations—to re-Islamize Muslim society, reassert the authority of the Koran, and revitalize Islamic culture.

The movement is not driven by a "fundamentalist" interpretation of religion. There is little debate in Islam over core doctrines or the divine origin and inerrancy of Scripture. Rather, Islamic fundamentalism is concerned with the renewal of Muslim life. In practice, the ideology has fostered Taliban repression and AL-QAEDA terrorism, but it also provides the underpinnings for the government of SAUDI ARABIA, one of the United States' most important strategic allies in the Middle East.

Scholars of Islamic fundamentalism argue that it must be understood within the context of 19th- and 20th-century geopolitics. Beginning with Napoleon's invasion of Egypt in 1798, Western colonial powers steadily encroached on historically Muslim lands, bringing with them the imperative to modernize and secularize, to abandon Islamic culture and adopt Western styles of dress, entertainment, and education. At the same time, the colonial powers secured "capitulations" that enabled them to exploit most of the region's significant economic activities. With the demise of the Ottoman Empire at the end of World War I, the Muslim world fell under the control of European powers that arbitrarily fixed the national boundaries of countries such as Saudi Arabia, IRAQ, and Syria following the Treaty of Versailles.

The very idea of the nation-state is a Western concept that contravenes Islamic tradition, which

Behind the Veil

THE KORAN contains no injunctions about women's clothing, only noting that both sexes are to dress modestly. There is, however, one passage stating that men visiting the Prophet at night should address his wives from behind a "curtain." This evidently became the basis for the Muslim practice of veiling women, although it was not widespread until several generations after the Prophet's death. After September 11, Americans learned about a particularly brutal example of veiling: the TALIBAN law that women must wear burkas—tent-like garments that conceal the entire body—and slippers, so as not to make noise while walking. The Taliban routinely beat women on the streets that were in violation of this law.

The Taliban were no doubt extreme, but veiling has also been an important marker of identity in fundamentalist Islam. During the 1970s, radical female university students in Egypt voluntarily assumed traditional Islamic dress as a way to reject foreign influences. They reasoned that Western clothing revealed the figure, in keeping with the Western ethos of individualism. By concealing the body, Muslim clothing signified the Koranic ideals of community and equality.

BELOW *Women are veiled in traditional burkas in Herat, Afghanistan. Under the Taliban, females lived under strict rules with beatings common for violating laws.*

emphasizes the primacy of the *ummah*, the entire community of Muslim believers across the world. Authoritarian, oppressive governments almost invariably ruled the Middle Eastern nation-states granted independence during the twentieth century. Muslims witnessed the imposition of "alien" political ideologies, such as nationalism and socialism; they saw power and wealth accrue to a relatively small, corrupt elite; they felt that many of their own *ulama* (clerical leaders) had been marginalized by the state. Moreover, Muslims feared that their own culture was decaying because of pervasive Western and secular cultural influences. This history became the fertile ground for the rise of Islamic fundamentalism.

The "founding father" of the Islamic fundamentalism movement, Hassan al-Banna, an educator in Cairo who founded the Muslim Brotherhood, was a political moderate. Al-Banna felt that Muslims had been humiliated by colonialism and could only regain their dignity through their Islamic faith. Railing against Western values of secularism, materialism, radical individualism, and gender equality, al-Banna asserted traditional Islamic values: personal piety,

Muslim community and fraternity, charity, social justice, and domestic roles for women. In his view, the Western notion of the separation of church and state was pernicious. He wrote of the Islamic "unity of life," in which the public and private, the political and the religious, were one. Al-Banna believed that when individual Muslims changed internally, society would also change.

Through the decades, the Muslim Brotherhood, usually standing for nonviolent, gradualist reform, has attracted millions of adherents across the Middle East. Historian Lawrence Davidson notes that the organization's ongoing popularity "speaks to the depth of Islamic feeling among the masses of people for whom secular government has meant cultural alienation." However, the organization has often been brutally suppressed by nondemocratic Middle Eastern governments, and some offshoots of the group have fought back through violence and terror. The turn toward extremism in fundamentalist thinking is epitomized by the influential writings of two men with ties to the Brotherhood. SAYYID QUTB, a scholar who wrote during the 1950s and 1960s, denounced all Muslim efforts toward political and social reform as *jahiliyyah*, the apostate worship of humanity instead of God. In his view, the only permissible response to Western secularism was for an elite vanguard of truly faithful believers to foment revolution in the name of God, using physical power if necessary. Writing during the 1980s, Abd al-Salam Faraq reinterpreted the Muslim concept of JIHAD, traditionally connoting an internal struggle for righteousness, to mean an external "holy war." According to Faraq, this jihad was the "sixth pillar of Islam" and a sacred duty that had been neglected for centuries. The theories of Qutb and Faraq flew in the face of the Koran, which explicitly states: "There shall be no coercion in matters of faith." Nevertheless, their writings have heavily influenced Islamic fundamentalist terrorist organizations such as AL-QAEDA.

The Islamic fundamentalist movement is dynamic rather than monolithic, and fundamentalist practices have varied by time and place. The TALIBAN outlawed television in Afghanistan while Wahhabi Muslims in Saudi Arabia enjoy a sleek, technology-focused modernism. Saudi women are forbidden to participate in most aspects of public life while Iranian women are allowed to vote and hold public office. Islam specialist Bruce B. Lawrence writes, "Whether frustrated engineers, disaffected doctors, or underpaid bureaucrats in meaningless public jobs, potential Islamic fundamentalists are *petits bourgeois* in search of a purpose from the meaningful past to preempt the uncertain future." These fundamentalists claim to return to the pure Koranic revelation, dismissing Islamic jurisprudence, theology, religious practice, and mysticism as *al-bida'* or adulterated "innovations." In part this reflects their belief that many of the Sunni clergy, the *ulama*, have been co-opted by Western powers. In contrast, in Shia Islam clerical mysticism is revered, and clergy retain their unquestioned authority to make pronouncements about sacred Scripture. In Shia fundamentalism, change has largely been instigated from the top down. One man, the activist cleric Ayatollah Ruhollah Khomeini, largely propelled the 1979 Iranian Revolution.

Further Reading: Karen Armstrong, *The Battle for God* (Alfred A. Knopf, 2000); Lawrence Davidson, *Islamic Fundamentalism* (Greenwood Press, 1998); Carl W. Ernst, *Following Muhammad: Rethinking Islam in the Contemporary World* (University of North Carolina Press, 2003); Mark Juergensmeyer, *Terror in the Mind of God: The Global Rise of Religious Violence* (University of California Press, 2003); Bruce B. Lawrence, *Defenders of God: The Fundamentalist Revolt against the Modern Age* (University of South Carolina Press, 1995); Bernard Lewis, *The Crisis of Islam: Holy War and Unholy Terror* (Random House, 2003).

— TOM COLLINS

J

Jihad

The concept of jihad is central to the Islamic faith, but has several meanings. Derived from the root word Jahada, "to strive for a better way of life," Greater jihad involves the personal struggle to do right—an ongoing, nonviolent spiritual process. Lesser jihad is the defense of Islam itself, inclusive of violence. To the extremists, Muslims who interpret Islam differently than they are the same as Western infidels, and they use the concept of jihad as justification for attacks such as the September 11, calling it "holy war."

Lesser jihad's purpose is not to spread the faith but to extend boundaries, with world domination the ultimate goal; faith will follow. The rule of most of the Arabian Peninsula goes back to the time of Muhammad's death in 632, and Islam spread from Spain to Afghanistan within a century. Since then, lesser jihad has been used as justification for expansion into such areas as the Balkans, India, and Sudan. Moderate Muslims claim that holy war does not exist, and that faith cannot be coerced. Some claim jihad is not to defend Islam, but to oppose unjust regimes—people are to be freed so that they might come to Islam. Islamic rules of war prohibit terrorism, kidnapping, hijacking and harming of civilians or the destruction of their property, deforestation, harming the old, women, children, and the religious, including priests and rabbis. Those who commit such acts are in violation of Islamic law.

The most extreme jihadists believe they are not breaking Islamic law because they are careful how the term innocent is applied.

BIN LADEN SUPPORTERS *Religious students carry posters of Osama bin Laden and chant slogans during a rally against the United States in Karachi, Pakistan on September 19, 2001. The protesters vowed to wage a jihad against the United States if Afghanistan was attacked.*

Kuffar, or infidels—those who are not Islamic, not of a particular form of Islam, or not living under Islamic rule—are not considered innocent, regardless of gender, age or status. To the terrorist extremists, jihad is a straight road to paradise.

Further Reading: Andrew G. Bostom, ed., *The Legacy of Jihad: Islamic Holy War and the Fate of Non-Muslims* (Prometheus Books, 2005); Josh Burek and James Norton, "Q&A: Islamic Fundamentalism," www.csmonitor.com/2001/1004/p25s1-wosc.html, *Christian Science Monitor* (October 4, 2001); University of Southern California, "Compendium of Muslim Texts," www.usc.edu/dept/MSA/reference/glossary/ term.jihad.html (cited May 2006).

— **ELIZABETH A. KRAMER**

Joint Congressional Inquiry into Intelligence

In 2002, the U.S. Senate and House of Representatives conducted a joint inquiry into intelligence failures that contributed to the September 11 attacks. Senate leaders were Bob Graham, Democrat from Florida, and Richard Shelby, Republican from Alabama; House leaders were Republican Porter Goss (later to be appointed as Director of Central Intelligence) of Florida and Nancy Pelosi, Democrat from California. The joint investigation released an unclassified version of its findings in December 2002. The hearings were marked by a degree of political partisanship.

The joint inquiry raised many issues also addressed by the 9/11 Commission (see NATIONAL COMMISSION ON TERRORIST ATTACKS UPON THE UNITED STATES), but the Congressional body focused solely on intelligence problems. The final report provided conclusions about what went wrong and what needed to be changed, in both classified and unclassified versions.

There was an upsurge in threat warnings about possible terrorist attacks beginning in 1998 and continuing into 2001. Specifics were not received by U.S. INTELLIGENCE agencies, but as the Joint Inquiry noted "the [Intelligence] Community did have information that was clearly relevant to the September 11 attacks, particularly when considered for its collective significance." However, the assumption had been that potential attacks against U.S. interests most likely would take place overseas.

A key finding of the commission was that "Although relevant information that is significant in retrospect regarding the attacks was available to the Intelligence Community prior to September 11, 2001, the Community too often failed to focus on that information and consider and appreciate its collective significance in terms of a probable terrorist attack. Neither did the Intelligence Community demonstrate sufficient initiative in coming to grips with the new transnational threats. Some significant pieces of information in the vast stream of data being collected were overlooked, some were not recognized as potentially significant at the time and therefore not disseminated, and some required additional action on the part of foreign governments before a direct connection to the hijackers could have been established. For all those reasons, the Intelligence Community failed to fully capitalize on available, and potentially important, information."

Other key conclusions included: "The Intelligence Community acquired additional, and highly significant, information regarding Khalid Almindar and Nawaf Alhazmi in early 2000. Critical parts of the information concerning al-Almindar and Alhazmi lay dormant within the Intelligence Community for as long as 18 months, at the very time when plans for the September 11 attacks were proceeding. The CIA missed repeated opportunities to act based on information in its possession that these two OSAMA BIN LADEN-associated terrorists were traveling to the United States, and to add their names to watchlists.

"This Joint Inquiry confirmed that these same two future hijackers, Khalid Almindar and Nawaf Alhazmi, had numerous contacts with a long-time FBI counterterrorism informant in California and that a third future hijacker, Hani Hamjour, apparently had more limited contact with the informant. In mid- to late-2000, the CIA already had information indicating that Almindar had a multiple-entry U.S. visa and that Alhazmi had in fact traveled to Los Angeles, but the two had not been watchlisted and information suggesting that two suspected terrorists could well be in the

United States had not yet been given to the FBI. The San Diego FBI field office that handled the informant in question, did not receive that information or any of the other intelligence information pertaining to Almindar and Alhazmi, prior to September 11, 2001.

"On July 10, 2001, an FBI Phoenix [Arizona] field office agent sent an electronic communication to four individuals in the Radical Fundamentalist Unit (RFU), to two people in the Usama Bin Ladin Unit (UBLU) [alternate spelling] at FBI headquarters, and to two agents on International Terrorism squads in the New York Field Office. In the communication, the agent expressed his concerns, based on his first-hand knowledge, that there was a

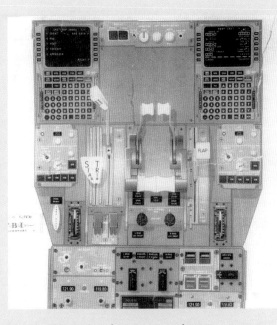

ABOVE *This portion of a torn poster of a 757 cockpit found in a trash compactor at the Days Inn, Newark Airport, in New Jersey was part of the evidence filed in the Zacarias Moussaoui trial.*

coordinated effort underway by Bin Ladin to send students to the United States for civil aviation-related training. He noted that there was an 'inordinate number of individuals of investigative interest' in this type of training in Arizona and expressed his suspicion that this was an effort to establish a cadre of individuals in civil aviation who would conduct future terrorist activity... The communication generated little or no interest at either FBI Headquarters or the FBI's New York field office.

"In the period from September 8 to September 10, 2001, NSA intercepted, but did not translate or disseminate until after September 11, some communications that indicated possible impending terrorist activity.

"Within the Intelligence Community, agencies did not adequately share relevant counterterrorism information, prior to September 11. This breakdown in communications was the result of a number of factors, including differences in the agencies' missions, legal authorities, and cultures. Information was not sufficiently shared, not only between different Intelligence Community agencies, but also within individual agencies, and between the intelligence and the law enforcement agencies. Serious problems in information sharing also persisted, prior to September 11, between the Intelligence Community and relevant non-Intelligence Community agencies.

"In short, for a variety of reasons, the Intelligence Community failed to capitalize on both the individual and collective significance of available information that appears relevant to the events of September 11. As a result, the Community missed opportunities to disrupt the September 11th plot by denying entry to or detaining would-be hijackers; to at least try to unravel the plot through surveillance and other investigative work within the United States; and, finally, to generate a heightened state of alert and thus harden the homeland against attack. No one will ever know what might have happened had more connections been drawn between these disparate pieces of information. We will never definitively know to what extent the Community would have been able and willing to exploit fully all the opportunities that may have emerged. The important point is that the Intelligence Community, for a variety of reasons, did not bring together and fully appreciate a range of information that could have greatly enhanced its chances of uncovering and preventing Usama Bin Ladin's plan to attack these United States on September 11, 2001."

Further Reading: Loch K. Johnson and James Wirtz, eds., *Strategic Intelligence: Windows into a Secret World* (Roxbury, 2004); Mark M. Lowenthal, *Intelligence: From Secrets to Policy* (Congressional Quarterly Press, 2005); Jeffrey T. Richelson, *The U.S. Intelligence Community* (Westview, 1999); Abram N. Shulsky, *Silent Warfare: Understanding the World of Intelligence* (Potomac Books, 2002).

— LAWRENCE E. CLINE, PH.D.

Judge, Mychal (1933–2001)

Reverend Mychal Judge, a Franciscan priest known as "Father Judge" and "Father Mike," was one of five chaplains serving the FIRE DEPARTMENT OF NEW YORK (FDNY) on September 11. Hearing of the morning's events, Judge was one of the first members of the FDNY to arrive at the World Trade Center.

The priest was only one of 343 firefighters killed in the collapse of the Twin Towers, but he captured the hearts of America because he gave an identifiable face to the attacks. Reuters photographer Shannon Stapleton took a photograph that was widely distributed of four firefighters carrying Judge's body out of the collapsed South Tower. Judge earned his reputation from his work with New York's firefighters and with the families of the 230 people who died when TWA Flight 800 exploded shortly after leaving Long Island on July 17, 1996. "Father Mike" was family to most New York firefighters. He officiated at their weddings, baptized their children, heard their confessions, and comforted the loved ones of those who died on the job. The popular chaplain received so many messages on his office answering machines in the firehouse on West 31st Street that he wore out message tapes every few months.

Because Judge was the first casualty identified on September 11, his death certificate bears the number "0001." Yet at least one other firefighter was already dead because Judge died while administering last rites to an unidentified firefighter from Company 216. Early reports stated that a body falling from the building had killed the firefighter, and that Judge, who had removed his helmet, was killed by falling debris as he knelt over him. Later reports indicated that the priest was inside the South Tower when it came down. After the dust had settled somewhat, a firefighter aimed his flashlight on the ground, found Judge, but could detect no pulse. Other reports state that the story of Judge's death has become an urban myth, and that he actually died of a heart attack.

The firefighters carried the priest to the ambulance and then to St. Peter's, the oldest Catholic church in Manhattan, where they covered him with a white cloth and laid him on the altar with his helmet on his chest. Later, Judge's body was taken back to Engine 1 and Ladder 24 so that the priests, firefighters, neighbors, street people, and strang-

ABOVE *Father Mychal Judge, a chaplain with the Fire Department of New York, stands on the beach at a service for the 230 victims of the July 1996 crash of TWA Flight 800.*

ers who came could pay their respects. Three thousand people attended Judge's funeral on September 15 at the St. Francis of Assisi Church. Millions watched the service on television. Archbishop Edward Egan presided; former president Bill Clinton gave one of the eulogies. A smaller, informal service was held a month later at the Good Shepherd Chapel of an Episcopal Church on Ninth Avenue in New York City. Guests attending this informal memorial ranged from priests and firefighters to politicians and rock stars. The music by Morning Star, an Irish band, included jigs and reels.

Further Reading: Michael Ford, *Father Mychal Judge: An Authentic American Hero* (Paulist Press, 2002); Terry Golway, *So Others Might Live: A History of New York's Bravest* (Basic Books, 2002); *New York Magazine* Editors, *September 11, 2001: A Record of Tragedy, Heroism, and Hope* (Harry N. Abrams, 2001); Jennifer Senior, "The Fireman's Friar, *New York* Magazine (November 12, 2001); Hampton Sides, "The Chaplain," *Men's Journal* (November 2001).

— ELIZABETH PURDY, PH.D.

K

Khalid Sheikh Mohammed (1964?–)

Khalid Sheikh Mohammed was the mastermind behind the September 11 attacks, which he called the "planes operation." Born in 1964 or 1965 in the Pakistani tribal region of Baluchistan, he was raised in Kuwait. In the early 1980s he entered Chowan College, a rural Southern Baptist college in Murfreesboro, North Carolina. Chowan had a small Muslim contingent that reportedly was the subject of practical jokes by other students.

After two years at Chowan, Khalid attended North Carolina Agricultural and Technical State University, graduating with a bachelor's degree in mechanical engineering. In 1987 he joined his three brothers in AFGHANISTAN to support the Arab MUJAHIDEEN fighting the Soviets. During this time, he worked closely with his nephew RAMZI AHMED YOUSEF, the man responsible for the first World Trade Center bombing (see WORLD TRADE CENTER 1993).

Khalid is reported to have fought at least once in Afghanistan, but his skill was in planning and organization. Even though he believed in the principles of AL-QAEDA, he was known as a playboy. Contrary to Muslim custom, he drank alcohol, visited discos, and dressed lavishly. Initially, he did not want to join al-Qaeda, but served as a consultant for several years.

Once Khalid pledged allegiance to OSAMA BIN LADEN, he took over command of all operational elements and media coordination within the organization. Khalid had a hand in every attack carried out by al-Qaeda,

"PLANES OPERATION" *A New York firefighter stands in front of the wreckage. The mastermind of the September 11 attacks on the United States, Khalid Sheikh Mohammed, sought to bring jihadist believers from around the world together under al-Qaeda.*

ABOVE *Nineteen Airmen died and hundreds were injured in the terrorist attack at Khobar Towers in Dhahran, Saudi Arabia, on June 25, 1996. The front of Bldg. 131 was destroyed when a fuel truck parked nearby was detonated by terrorists.* **BELOW** *A memorial at the former Prince Sultan Air Base, Saudi Arabia, to honor those who lost their lives at Khobar Towers.*

from the first World Trade Center attack in 1993 to the bombing of the USS *Cole* in 2000, and the murder of *Wall Street Journal* reporter Daniel Pearle. He sought to bring jihadist elements throughout the world together under the al-Qaeda umbrella. In 1999 he launched his most ambitious plan when he secured funding from bin Laden for the "planes operation."

On March 2, 2003, Khalid was captured when the Pakistani INTELLIGENCE service raided a house in Rawalpindi, and transferred to U.S. custody. In September 2006, the White House announced that Khalid was one of 14 high-level al-Qaeda operatives transferred from Central Intelligence Agency custody to Camp Delta at Guantanamo Bay, Cuba, for eventual trial by military tribunal.

Further Reading: Yosri Fouda and Nick Fielding, *Masterminds of Terror: The Truth Behind the Most Devastating Terrorist Attack The World Has Ever Seen* (Arcade Publishing, 2003); Simon Reeve, *New Jackals: Ramzi Yousef, Osama Bin Laden, and the Future of Terrorism* (Diane Publishing, 2005); "A Timely Arrest," *The Economist* (March 8, 2003).

— WADE K. EWING

Khobar Towers

On June 25, 1996, radical Islamists attacked a military housing facility, Khobar Towers, in Saudi Arabia. The building was part of an apartment complex for U.S. Air Force personnel, near the city of Dhahran. Although far smaller in scale than the September 11 attack, the Khobar Towers incident bore many of the earmarks of the later conspiracy: careful planning, an attack on a high-rise building, a detonation designed to kill and wound as many people as possible, and a pattern of motivation that resembled that of the September 11 event. The blast killed 19 Air Force service people and one Saudi, and 372 people were wounded. The bombing was blamed on members of the Saudi Hizbullah who wanted the United States out of Saudi Arabia.

The Khobar Towers complex housed U.S. and other foreign troops deployed in support of Operation Southern Watch, the air force mission implemented after Desert Storm to enforce no-fly and no-drive zones in southern IRAQ. The apartments had been built to house Saudi Bedouins, but remained vacant until Desert Shield. Because they offered comfortable quarters and were considered sufficiently secure, the U.S. military was happy to accept their use.

The high-rise apartments were located in the center of an urban environment. Although the compound housing U.S. troops was fenced off from the rest of the buildings, the closest perimeter fence was only 85 feet from the nearest U.S. barracks, and ran down the middle of a four-lane road. U.S. Air Force security personnel had identified security weaknesses and implemented improved security procedures; however, the changes focused on improving security inside the compound.

The terrorist group attempted to enter the compound through the main checkpoint. After being denied entrance, at about 10:00 P.M. a fuel truck and two cars approached a parking lot near Building 131, housing the airmen. The truck, packed with 3,000 to 5,000 pounds of explosives, was parked next to the fence. The driver and passenger left in one of the cars, a few moments later, the bomb exploded.

The explosion left a crater 85 feet wide and 35 feet deep. The "Jersey" dividers—concrete barricades as used in road construction and highway medians—that had been placed along the fence deflected the blast upward, probably preventing the total collapse of Building 131. Even so, the force of the explosion sheared away the front of Building 131, and the entire compound was damaged to some extent. The blast was so powerful that it was felt in Bahrain, 20 miles away.

Some 13 Saudi Shia dissidents and one Lebanese were suspected in the operation. According to sketchy INTELLIGENCE released by the U.S. government, the government of Iran was implicated as a sponsor of the attack. There have been hints of some AL-QAEDA involvement, possibly as a source for the explosives, but evidence of this connection remains vague.

Further Reading: James F. Record, "Independent Review of the Khobar Towers Bombing," Federation of American Scientists, www.fas.org/irp/threat/khobar/ (cited August 2006); Secretary of Defense, "Report: Personal Accountability for Force Protection at Khobar Towers," www.defenselink.mil/pubs/khobar/report.html (cited August 2006).

— LAWRENCE E. CLINE, PH.D.

The 1995 Attack

THE KHOBAR Towers attack was not the first against American troops in SAUDI ARABIA. On November 13, 1995, a car bomb was detonated outside the headquarters of the U.S. training mission to the Saudi Arabian National Guard, the OPM-SANG. This bomb, containing about 250 pounds of explosives, killed five Americans and wounded 34; it also killed two officials from India.

The Saudi government arrested four suspects who claimed that they had been influenced by OSAMA BIN LADEN. A short time after their confessions, they were executed. Reportedly, U.S. INTELLIGENCE officials learned that AL-QAEDA had decided a year before the bombing that they wanted to attack U.S. targets in Saudi Arabia and had provided explosives to conduct an operation. After the attack, al-Qaeda took public credit, but it is difficult to determine its actual involvement.

L

Lawsuits

After the September 11 attacks, the U. S. government created a Victim Compensation Fund intended to provide recompense to those who had been injured or had lost loved ones in the attacks, and protect them from the anguish of having to file lawsuits against the airlines or other potentially responsible parties. In return for accepting money from the fund, victims and their families waived the right to sue.

Although many families chose to accept compensation, generally calculated as the amount the person would have earned in his or her remaining working years plus a sum for pain and suffering, about 90 opted to pursue lawsuits, either individually or as a class action. Many of them considered the Victim Compensation Fund "blood money" offered to buy off the families and keep them from asking difficult questions about the systemic failures of INTELLIGENCE and security (see AIRPORT SECURITY) that had made the disaster possible.

Ellen Mariani, widow of Neil Mariani, a passenger on UNITED AIRLINES FLIGHT 175, was one of the litigants who emphasized that her quest was not about money. By refusing to accept a settlement from the Victim Compensation Fund, she gave up about $500,000 for the uncertainty of the civil court system. It was far more important for Mariani that the government account for the events of September 11 than it was to receive money.

She believed that the government knew the attacks were coming and failed to act, or worse, allowed them to happen in order to create sentiment for a war. By pressing a lawsuit, she hoped to force the government to open its files, to allow the black box recordings and the surveillance camera tapes from the airports where the terrorists boarded to be seen in a court of law. The fact that the government was willing to give victims and their families such large compensation checks reinforced her conviction that something was being hidden at the highest levels.

However, those lawsuits soon ran into roadblocks. By law, the government can decide whether it chooses to be sued, under the doctrine of sovereign immunity, a remnant of the concept that "the king can do no wrong." The government also rejected suits against the airlines, ostensibly to protect them from financial hardship.

Caroline O'hare, whose mother Hilda Marcin was aboard UNITED AIRLINES FLIGHT 93, Kathleen Ashton, whose son Thomas Ashton was in the World Trade Center, and Jacques Debeuneure, whose father James Debeuneure was aboard AMERICAN AIRLINES FLIGHT 77 also opted out of the Victim Compensation Fund and pursued independent suits. Although some of the suits did have to do with monetary compensation, many others focused on whether systemic weaknesses contributed to the hijackers' success and thus constituted actionable negligence.

Some who participated in the Victim Compensation Fund later looked to the court system for recourse. Several filed a class-action suit against fund administrator Kenneth R. Feinberg, claiming that he was arrogant and unfair in his distribution of awards. One beneficiary, Laura Balenian, sued her lawyer, Thomas Troiano, for having taken nearly a third of her award in legal fees, an amount she considered excessive. By September 11, 2006, about one-third of the 90 lawsuits filed by claimants who opted out of the fund had been settled. Although the settlements are confidential, observers suspect that the settlements have run somewhat higher than the average of $2 million paid per claim.

Further Reading: David Ray Griffin, *The New Pearl Harbor: Disturbing Questions About the Bush Administration and 9/11* (Olive Branch Press, 2004); Jim Marrs, *Inside Job: Unmasking the 9/11 Conspiracies* (Origin Press, 2004); Rowland Morgan and Ian Henshall, *9/11 Revealed: The Unanswered Questions* (Caroll and Graf, 2005).

— LEIGH KIMMEL

Literature of September 11

The attacks generated more books than any other news event in history. In less than a year, Amazon.com had almost 700 related titles available, and the country's largest wholesale book distributor, Ingram Book Group, planned to release 150 new September 11 books in the fall of 2002.

The initial offerings were commonly compilations of contemporary reporting and photography. Reuters, *Life,* the *New York Times,* and others produced collections that covered the events of September 11 from the first hit through the rescue and recovery phase. Also abundant were memoirs such as those of Thomas Von Essen and Bernard Kerik, the fire and police commissioners at the time, and Mayor RUDOLPH GIULIANI. Biographers were quick to eulogize those killed in works such as *Let's Roll* (see TODD BEAMER) and *Father Mychal Judge: An Authentic American Hero* (see MYCHAL JUDGE).

Included in the early literature was David Halberstam's *Firehouse,* and Bernard Lewis produced *What Went Wrong?,* dealing with the history of

Islam. Thomas Von Essen's memoir was *Strong of Heart*. James DeFede's *The Day the World Came to Town* dealt with the influx of international passengers to GANDER, NEWFOUNDLAND, when the United States shut down its airways.

Comic Books

ART SPIEGELMAN, author and illustrator of *Maus*, produced the comic book *In the Shadow of No Towers* in 2004. In this work, the Pulitzer Prize winner deals with both the events of September 11 and the political uses people have made of them.

Marvel Comics published books and comics dealing with firefighters and rescuers and donated the proceeds to relief funds. Included were the Black Issue (Vol. 2, No. 36, with an all-black cover) of *Amazing Spider-Man*. Marvel's book, *Heroes*, featured various artists' pin-ups with the aim of expressing appreciation for and admiration of the rescue workers and patriotism. Another Marvel book was the anthology *A Moment of Silence*, which included the true story of a Marvel employee who died in the rescue effort. Marvel also produced a new series focused on firefighters, *The Call to Duty*.

DC Comics contributed the two-volume *9-11: Artists Respond*, which included short stories and single-page art from various artists. Alternative Comics' *9-11 Emergency Relief* was similar. Wildstorm/DC published Brian K. Vaughan's *Ex Machina*, set in a world where the Great Machine saves one tower and becomes mayor of New York.

Early analytical works include Richard Bernstein's *Out of the Blue*, which used the rise of Islamist movements to explain the attacks. Bill Gertz's *Breakdown* and John Miller's *The Cell* emphasized INTELLIGENCE failures. Noam Chomsky blamed U.S. foreign policy. Also in this genre was Alan Dershowitz's *Why Terrorism Works*.

Science fiction includes "In Spirit," a novella of spiritual time travel by Pat Forde published in *Analog* in September 2002. William Gibson's *Pattern Recognition* in 2003 was the first novel to deal with the attacks directly, with the main character a marketing consultant whose father disappeared in Manhattan on September 11. *Windows on the World*, written by Frederic Beigbeder in 2003, is the story of a family's escape from the top of the North Tower.

Another novel, Jonathan Safran Foer's 2005 *Extremely Loud and Incredibly Close*, is narrated by a nine-year-old seeking his father's most illuminating secret. In 2002 Iain Banks published *Dead Air*, a novel set in London on September 11. Also dealing with the subject are *Twilight of the Superheroes* by Deborah Eisenberg and Jay McInerney's *The Good Life*. Ian McEwan's *Saturday* is set in London after September 11 but before July 7, 2005, the date of the LONDON BOMBINGS.

Poetry includes Richard Howard's "Fallacies of Wonder," dealing with the difficulty of remembering what the towers were really like. Dennis Loy Johnson and Valerie Merians produced the poetry anthology *Poetry After 9/11: An Anthology of New York Poets* on the first anniversary. Their volume included poems that deal not with the event but with the feelings it engendered—dread, mystery, loss. Naomi Shihab Nye produced *19 Varieties of Gazelle*.

Books for children and young adults include a *New York Times* compilation of the newspaper coverage.

Maira Kalman's *Fireboat: the Heroic Adventures of John J. Harvey* is a true story of a fireboat recalled to service on September 11. *Bravemole* was Lynne Jonell's story of courage for intermediate and middle schoolers. Christine Maclean's *Even Firefighters Hug Their Moms* is a picture book for primary and intermediate levels.

In theology and spirituality, the archbishop of Canterbury, Rowan Williams, produced *Writing in the Dust: After September 11* in 2002.

Further Reading: *Gotham Gazette*, "9/11 In Art and Culture: September 11 Books," http://www.gothamgazette.com/rebuilding_nyc/topics/culture/books.shtml (cited August 2006); Julia Keller, "Literature: A Rush of Books Helps Nation Come to Terms with 9/11," *Chicago Tribune* (August 25, 2002).

— JOHN H. BARNHILL

London Bombings

On July 7, 2005, at 8:50 A.M., four bombs exploded in London—three within 50 seconds of each other in the subway, and a fourth on a bus an hour later. The attacks killed 56 people, including four bombers, and injured 700. The explosions were the worst terrorist attack on the United Kingdom since the Lockerbie, Scotland, bombing of Pan Am Flight 103, which killed 270 people in 1988, and the worst in London since World War II.

Officials first thought that a power surge was responsible for the Underground explosions, but quickly realized they were acts of TERRORISM. The explosions completely shut down the subway network and many nearby roads.

The Secret Organization and Jihad Organization of Al-Qaeda in Europe, a group associated with AL-QAEDA, claimed responsibility, and authorities identified the suicide bombers. On the day of the bombing, the United Kingdom was hosting the G8 Summit in Perthshire. The day before, London had been chosen to host the 2012 Summer Olympic Games.

Two weeks after the bombing, on July 21, four more bombs went off, again three in the Underground and one on a bus. Because the bombs failed to detonate properly, there were no fatalities and only one injury. The bombers escaped but were captured later.

According to the preliminary official report in May 2006, the four plotters spent only a few hundred pounds sterling and obtained much of their information from the internet. They had visited Pakistan but had no direct support or planning by al-Qaeda.

Responsibility

THREE OF the four suspected London bombers had no police record. The alleged terrorists were Mohammed Sidique Khan, Shehzad Tanweer, Germaine Lindsay, and Hasib Hussain. When al-Qaeda in Europe claimed responsibility on the internet, it cited the U.S. invasion of AFGHANISTAN and the British support for the invasion of IRAQ as motive. It also warned Denmark, Italy, and other European nations with troops in Iraq and Afghanistan to withdraw. Experts noted the similarities of the London and Madrid attacks and their common use of AL-QAEDA methods of synchronization. Al-Qaeda officially claimed responsibility on September 1, 2005.

ABOVE *The front pages of British national newspapers covering the terrorist bombing on July 8, 2005. The attacks on London public transportation killed more than 50 people and wounded 700.*

Police destroyed two additional suspicious packages and determined that they were not bombs.

After the London bombings, security in the United Kingdom was raised to the highest levels, including security alerts and controlled destruction of suspicious packages, but there were no more terrorist acts. Canada, the United States, France, and Germany were among the states that also raised alerts for transit systems.

Although initially anti-Muslim incidents increased in Britain and Europe, these quickly waned as Muslim organizations condemned the attacks and as governments and the media supported the local Muslim communities.

Further Reading: Nafeez Mosaddeq Ahmed, *The London Bombings: An Independent Inquiry* (Penguin Group, 2006); Milan Rai, *7/7: The London Bombings, Islam and the Iraq War* (Pluto Press, 2006).

— JOHN H. BARNHILL

M

Madrid Bombings

On March 11, 2004, three days before national elections, 191 people died and more than 1,800 were wounded in the bombing of four commuter trains in Madrid, Spain. The government of Prime Minister Jose Maria Aznar immediately blamed the Basque separatist organization ETA *(Euskadi ta Askatasuna).* On March 12 in government-orchestrated demonstrations, 28 million Spaniards protested against ETA. ETA had a history of bombings, but the scale of the commuter train attacks was beyond their previous attempts. ETA usually warned before bombing, but there was no warning this time. The tactics employed seemed more like those of AL-QAEDA.

One day before the elections a videotape was discovered near a Madrid mosque. The tape stated that the attacks were al-Qaeda's punishment of Spain for the presence of Spanish troops in IRAQ. Again Spain took to the streets, this time protesting Aznar's accusation of ETA in an effort to sway public opinion and win the election.

The Spanish public opposed the Iraq War, and now there was a perception that Aznar had manipulated public opinion for political advantage. The Socialists of Jose Luis Rodriguez Zapatero took power in the election and announced that Spain would withdraw its 1,300 troops from Iraq.

Investigation revealed that the perpetrators of the Madrid train bombings were a Moroccan Islamist group, and on March 13 authorities arrested the Moroccans. The ousted Partido Popular and newspapers

TERROR IN MADRID *Rescue workers shield the removal of victims' bodies from cameras as they search the train for survivors. Bombs were timed to explode nearly simultaneously on three trains in Madrid during morning rush hour. Explosions rocked one long-distance, high-speed train and two suburban trains packed with commuters.*

such as *El Mundo* continue to claim that the attacks were part of a conspiracy to oust Aznar. Variously, the conspiracy theorists blame the Socialists, the ETA, and Spanish, French and/or Moroccan security forces.

European anti-Muslim sentiment increased after the bombings. Europeans were uncomfortable with Muslim culture and values and with the knowledge that a small but violent minority of the 20 million European Muslims were hostile. The bombings also raised concerns about the admission of predominantly Muslim Turkey into the North Atlantic Treaty Organization (NATO).

The bombings reminded the European Union that it was a target for Islamic radical terrorists, possibly an easier target than the United States because of proximity, economic ties, and cultural influences dating back 600 to 800 years. The European Union states increased sharing of INTELLIGENCE to improve collective security.

Further Reading: Sebastian Balfour, ed., *Politics of Contemporary Spain* (Taylor and Francis, 2005); Council on Foreign Relations, "Basque Fatherland and Liberty (ETA)," www.cfr.org/publication/9271/(cited June 2006).

— JOHN H. BARNHILL

Basque Separatism

THE BASQUES are not Spanish. They are a distinct group that has lived since the Stone Age in the western Pyrenees Mountains between Spain and France, and has long sought independence from Spain. In 1959 the Euskadi ta Askatasuna, which means "Basque Fatherland and Liberty," was formed to bring about a Basque state from parts of Spain and France. For decades the Basques fought through TERRORISM. They attempted to assassinate Prime Minister Jose Maria Aznar and King Juan Carlos in 1995. After 2001 their attacks became less frequent and less violent, and by 2003 they were warning of coming attacks so that targets could be evacuated. In 2005 when parliament proposed negotiations with the Basques, 250,000 Spaniards protested. In March 2006 the Basques unilaterally announced a cease-fire.

Malaysia

Malaysia served as a transportation hub for terrorists traveling to the United States to hide their travel origins, particularly when leaving Pakistan from AFGHANISTAN. Khalid Sheikh Mohammed, the mastermind behind September 11, organized a support network from Malaysia that worked closely with RAMZI BIN AL SHIBH.

Most well-known of the connections between Malaysia and September 11 is the 2000 meeting in Kuala Lumpur, where two of the high-profile hijackers met with other terrorists before moving to Southern California (see TERRORISTS OF SEPTEMBER 11). Khalid Almindar departed Kuala Lumpur for Bangkok and eventually Los Angeles. Twenty months later, he was aboard AMERICAN AIRLINES FLIGHT 77 when it plunged into the Pentagon. So were Nawaf Alhazmi and his younger brother, Salem, both of whom were present at the Kuala Lumpur meeting. Prior to the meeting, the Central Intelligence Agency (CIA) had been tracking Khalid Almindar and Nawaf Alhazmi during a trip to Malaysia, but lost them in Bangkok. Only when they resurfaced in the aftermath of the attacks was it discovered that they had entered the United States shortly after this meeting.

ABOVE *The Petronas Twin Towers are a landmark of Kuala Lumpur and feature geometrics typical of Islamic architecture. The towers were the world's tallest from 1996 to 2003, although only 88 floors are occupied as compared with 110 occupied floors in the former World Trade Center towers.*

In January 2001, it was learned that another important member of AL-QAEDA had met with Almindar and Alhazmi during the Kuala Lumpur meeting in 2000, a man named "Khallad," who was then believed to be Almindar. Khallad had been associated with both the East Africa EMBASSY BOMBINGS in 1998 and the USS *Cole* bombing in 2000, but later investigations proved that he and Almindar were different people.

A spurious connection between al-Qaeda, Malaysia, and IRAQ surfaced in 2004 when journalist Stephen F. Hayes outlined a meeting at the airport between a supposed member of Iraqi intelligence and Khalid Almindar. Another connection came to light during the trial of ZACARIAS MOUSSAOUI when it was revealed that he maintained one of his many e-mail addresses through a server in Malaysia. He also received letters from Infocus Tech, a Malaysian company, stating that he was appointed that company's marketing consultant in the United States, the United Kingdom, and Europe, and that he would receive, among other things, an allowance of $2,500 per month.

Further Reading: "Four Moments When 9/11 Might Have Been Stopped," *Christian Science Monitor* (April 19, 2004); Stephen F. Hayes, "The Connection," *The Weekly Standard* (June 7, 2004); Indictment, *USA v Zacarias Moussaoui*, http://news.findlaw.com/hdocs/ docs/terrorism/moussaoui1201.pdf (December 11, 2001); "Inside the Mind of a Terrorist," *The Guardian Observer* (August 22, 2004).

— **WADE K. EWING**

Media Coverage

Television cameras were broadcasting live coverage of the devastation from AMERICAN AIRLINES FLIGHT 11's crash into the North Tower when UNITED AIRLINES FLIGHT 175 flew into the South Tower. September 11 provided a plethora of human-interest stories, allowing the media to show the pain of those searching for loved ones without sensationalism or embellishment.

Many reporters were forced to turn to alternative transmission methods because much of New York's communication network was hit during the attacks. Ten cellular communication towers, which provided service to 200,000 phone lines, were knocked out by the attacks, rendering cell phones useless. With landlines for phones also out of service, cable and satellite e-mail and internet service were the only methods of sending information to news services and networks. Forced to evacuate its offices amid rumors that its chief editor was dead, the *Wall Street Journal* set up shop 50 miles away in New Jersey.

For four days, the broadcast industry devoted itself almost solely to covering the events and aftermath of September 11, and advertisers lost millions of dollars by foregoing all commercials. Commentators worked without sleep. CNN provided coverage by running multiple text lines across the screen. For the first time in the history of television, rival networks shared information, and radio stations broadcast live television feeds.

Without concern for budgets, newspapers rushed to turn out special editions. The *Chicago Tribune* published two special editions in one day. Biweekly newspapers turned into weeklies. For the first time in its history, the front page of the *Atlanta Constitution* covered only a single story. Newsmagazines discarded planned editions and staffs worked around the clock to compile new material. Supplying extended coverage, all major newsmagazines put out special editions devoted exclusively to September 11.

IMPACT OF MEDIA COVERAGE

Before the day ended, the media had begun comparing September 11 to December 7, 1941, the "infamous" day when the Japanese launched a surprise attack on the Pacific fleet at Pearl Harbor at a cost of 2,400 Americans lives. On CBS, Dan Rather was one of the first to identify September 11 as "the Pearl Harbor of terrorism." Peter Jennings of ABC admitted that he wanted to go home and hug his children, and more than one reporter wiped away tears. Some members of the media joined the far right to present the Arab people as "the enemy," and Arab Americans reported a backlash against them as a group. Such actions led to a public call for restraint in assigning blame, and

an effort was made to include the Arab community in public expressions of mourning.

On September 12, a poll reported in *USA Today* revealed that 86 percent of Americans considered the terrorist attacks as acts of war. Some 80 million viewers watched prime-time broadcasts and cable news coverage during the four days of continuous television coverage. Initially, media approval ratings rose sharply, with 85% of respondents approving of the September 11 coverage. Later, as the full extent of the powers granted to the federal government by the USA PATRIOT ACT (Public Law 107–56) became known, the media was criticized for not informing the public of the threat to civil liberties. Criticism was also levied against the media for insufficiently informing the American public about AL-QAEDA and other terrorist groups that presented a threat to American lives and property.

Early unverified reports resulted in a number of inaccuracies. Networks reported that a bomb had exploded at the State Department; reports were issued that people had been rescued from the rubble of the World Trade Center and that survivors were using cell phones to call for help. Another rumor surfaced claiming the United States had initiated a retaliatory attack against AFGHANISTAN.

MEDIA AND PUBLIC REACTIONS

Like firefighters, police officers, and other rescue workers, journalists and photographers ran toward the disaster. Those who could traveled to the site in taxis, on foot, by bicycle, even by hitching rides with complete strangers. With air traffic into New York banned at 9:17 A.M, a photographer for the *Los Angeles Times* drove nonstop from Los Angeles to New York. After the Federal Aviation Administration (FAA) suspended all air traffic for 24 hours at 2:30 P.M., the media was forced to pursue other methods

Memorable Images

ON SEPTEMBER 11, digital cameras provided graphic illustrations for immediate dispatch. Photos of firefighters (see FIRE DEPARTMENT OF NEW YORK), captured the spirit of the day, providing symbols of both horror and hope. Memorable photographs of September 11 included firefighters carrying the body of Father MYCHAL JUDGE, a Fire Department chaplain who died during the collapse of the South Tower; a picture of a firefighter trudging up the staircase as workers hurried down and evacuated the building; the depiction of three firefighters planting U.S. flags in the rubble of the Twin Towers; evacuees covered in ash streaming down the streets of Manhattan; and medical personnel waiting at area hospitals to treat survivors that never arrived. Photographs and media portrayals of New York City Mayor RUDOLPH GIULIANI came to symbolize the American spirit of resilience in the face of tragedy.

TOP LEFT *Survivors of the terrorist attacks make their way through smoke, dust, and debris about a block from the collapsed towers.* TOP RIGHT *Firefighters raise the U.S. flag as they continue their recovery efforts.* BOTTOM RIGHT *A Staten Island firefighter heads upstairs to evacuate people from Tower One. The rescue worker barely escaped before the towers collapsed. This photograph was taken by John Labriola, who escaped from his office on the 71st floor.*

of travel to the crash sites near Washington, D.C. (see PENTAGON), and Shanksville, PENNSYLVANIA.

While the media was not directly involved in rescue efforts, they performed a valuable service in keeping the public informed and helping to diminish the spread of uncontrolled panic. Some reporters and photographers who covered the attacks and the recovery work at Ground Zero paid a price for their dedication to pursuing the story—post traumatic stress disorder (PTSD). The Dart Center for Journalism and Trauma reported that after September 11, some members of the media experienced nightmares, flashbacks, emotional detachment, insomnia, and debilitating headaches. In extreme cases, such symptoms were the precursors of more serious problems, including substance abuse, memory and cognition impairment, and severe mental and physical incapacitation.

Further Reading: Lee Artz and Yahya R. Hakalipour, *Bring 'Em On: Media and Politics in the Iraq War* (Rowman and Littlefield, 2005); CBS News, *What We Saw* (Simon and Schuster, 2002); Wheeler Winston Dixon, ed., *Film and Television after 9/11* (Southern Illinois University Press, 2004); Douglas Kellner, *Media Spectacle and the Crisis of Democracy: Terrorism, War, and Election Battles* (Paradigm, 2005); Howard Kurtz, "Americans Tune in and Stress Out," *New York Times* (September 20, 2001).

— ELIZABETH PURDY, PH.D.

Memorials

The first September 11 memorials took shape online before the day ended. Hundreds e-mailed family and friends, linked to rescue agencies, posted photographs and eyewitness accounts. People gathered at U.S. embassies and consulates around the world.

Breaking Ground After Ground Zero

IN AUGUST 2005, the brokerage firm Goldman Sachs decided to build its $2.4 billion world headquarters across from the World Trade Center site. The company's decision to build in this location depended on state and city leaders agreeing to finance the construction with $1.6 billion in tax-exempt bonds and other incentives.

In November 2005, Governor George Pataki, Mayor Michael Bloomberg, and Senators Hillary Rodham Clinton and Charles Schumer attended the groundbreaking ceremony. Henry M. Paulson, chairman and chief executive officer of the company, said that "Goldman Sachs has called Lower Manhattan its home for 136 years and we are proud to reaffirm our commitment to this neighborhood and to the city of New York."

Five months later in January 2006, a new upscale restaurant called Colors opened in Greenwich Village, just a walk from Ground Zero. The owners of Colors are former employees of WINDOWS ON THE WORLD, the 107th-floor restaurant destroyed in the World Trade Center collapse. They lost 73 of their friends and coworkers in the attacks. The Colors waiters, busboys, bartenders, chefs, and dishwashers all have a stake in the venture, financed with about $2.2 million. The consortium Good Italian Food offered $500,000 as an equity investment, and the Nonprofit Finance Fund put up $1.2 million for the project from 15 smaller lenders. Modest funds came from Roman Catholic nuns in California, Michigan, and Ohio.

ABOVE LEFT *The 2002* Tribute in Light *marked the six-month anniversary of the tragedy, the beams representing the fallen twin towers.* **ABOVE RIGHT** *At the Pentagon, beams of light were projected to honor each life lost.*

Candlelight vigils glowed throughout NEW YORK CITY. In Washington, D.C., thousands of citizens marched in a candlelight vigil onto the National Mall, just across the Potomac River from the PENTAGON.

On September 13, England's Queen Elizabeth broke with decades of tradition and ordered the changing of the Guard at Buckingham Palace to stop for two minutes of silence and the playing of "The Star-Spangled Banner." On September 14, Queen Elizabeth and British officials attended a memorial service in St. Paul's Cathedral in London, and at noon Paris time, a three-minute silence was observed throughout Europe. Over 100,000 people attended a memorial service on Parliament Hill in Ottawa, Canada, presided over by Prime Minister Jean Chretien, Governor General Adrienne Clarkson, and U.S. ambassador Paul Cellucci. Reverend Billy Graham led a service at the Washington National Cathedral, with President GEORGE W. BUSH, Congressional leaders, and other politicians attending.

On Sunday, September 16, families of the victims of UNITED AIRLINES FLIGHT 93 gathered at the crash site in PENNSYLVANIA for a private ceremony, then joined a service with Governor Tom Ridge and First Lady Laura Bush.

At Washington Square in New York City, people placed hundreds of candles and flowers, and at Union Square Park thousands congregated, grieved, and prayed. The American flag appeared on front porches, flagpoles, cars, clothing, and public buildings across the United States. On October 4, Reverend Brian Jordan, a Franciscan priest, blessed two beams found in the World Trade Center wreckage that had spontaneously formed a cross and then had been welded together by ironworkers. The Firefighters Association of Missouri donated a previously commissioned statue

ABOVE *Residents of Hoboken, New Jersey, set up a spontaneous memorial along the Hudson River, facing the former World Trade Center towers.*

of fallen firefighters to New York City to honor the firefighters who died in the attacks.

On March 11, 2002, the city of New York dedicated the damaged sphere sculpture that had stood in the World Trade Center as a temporary memorial in Battery Park City. Beginning on March 11, the Tribute in Light project—88 searchlights placed next to the site of the World Trade Center—created two vertical columns of light and shone until April 14. On May 28, the last steel beam standing at the site of the World Trade Center was cut down and placed in a flatbed truck.

On September 11, 2002, representatives from 90 countries came to Battery Park and New York mayor Michael Bloomberg lit an eternal flame to commemorate the first anniversary of the attacks.

PERSONAL MEMORIALS

Officials of the tiny community of Colts Neck, New Jersey, which lost five of its citizens in the attacks,

commissioned resident sculptor Jim Gary to create a memorial garden.

Many people watched the events of September 11 unfold from Pier A in Hoboken, New Jersey, with a clear view of the World Trade Center. At dusk on March 11, 2002, the Tribute in Light was turned on, marking the six-month anniversary of the terrorist attack. In September 2004, a permanent September 11 memorial called *Hoboken Island* was chosen.

Eighty-one streets in New York City were renamed in honor of September 11 victims. The city of Newark renamed its airport to honor the people who died. On September 11, 2004, Russian artist Zurab Tsereteli dedicated his sculpture *Tear of Grief* to the people of September 11. An official gift of the Russian government, the 10-story-high tribute is to be built on the Jersey City waterfront across the Hudson River from where the World Trade Center stood. On the evening of September 11, 2004, the Empire State Building went dark for eleven minutes at 9:11 P.M.. The Massachusetts Port Authority created a memorial at Logan International Airport (see AMERICAN AIRLINES FLIGHT 11; UNITED AIRLINES FLIGHT 175.

The Los Angeles Fire Department unveiled a memorial on September 11, 2003, at its Frank Hotchkin Memorial Training Center in Elysian Park. The 23-ton, approximately 22-foot-tall steel column was originally part of the lobby supports of the World Trade Center and is considered to be the largest artifact of the attacks on the West Coast.

In Sandwich, Massachusetts, the family of a Navy captain killed in the September 11 attacks pledged $250,000 to help build a sports complex at Sandwich High School in the spring of 2006. Captain Gerald F. "Jerry" Deconto, who graduated from Sandwich High in 1974, was in his first-floor office in the Pentagon when AMERICAN AIRLINES FLIGHT 77 smashed through the walls.

WTC MEMORIAL

On January 4, 2005, the World Trade Center Foundation, a nonprofit corporation, held its inaugural meeting. Formed to collect donations to build a World Trade Center memorial, the foundation planned to raise up to $1 billion to build a memorial and museum on the building footprints of the Twin Towers, scheduled to open on September 11, 2009.

Plans for the memorial were plagued by controversy from the beginning. In the spring of 2003, the Lower Manhattan Development Corporation announced an international competition to design the memorial. Some 5,201 individuals and teams from around the world contributed proposals. On January 6, 2004, the 13-member jury selected *Reflecting Absence*, New York City Housing Authority architect Michael Arad's design for a street-level plaza overlooking two pools of water as the winning design.

The memorial's primary features are two 30-foot-deep pools with waterfalls in the footprints of the buildings. The heart of the memorial is located behind a curtain of water at the base of a waterfall in the grotto-like gallery where the names of the September 11 dead would be inscribed. A major issue arose over how the names would be displayed.

Critics said that *Reflecting Absence* would be too expensive and too complicated, citing, for example, that there was no practical, cost-effective way to keep the waterfalls from freezing in winter. Cost was another point of contention. Estimates placed the cost of the memorial alone at about $500 million. Plans for additional buildings, including a museum and performing arts center, could push the cost to more than $1 billion. The steep cost and poor fund-raising would make it necessary to charge admission to all visitors to the memorial except relatives of the victims.

Estimated construction costs have risen to over $1 billion, matching the cost of the World Trade Center itself, which was completed in 1970. New York Mayor Michael Bloomberg said that construction costs must be capped at $500 million and a higher

AT LEFT *A touching memorial to the World Trade Center rescue workers near Battery Park.* **ABOVE** *In Shanksville, Pennsylvania, handmade "Angels of Freedom" honor the 40 passengers and crew members killed when Flight 93 crashed.*

figure would be "inappropriate, even if the design has to be changed."

FLIGHT 93 MEMORIAL

The Flight 93 National Memorial in a grassy, Shanksville, Pennsylvania, meadow, will recognize and honor the sacrifice of the passengers on United Airlines Flight 93. One of the memorial's chief features will be a 93-foot-tall *Tower of Voices*, set on high ground to mark the entrance to the memorial park. The circular tower with a canted top will contain 40 wind chimes, one for each passenger and crew member, and each with a different tone. The memorial, to be completed in 2011, and designed by the Los Angeles firm of Paul Murdoch Architects, assisted by Nelson Byrd Woltz Landscape Architects, will encompass more than 2,000 acres surrounding the crash site near Shanksville.

PENTAGON MEMORIAL

About 150 family members and guests including Secretary of Defense DONALD RUMSFELD attended the invitation-only groundbreaking ceremony for the Pentagon Memorial on June 15, 2006. Also attending were architects Julie Beckman and Keith Kaseman who won a worldwide competition to design the memorial. Covering 1.93 acres, the memorial will feature 184 cantilevered benches, in memory of each victim of the Pentagon attack. Eighty paperbark maple trees will shade the memorial. According to James J. Laychak, who lost his brother in this attack, about $10.8 million dollars was raised to build the memorial, most of it from private donations. Construction is expected to be completed in September 2008.

FIFTH ANNIVERSARY MEMORIALS

September 11 occurred on a Monday in 2006, and during the previous weekend the fifth anniversary of the attacks was commemorated throughout the country. President Bush visited each of the attack sites and made speeches that were criticized by some Democrats for being political and linking the war in Iraq with September 11. In Phoenix, Arizona, the Phoenix Bach Choir remembered the events with a commemorative concert and featured September 11-inspired musical reactions from composers and poets around the country.

NEW YORK CITY marked the fifth anniversary with sculpture shows, quilt dedications, candlelight vigils, and a conference examining "the economic, cultural, environmental, educational, and political consequences of the day that changed everything."

In Shanksville, Pennsylvania, the Families of Flight 93, the National Park Service, the Flight 93 Memorial Task Force, and the Flight 93 Advisory Commission hosted a Commemoration Service, which included the reading of the names of the victims on United Airlines Flight 93 and the traditional tolling of the bells of remembrance.

Further Reading: Timothy Dwyer, "Groundbreaking for 9/11 Memorial at Pentagon Set," *Washington Post* (June 7, 2006); David Simpson, *9/11: The Culture of Commemoration* (University of Chicago Press, 2006); Brian W. Vaszily, *Beyond Stone and Steel: A Memorial to the September 11, 2001 Victims* (Hard Shell Word Factory, 2001).

— **KATHY WARNES**

Moussaoui, Zacarias (1968–)

Zacarias Moussaoui has been described as the 20th hijacker, a replacement for RAMZI BIN AL SHIBH, who was denied an entry visa into the United States. A French citizen of Moroccan descent who moved to London, Moussaoui attended the Fins-

ABOVE *The A Pan-Am Flight Simulator similar to the one Zacarias Moussaoui trained on in Minnesota.* **AT LEFT** *FBI photo of Moussauoi after his arrest on immigration charges in August 2001.*

bury Park mosque, home to extremist Abu Hamza. He reportedly visited the Khaldan training camp in AFGHANISTAN in 1998 and 1999, entered the United States in February 2001 and spent three months at the Airman Flight School in Norman, Oklahoma. He then moved to the Pan-Am International Flight Academy in Eagan, Minnesota, for training in a 747-400 simulator.

Moussaoui was arrested by the Federal Bureau of Investigation (FBI) on August 16, 2001, and charged with an immigration violation. His Minnesota flight instructor, Clancy Prevost, had contacted the FBI after becoming suspicious of Moussaoui's actions and his lack of knowledge regarding the plane's operating systems. The FBI was denied a special warrant to search Moussaoui's computer on the grounds of insufficient probable cause. On

September 11, Moussaoui was in a Minnesota jail on immigration charges. His cellmates reported that he cheered when he heard of the attacks.

Moussaoui was indicted by a federal grand jury on December 11, 2001, for his role in the murder of thousands of people in New York, Virginia, and Pennsylvania. Moussaoui maintained that he was not involved in the September 11 plot, but in a separate plan to free Omar Abdel-Rahman, convicted for the first attack on the World Trade Center (see WORLD TRADE CENTER 1993). In April 2005 Moussaoui reversed himself and pleaded guilty to the charges. On May 3, 2006, a federal jury levied a life sentence without parole. He is currently serving the sentence in a maximum-security prison in Colorado.

Further Reading: Sarah Downey, "Who is Zacarias Moussaoui?" www.msnbc.com (December 14, 2001); BBC News, "Profile: Zacarias Moussaoui," http:/news.bbc.co.uk (April 25, 2006).

— ABBE ALLEN DEBOLT

Mujahideen

In response to the December 1979 invasion of AFGHANISTAN by the Soviet Union, a myriad of indigenous, grassroots resistance groups sprang up and began attacks on Soviet forces. Despite the media attention that surrounded the Afghan struggle against the Soviets after September 11, 2001, the first Afghan "Islamic resistance fighters" or Mujahideen were not members of AL-QAEDA but practitioners of a localized, lived Islam as opposed to a doctrinal, scholarly Islam. By the early 1980s the Afghan struggle against the Soviets and the communist regime in Kabul had become a popular cause through-

The "Arab Afghans"

DURING THE ten years of the Afghan-Soviet conflict, tens of thousands of volunteers from the Arab world came to AFGHANISTAN to participate in the jihad against the atheistic Soviets. Although the vast majority of Mujahideen were indigenous Afghans, the Arab volunteers were eager participants and many of the Persian Gulf Arabs brought in large amounts of money to fund the Mujahideen. Referred to as "Arab Afghans," these fighters were not always welcomed; the money from Arab states was of much greater value to the Afghan victory over the Soviets than the participation of the Arab volunteers.

out the Islamic world and thousands of volunteers from the Arab world and Asia traveled to Afghanistan to participate in the JIHAD.

OSAMA BIN LADEN, a wealthy Saudi student of the radical Palestinian Muslim scholar Abdullah Azzam, began raising financial support for the Afghan cause in early 1980 and traveled frequently between his native country and Peshawar, Pakistan, on the border of Afghanistan. He developed contacts within the Mujahideen, primarily with Burhanuddin Rabbani, head of the modernist Islamic party Jami'at-e Islami, and 'Abd al-Rab al-Rasul Sayyaf, the leader of the small Ittehad-e Islami Afghanistan party that received a sizeable amount of aid from the Saudi government.

By 1984 bin Laden had moved to Peshawar where he worked on Azzam's Arabic-language *al-Jihad* newspaper, which reported on the Afghanistan conflict and served as an influential recruiting tool for Mujahideen in the Arab world.

There have been charges that the U.S. Central Intelligence Agency directly funded bin Laden or Azzam, but funding was in support of the Afghan groups and was channeled through Pakistan's Inter Services Intelligence agency. In addition to American financial support, the Mujahideen received significant monetary backing from wealthy Arab Muslim states in the Persian Gulf, including Saudi Arabia and Kuwait. Official Saudi funding equated approximately with the hundreds of millions of dollars in U.S. aid that was flowing to the Mujahideen by 1985. Large amounts of money also came from private Islamic charities, mosque fund-raisers, and wealthy private donors.

In effect, bin Laden's ties with the Mujahideen provided a platform for his later activities in Afghanistan. After Azzam's assassination in 1989, the Saudi took over his mentor's organization and continued to participate in Islamic politics in Afghanistan after the Soviet withdrawal in January. It was around this time that bin Laden set up the first military training camp. A year later he left Afghanistan, which had descended into civil war, and went back to his native Saudi Arabia where he remained until 1992, when he relocated to Sudan. After his Saudi citizenship was revoked in 1994 for criticizing the monarchy, bin Laden was asked to leave Sudan by the country's ruling National Islamic Front under intense pressure from the United States, and he returned to Afghanistan.

By 1996 he had established close ties with the TALIBAN, and his amorphous al-Qaeda movement operated relatively freely there until the multinational invasion led by the United States in the winter of 2001.

Further Reading: Jason Burke, *Al-Qaeda: Casting a Shadow of Terror* (I.B. Tauris, 2003); Gilles Dorronsoro, *Revolution Unending: Afghanistan, 1979 to the Present* (Columbia University Press, 2005); Roland Jacquard, *In the Name of Osama Bin Laden: Global Terrorism & the Bin Laden Brotherhood* (Duke University Press, 2002); Ahmed Rashid, *Taliban: Militant Islam, Oil and Fundamentalism in Central Asia* (Yale University Press, 2000); Olivier Roy, *Islam and Resistance in Afghanistan* (Cambridge University Press, 1986).

— **CHRISTOPHER ANZALONE**

ABOVE *The Mujahideen during the rebel assault on Jalalabad, Afghanistan. The Islamic resistance fighters were primarily funded by wealthy Arab states, including Saudi Arabia and Kuwait.*

N

National Commission on Terrorist Attacks Upon the United States

The National Commission on Terrorist Attacks Upon the United States, known as the 9/11 Commission, was created in November 2002. Headed by Thomas H. Kean and Lee H. Hamilton, the commission's objectives were to investigate "facts and circumstances relating to the terrorist attacks of September 11, 2001, including those relating to intelligence agencies, law enforcement agencies, diplomacy, immigration issues and border control, the flow of assets to terrorist organizations, commercial aviation, the role of congressional oversight and resource allocation, and other areas determined relevant by the commission." The commission began hearings at the end of March 2003, and received testimony from 160 witnesses during 19 days of hearings. The last hearing was in July 2004.

The commission conducted a wide-ranging investigation of the events of September 11, earlier aspects of AL-QAEDA operations, and overall U.S. COUNTERTERRORISM responses.

SEPTEMBER 11: THE NATIONAL RESPONSE

The commission examined the immediate response to the hijacked aircraft and pointed out that this HIJACKING did not conform to others; therefore the standing protocols did not provide adequate guidance on how to deal with the event. The commission concluded that

PENTAGON RUINS AT NIGHT
The 9/11 Commission investigated why the Pentagon—the military headquarters of the United States—was so easy a target on September 11.

the Defense Department and the Federal Aviation Administration (FAA) did the best they could under the circumstances.

Because of dual and overlapping communications, some leaders in Washington believed that the Defense Department had launched fighter aircraft to shoot down the hijacked aircraft, while the actual orders sent to the fighter pilots were only to identify the type of aircraft and to tail them. As a consequence, Vice President RICHARD B. CHENEY "was mistaken in his belief that shoot down authorization had been passed to the pilots flying at NORAD's direction."

One set of fighter planes, part of the 113th Wing of the District of Columbia Air National Guard, flew over Washington by 10:38 on September 11. They had been launched from Andrews Air Force Base in nearby Maryland in response to informa-tion from the Secret Service. Aircraft launched from Langley Air Force Base under NORAD direction could only tail suspicious planes. Andrews National Guard aircraft operated under orders allowing them to fire on hijacked planes. Not until much later was it realized that two sets of rules of engagement had been issued. Although NORAD claimed for a period that if the passengers aboard UNITED AIRLINES FLIGHT 93 had not succeeded in bringing down the airplane near SHANKSVILLE, PENNSYLVANIA, it would have been shot down by NORAD aircraft, the commission found that to be "incorrect." In the complex events of the morning, NORAD officials did not even know that United Airlines Flight 93 had been hijacked, and its aircraft did not have time to intercept the flight nor authorization to shoot it down.

Criticisms of the Commission's Work

CRITICISMS OF the 9/11 Commission soon surfaced. One was that the U.S. government had a plethora of commissions, special hearings, Congressional joint committees, and the like throughout the 1990s covering many of the same national security and INTELLIGENCE issues as those addressed by the 9/11 Commission. With earlier commissions, much ink was spilled but the follow-up actions based on their recommendations were limited. Much of the same was expected from the 9/11 Commission. After the commission finished its work, however, the Bush administration—with some prodding—adopted many of its recommendations. Members of the commission continued their involvement with the issues raised during the hearings, despite the commission having formally ended, in an effort to keep pressure on for reforms.

The second major criticism of the 9/11 Commission was that it did not single out individual culpability for failures. The commission members considered it their role to examine systemic failures, and their unwillingness to identify individual mistakes left some observers unsatisfied.

There also have been criticisms of the 9/11 Commission's thoroughness in examining all the aspects of the attacks and the lead-up to them. Although the commission and its staff conducted extensive studies and hearings, there are indications that it may have either missed or ignored other information.

This criticism became particularly sharp after reports surfaced regarding a U.S. military intelligence operation called Able Danger that tried to track some of the hijackers. Its reports were not shared with the Federal Bureau of Investigation (FBI) or other agencies; some claimed that the commission had been briefed but chose not to pursue it further.

The members of the 9/11 Commission held twelve public hearings in Washington, D.C., and New York City.

In examining command, control, and communication even within single agencies such as the Port Authority (see PORT AUTHORITY OF NEW YORK AND NEW JERSEY), the NEW YORK POLICE DEPARTMENT, and the FIRE DEPARTMENT OF NEW YORK, the commission identified problems. Communication and coordination among such agencies was a large issue. The 9-1-1 operators in the police department and the fire department dispatch offices were not integrated into the emergency response. The 9-1-1 system was not prepared to cope with a major disaster.

COMMISSION RECOMMENDATIONS

The 9/11 Commission made a series of recommendations, from broad strategic judgments to very technical issues. Some of the major recommendations in the final report are these:

1. The U.S. government should identify nations and regions that are potential terrorist sanctuaries.

2. The United States and the international community should help the Afghan government (see AFGHANISTAN) gain authority over its own country.

3. The United States and SAUDI ARABIA had to confront the problems in their relationship openly.

4. The United States should define its message to the world regarding humane treatment, the rule of law, and respect for human dignity and opportunity.

5. The United States must recognize that cooperating with repressive and brutal governments is a bad policy, and must stand for a better future in countries that do not respect the principles of human dignity and rule of law.

6. The United States has to defend its ideals abroad in a vigorous fashion.

7. A strategy to counter TERRORISM should include economic policies that encourage economic development and more "opportunities for people to improve the lives of their families and to enhance prospects for their children's future."

8. The United States should work with other nations to develop a comprehensive coalition strategy against Islamist terrorism and develop a common approach toward detention and treatment of captured terrorists.

9. The United States should work against the proliferation of weapons of mass destruction, since their acquisition has been a goal of AL-QAEDA.

10. U.S. counterterrorism efforts should focus on terrorist financing and travel.

The commission went on to make more than 20 other specific security recommendations, and urged the government to take the lead in ensuring that civil liberties be protected while increased security measures were put in place.

Further Reading: *The 9/11 Commission Report: Final Report of the National Commission on Terrorist Attacks Upon the United States* (Authorized Edition) (W.W. Norton, 2004); David Ray Griffin, *The 9/11 Commission Report: Omissions and Distortions* (Interlink Publishing Group, 2005).

— RODNEY P. CARLISLE
LAWRENCE E. CLINE, PH.D.

NATO

Article 5 of the North Atlantic Treaty Organization (NATO) charter, which states that an attack on any member is considered an attack on all the members, was invoked for the first time in history on October 5, 2001, in response to the September 11 attacks. The U.S. ambassador to NATO, R. Nicholas Burns, asked for an emergency meeting of the North Atlantic Council (NAC) to discuss the attacks. At this meeting, he did not ask to have Article 5 invoked; however, after the meeting, the Canadian ambassador, David Wright, suggested to Burns that this might be a good time to do so. Burns consulted with National Security Advisor Condoleezza Rice on September 12 about the possibility of invoking Article 5, and the decision was made to tell the NAC that the United States would support invoking the article.

Lord George Robertson, NATO's secretary general, led the discussions in the NAC about whether to approve the use of Article 5. Robertson believed that NATO needed to invoke Article 5 and personally communicated with various heads of state and foreign ministers to make sure that they would sup-

Article 5

FROM THE NATO Charter: "The Parties agree that an armed attack against one or more of them in Europe or North America shall be considered an attack against them all and consequently they agree that, if such an armed attack occurs, each of them, in exercise of the right of individual or collective self-defense recognized by Article 51 of the Charter of the United Nations, will assist the Party or Parties so attacked by taking forthwith, individually and in concert with the other Parties, such action as it deems necessary, including the use of armed force, to restore and maintain the security of the North Atlantic area.

"Any such armed attack and all measures taken as a result thereof shall immediately be reported to the Security Council. Such measures shall be terminated when the Security Council has taken the measures necessary to restore and maintain international peace and security."

port him. Robertson thus cleared the way for the NAC to approve the request, and NATO was ready to help defend the United States.

To invoke Article 5, NATO needed evidence that the attack had come from abroad. On October 2, the U.S. coordinator for COUNTERTERRORISM presented that evidence to the NAC, and Article 5 went into operation on October 5.

Part of the aid provided by NATO to the United States was to send AWACS (airborne radar) aircraft from their bases in Germany to the United States to help protect U.S. airspace and to relieve U.S. planes for use elsewhere. This was the first time the United States had received aid to deal with a domestic security issue from a foreign power since the Revolutionary War. It was also the first time NATO resources were used in North America for activities other than training or testing. Additionally, members of NATO granted the United States access to their airspace, airfields, ports, and refueling facilities. The NATO allies also took on a greater role in patrolling the Mediterranean Sea to free up U.S. naval forces for use in the war on terrorism. NATO approved the U.S. decision to attack AFGHANISTAN and agreed on October 9, 2001, to send troops to help. NATO members enhanced their cooperation in gathering intelligence about various terrorist organizations and activities, agreed to help increase security at U.S. and allied facilities, and to help each other if any of them became the target of increased terrorist threats because of support for the war on terrorism.

Further Reading: Ryan C. Hendrickson, *Diplomacy and War at NATO: The Secretary General and Military Action after the Cold War* (University of Missouri Press, 2006); Dieter Mahncke, Wyn Rees, and Wayne C. Thompson, *Redefining Transatlantic Security Relations: The Challenge of Change* (Manchester University Press, 2004); North Atlantic Treaty Organization, "NATO and the Fight Against Terrorism," www.nato.int (cited June 2006).

— **DALLACE W. UNGER, JR.**

New York City

New Yorkers woke on the morning of September 11 to bright blue skies and comfortable temperatures. Millions began their workday trek into the city by train, subway, bus, ferry, or car. They were joined by more than a million schoolchildren, whose summer vacations had ended a few days before.

People walking along the streets of lower Manhattan noticed the plane first, their eyes drawn up to the sound of a jet engine flying too low and too fast. Seconds later, at 8:45 A.M., AMERICAN AIRLINES FLIGHT 11 slammed into the North Tower of the World Trade Center. "It was as if the plane was absorbed into the building," said Alex Zaitsved. Watching from the sidewalk, David Blackford said, "you could see the concussion move up the building."

Confused bystanders crowded the streets, watching thick black smoke pour out of the North Tower, and dark objects – quickly identified as bodies – fall from the upper floors. "They looked like rag dolls being tossed," said Edguardo Villegas, who himself barely escaped the building. "Their bodies were lifeless; just twirling in the air, dressed in suits." It is estimated that 50 to 200 people jumped from the upper floors.

It was just after 9 A.M. when Lakshman Achuthan, managing director of the Economic Cycle

ABOVE *Attendees of the NATO-Russia Council Conference on Terrorism listen to speakers through their translation headsets.*

ABOVE *An ash-covered man assists a woman as both evacuate Ground Zero. Many noted the kindness of strangers during the surreal time following the attack.* **AT RIGHT** *A map showing the World Trade Center area in lower Manhattan and a detailed inset.*

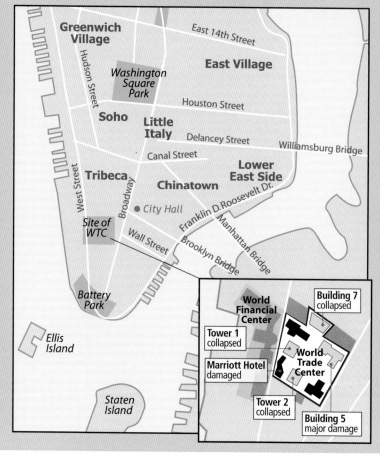

Research Institute, made his way out of the North Tower. "I looked over my shoulder and saw the United Airlines plane coming," he said. "It came over the Statue of Liberty. It was just like a movie. It just directly was guided into the second tower." UNITED AIRLINES FLIGHT 175 hit the South Tower at 9:03, at approximately 500 miles per hour. Pieces of the plane were later found six blocks away.

At 10:03, the South Tower fell. David Rohde, a reporter for the *New York Times*, described it as sounding "...like a waterfall, thousands of panes of glass shattering as the north side of the tower buckled. Then a slow, building rumble like rolling thunder that will not stop as the tower cascades toward the ground. And finally the silence of dozens of people running for their lives focused on nothing but themselves and survival as the thick brown cloud of debris surges down the street."

Joe Disordo was describing his escape from the 72nd floor of the South Tower when he suddenly realized it was not there. "Where is the building? Did it fall down? Where is it?"

THE CITY STOPS

The usual frenetic pace of city life came to a stop. The *New York Post* reported the next day that "New Yorkers were members of a tribe in shock, tied in knots and easily moved to sudden tears and swift kindnesses. People moved through Midtown without the ordinary get-out-of-my way pace…They waited quietly in long lines—no shoving, no impatient words—at the pay phones on street corners. The hundreds who sat or stood under outdoor jumbo electronic television screens were virtually silent; it was no time for small talk."

The Port Authority, which ran the major transit systems in Manhattan (see PORT AUTHORITY OF NEW YORK AND NEW JERSEY), was buried under tons of rubble at the World Trade Center, with 84 of its employees among the dead. Most of the transit and commuter rail systems were shut down, and bus service was limited.

Tens of thousands crossed the Brooklyn and Manhattan bridges on foot. Rescue workers from the Long Island College Hospital and Brooklyn Hospital Center were waiting on the other end of the Manhattan Bridge with cold water and offers of medical assistance.

Commuters packed into Grand Central terminal to try to catch Metro North trains. Both passengers and officials were aware that Grand Central was a landmark building and so a potential target for terrorism. The day was punctuated with evacuations and rumors of a shutdown.

Others headed for the piers, hoping to catch a ferry to New Jersey. NY Waterway had 24 boats in operation. Circle Line and World Yacht added their 20 boats to the evacuation effort, and together the ferry companies moved thousands of people out of Manhattan. (See also EVACUATION, LOWER MANHATTAN.)

As night fell, the city was quiet. Dust was thick on the ground and in the air. Only 290,000 people out of a population of 8 million lived in the area below 14th Street, but it was home to a large number of popular restaurants, nightclubs, and galleries—a lively,

exciting place on a normal Tuesday in September. This night, it was a ghost town. Broadway was dark.

Dozens of the city's churches stayed open that night, offering food, cool drinks, and solace. "There's nothing but death in the air today," said a paralegal interviewed by the *Post* as she sat in the Middle Collegiate Church on Second Avenue. "I don't want to hate anybody. I don't want to judge anybody. So in order to keep my peace, I had to be here for a little bit."

Further Reading: David Friend, *Watching the World Change: The Stories Behind the Images of 9/11* (Farrar, Straus and Giroux, 2005); Magnum Photographers, *New York September 11* (Powerhouse Books, 2001); *New York Times, Portraits 9/11/01* (Henry Holt, 2003); Annie Thoms and Taresh Batra, *With Their Eyes: September 11th: The View from a High School at Ground Zero* (HarperCollins, 2002).

— HEATHER K. MICHON

New York Police Department

Comprised of approximately 40,000 employees, the New York Police Department, popularly known as the NYPD or "New York's Finest," played an essential role on September 11. About 50 of the police officers dispatched to the World Trade Center were members of the elite Emergency Services Unit, trained to deal with hostage situations and high-risk rescues. As workers streamed out of the Towers, members of the NYPD's Emergency Services Unit, led by Lieutenant Vic Hollifield, remained inside searching offices on accessible floors, providing oxygen masks and basic first aid, and guiding office workers to safety.

The New York Police Department arrived on the scene almost immediately after the North Tower was struck at 8:45 A.M. by AMERICAN AIRLINES FLIGHT 11. Eleven minutes later, Joseph Esposito,

Lessons Learned

THE NEW York Police Department (NYPD) has learned much about fighting TERRORISM since September 11 and has become more vigilant on those occasions when large crowds are gathered. On New Year's Eve 2001, for instance, NYPD officers carried radioactivity detectors borrowed from the U.S. Customs department to patrol the celebration at Times Square. Counterterrorism equipment has also become more sophisticated. In 2005, the NYPD announced that it was purchasing Barrett 50-caliber semiautomatic rifles, which have been used by the U.S. military to penetrate armored vehicles. Mounted on police helicopters, the rifles are capable of disabling aircraft that might be used to target buildings such as the World Trade Center and the Pentagon. Bullets from these rifles can penetrate windshields and concrete barriers. The rifles are only one element of the NYPD's improved COUNTERTERRORISM capabilities.

the chief of the department, placed the department on Level 4 mobilization, calling up 22 lieutenants, 100 sergeants, and 800 police officers from all over the city. Most NYPD officers were stationed in the lobbies and outside the World Trade Center buildings. As people evacuated the buildings, the NYPD steered them to safety or to medical help. The NYPD command post was established on West and Vesey Streets by 9:01 A.M., ready to provide organization and oversight to the rescue operation.

The NYPD Aviation Unit was in the air by 8:50. Within ten minutes, three NYPD helicopters were observing events at the World Trade Center. Aviation officers immediately informed air traffic control, which no one else had done. Police officers aboard the helicopters took photographs as they tried to get close enough to attempt roof rescues similar to those during the 1993 bombing of the World Trade Center (see WORLD TRADE CENTER 1993). However, World Trade Center security officials had locked the doors to the roof, reportedly for security reasons. Hundreds of workers who had climbed upward were trapped inside the buildings.

INSIDE THE TOWERS

NYPD commanders immediately dispatched six-member Emergency Services Unit (ESU) teams up the stairwells in each of the Towers. The first team began climbing the stairs of the North Tower around 9:15 A.M. By 8:59, an additional ESU team was ascending the stairs and a fifth team was headed toward the North Tower from 6 World Trade Center. At the 31st floor of the North Tower, the first ESU team administered oxygen to some firefighters who had climbed the stairs in full gear in the scorching heat.

The ESU team on the 11th floor continued to evacuate the North Tower with officers holding flashlights to guide evacuees down the stairwells. Once everyone was out, they transferred operations to 6 World Trade Center and continued searching. Only two members of this team survived. The ESU team that had exited from 5 and 6 World Trade Center onto Vesey Street survived intact.

A radio exchange between the command post and an ESU team in the South Tower around 9:56 placed the team at about the 20th floor. NYPD members reported that a number of civilians were still descending the stairs. In the North Tower, three plainclothes officers checked every other floor beyond the 12th for stragglers but reported finding few civilians. The detectives checked in with the command post by ground phones but refused to leave the North Tower when commanded to do so. They arrived at the 54th floor at about 10 A.M. and reported on stairwells A and C.

The detectives stated that other police officers, two Secret Service agents, and members of the Port Authority Police Department were still in the building assisting evacuees. The three plainclothes officers also reported meeting members of an FDNY engine company who refused to leave the building themselves but told the detectives to do so because they were not wearing protective gear.

Most civilians who were able to walk or who had not been trapped by fire or debris were out of the two main buildings by 9:55. Shortly after reporting that the South Tower was "glowing red," officers in the NYPD helicopters radioed that the building had collapsed. However, many rescue workers inside

the North Tower remained ignorant of the collapse. Some who heard it believed that bombs were going off in both buildings. At approximately 10 A.M., NYPD commanders ordered their teams to evacuate all tower buildings. Around 10:08, the officers reported from the helicopter that the North Tower would soon follow its twin to the ground.

Some ESU teams inside the building, who had learned by radio of the collapse of the South Tower, later stated that they had transmitted this information and the evacuation orders to firefighters, but radio communication problems between the departments may have kept the orders from reaching the firefighters. Some firefighters were searching for missing colleagues, were injured, or trapped. Several NYPD officers died when the South Tower collapsed onto the concourse below, and at least one officer died when the North Tower collapsed. Fourteen

ABOVE *New York Police officers in the area north of the World Trade Center, which resembled a war zone rather than the usually busy streets of Manhattan. The NYPD radios were more powerful than those used by firefighters and because of this, officers on site knew in advance that the towers were in danger of collapsing. The NYPD lost 23 officers, a fraction of the 343 lost firefighters.*

members of the elite ESU teams were killed. Other rescue workers were killed when SEVEN WORLD TRADE CENTER fell after receiving major structural damage from the collapse of the South Tower.

TALLYING LOSSES

Early reports suggested that at least 85 police officers were missing. However, the NYPD radios were more powerful than those used by firefighters, designed to communicate over longer distances. By using 35 distinct radio zones, members of the NYPD had access to 20 radio channels. Commanders of the NYPD rescue efforts also received regular updates from the helicopters flying overhead, manned by members of the NYPD Special Operations Division. In this way, police officials learned that both towers were in imminent danger of collapse, and officers on the scene were able to hear the command to evacuate. As a result, the number of NYPD deaths was 23, compared to 343 for the FDNY. The FDNY did not have access to police radios or to updates from the police helicopters, although, according to protocol, there should have been at least one representative of the FDNY aboard each helicopter. However, FDNY commanders had assigned no one to report for aviation duty on September 11.

The 9/11 Commission Report issued three years after the attacks cited the lack of communication and cooperation between the NYPD and the FDNY as contributing factors in the deaths of the 343 firefighters. Even though city officials attempted to address the problem after the 1993 attack on the World Trade Center, both departments were slow to coordinate emergency responses.

Officer Moira Smith, 38, was the only female member of either the New York police or fire departments to lose her life on September 11. Smith was with fellow officer Robert Fazio when they rushed to the site. Officer Smith established herself in the lobby of the South Tower and began guiding evacuees to safety, repeatedly telling them not to look up but to keep moving. Smith had demonstrated her bravery in 1991 following a subway crash at Union Square and was awarded the Distinguished Duty Medal for her services. In February 2002, the Policewoman's Endowment Association named Smith their Woman of the Year for 2001.

Four sergeants, two detectives, and 17 NYPD officers lost their lives. Sergeant Michael Curtin, 45, was an ex-Marine who had served in Operation Desert Storm; he had participated in rescues at the World Trade Center 1993 bombing and had worked with FEMA in the aftermath of the Oklahoma City bombing in 1995.

Detective Claude "Dan" Richards, 46, of the NYPD Bomb Squad, was devoted to his job, and Detective

BELOW *Quilt tile for the United In Memory 9/11 Victims Memorial Quilt in memory of Officer Moira Smith. Smith was the only female member of either the New York police or fire departments to lose their life during the rescue efforts.*

Joseph Vigiano, 34, was one of the most decorated officers in the department. Vigiano's brother John, 36, a firefighter, also died on September 11. Jerome Dominguez, 37, was a fisherman and diver who had saved several Texas children from a burning school bus in 1999. Officer Mark Ellis, 26, had just become engaged to be married; his acceptance to the elite Secret Service arrived after his death.

Officer Tommy Langone, 39, and his firefighter brother Peter, 41, both died on September 11. Tommy Langone had headed straight for the World Trade Center after hearing about the attacks, and Peter Langone reported for rescue duty after coming off an overnight shift. John Perry, 38, one of the most versatile members of the NYPD, was also a lawyer, an actor, a linguist, a social worker, and a dedicated volunteer. Perry had just handed in his badge when he heard about the attacks. He asked for the badge back and set out for the World Trade Center.

The family of Ramon Suarez, 45, recognized him in a published photograph leading rescuers out of the South Tower after they had received news that he was missing. (See APPENDIX for a complete list of victims of September 11.)

AFTERMATH

One police officer trapped by falling debris for 11 hours was rescued around 8 A.M. on September 12. However, over time, rescuers gave up hope that others would be found alive. Members of the NYPD participated in the recovery efforts at Ground Zero, searching for the remains of their fellow officers and saluting and escorting any remains that were recovered, according to NYPD tradition.

Several thousand of those who worked on the World Trade Center cleanup continue to be monitored for chronic health problems related to site contamination, including Detectives John Walcott and Richard Volpe of the Narcotics Division, who filed suit in June 2004 after being diagnosed with cancer and kidney disease, respectively. In addition to police officers that have been diagnosed with health problems, some 332 firefighters have identifiable respiratory problems. It is probable that the full extent of the environmental impacts will not be known for years because some problems, such as asbestos-related illnesses, may not appear for decades (see HEALTH, LONG-TERM EFFECTS).

Hoping to alleviate the financial burdens of the survivors of the police and fire departments, the City of New York provided each family with one year's salary and a one-time death benefit of $250,000 in addition to about $355,000 received from the Twin Towers Fund established by Mayor RUDOLPH GIULIANI. The federal government paid a tax-free death benefit of $250,000 and a $1 to $2 million benefit from other government programs. Survivors also received payments from Social Security, private insurance companies, private and corporate donors, and $293,000 from the New York Police and Fire Widows and Children's Benefit Fund. Children of police officers and firefighters killed on September 11 will be given free college tuition at public colleges and universities in New York. Total benefits for the families of police officers were estimated at approximately $5 million per family.

Further Reading: Steven Brill, *After: How America Confronted the September 12 Era* (Simon and Schuster, 2003); CBS News, *What We Saw* (Simon and Schuster, 2002); Jim Dwyer and Kevin Flynn, *102 Minutes: The Untold Story of the Flight to Survive Inside the Twin Towers* (Times Books, 2005); Jacob Gershman, "NYPD Greatly Strengthens Anti-Terrorism Arsenal," *New York Sun* (August 26, 2005); James Lardner and Thomas Reppetto, *NYPD: A City and Its Police* (Henry Holt, 2000); Dean E. Murphy, *September 11: An Oral History* (Doubleday, 2002); Christopher Sweet, ed., *Above Hallowed Ground* (Viking, 2002).

— **ELIZABETH PURDY, PH.D.**

P

Patriotism

Patriotism is an ideology—a set of beliefs and values—and often defined as support, devotion, and loyalty to one's country, and a willingness to sacrifice for it. Since the terrorist attacks on September 11, there has been a resurgence of patriotism in the United States.

Some expressions have centered on flying the American flag, having flag stickers on cars and other items, and buying towels, clothes, mugs, cups, key chains, plates, napkins, stationery, and posters emblazoned with the flag.

Yellow ribbons show support for veterans, while red, white, and blue ribbons show support for soldiers currently serving in the armed services. Many are placed on mailboxes and automobiles, or tied to trees.

Expressions of patriotism also include poems, articles, letters, manuscripts, proclamations, tributes, and especially music. Patriotic songs express a love for one's country, have nationalist sentiment, and sometimes illustrate self-sacrifice and militarism. Toby Keith, a country musician, wrote a song entitled "The Angry American: Courtesy of the Red, White and Blue." This song portrays anger as a form of patriotism and many in the United States identified with the song. There are over 27,000,000 websites associated with American patriotism.

Patriotism can be seen when individuals strive to be stewards of the United States and represent the nation in a positive, nonjudgmental way, such as an increase in the parades honoring military personnel, and more elaborate July 4 celebrations. Some Muslim and Arab

FIELD OF FLAGS *The Healing Field flag memorial originated in Utah on September 11, 2002, emerging from a patriotic desire to honor the memory of the victims. Since then, a foundation has been created, and acres of full-sized American flags are displayed in host cities to raise money for local charities. The flags at left were displayed in Vacaville, California, on September 11, 2004.*

ABOVE LEFT *Tributes and the display of flags were frequent in the days following the attacks, such as this American flag and the words "Let us never forget—9-11-01" painted on a garage door.* **ABOVE CENTER** *A rough-hewn sign seen in the California desert in 2006.* **ABOVE RIGHT** *Rescue workers took comfort in displaying the American flag at Ground Zero.*

Americans have experienced a negative side of patriotism, expressed through varying levels of hostility, racism, prejudice, and discrimination.

Following the September 11 attacks, President GEORGE W. BUSH passed the USA PATRIOT ACT and declared September 11 Patriot's Day in the United States, to be an annual day of remembrance and national unity. Many Americans fly the nation's flag at half-staff on September 11 and observe a moment of silence beginning at 8:45 A.M. Eastern Daylight Time.

Further Reading: Samuel P. Huntington, *Who Are We: The Challenges to America's National Identity* (Simon and Schuster 2005); Richard Nelson, *Patriotism and the American Land* (Orion Society, 2005); "Patriot Day, 2003," www.whitehouse.gov (cited September 2006); United States Department of Justice, "The USA Patriot Act: Preserving Life and Liberty," www.lifeandliberty.gov (cited September 2006).

— **MARGARET H. WILLIAMSON, PH.D.**

Pennsylvania, Shanksville

A few minutes before 10 A.M., air traffic coordinators reported to Richland Township Pennsylvania police chief Jim Mock that a large plane was headed toward John Murtha Johnstown Cambria County Municipal Airport. The plane did not respond to requests for identification. At 9:57, the caddie master at the Laurel Valley Country Club in nearby Ligonier, Pennsylvania, saw the plane wobble as it disappeared over the horizon.

At 10:10 A.M. Michael and Amy Merringer were riding mountain bikes in Shanksville when they heard an airplane gun its engine, a loud bang, and then an explosion that rattled the windows of houses for miles around. From the Rollock Scrap Metal Company, Lee Purbaugh saw an airliner invert and drive into the ground at a 45-degree angle. Shanksville immediately lost electricity and phone service.

The plane was UNITED AIRLINES FLIGHT 93, bound for San Francisco and carrying seven crew members, 37 passengers—four of which were hijackers. Shanksville is less than 20 flight-minutes away from Washington, D.C., and many people believe Flight 93 was headed for either the White House or the Capitol Building. Others speculated that Flight 93 was headed for Camp David some 85 miles to the southwest.

The first witnesses on the scene expected to find survivors, or at least human remains and a wrecked plane. Instead, they found only a huge, charred crater, 8 to 10 feet deep and 15 to 20 feet long, surrounded by scattered debris and the smell of jet fuel.

When the families and friends of the passengers and crew of United Airlines Flight 93 arrived in

ABOVE CENTER *A memorial wall set up in Shanksville, featuring a flag with a "93" in the blue field, and the words "Our nation will eternally honor the heroes of Flight 93" appearing on the white stripes.* **ABOVE FAR RIGHT** *Tributes appeared across the country, as in this flag painted on a Vermont barn, flanked by yellow ribbons and bearing painted numbers 9-11-01.*

Shanksville on Sunday, September 16, a line of local officers saluting them met their chartered buses. Their route to the crash site was lined with locals who had come out to pay their respects to the heroes of Flight 93. Some held homemade signs displaying prayers and words of encouragement. The people of Shanksville continued to welcome the families of the victims of Flight 93 and express their gratitude for the heroic efforts that prevented the plane from reaching its target.

On April 28, Universal Studios released *United 93*, directed by Paul Greengrass, amid controversy that the movie was being released too soon after September 11 for the healing process to have been completed (see FILMS OF SEPTEMBER 11). Physical MEMORIALS have also been created, including one in Somerset County. On September 11, 2002, about 5,000 individuals, including 500 family members and friends and 50 airline employees, gathered at the crash site to pay tribute to the passengers and crewmembers who lost their lives one year earlier.

The memorial service, "A Time for Honor and Hope," was led by Tom Ridge, who was governor of Pennsylvania on September 11. Ridge had since become the director of the new DEPARTMENT OF HOMELAND SECURITY. Sandy Dahl, the wife of pilot Jason Dahl, spoke of her pride in her husband and the others who had pulled together to thwart another disaster. Eleven-year-old Muriel Borza, sister of 20-year-old passenger Deora Bodley, expressed her desire for a moment of worldwide peace in honor of the victims of United Airlines Flight 93. An antique iron bell tolled 40 times as each of the victims' names was read.

Shanksville at a glance

SHANKSVILLE IN Somerset County, Pennsylvania, is a town of 0.2 square miles with a population of about 245 people. Less than 80 miles from Pittsburgh and approximately 260 miles from Philadelphia, the town is extremely homogeneous. Residents are mostly of German ancestry, with smatterings of English, Irish, Polish, Scottish, and Dutch. The median age of Shanksville residents is 35.5 years, and the average annual income is $29,792.

Further Reading: Lisa Beamer, *Let's Roll: Ordinary People, Extraordinary Courage* (Tnydale House, 2002); *Life* Magazine, "Heroism Large and Small," *One Nation: America Remembers September 11, 2001* (Little, Brown, 2001); Jerre Longman, *Among the Heroes: United Flight 93 and the Passengers and Crew Who Fought Back* (HarperCollins, 2002).

— ELIZABETH PURDY, PH.D.

Pentagon Attack

At approximately 9:35 A.M. on September 11, controllers at Dulles International Airport spotted an airplane heading east-southeast toward the White House. Charles Burlingame had been piloting the Boeing 757-223 AMERICAN AIRLINES FLIGHT 77 when it took off from Dulles, but then it suddenly thundered toward the U.S. Capitol, banked in a circle, and came around toward the Pentagon from the west.

Father Stephen McGraw took the wrong highway exit that morning and witnessed Flight 77's crash into the Pentagon. "I saw it crash into the building… I saw an explosion of fire billowing through two windows," he later recalled.

Henry Ticknor, intern minister at the Unitarian Universalist Church of Arlington, Virginia, saw American Airlines Flight 77 coming in fast and low over his car as he drove to his church. "There was a puff of white smoke and then a huge billowing black cloud," he said. Tim Timmerman, a pilot, knew it was an American Airlines Boeing 757. "It added power on its way in. The nose hit, and the wings came forward and it went up in a fireball."

The Boeing 757-223 banked sharply and swooped so low that it clipped light poles. At 9:43 A.M., the jet slammed into the west side of the Pentagon, first hitting the helipad, and then penetrating the outer three rings of the building. Exploding jet fuel sent a fireball outward from the point of impact.

Fireman Alan Wallace was walking to the front of the Pentagon fire station when he saw the jetliner about 25 feet above the ground, only a few hundred yards away and barreling straight at him. He ran about thirty feet before he heard a roar and felt the heat of the explosion. He dove underneath a van. A few seconds later he slid out and raced back to the fire truck. The truck would not start—the rear end

"Where Does Your Husband Work?"

ON THE morning of September 11, 2001, Army Lieutenant Colonel Robert Snyder sat in his office on the first floor of the D Ring of the Pentagon. As he surfed the Web, he heard a crack and a boom. Instantly, flames danced around him. The lights in the room went out and his digital watch stopped.

Following his military training, he slammed himself to the floor. A series of small fires burning around the room provided the only light. He stood up and bumped into a civilian secretary. Together they negotiated their way to Corridor 5 and safety.

While Colonel Snyder was escaping the inferno at the Pentagon, his wife Margaret was at her job as an elementary school teacher in Springfield. Her coworkers told her about the events at the World Trade Center. She tried to phone her brother-in-law who worked on the 82nd floor of one of the towers and her brother who worked across the street from the World Trade Center, but could not get through. A teacher came in and asked, "Where does your husband work?"

"Not my husband, my brother and brother-in-law," she cried.

"No," the teacher repeated. "Where does your *husband* work?"

had been torn apart and the cab was on fire. Wallace grabbed the radio headset and reported to the main station at Fort Myer.

ESCAPING THE INFERNO

Inside the building, Shelia Moody in Room 472 felt blasts of air and fire. She looked down and shook her burning hands. A man called out to her; she felt the swoosh of a fire extinguisher and glimpsed her rescuer through a cloud of smoke. He led her out and calmed her fears that she would never see her grandchildren again.

Carl Mahnken and David Theall, colleagues in the army public relations office, had been in the first-floor studio, just a few dozen feet from where the plane hit. A computer monitor hit Theall on the head, but he remained conscious. When they reached the D Ring hallway, they heard people crying, moaning, talking. They coaxed stunned and bewildered people down the hallway and out of the building, then helped others throughout the day. Finally persuaded to leave, Mahnken and Theall walked miles to Theall's house in Alexandria. They did not want to leave each other after surviving together.

Army librarian Ann Parham and Mena Whitmore, acting director of the Pentagon Library, worked in the D Ring, the second ring in from the exterior on the west side of the Pentagon. Parham had been watching the attacks on the World Trade

ABOVE *The Pentagon in flames just minutes after the hijacked plane crashed into the building.*

An aerial view of the Pentagon site, showing the extent of damage to the building.

Center on the television around the corner from her desk; she was heading back to her desk when she heard a huge explosion, the lights went out, and everything fell from the ceiling. The blast knocked her to the floor and when she stood up, she was covered with jet fuel. She yelled for Patrick, a coworker. Patrick took her arm, and guided her to the A ring and safety.

About 10:10 A.M. a walled section of the Pentagon collapsed. The intense heat prevented firefighters from approaching the point of impact until about 1 P.M. The collapsing wall and roof fires created a gaping hole, making the courtyard between the two outer rings visible from outside. By Wednesday, September 12, 2001, the fires were finally contained. On Friday, September 14, both black boxes from American Airlines Flight 77 were recovered and sent to the National Transportation Safety Board for analysis.

On September 13, 2002, more than a thousand family members of the Pentagon victims attended a funeral with full military honors at the Tomb of the Unknowns in Arlington National Cemetery, in the shadow of the Pentagon. The mourners faced a single flag-draped casket containing the remains of 25 victims. The ceremony honored all of the 125 people killed at the Pentagon and the passengers and crew of American Airlines Flight 77, but singled out five people whose remains were not found: Rhonda Rasmussen, an army budget analyst; Retired Army Colonel Ronald Golinski, a civilian Pentagon worker; Ronald John Hemenway, a Navy electronics technician and native of Kansas City, Kansas; James T. Lynch, a civilian electronics technician in the navy's command center; and three-year-old Dana Falkenberg, a passenger on Flight 77.

The mourners sang "Amazing Grace" and watched an eight-man casket team—two soldiers, two sailors, two marines, and two airmen—carry the coffin from the amphitheater to the waiting caisson. After army chaplain Lieutenant Colonel James May committed the body, a rifle party fired three rounds in salute and a navy bugler played taps. The casket team folded the flag as the Army Band played "America the Beautiful." (See APPENDIX for a complete list of victims of the Pentagon attack.)

Further Reading: Eric Hufschmid, *Painful Questions: An Analysis of the September 11th Attacks* (Endpoint Software, 2002–2009); *Life* Magazine, *One Nation: America Remembers September 11, 2001* (Little Brown, 2001); "Pentagon Eyewitness Accounts" *The Guardian* (September 12, 2001); Paul Virilio and Chris Turner, *Ground Zero* (Verso, 2005); Steve Vogel, "Lost and, Sometimes, Never Found: Pentagon Families Bury Their Dead Together and Mourn Five Not Identified," *Washington Post* (September 13, 2002) .

— KATHY WARNES

Pentagon Building

O n September 11, approximately 20,000 people were working in the headquarters of the Department of Defense—the largest office building in the world. Yet the Pentagon casualty list numbered only 125 employees killed, in addition to the 64 aboard the plane (see APPENDIX for a complete list of victims of the Pentagon attack). The recent renovation of the impact area, referred to as Wedge One, was the primary reason for the low casualty figures. The Department of Defense had embarked on an extensive renovation in 1993, upgrading the mechanical and electrical systems and addressing security issues raised by earlier terrorist attacks in Oklahoma City and U.S. installations abroad. In addi-

Initial Construction of the Pentagon

THE OUTBREAK of World War II in September 1939 led to a growing workforce for the War Department and an urgent need for additional office space. Brigadier General Brehon B. Somerville, chief of the Construction Division of the U.S. Army Quartermaster General, and his staff developed a plan for the five-sided building with three floors in just four days; two additional floors were added to the plan after the attack on Pearl Harbor on December 7, 1941. In the end, the building consisted of five concentric rings—A, B, C, D, and E, with the A Ring being the innermost—and 6.5 million square feet of floor space.

A study conducted by the American Society of Civil Engineers (Pentagon Building Performance Report) after the September 11 attack found that 56 support columns were destroyed due to the impact of the plane. Even with the loss of support columns, the original structural system successfully redistributed the weight, limiting the collapse to floors directly above the point of impact. The Phoenix Project to reconstruct the damaged areas was launched within days of the attack and allowed Wedge One to be fully reoccupied one year after the attack.

tion to an overhaul of the mechanical and electrical systems, the renovation addressed the fire sprinkler systems, automatic fire doors, and structural issues. New blast-resistant windows were installed that either remained intact after the impact or fell out of their frames without shattering.

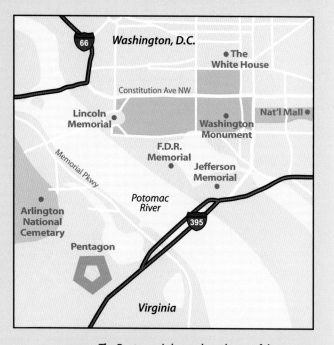

ABOVE *The Pentagon is located southwest of downtown Washington, D.C., across the Potomac River in Virginia.*

Persian Gulf War

When IRAQ invaded neighboring Kuwait in August 1990, it triggered a unified international response in which a broad-based coalition of nations led by the United States built up a military force in the deserts of SAUDI ARABIA, and then successfully liberated Kuwait after a lengthy air bombardment. In the waning days of the Cold War, the absence of superpower maneuvering was particularly notable. Where only a few years earlier the Soviet Union might have deliberately protested every move the United States made in the region, Soviet foreign minister Edvard Shevardnadze was very supportive of U.S. president George H. W. Bush's actions.

The Persian Gulf War was unusual in other ways. For the second time in history–the first was during the Korean Conflict—the United Nations Security Council authorized the use of military force to repel an invasion. The coalition included Western nations such as the United States, the United Kingdom, and Canada, but also a number of Muslim nations. Although Arab states initially resisted joining in actions against Iraq, concern about further Iraqi aggression, combined with promises of debt relief, brought several important Arab nations on board, including Saudi Arabia, and non-Arab Muslim nations such as Turkey.

Because of internal divisions, the coalitions ability to carry out decisive action was limited. Furthermore, the UN resolution that gave Operation Desert Storm its international legitimacy also restricted the ability of commanders on the ground to take advantage of some opportunities. When Iraqi forces proved weaker than anticipated, General H. Norman Schwartzkopf wanted to complete the liberation of Kuwait with absolute destruction of the retreating Iraqi army, followed by a drive to Baghdad

Kevlar cloth was installed on exterior walls between the steel columns to keep building materials from becoming projectiles in an explosion. The exterior walls were reinforced with steel beams and columns bolted down at each point where they met other floors. These reinforced walls held for 30 minutes after the attack, allowing sufficient time for employees to evacuate the building. The reinforcement was so effective that the Pentagon reported a glass display case just 40 feet from where the plane entered the building survived the impact and explosion.

Further Reading: "Engineering Report on Pentagon Disaster," *Architecture Week* (February 12, 2003); Carolyn Gard, *Attack on the Pentagon on September 11, 2001* (Rosen, 2003); "Pentagon Rebuilt," *Architecture Week* (September 4, 2002).

— **ABBE ALLEN DEBOLT**

to oust Hussein from power. However, prominent Arab members of the coalition were wary of a U.S.-led military force toppling an Arab leader, even one as disliked as Hussein. As a result, President Bush ordered Schwartzkopf to halt just inside Iraqi territory, staying strictly within the letter of the UN resolution. Many Americans expressed a sense of frustration and would later blame that act of restraint for subsequent troubles in the area.

The coalition forces were subsequently withdrawn to inside the borders of Kuwait and Saudi Arabia, although U.S. aircraft routinely enforced the "no-fly zone" against the Iraqi air force that had been established in the UN-brokered ceasefire. Iraq was also subject to inspections to ensure it was not building prohibited chemical and nuclear weapons. Hussein remained in power and his elite Republican Guard and Special Republican Guard forces remained a threat to peace and stability in the region. American and other forces of the former coalition remained stationed in Kuwait and Saudi Arabia for the long term to ensure that Saddam could not make a second bid for hegemony.

Although Kuwaitis remained steadfastly grateful for the presence of Western military, many in Saudi Arabia came to see the presence of non-Muslim forces as an affront. Although U.S. and other commands emphasized in their general orders to their troops the need to be culturally sensitive, and the bases were all on the opposite side of the Arabian Peninsula from the holy cities of Mecca and Medina, a segment of the most intensely religious Muslims came to consider the presence of any infidels on Arabian soil as sacrilegious.

OSAMA BIN LADEN was among the Muslims who found the continuing U.S. presence in the desert kingdom offensive. This former "playboy" son of a wealthy Saudi construction contractor had become seriously religious in the 1970s and gone to AFGHANISTAN to help the local resistance (see MUJAHIDEEN) oust the Soviet Union. With that war won, bin Laden directed his interest to forcing the United States to leave what he regarded as holy soil. Thus he turned the substantial resources of his terrorist network AL-QAEDA to striking the United States.

Further Reading: Peter L. Bergen, *The Osama bin Laden I Know* (Free Press, 2006); Lawrence Freedman and Efraim Karsh, *The Gulf Conflict 1990-1991: Diplomacy and War in the New World Order* (Princeton University Press, 1993).

— LEIGH KIMMEL

A War for Oil?

DURING THE 1991 Persian Gulf War, a frequent refrain of the antiwar protesters in various parts of the United States was "No Blood for Oil." The protesters thus accused the government of using the humanitarian issues of Saddam's invasion of Kuwait as a façade to conceal its true intention, namely securing America's access to cheap oil.

But was the Persian Gulf War really about oil? Scholars and pundits have been arguing both ways almost continuously. Those who claim the Gulf War was not about oil point to the blatant human rights abuses committed against ordinary Kuwaitis by the invading Iraqi forces. Those who oppose this interpretation point to other countries in which equally bad or worse abuses were occurring, but which were not the object of U.S.-led interventions simply because the countries in question had no oil or other resources vital to the United States. The arguments were still ongoing when the 2003 invasion of IRAQ occurred .

Port Authority of New York and New Jersey

The Port Authority of New York and New Jersey operated most of the major international and interstate transportation facilities in New York City and northern New Jersey, owned the World Trade Center (WTC) complex, had its own police force, police academy and art collection, and in various ways was involved in other official, commercial, and industrial undertakings throughout the area.

The Port Authority's executive offices were in the WTC's North Tower, with approximately 2,000 of its officers, managers, professionals, and staff based there. Towering over the east bank of the Hudson River, the WTC had been the largest, the most significant, and the most controversial addition to the Port Authority's facilities.

Officers of the Port Authority Police Force were the first EMERGENCY WORKERS on the scene after AMERICAN AIRLINES FLIGHT 11 crashed into the North Tower. Bridges and tunnels into Manhattan were ordered closed at 9:21 A.M., the South Tower collapsed at 10:03 A.M., and the North Tower collapsed at 10:28 A.M. In less than two hours, the space occupied by the Twin Towers was empty. The bases of the Towers and the outdoor Tobin Plaza were filled with smoke and debris and became the sites of frantic evacuation and rescue efforts.

Executive Director Neil Levin had gone for breakfast at the Wild Blue restaurant on the North Tower's 107th floor before American Airlines Flight 11 struck. By nightfall, he and 73 other Port Authority employees were dead or dying. It would be April 2002 before his body was recovered; others remain missing. In Levin's absence, Ernesto Butcher, the Port Authority's chief operating officer, assumed his

Port Authority's Art Collection

THE PORT Authority entered the art world in 1957, when it commissioned sculptor Alexander Calder to construct a mobile for the international arrivals building at Idylwild Airport. It established its own Committee on Art in 1969, and by 1985 its collection was substantial enough to be the subject of a coffee-table art book. Most of its collection, then valued at $26.7 million, was sold at auction in February 1997, as the Port Authority began its efforts to refocus on transportation and economic development. The Port Authority did, however, keep its publicly displayed artworks and a few others.

The Port Authority's art collection on display at its other facilities survived September 11, but those at the World Trade Center suffered differing fates. Its model of Japanese sculptor Masayuki's *Cloud Fortress*, its portrait of Austin Tobin in the boardroom, a silk kimono at the entrance of its World Trade department that had been a gift of the Japanese government, Chinese cloisonné vases in its boardroom, a Joan Miro tapestry, and other paintings and sculptures inside WTC buildings were destroyed. One outdoor sculpture, Alexander Calder's red 25-foot-high *World Trade Center Stabile* or *Bent Propeller*, had been moved from its original location in front of the North Tower to the plaza in front of SEVEN WORLD TRADE CENTER. It was crushed by falling debris, with only half of its parts recovered. Sculptor Fritz Koenig's *The Sphere*, a 25-foot-high bronze resting on a black granite base in Tobin Plaza's fountain representing the dream of world peace through world trade, was knocked off its axis and overturned. The sculpture is now displayed as part of a World Trade Center memorial in Battery Park in Manhattan .

duties. The Port Authority's airports, bridges, tunnels, Port Authority Bus Terminal, and marine terminals were promptly closed.

By 4:45 P.M. on September 11, the westbound lanes of the George Washington Bridge, Lincoln Tunnel, and Staten Island bridges were reopened, along with the westbound PATH line from 33rd Street into New Jersey. The eastbound PATH line from New Jersey to 33rd Street was reopened by 5:30 P.M. But the eastbound bridge and Lincoln Tunnel lanes, the bus terminal, the Holland Tunnel, the airports, and the marine terminals remained closed.

Eastbound traffic on the bridges and through the Lincoln Tunnel was opened on September 13, but the Holland Tunnel remained closed to the public to allow emergency vehicles exclusive use. That same day, in the evening, the Port Authority's airports were reopened, but only to allow completion of inbound flights that had been rerouted and grounded on September 11. Regular airport service began the next day.

ABOVE *A memorial at the Ground Zero site displays artifacts from police, fire, and military units around the world, honoring fallen rescue workers.*

Port Authority Police Force

THE PORT Authority Police Force suffered the largest loss of police officers—37—ever suffered by a U.S. police department on a single day (see APPENDIX for a complete list of victims). Before September 11, only eight officers had died in the line of duty in the force's entire 73-year history. Formed in 1928 to patrol the bridges between New Jersey and Staten Island, the force now has over 1,600 members, whose duties include policing the Port Authority's airports, marine terminals, docks, bridges, tunnels, bus stations, and PATH trains.

Because the PATH's WTC Station was destroyed, there was no PATH passenger service between New Jersey and downtown Manhattan until March 2002, when PATH contracted with a ferry company, New York Waterway, to provide temporary passenger service from the old Hoboken railway terminal on the Hudson's west bank to two downtown Manhattan piers. Regular PATH rail service from New Jersey into downtown Manhattan was restored on November 23, 2003, when a temporary $556 million PATH station opened as the first new facility on the WTC site.

Further Reading: Erwin Wilkie Bard, *The Port of New York Authority* (AMS Press, 1968); Eric Darton, *Divided We Stand: A Biography of New York's World Trade Center* (Basic Books, 1999); Jameson W. Doig, *Metropolitan Transportation Politics and the New York Region* (Columbia University Press, 1966); James Glanz and Eric Lipton, *City in the Sky: The Rise and Fall of the World Trade Center* (Henry Holt, 2003); Paul Goldberger, *Up From Zero: Politics, Architecture, and the Rebuilding of New York* (Random House, 2004).

— STEVEN B. JACOBSON

Q

Quilt Project

In the weeks following September 11, shock and grief gave way to a need to pay lasting tribute to the memory of the almost 3,000 people who died as a result of the attacks. Long Beach, California residents Corey Gammel, a graphic artist, and Peter Marquez, an operations manager for a moving company, took action. Moved by a visit to Ground Zero in NEW YORK CITY, and inspired by the success of and sentiment behind the AIDS Quilt, Gammel and Marquez founded United In Memory 9/11 Victims Memorial Quilt, a nonprofit volunteer association dedicated to producing a huge quilt in memory of the September 11 victims. Word of the project spread, a Web site was created, and soon volunteers from around the world were contributing to the project.

By early 2002 the United in Memory 9/11 Victims Memorial Quilt had received hundreds of individual textile blocks from the United States and eighteen foreign countries. Working primarily on the weekends, several dozen experienced quilters pieced the blocks into large panels.

The completed quilt covers more than 15,000 square feet and consists of 142 panels, each of which is 10.5 square feet. Each panel, in turn, is made up of 25 blocks that are 18.5 inches square, and each block is dedicated to a victim of the terrorist attacks. The quilt made its debut on August 30, 2002, in the exhibition hall of the *Queen Mary* in Long Beach, California.

MOVING TRIBUTE *Quilt tiles created for the United In Memory 9/11 Victims Memorial Quilt often represented the personalities, interests, career, and character of the loved ones lost in the September 11 attacks. Installation of the traveling exhibit needs 15 workers and a full day to complete.*

Mission statement of the United in Memory 9/11 Victims Memorial Quilt

MISSION STATEMENT of the United in Memory 9/11 Victims Memorial Quilt: "The United in Memory 9/11 Victims Memorial Quilt, Inc. is a non-profit organization whose purpose is to keep alive the memories of the victims of September 11, 2001 through the United in Memory Victims Memorial Quilt. This organization is committed to honoring the victims and comforting the world by making the quilt available for public viewing throughout the nation and around the world. The organization also strives to honor with courage and compassion the thousands of surviving families, those who risked their lives to save others, and those who supported the United States of America during its darkest hour. May their lives serve as a healing balm to our wounded spirits and as eternal beacons, reaffirming our respect for life and freedom and inspiring an end to hatred, bigotry, ignorance and intolerance."

AT LEFT *The United in Memory 9/11 Victims Memorial Quilt as it appeared installed in September 2006. The 15,500 square-foot quilt will tour the country until a permanent home can be found.*

As the exhibit moved through towns and cities across America, thousands of people viewed the quilt and paid their respects to the September 11 victims and their families. Because the quilt is so large, moving it from one place to another is a significant project.

Preparing the quilt for display requires a full day of work for 15 people and involves unpacking, setting pipes, climbing ladders, and hanging the quilt panels and other decorations. Taking down the exhibit requires less time, only about four hours for the same 15 workers. Future plans for the quilt include finding a permanent home in Washington, D.C., or New York City.

While the United in Memory 9/11 Victims Memorial Quilt is probably the best known project of its kind, other individuals and groups also have produced quilts that pay tribute to the September 11 victims. Some are dedicated to all the victims; others are more specific, paying tribute to firefighters, police officers, or those who died on individual flights. Prominent among the groups that have sponsored quilt projects is America's 9/11 Quilts Organization, founded by Jeannie Ammermann. Since the September 11 attacks, this group has produced quilts paying tribute to EMERGENCY WORKERS, New York firefighters (see FIRE DEPARTMENT OF NEW YORK), the NEW YORK POLICE DEPARTMENT, the PENTAGON, the PORT AUTHORITY OF NEW YORK AND NEW JERSEY police and staff, UNITED AIRLINES FLIGHT 93, New York State courts, and victims in general. These works of art also tour the country.

Further Reading: Jean Spencer, "Quilt Visions," July/August 2002, www.fabrics.net/Jean802.asp (cited May 2006); Helen Squire, ed., *United We Quilt and Anchor Project* (Collector Books, 2002); "United In Memory: The 9/11 Victims Memorial Quilt Project," www.unitedinmemory.net (cited May 2006).

— BEN WYNNE, PH.D.

Qutb, Sayyid (1906–1966)

Sayyid Qutb led the revival of radical ISLAMIC FUNDAMENTALISM while developing *jihadi Salafi* ideology and the beginning of modern political Islam. He was the most influential advocate of JIHAD in the 20th century, and the architect of dogma that legitimizes violent Muslim resistance against regimes that claim to be Muslim yet fail to implement Islamic religious law. Qutb's writings have influenced radical Islamic leaders such as Mullah Omar and OSAMA BIN LADEN and direct lines can be traced from Qutb to bin Laden, Ayman al-Zawahiri (AL-QAEDA leader), and Mohamed Atta.

Qutb was born in 1906 in Egypt in a devoutly Muslim world. As a 10-year-old, he memorized the Koran. In his early life he was an educator, novelist, and literary critic. In 1948, his political views brought him unwanted attention, so he was sent to the United States to study for a master's degree in education.

Qutb was shocked by the racism, especially against Arabs, prevalent in the still-segregated United States. He decided, "Americans intentionally deride what people in the Old World hold sacred." To Qutb, Americans had become numb to "faith in religion, faith in art and faith in spiritual values altogether."

Qutb returned to Egypt in 1951. His vocal political and religious philosophy was deemed so dangerous by Egyptian leader Gamal Abdel Nasser that Qutb spent much of the next 15 years in prison, during which he wrote the hallmark books *Jihadi Salafi: Fi zilal al-Qur'an* (*In the Shade of the Koran*), and *Ma'alim fi-l-Tariq* (*Milestones*).

Qutb was hanged in 1966, becoming a martyr for the cause of jihad, and his teachings were spread to a generation of young, radical Muslims who believed that the world required purification by jihad even if Islam itself was not being threatened, because it was only through bringing Islamic law to the entire world, by force if necessary, that all peoples would be free.

Qutb argued that Muslims must follow the *din*, the religious path set out in Koranic law. The *din* is a "universal declaration of man of the freedom of man from slavery to men and to his own desires…" Racial equality and one's relationship with God as well as the government's relationship with God were also key issues of the *din*. The ultimate goal is the restoration of the Islamic religion as critically relevant to world governance.

Further Reading: Mary Habeck, *Knowing the Enemy: Jihadist Ideology and the War on Terror* (Yale University Press, 2006); Mark Huband, *The Struggle for Islam* (Westview Press, 1999); Sayyid Qutb, *Milestones* (American Trust Publications, 1990).

— B. KEITH MURPHY, PH.D.

R

Rowley, Colleen (1954–)

Colleen Rowley, a Special Agent of the Federal Bureau of Investigation (FBI) and its chief division counsel in the Minneapolis office, was considered a whistleblower for her now famous 13-page memorandum to then FBI director Robert Mueller on May 21, 2002, eight months and 10 days after the attacks. Rowley raised serious concerns about the failure of FBI headquarters in Washington, D.C., to handle intelligence about suspected AL-QAEDA terrorist ZACARIAS MOUSSAOUI prior to, during, and after the September 11 terrorist hijackings. In essence, her memorandum pointed to ways the FBI failed to respond to suspicions about Moussaoui, who had taken flight training and whom the French intelligence community had identified as a possible al-Qaeda operative prior to the September 11 attacks. Rowley believed that positive action in response to the Moussaoui situation might have prevented the terrorists from carrying out their attacks.

On June 6, 2002, Rowley testified before the Senate Committee on the Judiciary Oversight Hearing on Counterterrorism. In her testimony, Rowley cited serious problems with the FBI bureaucracy and recommended making procedural changes, removing obstacles, and re-creating the organizational culture at the FBI. She concluded her testimony by advocating the need for integrity in the agency. She was one of three women selected as *Time* magazine's Persons of the Year 2002. In December 2004, after 24 years of service, she retired from the FBI.

THE VIEW FROM SPACE *The Satellite Landsat 7 captured an image of Manhattan on September 12, 2001. The picture shows the smoke plume still drifting over much of the city.*

Whistleblowers

ORGANIZATIONAL WHISTLEBLOWERS place their physical and emotional health, personal privacy, and present and future employment in grave danger. When they "blow the whistle" on their organizations, they are often summarily dismissed from their jobs, blackballed in their industry, and are unable to find new employment. Colleen Rowley and other whistleblowers like her have also been viewed as public heroes for their bold and ethical actions. In recent years the federal government has given whistleblowers some protection with the enactment of the Sarbanes-Oxley Act of 2002.

Further Reading: "The Bombshell Memo," *Time* (June 3, 2002); Richard Lacayo and Amanda Ripley, "Persons of the Year 2002," *Time* (December 30, 2002); Amanda Ripley and Maggie Siegler, "The Special Agent," *Time* (December 30, 2002).

— **JOSEPH C. SANTORA, ED.D.**

Rumsfeld, Donald (1932–)

Secretary of Defense Donald Rumsfeld first learned of the terrorist attacks from a staff member who passed him a note that AMERICAN AIRLINES FLIGHT 11 had crashed into the North Tower of the World Trade Center. Rumsfeld abruptly ended his breakfast meeting. Minutes later, he was informed that a second aircraft, UNITED AIRLINES FLIGHT 175, had crashed into the South Tower.

In response to the attacks, Department of Defense (DoD) staff initiated a crisis management process. Rumsfeld's first briefing was with the Central Intelligence Agency (CIA). Next he placed telephone calls from his office to discuss strategic matters with key government personnel. At 9:43 A.M., while Rumsfeld was engaged in a teleconference with Richard Clarke, the National Security Coordinator for Security, Infrastructure Protection and Counterterrorism, AMERICAN AIRLINES FLIGHT 77, crashed into the PENTAGON.

At approximately 9:55 A.M., after briefly talking with President GEORGE W. BUSH, Rumsfeld exited the damaged Pentagon. Security personnel insisted that he leave the area, but 30 minutes later, he reentered and went directly to the National Military Command Center–the "war room," and raised the nation's readiness level to DefCon 3, a level not seen since the 1973 Arab-Israeli War. At 6:40 P.M. Rumsfeld, from the Pentagon, announced that the badly damaged and burning Pentagon "will be in business tomorrow."

From 1975 to 1977, Rumsfeld served as the 13th secretary of defense in the Gerald Ford administration. On January 20, 2001, he was sworn in as the 21st secretary of defense in the George W. Bush administration. Rumsfeld has been both the youngest (43) and the oldest (almost 69) secretary of defense. In the intervening years, he held appointed positions in government and several executive positions in the private sector.

In 2003, Rumsfeld was in charge of executing the U.S. and coalition forces' invasion of Iraq. Bush and members of his policy team, including Rumsfeld, justified the war by linking Saddam Hussein with AL-QAEDA and proclaiming Hussein was intent on attacking the United States with weapons of mass destruction. As later information revealed that both these assertions were false, Rumsfeld came under heavy criticism not only for the war's justification but the actual conduct of the war. Critics said he was conducting the war "on the cheap" and that this strategy was responsible for continuing insurgent attacks in Iraq.

Rumsfeld developed a reputation for handling questions from journalists in a way that infuriated critics and won praise from administration supporters. To critics, he appeared to delight in evading questions or in demeaning the intelligence of his questioners. As the war continued into 2005 and 2006, critics of the administration focused their fire on Rumsfeld, suggesting that Bush should demand his resignation. The president refused, yet on November 8, 2006, one day after the Democratic Party won control of Congress in the midterm elections, Rumsfeld's resignation was announced.

Further Reading: Richard A. Clarke, *Against All Enemies: Inside America's War on Terror* (Free Press, 2004); Rowan Scarborough, *Rumsfeld's War: The Untold Story of America's Anti-Terrorist Commander* (Regnery, 2004).

— JOSEPH C. SANTORA, ED.D.

ABOVE *Secretary of Defense Donald H. Rumsfeld (C) leads Sen. Carl Levin (L), D-Mich. and Sen. John Warner (R), R-Va., to the crash scene at the Pentagon on September 11. Rumsfeld earlier conducted a news conference with reporters in the Pentagon briefing room.*

S

Saudi Arabia

"Follow the money" have long been the watchwords for investigators of organized criminal activity. The people actually committing the crimes are often the foot soldiers, while the masterminds are safely out of public view.

This has also been true of terrorism associated with radical IS-LAMIC FUNDAMENTALISM. Suicide bombers are often from the segment of Arab society mired in poverty, which sees little hope for its future. Such disaffected people can be wooed by promises that their families will be provided for after their own "martyrdom" in striking a blow to their enemies. Moreover, such martyrs believe they will enter paradise because of their actions.

Investigations following the September 11 attacks uncovered a system of payments to terrorists by various Muslim authorities, particularly in Saudi Arabia. Although some funds came from Saudi oil profits, a significant portion of the money used to fund international TERROR-ISM was collected from unsuspecting Muslims of modest or even little means, under the auspices of various Muslim charitable foundations. Closer investigations revealed an intricate system of nested shell organizations created to funnel money to Saudi Arabia, where it was then distributed to terrorist organizations, often to support violence in the very countries from which the donations originally came.

However, when the U.S. government tried to shut down a number of these charitable front organizations, there were complaints not only

MECCA *Muslim pilgrims pray near the Prophet Muhammad mosque in January 2006 in the holy city of Medina, Saudi Arabia.*

from Muslims but from many non-Muslim Americans about discrimination.

The relationship between the United States and Saudi Arabia has been long and complex. Because of its dependency on Saudi oil, the United States has often overlooked signs of Saudi complicity in various acts of terror.

For example, 15 of the 19 suicide terrorists of September 11 were Saudi citizens. Investigations have shown that two of the hijackers of the plane that hit the Pentagon were receiving $3,500 a month from Saudi sources. But Saudi authorities have been quick to point to the conclusion of the 9/11 Commission (see NATIONAL COMMISSION ON TERRORIST ATTACKS UPON THE UNITED STATES):

> "We found no evidence that the Saudi government as an institution or senior officials within the Saudi government funded al-Qaeda."

Still, the question of just how much funding the terrorists received directly or indirectly from charitable organizations operating in Saudi Arabia remains unresolved.

The New Remittance Men

IN VICTORIAN England, a remittance man was a young man who was regularly paid a sum of money to stay away from London and from the family estates. The idea was that he would carry out his wastrel life someplace where he would not disgrace a respectable family's reputation. During the latter part of the 20th century, Saudi Arabia developed a similar pattern of paying certain people to cause trouble somewhere else. However, these troublemakers were not leading worldly lives, but were the most extreme of the radical Muslims who conceived of their faith primarily in terms of striking a blow against the infidel. Many of the Saudi nationals who fought in AFGHANISTAN alongside the MUJAHIDEEN and often served as military advisors in the battle against the Soviet Union were just such remittance men, given funding for their ventures primarily to remove them from the desert kingdom. OSAMA BIN LADEN appears to have gotten his start in this manner.

Further Reading: Douglas Farah, *Blood from Stone: The Secret Financial Network of Terror* (Broadway Books, 2004); Richard Labévière, *Dollars for Terror: The United States and Islam* (Algora Publishing, 2000); National Commission on Terrorist Attacks, *The 9/11 Commission Report* (W.W. Norton, 2004).

— **LEIGH KIMMEL**

Seven World Trade Center

Seven World Trade Center (7 WTC) fell at 5:20 P.M. on September 11, damaged and set on fire by debris falling from the towers that ignited the diesel fuel lines running beneath the structure.

The Commerce Department's National Institute of Standards and Technology (NIST) and various private institutions subsequently conducted a three-year, $24-million study involving the structural failure of all of the buildings.

Located north of the main buildings, on the far side of Vesey Street, 7 WTC had 47 floors reaching 570 feet high. It was built on a trapezoid-shaped plot on Port Authority land, and was part of the World Trade Center but had a separate lease and tax lot from the rest of the complex.

It connected to the main complex via a Plexiglas-covered pedestrian bridge, and had two different facings: horizontally striped glass on the Vesey and Barclay sides, and red granite with smaller windows on the others.

Designed by Emery Roth & Sons, it was architecturally different from the main towers. A plaza at its front contained Alexander Calder's 8-meter high *Three Red Wings*. Beneath it was the substation that supplied electrical power to most of downtown Manhattan.

Seven World Trade Center housed a number of government agencies, financial institutions, and insurance companies: the Department of Defense, Immigration and Naturalization Service, Internal Revenue Service, Central Intelligence Agency, Secret Service, Securities and Exchange Commission, Mayor's Office of Emergency Management, American Express Bank International, Federal Home Loan Bank, Standard Chartered Bank, Provident Financial Management, First State Management Group,

Salmon Smith Barney, NAIC Securities, and ITT Hartford Insurance Group. The 1988 movie *Working Girl* used 7 WTC as a setting.

Further Reading: Donald Friedman, *After 9-11: An Engineer's Work at the World Trade Center* (Xlibris, 2002); "Seven World Trade Center," www.emporis.com/en/wm/bu/?id=114932 (Emporis, 2004) "World Trade Center—Minoru Yamasaki," Great Buildings Online, www.great-buildings.com (Kevin Matthews and Artifice, 1994-2006).

— **ELIZABETH A. KRAMER**

ABOVE *Seven World Trade Center was damaged and set aflame by falling debris from the towers, which set off diesel fuel lines below the building.*

SimCenter Inc.

SimCenter Inc. is a flight simulation center located in Opa-Locka, Florida, near Miami in Dade County. Terrorist hijackers Mohamed Atta and Marwan Alshehri attended SimCenter on December 29 and 30, 2000, after receiving their commercial pilot's licenses from Huffman Aviation. Under the tutelage of flight instructor Henry George, Atta and Alshehri took two courses for a total of six hours of in-flight training on a simulation Boeing 727 commercial airliner. With nearly 300 hours of flight time in smaller aircraft, the two students had experience in the air, but none piloting larger craft.

The Boeing multiengine simulator gave Atta and Alshehri experience on instruments standard for most commercial airliners, and enough knowledge to control an aircraft in flight. Following their attendance at SimCenter, Atta and Alshehri traveled to Spain, returning to Florida in January 2001 to establish residency in the United States and aid fellow terrorists in Florida and New Jersey.

The ability of the terrorists to commandeer commercial aircraft and fly them to their targets highlights the fact that most commercial aircraft in the United States utilize a standardized set of instruments. This standardization in Boeing aircraft, including the 727, 747, and 757, enables pilots throughout the nation, and many globally, to be mobile in the airline industry. In interviews after the attacks, SimCenter instructor George noted that Atta and Alshehri had no experience on large craft before attending the school but were able to use their six hours under his tutelage to pilot the hijacked planes.

Further Reading: Damion Dimarco, *Tower Stories: The Autobiography of September 11, 2001* (Revolution Publishing, 2004); Steve Perseus, ed., *The 9/11 Investigations* (Perseus Publishing, 2004).

— **NICHOLAS KATERS**

ABOVE *An airport surveilance camera captured the western dress style of hijackers Mohamed Atta (R) and Abdulaziz Alomari (C) as they passed through Portland International Airport Security on September 11, 2001. Western dress and lifestyles for terrorists are permitted under a belief that "the necessary permits the forbidden."*

Sleeper Cells

Terrorist sleeper cells are shrouded in secrecy. Islamist terrorist groups have elevated secrecy, operational security, deception, and cover to the highest levels. Not all terrorist cells, or even a majority, carry out attacks. Some are dedicated to intelligence gathering and reconnaissance. Others are concerned with recruitment, education, and indoctrination, or focus on financial matters and logistics. The attack cells are called "sleepers" because the terrorists seemingly lie dormant until "awakened" when needed.

Terrorists live a double life, with extraordinary concerns for the security of the mission. Significant time is required to carry out a mission because terrorists have a standard strategy: targeting, casing and surveillance, rehearsal, and attack.

Targeting requires research, comparing the desirability and accessibility of the target. Terrorists seek four results from an attack: mass casualties, spectacular images, economic impact, and iconic value. Mass casualties are important, particularly against U.S. targets.

Casing and surveillance comprise the most laborious element of a terrorist operation. Terrorists want to know everything about a target, including the best time to inflict casualties, the presence of local law enforcement, professionalism of the workforce, response time of emergency services, means of access, location of security cameras, access controls, composition of target construction, points of vulnerability, and means of egress. Those carrying out the surveillance generally are not the attack team, and may take cover as taxicab drivers, vendors, people working in nearby retail, students, and tourists.

There are probably several rehearsals carried out by the attack team, and probably a simulation carried out in a place remote from the target. There is also a dry run as close as possible to the actual target. Actor James Woods witnessed a rehearsal on a flight from Boston's Logan Airport on August 1, 2001. He thought he was seeing an actual operation and reported it to airport authorities, who did not initially follow up, according to ABC News. On September 12, the FBI confirmed that what he witnessed was a rehearsal by the September 11 hijackers. OSAMA BIN LADEN personally approved the final selection of the 19 hijackers. His final requirement for selection was patience, as he knew it would be a long time before all preliminary tasks were completed. Spanish investigators determined that the perpetrators of the March 11, 2004 attacks on the Madrid light rail system (see MADRID BOMBINGS) conducted three years of surveillance prior to their attack, which killed 191 people and wounded more than 1,800.

All the while prior to an attack, the terrorists need means of support to provide food, housing, medical

Infiltration

FOR THREE months in late 2002, French journalist Mohamed Sifaoui integrated himself into a Parisian terrorist cell and chronicled the hatred Islamist terrorists have for anyone and anything not their own. He was told not to wear a beret because it was too much like a yarmulke. He was told that British prime minister Tony Blair and French president Jacques Chirac must convert to Islam.

Sifaoui is a French citizen, a print and electronic journalist, and an Algerian-born Muslim. He began his contact with AL-QAEDA while covering trials of terrorists involved in the 1995 Armed Islamic Group's subway bombing campaign in Paris. Sifaoui had lost friends in the underground bombings and had been an outspoken critic of those who would pervert his religion to justify murder.

Yet, though his name and even his face were not unknown to those he criticized, he was able to ingratiate himself and even become recruited to al-Qaeda's cause. In a nerve-racking and perilous journey to the heart of TERRORISM, Sifaoui passed numerous tests of dedication and trustworthiness. During this process, he discerned inconsistencies in the terrorist's worldview, and their misinterpretation of their own faith. He learned about targeting criteria, concluded that his newfound cohorts were essentially "neofascists," and even traveled to the nerve center of al-Qaeda in Europe—which was London.

In January 2003, Sifaoui published his findings and was placed under a death sentence by al-Qaeda. Yet he felt compelled to portray what he had witnessed. No apologist for all things Western, he believed his own identity and value system had been perverted and hijacked by the Islamists. Many Muslims in France have thanked him for his work.

care, and transportation. Weapons need assembly and transportation to the target must be arranged. The operation can in no way be compromised or disclosed. Operatives try to live in new communities where people do not know one another. In apartments, lower floors are preferred to allow means of escape. Holding to the dictum that "the necessary permits the forbidden," they adopt Western modes of dress and leisure activities. Overt religiousness is avoided. All laws are to be obeyed. Meetings are avoided, and when necessary involve elaborate schemes to avoid being followed or observed, with prearranged signals to warn of suspected danger.

Cell members know only their assigned task, not the full plan, so there is minimal damage to the mission if they are apprehended. A cell member often has no knowledge of other associated cells. The leader knows whom to report to, but as little else as possible. Most of the September 11 hijackers knew only their role on the planes, but, the targets probably remained unknown except to the pilots. That there were near-simultaneous attacks occurring was probably not known to the hijackers.

Further Reading: Jason Burke, *Al-Qaeda: The True Story of Radical Islam* (I.B. Tauris, 2003); Steve Emerson, *American Jihad: The Terrorists Living Among Us* (Simon and Schuster, 2002); Simon Reeve, *The New Jackals: Ramzi Yousef, Osama bin Laden and the Future of Terrorism* (Avalon, 2002); Mohamed Sifaoui, *Inside al-Qaeda: How I Infiltrated the World's Deadliest Terrorist Organization* (Avalon, 2004).

— **RAY BROWN**

Sorbi's Flying Club

Sorbi's Flying Club, an aviation school located 20 miles north of San Diego, California, gained notoriety as one of the schools attended by the terrorists. Saudi nationals Nawaf Alhazmi and Khalid Almindar arrived in Los Angeles on January 15, 2000, and settled in San Diego on February 4, 2000. Through connections at the Islamic Center of San Diego, they obtained an apartment and a vehicle.

After an introductory course at National Air College of San Diego in April 2000, Alhazmi and Almindar attended Sorbi's Flying Club in May 2000. Their attitudes, unrealistic goals, and inability to communicate caused flight instructor Rick Garza to permanently ground the two students by June. Almindar departed San Diego for Yemen in June 2000 and Alhazmi left soon after.

Alhazmi and Almindar had a difficult time acclimating to American life. The two terrorists lived in several apartments in their six months in the United States and did not easily learn the English language. The San Diego pair was not the only one to struggle in the United States and had many parallels with another group of terrorists living in Paterson, New Jersey.

This group, recruited to strong-arm passengers aboard the airliners, often did not observe Muslim customs and embraced American cultural norms like wearing shorts, drinking alcoholic beverages, and consuming fast food.

While the first groups of terrorists were engaged in the more challenging and long-term goals of gaining residency and pilot's licenses, this second group was brought to America to weight-train and keep the terrorist pilots out of trouble on September 11.

Further Reading: Damion Dimarco, *Tower Stories: The Autobiography of September 11, 2001* (Revolution Publishing, 2004); Terry McDermott, *Perfect Soldiers: The Hijackers: Who They Were, Why They Did It* (HarperCollins, 2005).

— **NICHOLAS KATERS**

T

Taliban

From September 27, 1996, until November 12, 2001, the Taliban controlled the capital city of Kabul, along with about 80 percent of the rest of AFGHANISTAN. The regime was a radical Islamic fundamentalist theocracy led by extremist cleric Mullah Mohammad Omar and comprised of ethnic Pashtuns.

Its interpretation of Sunni Islam and the application of its own brand of medieval Sharia (Islamic law) were possibly the most repressive on earth. It was a haven for terrorists and their camps. Government participation was open only to religious students and the men of Kandahar. In 2001, military commanders reported to Mullah Omar alone.

The Taliban admired OSAMA BIN LADEN for his JIHAD against Soviet occupation forces. The Taliban depended on him for the training his camps supplied its elite brigade and the military aid of his "Arab Afghan fighters." The relationship, already ideologically mated, was furthered by the alleged marriage of bin Laden's daughter to Mullah Omar.

During the Taliban's reign, the government was recognized only by Pakistan, Saudi Arabia, and the United Arab Emirates. The United Nations recognized the Taliban's predecessors. Internal opposition to the Taliban came from the Northern Alliance, a coalition of ethnic minorities and supporters of the former Soviet-installed state. On September 9, 2001, suicide bombers assassinated Ahmed Shah Masood,

TALIBAN FIGHTERS *Taliban members at their 1995 headquarters near Kabul, Afghanistan. By 1996, the Taliban had established themselves as the rulers of most of Afghanistan.*

175

Life Under the Taliban

WOMEN AND girls were not allowed to pursue education under the Taliban regime, and were held virtual prisoners within their homes. Seen as chattel, and not allowed to work in most occupations, many were forced to beg. Should so much as a stray hair or glimpse of wrist peek out from beneath a burka, a woman could be beaten. She could not go out without the escort of a male relative, even if lack of one meant starvation. Hospitals were segregated, infant mortality at an all-time high, women's mental and physical health an all-time low. Only women could be doctors to women, and many of these had fled the country.

Torture and public executions were common practices. Minority Shiites were murdered. Ethnic purges have been alleged. Refugees poured over the border into Pakistan. Sports, secular music, western clothes, even kite flying were forbidden. Men were not allowed to shave, beards were measured. Even those leaving the country would have their shaving lotion confiscated. Prayer time was mandatory. In 2001, Taliban artillery and explosives blasted the Bamiyan Buddhas, priceless statues from the 3rd and 5th centuries, and part of the heritage of Afghanistan. Ordered by Mullah Omar, this was the destruction of "dead false gods."

AT LEFT *Two Afghani women dressed in religious attire during the hajj, part of the pilgrimage to Mecca, a religious obligation of adult Muslims. The women are careful to keep everything but their eyes hidden.*

leader of the Northern Alliance. Bin Laden's backing was suspected.

In spite of urgings by some factions within his own government, including foreign minister Maulana Muttawikil (who thought bin Laden should be kept under surveillance), Mullah Omar did nothing to improve relations with the rest of the world. His "diplomatic" orders included that no non-Muslim leader should receive birthday congratulations, nor wishes for good health or long life, and that no nation having suffered a natural disaster receive messages of sympathy or solidarity, as he viewed such events as acts of God.

By September 11, conditions were already in place that would lead to the end of the Taliban regime. Pakistan, formerly quite supportive, worked to maintain friendly relations with the West. Iran hated the Taliban for its persecution of Shiites. China was generally supportive of the U.S. position against terrorists, and the terrorists that Afghanistan harbored were apparently of some concern.

Both Tajikistan and Uzbekistan had ethnic ties to the Northern Alliance, and Uzbekistan also had Islamic insurgency problems of its own. The only other bordering state, Turkmenistan, remained ideologically neutral but would do as Moscow said.

Further Reading: Peter L. Bergen, *The Osama bin Laden I know, An Oral History of al Qaeda's Leader* (The Free Press, 2006); Tony Karon, "Understanding Bin Laden's Hosts, the Dilemma He Poses for Them, and the Politics of the Neighborhood," *Time* Magazine (September 18, 2001); Gerald Posner, *Why America Slept, The Failure to Prevent 911* (Random House, 2003).

— ELIZABETH A. KRAMER

Terrorism, Causes of

Analysts and governments around the world have spent considerable time trying to determine why people turn to terrorism. Studies before the rise of jihadist (see JIHAD) terrorism could reach no generally accepted results, even with many former terrorists volunteering lengthy interviews.

Debates over jihadist terrorism generally hold one of two positions. If the jihadist cause is based on politics, diplomacy, and military deployments, changes in policy may undercut the radicals' cause. If, conversely, it is based on culture, societal norms, and belief in democracy, any action is likely to provoke wrath. The provocation of those inclined to jihadist violence may be a mix of both.

POVERTY AND EDUCATION

Beyond this basic issue, many analysts blame poverty and lack of education for both jihadist terrorism and the formation of terrorist groups, but many of the principal terrorists of concern to the West, including the September 11 hijackers and their leaders, fit a different profile. Most come from middle-class backgrounds and have higher than average education. Many of the more important AL-QAEDA terrorists and leaders studied technical subjects such as engineering or medicine in college.

Some jihadists—particularly the Saudis—come from strongly religious families and have been brainwashed into radicalism. Many others were raised in largely secular environments and became radicals later in their lives, after entering a new environment in the West. Some argue that the radicals hate the West out of cultural ignorance. But most of the most prominent terrorists have lived or traveled in the West, particularly Europe, and therefore have seen and experienced life in the Western world.

One analyst, Marc Sageman, has argued that contacts with the West have been critical in the formation of a jihadist identity. The isolation and alienation that young Muslim males have felt in Europe and other Western countries have driven them to form strong social bonds with other Muslims who have similar reactions. For a small minority, these bonds result in radicalism, particularly if guided by a charismatic leader. For the most radical, this could take the form of global jihad.

POLITICAL MOTIVATION

Those who point to a more politically driven motivation for the jihadist movement argue that specific U.S. and European policies are generating and maintaining the movement. The jihadists have issued specific political demands. The first is to end U.S. occupation of SAUDI ARABIA.

Although the U.S. military presence in Saudi Arabia is in fact rather small—basically the forces remaining from Desert Storm who stayed to enforce

ABOVE *A U.S. convoy-security team in Iraq passes a billboard that loosely translated says "The terrorists give bad ideas—like poison—to our children. Do not let terrorists take advantage of your children."*

Causes of Religious Terrorism

TERRORIST MOVEMENTS include traditional ideological groups, those with ethnic or nationalist aspirations, single-issue groups such as fringe environmentalists or anti-abortionists, and religious. Those based on religion have increased sharply in recent years and now represents the majority of terrorist groups. Even small religious terrorist groups commonly have an extensive network of supporters.

Sociologist and author Mark Juergensmeyer describes the underlying motivator of religious groups as "cosmic war," a struggle of good versus evil that may never be won but is essential to fight. Individuals and groups believe that their communities are under "attack," either physically or socially. Their goals are to gain collective justice and to fight cultural domination. "Enemies" can include not only those who directly oppose the group, but also co-religionists and moderates who do not support the concept of a war to the death.

A distinction should be made between religion as the underlying cause of terrorism versus religion as a "marker" for other grievances. "Religious" groups fighting primarily for social or political grievances may stop once their grievances are satisfied. Groups fighting a "cosmic war" are unlikely to ever have their demands met. Although these groups are commonly identified by a particular religion, their aims are essentially political and social. Other groups, such as Aum Shinrikyo and Christian Identity, are engaged in a "cosmic war."

Groups such as AL-QAEDA and Hamas present a particular difficulty. They are intensely religious but at the same time have specific political demands. As individuals and groups become more radicalized, the more likely they are to believe in "cosmic war" and the less likely to accept compromise.

sanctions on IRAQ—their presence in the cities of Mecca and Medina is a particularly sensitive issue for the radicals. Others have pointed to U.S. and Western support for oppressive governments in the Middle East and elsewhere.

The other major issue for many jihadist groups is the U.S.-Israel relationship. Many of their ideological documents emphasize the threat of the alliance between "Crusaders and Zionists." Just how critical this issue is for many of the jihadist groups may be debatable. Some analysts view it as the number one issue and argue that if the Israeli-Palestinian issue were resolved, the jihadist groups would wither. This view may be overstated. Although a resolution of the Israeli-Palestinian conflict may reduce terrorist recruitment and support, it is unlikely to eliminate the jihadist movement.

One key reason for this is the goal of most of the jihadist groups—to "liberate" all Muslim lands and to establish a caliphate to be ruled by Sharia (Islamic law). The jihadists view local regimes ruling Muslim majority populations as having abandoned their religiosity, requiring overthrow and replacement with religiously guided rule. Most jihadist ideologues explicitly reject democracy because this implies rule by man rather than God.

This brings us back to the question of whether jihadist attacks are politically or socially based. Several policy changes could have a positive impact: efforts to resolve the Israeli-Palestinian issue; encouraging authoritarian regimes in the Middle East and elsewhere to liberalize; helping to improve education, living conditions, and society for Muslim populations wherever they are; reducing the "footprint" of the United States in the Middle East. However, the most radical of the jihadists may continue to view anything Western as inherently inimical to Islam.

ABOVE *A bottle of cologne is displayed at a Pakistani cosmetic shop in March 2004 depicting Osama bin Laden. Although support for bin Laden is believed to be waning in Muslim states, he is still hailed as a hero by many devout Islamists, particularly in Pakistan.*

THE 'SCHOOLS' OF ANALYZING TERRORISM

The emphasis in the 21st century has been on explaining jihadist terrorism, but analysts for many years have been trying to analyze and explain the phenomenon of terrorism in in one of three frameworks: psychological, strategic, and organizational.

The psychological approach argues that members join terrorist groups because they want to commit acts of violence. This approach focuses on motivations, how decisions are made, group behaviors, and personalities. Even those analysts who stress this argument acknowledge that there is no single terrorist profile. The strategic approach argues that a particular group has a set of political objectives, and persons join because they agree with these objectives. Groups have certain strategic objectives and rationally choose terrorism from a range of strategic alternatives.

The organizational approach focuses on the internal dynamics that drive the actions of groups. The basic tenet is that terrorism is a social activity. Distribution of beliefs among members of the group is uneven, with some being more 'true believers' than others. The aim of the terrorist leaders is to inculcate all members with deeply held beliefs. Socialization of the members is intense, and group cohesion is critical.

No single approach does a particularly good job of explaining the roots of terrorism. Despite many efforts, no one has successfully identified a "terrorist personality." The strategic, rational approach may help identify overall strategic goals, but not necessarily why particular groups find terrorism to be their best choice for achieving these goals. The organizational approach can be useful in explaining group dynamics, but is not as effective in explaining why groups form in the first place. Taken together, however, these various approaches may help in making sense of terrorism.

Further Reading: Mia Bloom and Robert A. Pape, *Dying to Win* (Random House, 2005); Mark Juergensmeyer, *Terror in the Mind of God* (University of California Press, 2000); Walter Reich, ed., *Origins of Terrorism: Psychologies, Ideologies, Theologies, States of Mind* (Woodrow Wilson Center Press, 1998); Marc Sageman, *Understanding Terror Networks* (University of Pennsylvania Press, 2004); Michael Scheuer, *Through Our Enemies' Eyes* (Potomac Books, 2006).

— **LAWRENCE E. CLINE, PH.D.**

Terrorism, Results of

Eight months after the July 7, 2005, subway and bus bombings in London, Reverend Julie Nicholson stepped down as vicar at St. Aidan with St. George, an inner-city parish in Bristol, England. Her 24-year-old daughter, Jennifer, was among the 56 victims of the bombings. According to the *Times of London*, the vicar was no longer able to preach the message of "peace and reconciliation," when she found it impossible to forgive the terrorists.

On November 2, 2004, Dutch filmmaker Theo van Gogh was murdered after filming a movie of a naked woman painted with the words of the Koran. The 26-year-old radical Islamic terrorist left a note on van Gogh's body threatening Hirsi Ali, a former Muslim Dutch parliamentarian who fled from Somalia because of abuse. The note also attacked "infidel" Dutch society in general. Only a few years

ABOVE *Two U.S. Army Military Police escort a detainee to a cell in Guantanamo Bay Navy Base, Cuba. Prisoners were held without charges or trials, sparking outrage from Muslims and human rights groups.*

before, security was so relaxed that the prime minister was able to ride to work on a bicycle. Now several members of Parliament are forced to live under high-security protection, the country is faced with a growing social crisis, and unemployment for minorities has doubled. The country is forced to reconsider the ideal of multiculturalism as Muslim minorities are increasingly treated with suspicion. One parliamentarian, Geert Wilders, suggested the suspension of due process for suspected terrorists.

A country like the United States, founded on the principles of a strong judiciary and due process, can find itself making questionable arrangements in dealing with terrorists. Camp Delta, a prison for terrorist suspects in Guantanamo Bay in Cuba, was opened in January 2002. The prisoners were held in legal limbo without charge or trials. Vice President Dick Cheney (see RICHARD B. CHENEY) defended the indefinite detention of the prisoners: "They're facilitators of terror... If you let them out, they'll go back to trying to kill Americans."

Nearly five years after some of the terrorist suspects were apprehended, Congress approved a bill that began to delimit the treatment of detainees. "The bill would set up rules for the military commissions that will allow the government to proceed with the prosecutions of high-level detainees... It would make illegal several broadly defined abuses of detainees, while leaving it to the president to establish specific permissible interrogation techniques. And it would strip detainees of a *habeas corpus* right to challenge their detentions in court," reported the *New York Times* on September 29, 2006.

Guantanamo Bay, coupled with abuse at the Abu Ghraib prison in IRAQ, created a backlash in the Muslim world and outrage from some European governments and groups like Amnesty International. America is seen as following a double standard, claiming

to promote freedom and democracy even as it detained suspects arbitrarily. President GEORGE W. BUSH and his administration claimed extensive and extraordinary executive powers as the war continued, not only to detain suspects without trial but also to wiretap international telephone conversations without a warrant.

On March 11, 2004, hundreds died after a series of bombs exploded in the Atocha train station in Madrid, Spain. President Jose Maria Aznar, up for election three days later, immediately blamed the Basque terrorist group ETA. However, new evidence came to light showing the possible involvement of AL-QAEDA. It was learned that the attack was meant to target Spain for the participation of Spanish troops in the 2003 war against Saddam Hussein. The Spanish public elected the antiwar socialist leader Jose Luis Rodríguez Zapatero as president. Zapatero almost immediately recalled Spanish troops from Iraq, leading to charges by neoconservatives that Spain was allowing terrorists to manipulate the democratic process.

The results of terrorism are not found simply in the rubble and twisted wires, in the rows of body bags, or even in the memory of murdered innocents. The American, Spanish, and British economies were not fundamentally shaken by brutal terrorist attacks. The number of dead was relatively small compared with deaths from common diseases and accidents. The deepest wounds and the most important results of terrorism are found in the collective social consciousness, exploded and scattered like psychological

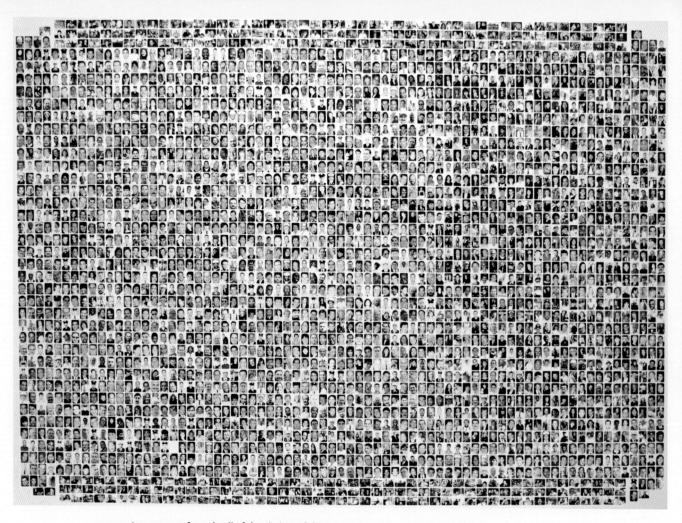

ABOVE *A montage of nearly all of the victims of the September 11 terrorist attacks (92 victim photos were not available), presented as evidence in the Zacarias Moussaoui trial. Almost 3,000 people were killed that day in a matter of hours.*

shrapnel. Even the fundamental, constitutional values and principles, the core of a society's identity and character, can be altered by terrorism, as a population is pushed to give up basic freedoms to the state in the name of protection.

WHAT TERRORISTS WANT

In almost every case, terrorists have at least three goals: short-term media attention; the long-term polarization of society; and the creation of a state of panic and terror. The long-term goal of terrorism is the fulfillment of political, religious, or, in the case of some terrorist groups like al-Qaeda, millennial or apocalyptic goals. Terrorist insurgency is often the most effective weapon of a weaker group when facing a more powerful adversary. A relatively small number of TALIBAN are still able to mount attacks from the mountains of

AFGHANISTAN because they do not confront their enemy on the open battlefield.

The increasing democratization and globalization of the world has made some of the terrorists' short-term goals easier. By targeting civilians who control democratically elected leaders, terrorists expect nations to react emotionally, sometimes against their own best interests. Modern, democratic nation-states are manifestations of shared media and identity; the national community makes it possible to feel as if one knows the victims when they are seen on television and in newspapers. Thus the first desired result of almost every terrorist is the manipulation of worldwide media, and an enormous increase in attention for the terrorists' agenda. Terrorists hope to provoke a polarization of society. A society that has been attacked looks for the "enemy within," which can lead to the denial of human rights for those who share the same ethnic or religious origin as the terrorists. This alienation further justifies terrorist claims.

HAS TERRORISM WORKED?

Although terrorism destabilizes a state, it often does not provide a viable alternative to the structures of state control. It has been claimed that the end of British colonial control of Aden in Southern Yemen, Palestine, and Cyprus was the result of terrorism, but larger factors that weakened the British empire were probably the main causes of British retreat. Political control is often not the sole objective of terrorist organizations– prestige is often more important. Prestige and leadership in a global environment does not require the existence of a state. Every time OSAMA BIN LADEN makes a video or tape, his face is seen or his words are heard around the world.

Some terrorists commit violence because they genuinely believe that it is religiously correct and justified. They want terrorism to change the world,

prepare it for ultimate justice, and the end of time. With this self-destructive mentality and philosophy, a welcoming of death and the end of the world, it is difficult, if not impossible, to negotiate with or moderate the ways of millennial religious terrorists. Paul Wilkinson, a scholar of terrorism and international relations and director of the Center for the Study of Terrorism and Political Violence at the University of St. Andrews, suggests that as terrorists are appeased through quiet diplomacy and sometimes payoffs, the tactic of terrorism becomes more popular and frequent.

Further Reading: Thomas L. Friedman, *Longitudes and Attitudes: The World in the Age of Terrorism* (Alfred A. Knopf, 2003); Karen Greenberg, ed., *Al Qaeda Now: Understanding Today's Terrorists* (Cambridge University Press, 2005); Walter Laqueur, *No End to War: Terrorism in the 21st Century* (Continuum, 2003); Jamal Nassar, *Globalization and Terrorism* (Rowman and Littlefield, 2005); Paul Wilkinson, *Terrorism versus Democracy: The Liberal State Response* (Frank Cass, 2001).

— **ALLEN FROMHERZ**

Terrorists of September 11

AL HAZNAMI, AHMED IBRAHIM
United Airlines Flight 93
BORN: *October 10, 1980, Baljurshi, al Ban'ah Province, Saudi Arabia*

The son of a Muslim cleric from the town of Baljurshi, Ahmed Al Haznami was selected for the mission while living in Kandahar, Afghanistan, and attending the al-Farooq camp. Outwardly religious, he announced to his family in 1999 that he was planning to fight in

Chechnya even though his father forbade him to do so. Unlike many other hijackers, Al Haznami remained close to his family.

On June 8, 2001, he arrived in Miami, Florida. He was one of nine hijackers to open a SunTrust bank account. It is believed he shared an apartment at 4641 Bougainvilla in Lauderdale-by-the-Sea with Ziad Jarrah. The landlord later turned over photocopies of their German passports to the Federal Bureau of Investigation (FBI). On September 7, Al Haznami purchased two first class one-way tickets on United Airlines Flight 93 from Newark, New Jersey, to San Francisco, California. On September 11, Al Haznami was selected for additional security screening, but boarded the aircraft without incident. He is believed responsible for killing at least one of the flight crew and securing the cockpit door from the efforts of the passengers to retake the flight.

AL SUGAMI, SAFAM M.A.
American Airlines Flight 11
BORN: *June 28, 1976, Riyadh, Saudi Arabia*

A muscle hijacker on American Airlines Flight 11, Safam Al Sugami was born in the capital city of Saudi Arabia, had very little formal education, and a minor criminal record. He was known not to be devout, and drank alcohol. He trained along with several other plot members at the al-Farooq camp in AFGHANISTAN.

Prior to his arrival in the United States, Al Sugami made one suspicious move, traveling with fellow hijacker Majed Moged from Bahrain to Iran in November 2000. Once in the United States, he made another unusual trip, with Waleed Alshehri to the Bahamas. The two were turned away by Bahamian Customs for not having valid visas and returned to Florida the same day. Al Sugami's passport was recovered at the WTC site after the attacks and, according to the 9/11 Commission, showed evidence of tampering. He was the only member of the plot not to obtain any U.S. identification.

ALGHAMDI, AHMED
United Airlines Flight 175
BORN: *July 2, 1979, Tasir Province, Saudi Arabia*

The Arabic newspaper *Al Watan* reported that Ahmed Alghamdi was a Saudi from Baha who left the country in late 1999 or early 2000 for Chechnya. Alghamdi was a muscle hijacker who arrived in the U.S. shortly before the attacks, one of three members of the Alghamdi clan to have participated in the attacks.

He grew up in the Tasir Province, an underdeveloped area of Saudi Arabia. A graduate of a religious high school, he last spoke to his family four months before the attacks and asked his parents to forgive him and pray for him. Before leaving to fight the JIHAD in Chechnya, Alghamdi studied engineering in Mecca, SAUDI ARABIA.

Alghamdi was responsible for keeping passengers at bay while Marwan Alshehri flew the aircraft into the South Tower of the World Trade Center. Alghamdi had at least three passports, and as with many of the muscle hijackers, is confused with the same last name.

ALGHAMDI, HAMZA

United Airlines Flight 175

BORN: *November 18, 1980, Baljurshi, al Ban'ah Province, Saudi Arabia*

Hamza Alghamdi, 20, from Baljurshi in southern Saudi Arabia, had what he considered a humiliating stockboy job when he was recruited by AL-QAEDA. He is believed to be the brother of Ahmed Alghamdi, purchased tickets for himself and Ahmed at a Kinko's in Delray Beach, Florida, and listed his address as the same postal box in Delray Beach, Florida.

He most likely trained in late 1999 or early 2000 in al-Qaeda camps. The Alghamdi tribe, from the al Ban'ah area of Saudi Arabia, is known as one of the more religiously observant Wahhabi groups within the kingdom.

He was a frequent travel companion of Mohand Alshehri. He spent his last days at the Day's Inn in Brighton, Massachusetts with Marwan Alshehri and Mohand Alshehri.

ALGHAMDI, SAEED

United Airlines Flight 93

BORN: *November 21, 1979, Abha, Al-Ban'ah Province, Saudi Arabia*

In November 2001, the FBI listed 11 aliases and four different dates of birth for Saeed Alghamdi. It is believed that he held the same tribal affiliation as several other hijackers from the southwest region of Saudi Arabia, and appears to be the first of the hijackers to depart from Saudi Arabia to Chechyna.

In March 2001, Alghamdi was filmed in a farewell video aired on *al Jazeera* television. In the video, many future September 11 hijackers swear to become martyrs, although no details of the plot are revealed. Alghamdi referred to America as "the enemy," and is seen studying maps and flight manuals.

There are theories that Alghamdi was not a member of the plot. The Arab newspaper *Al Sharq al-Awsat* reported that he may have been using a stolen identity. The newspaper spoke with the real Alghamdi, a Saudi Arabian Airlines pilot, who said he was shocked when he saw his photo and heard himself identified as a hijacking suspect in a media report.

ALHAZMI, NAWAF

American Airlines Flight 77

BORN: *August 9, 1976, Mecca, Saudi Arabia*

Nawaf Alhazmi joined the JIHAD when he was 17 years old. Born in Mecca, he left home sometime in 1993 and went to AFGHANISTAN, Bosnia, and Chechnya to fight for his beliefs. His brother Salem, also a September 11 terrorist, later joined him in Afghanistan. Alhazmi was one of the few members of the plot to have definite connections to AL-QAEDA prior to entering the United States.

Along with Almindar, he is known to have met with Tawfiq Attash Khallad, one of the al-Qaeda members responsible for the attack on the USS *Cole*. An attendee of the infamous Kuala Lumpur planning meeting in Bali, Alhazmi joined Almindar in San Diego and frequented the San Diego Islamic Center.

During the late summer of 2001, Alhazmi's name surfaced at the Central Intelligence Agency (CIA) as being connected to al-Qaeda. The FBI searched for him in New York and Los Angeles, but not in San Diego.

Alhazmi was also identified by the National Security Agency (NSA) and the CIA, but this information was not given to the FBI or the Federal Aviation Administration (FAA) in a timely manner. Alhazmi was able to purchase a ticket in his own name and board American Airlines Flight 77 without incident.

ALHAZMI, SALEM
American Airlines Flight 77
BORN: *February 2, 1981, Mecca, Saudi Arabia*

The younger brother of Nawaf Alhazmi, Salem Alhazmi was sitting in seat 5F on American Airlines Flight 77 on September 11. Born and raised in Mecca, Alhazmi grew up near the Caba, one of Islam's holiest sites. His older brother was a veteran of al-Qaeda who had fought against the enemies of OSAMA BIN LADEN since before the younger Alhazmi was in his teens. Recruited to be a muscle hijacker, Alhazmi was anything but physically imposing; but what he lacked in size, he made up for in religious fervor.

A Saudi from lower-middle-class surroundings, he found his way to al-Qaeda and volunteered for JIHAD operations. His father recounted that Alhazmi—who had had problems with alcohol and petty theft—stopped drinking and started attending mosque regularly three months before he disappeared. Like other hijackers with similar names, he is often confused in reports with his older brother Nawaf.

According to the 9/11 Commission Report, Salem traveled with his brother Nawaf to Kuala Lumpur prior to entering the United States. The new recruit was given the opportunity to observe how al-Qaeda conducted its business, but he did not continue on with Nawaf and Khalid Almindar to San Diego.

He did not arrive in the United States until June 29, 2001, along with hijacker Abdulaziz Alomari. The last two of the muscle hijackers, their arrival signaled that the final pieces of the "planes operation" were in place.

ALMINDAR, KHALID
American Airlines Flight 77
BORN: *May 5, 1975, Mecca, Saudi Arabia*

Of all the members of the September 11 plot, Khalid Almindar had the most definitive connections to al-Qaeda. He was one of the al-Qaeda operatives sought by U.S. intelligence after the Kuala Lumpur planning meeting. His father-in-law had also sworn allegiance to bin Laden. While the other plot members were working toward their studies in Germany or attending secondary schooling, Almindar was fighting in Bosnia against the Serbs and Croats.

Almindar also had combat experience in Chechnya and in AFGHANISTAN. One of the first operatives picked by bin Laden for the "planes operation,"

Almindar was slated to be a pilot, but proved to be a poor student. Instead of flight training, the experienced operative was used to ensure that AMERICAN AIRLINES FLIGHT 77 would reach its intended target: the Pentagon. Almindar had met with Tawfiq Attash Khallad, one of the operatives responsible for the attack on the USS *Cole*.

Almindar lived in San Diego prior to the attacks. He used a credit card in his own name and boarded American Airlines Flight 77 without identification.

ALNAMI, AHMED
United Airlines Flight 93
BORN: *December 7, 1977, Khamis Mushayt, Asir Province, Saudi Arabia*

Ahmed Alnami was born in the southern tribal region of Saudi Arabia. His father said that his son left for a pilgrimage to Mecca a year and a half before September 11 and never returned. He is believed to have been trained as a member of AL-QAEDA at the al-Farooq camp. After acquiring his U.S. visa in 2000, Alnami and other Saudi hijackers attended final training at the al Matar complex in AFGHANISTAN.

Alnami served as a muezzin—similar to a Catholic altar boy at the Seqeley Mosque. He later enrolled in King Khalid University in Abha to study Islamic law but stories vary about whether he finished his degree or dropped out to pursue JIHAD training in Afghanistan. He traveled in May 2001 through the United Arab Emirates, along with two other hijackers, and by early June was living in an apartment at the Delray Racquet Club condominiums in Delray Beach, Florida.

ALOMARI, ABDULAZIZ
American Airlines Flight 11
BORN: *May 28, 1979, Asir Province, Saudi Arabia*

Believed to have been a student of the radical Saudi cleric Sulayman al Alwan, Abdulaziz Alomari left the Saudi kingdom for training at the al-Farooq camp in Afghanistan. Unlike the other muscle hijackers, he had a degree from the Imam Muhammad Ibn Saud Islamic University, was married, and the father of a young girl.

Alomari was the last of the hijackers to enter the United States in late June 2001. On the morning of September 11, Alomari traveled with Mohamed Atta on a flight from Portland, Maine, to Boston's Logan International Airport, where they boarded AMERICAN AIRLINES FLIGHT 11. His passport was recovered at Ground Zero and showed evidence of tampering.

ALSHEHRI, MARWAN
United Airlines Flight 175
BORN: *May 9, 1978, Ras al Khaimah, United Arab Emirates*

The youngest of the Hamburg, Germany, cell members, Marwan Alshehri was born in Ras al Khaimah, one of the poorest areas of the United Arab Emirates (UAE) to parents of Egyptian origin. He was the cousin of Mohand Alshehri. Alshehri was a scholar of the Koran, and who convinced the members of the Hamburg cell that it was their duty to sacrifice their lives for Islam. Alshehri joined the Emirati military and received six months of basic training before gaining admission to a military scholarship program that would fund his continued study in Germany.

He was not a proficient scholar at the University of Bonn, studying general sciences and mathematics. When his father died, he broke away from his family and became more radicalized. In late 1997, he applied for permission to complete his coursework in Hamburg. He later moved with other hijackers and clerics into an apartment that they dubbed "Dar al Islam."

After attending AL-QAEDA training near Kandahar, AFGHANISTAN, in 1999, Alshehri returned to the United Arab Emirates and married. Cell members and other al-Qaeda associates were invited to the wedding. After acquiring a new passport and a U.S. visa on January 28, 2000, he traveled to Saudi Arabia and Bahrain.

ALSHEHRI, MOHAND
United Airlines Flight 175
BORN: *May 7, 1979, Asir Province, Saudi Arabia*

Mohand Alshehri was one of five hijackers to come from the poor Asir Province in Saudi Arabia. He graduated from a religious high school and dropped out of Imam Muhammad Ibn Saud Islamic University in Abha.

On UNITED AIRLINES FLIGHT 175, Alshehri was in seat 2B next to Fayez Ahmed, also known as Fayez

Banihammad, who quit the same university after one semester. Alshehri was sent to aid his cousin Marwan Alshehri on Flight 175 as a muscle hijacker.

Alshehri had originally planned to fight the Russians in Chechnya, but was turned away at the border. Afterward, he entered training at an al-Qaeda camp in Afghanistan and was recruited as a supplementary member of the "planes operation." Entering the United States during the summer of 2001, Alshehri rented a post office box in Delray Beach, Florida, with fellow hijacker Hamza Alghamdi. He also accompanied him on their flight to Newark prior to driving to Boston and taking United Airlines Flight 175.

ALSHEHRI, WAIL M.
American Airlines Flight 11
BORN: *July 31, 1973, Asir Province, Saudi Arabia*

Born in the Asir Province, a poverty-stricken region in southwestern SAUDI ARABIA near the border of YEMEN, Wail Alshehri was 28 years old at the time of the attacks. Alshehri was the older brother of fellow hijacker Waleed Alshehri.

While he is believed to have begun university studies prior to leaving for AFGHANISTAN, there is no evidence that he completed his degree. He most likely trained for JIHAD at the al-Farooq camp near Kandahar, Afghanistan, and was one of those recruited while on security detail at the Kandahar airport.

Alshehri was married and employed as a physical education teacher prior to the attacks. He also had a family member in the Saudi Passport Office who provided him and his brother with clean passports before entering the United States.

He arrived in the United States in June 2001 and settled with other hijackers in southern Florida. During the attack, his responsibility was keeping the passengers away from the cockpit.

ALSHEHRI, WALEED M.

American Airlines Flight 11

BORN: *December 20, 1978, Asir Province, Saudi Arabia*

Waleed Alshehri was recruited into JIHAD by his brother Wail. AL-QAEDA leaders did not want the young man on the operation but his brother insisted. Seated next to each other on AMERICAN AIRLINES FLIGHT 11, Waleed and Wail struck the first blows in the attack by stabbing two first class flight attendants preparing to serve beverages.

Alshehri, through his relative in the Saudi Passport Office, provided other Saudi hijackers with clean passports before deployment to the United States. He was also the first of the muscle hijackers to arrive in the United States, on April 23. He seems to have been an important link in bringing several of the muscle hijackers into the United States, and coordinated with the pilots to bring the rest of the hijackers into the country.

ATTA, MOHAMED

American Airlines Flight 11

BORN: *September 1, 1968,*

Kafr el-Sheikh, Egypt

Mohamed Atta is the most well-known of

the terrorists. The operational leader of the plot, Atta met with RAMZI BIN AL SHIBH on more than one occasion, to finalize the plans. The hijacker-pilot of AMERICAN AIRLINES FLIGHT 11, he was the first to crash a commercial airliner into a U.S. target.

Atta was the son of a wealthy Cairo attorney, grew up in a middle-class environment, and graduated with a bachelor's degree in architectural engineering in 1990 from Cairo University. His father, Mohamed Al Amir Atta, Sr., described his son as "effeminate and non-violent" and refused to believe that he could become the operational leader of such a heinous act.

After moving to GERMANY and initially pursuing a degree at the University of Hamburg, Atta transferred to the city engineering and planning program at the Technical University of Hamburg-Harburg, showed an interest in the preservation of Islamic cities, and eventually completed his thesis on the Syrian city of Aleppo. Of all the Hamburg plotters, Atta seemed the most serious about his studies. In late 1999, Atta and three others entered AFGHANISTAN to train as members of AL-QAEDA. Originally, Atta and his colleagues had wanted to travel to Chechnya to fight the Russians, but a chance meeting with Mohamedou Ould Slahi convinced them to travel to Pakistan instead. Following Slahi's advice, Atta traveled to Karachi, Pakistan, in November 1999 bound for Quetta and eventually Kandahar, Afghanistan.

Atta pledged allegiance to OSAMA BIN LADEN and became a covert operative for al-Qaeda. He wore Western clothing, shaved his beard, and no longer extolled extremist views or associated with any known extremists. He applied for flight training in the United States, obtained a new passport to conceal his travels to Pakistan and Afghanistan, and obtained a U.S. student visa.

On June 2, 2000, Atta traveled by bus from Hamburg to Prague, Czech Republic, and flew to Newark, New Jersey, the next day.

BANIHAMMAD, FAYEZ RASHID
United Airlines Flight 175
BORN: *March 19, 1977, Abu Dhabi, United Arab Emirates*

Fayez Rashid Banihammad was born near Abu Dhabi, United Arab Emirates. He arrived in Florida from Dubai with Saeed Alghamdi on June 27, 2001. Banihammad was admitted as a tourist for six months, even though he used two different names on his application forms. He opened a bank account at SunTrust, also had a bank account in the United Arab Emirates, opened on June 25 and administered by Mustafa Ahmed Al Hawsawi.

On July 10, Banihammad got a Florida State identification card. Eight days later, Al Hawsawi shipped him a Visa credit and ATM card. Banihammad used this Visa card on August 29, 2001, to purchase his and Mohand Alshehri's one-way first-class tickets for UNITED AIRLINES FLIGHT 175. After charging the $4,464.50 tickets, he listed their address as a Mailboxes, Etc. location in Florida. Banihammad traveled to Boston on September 8, 2001, and stayed in the Milner Hotel in Boston until September 10 with Marwan Alshehri, Mohand Alshehri, and Safam Al Sugami. On September 11, 2001, Banihammad drove Mohand Alshehri in a rental car to Boston's Logan International Airport, where they boarded United Airlines Flight 175.

HAMJOUR, HANI
American Airlines Flight 77
BORN: *August 30, 1972, Ta'if, Saudi Arabia*

At approximately 7:30 on the morning of September 11, Hani Hamjour, a Saudi-born Muslim

extremist, arrived at Dulles International Airport and checked in for AMERICAN AIRLINES FLIGHT 77. Hamjour was flagged by the airline's Computer Assisted Passenger Prescreening System (CAPPS), which resulted only in his bags being held off the plane until it was confirmed that he had boarded and taken his seat.

Hamjour went to AFGHANISTAN in the late 1980s and worked at a relief agency in support of the JIHAD. Reportedly a mediocre pilot, Hamjour was repeatedly discouraged from continuing his flight instruction, and was rejected by a civil aviation school in Jeddah, SAUDI ARABIA. But he persisted and completed several rounds of flight training, earning his commercial pilot certificate from the Federal Aviation Administration (FAA) in April 1999, and completing initial training on a Boeing 737 simulator at Pan Am International Flight Academy in Mesa, Arizona, in March 2001.

In early summer 2001, Hamjour received permission to fly the Hudson Corridor, a narrow, low-altitude route along the Hudson River that passes several New York City landmarks, including the World Trade Center. His request for a second flight was denied based on his poor piloting skills, which made him a hazard in the high-traffic corridor.

Hamjour took control of American Airlines Flight 77 at 8:54 a.m. At 9:29, with the plane 38 miles west of the Pentagon, Hamjour disengaged the autopilot. At 9:34, tracked by controllers at both Dulles and Reagan National airports, Hamjour took the plane through a 330-degree turn, pointed the nose of the plane down, and crashed into the Pentagon.

JARRAH, ZIAD SAMIR
United Airlines Flight 93
BORN: *May 11, 1975, Al Mazra'a, Lebanon*

The hijacker-pilot of UNITED AIRLINES FLIGHT 93 was born in a small town north of Beirut, Lebanon, to a family of financial means. Though Muslim, his family chose to send their son to a private Catholic school in Beirut, where he struggled to attain low grades, particularly in the sciences. According to his father, Jarrah always wanted to fly planes, but the elder Jarrah feared that his son would perish in a crash.

From June 2000 to January 2001, Jarrah was enrolled in the Florida Flight Training Center where he obtained his small-aircraft pilot's license. On September 7, 2001, Jarrah and his three accomplices flew from Fort Lauderdale, Florida, to Newark, New Jersey. Four days later they boarded United Airlines Flight 93.

His voice was heard on the cockpit voice recorder at 9:39 A.M., saying "Uh, this is the captain. Would like you all to remain seated. There is a bomb on board and are going back to the airport, and to have our demands [unintelligible]. Please remain quiet." About 30 minutes later the plane crashed into the PENNSYLVANIA countryside near Shanksville.

Jarrah was an anomaly among the September 11 hijackers. He drank alcohol, and did not frequent the mosque before the late 1990s in Hamburg. He had a Turkish girlfriend, to whom he wrote a goodbye letter on September 10.

Jarrah is the subject of conspiracy theories ranging from mistaken identity to beliefs that he was a passenger on United Airlines Flight 93, not one of the hijackers.

MOGED, MAJED
American Airlines Flight 77
BORN: *June 18, 1977, Annakhil, Saudi Arabia*

At 7:15 A.M. Khalid Almindar and Majed Moged checked in at the American Airlines ticket counter at Dulles International Airport to board AMERICAN AIRLINES FLIGHT 77. Moged was flagged for secondary screening by security personnel, then allowed to board the flight. He entered the country less than four months earlier at the same airport.

Moged came from a small town west of Medina named Annakhil, and had no known ties to extremists in SAUDI ARABIA before he volunteered for the operation. He trained at the Khaldan complex near Kabul, AFGHANISTAN. In the United States, Moged moved in with Nawaf Alhazmi and Hani Hamjour in Alexandria, Virginia, and eventually, Paterson, New Jersey. The details of his recruitment and family life have not been released. It is known that during interrogation, Khalid Sheikh Mohammed, the mastermind of the attacks, remembered little more than Moged's name and face.

Further Reading: Terry McDermott, *Perfect Soldiers: The 9/11 Hijackers: Who They Were, Why They Did It* (HarperCollins, 2006); National Commission on Terrorist Attacks, *The 9/11 Commission Report: Final Report of the National Commission on Terrorist Attacks Upon the United States* (W.W. Norton, 2004); Lawrence Wright, *The Looming Tower: Al-Qaeda and the Road to 9/11* (Alfred A. Knopf, 2006).

— WADE K. EWING

U

United Airlines Flight 93

United Airlines Flight 93 was scheduled to leave Newark International Airport at 8:00 A.M. Although the plane was ready to leave, takeoff was delayed, which would prove crucial in the chain of events that occurred once the plane was in the air. The plane lifted off at 8:42 A.M., carrying seven crew members and 37 passengers. Four Arab passengers were aboard: Saeed Alghamdi, Ahmed Ibrahim Al Haznami, and Ahmed Alnami, all from Delray Beach, Florida, and Ziad Jarrah, address unspecified. The four men were part of an AL-QAEDA plot to turn jetliners into weapons of mass destruction.

Pilot Jason Dahl and copilot Leroy Homer were in the cockpit. Senior flight attendant Debbie Welsh tended the 10 passengers in first class, while Lorraine Bay, Sandra Bradshaw, Wanda Green, and CeeCee Lyles looked after the 27 passengers in coach. The trip seemed routine until Flight 93 inexplicably turned back toward PENNSYLVANIA and failed to respond to air traffic controllers in Pittsburgh.

Passengers in coach were unaware that four hijackers had simultaneously risen from their first-class seats and tied red bands around their heads. One hijacker displayed a packet fastened around his waist with a red belt, declaring it to be a bomb. The hijackers incapacitated the pilot and the copilot, and it is believed that two people were lying on the floor. Voice recordings reveal that a woman, probably Welsh, was pleading for her life. It is believed that the only passenger attacked was Mickey Rothenberg who, according to his family, would have

PAYING RESPECTS *Visitors to a makeshift memorial wall in Shanksville, Pennsylvania, on September 11, 2002. Flags, hats, photos, and all manner of Americana decorated a chain link fence near the crash site.*

ABOVE *A photo of the Shanksville, Pennsylvania, crash site, presented as evidence in the Zacarias Moussaoui trial. The plane went down in an abandoned strip mine.*

resisted being taken hostage. Most passengers believed at first that it was a "normal" HIJACKING because they were told that the hijackers' demands had been relayed and the plane was heading back to Newark.

PASSENGERS AND CREW

A number of passengers aboard United Airlines Flight 93 were on the flight by happenstance (see APPENDIX for a complete list of passengers and crew). For Ed Felt, it was a last-minute business trip. JEREMY GLICK's plane had been grounded the previous afternoon because of a fire at Newark airport.

MARK BINGHAM missed his flight on September 10, and, the next day, he barely made it onto the plane. Louis Nacke had booked Flight 93 at the last minute. Sandy Bradshaw's husband repeatedly begged her to cancel her tour and stay in North Carolina with the family. Both TODD BEAMER and Glick expressed a disinclination to fly to San Francisco that week.

One hijacker stood guard over the passengers. He did not prevent their making outside contact, and more than 24 calls were made from Flight 93. Lauren Grandcolas left a message for her husband Jack stating that there was a "little problem with the plane" and assured him that she was "comfortable."

Grandcolas then lent her cell phone to her seatmate, Elizabeth Wainio, who called her stepmother. Linda Gronlund called her sister and gave her the combination to her safe deposit box. In addition to the calls that Glick and Tom Burnett (see THOMAS E. BURNETT) made to their wives, Bingham called his mother, and Beamer talked to GTC Airfone operator Lisa Jefferson. Andy Garcia made the last recorded call, to his wife, which was scrambled and disconnected.

The passengers aboard United Airlines Flight 93 were better trained than most people to face down terrorists. Don Greene was a licensed pilot of single-engine planes. Garcia had been an air traffic controller for the National Guard. Many of the passengers and crew were athletically active. Flight attendant Lyles was a former police officer. Rich Guadagno worked for the U. S. Office of Fish and Wildlife and was trained in hand-to-hand combat. Linda Gronlund had a brown belt in karate. William Cashman was a former paratrooper with the 101st Airborne and an avid hiker. Alan Beaven was a former Scotland Yard prosecutor and a rock climber.

A few minutes before 10:00 A.M., passenger Ed Felt locked himself in the plane's restroom and called 9-1-1 from his cell phone. Felt reached the Westmoreland County emergency operations center and informed dispatcher Glenn Cramer that United Airlines Flight 93 had been hijacked.

RUSHING THE COCKPIT

As news of the crashes at the World Trade Center spread through the plane, the passengers of Flight 93 understood that theirs was no common hijacking. Messages from passengers and crew and the tapes of the flight's voice recordings indicate that Todd Beamer, Mark Bingham, Tom Burnett, and Jeremy Glick were the instigators of the plan to regain control of the plane and that they led the group in carrying out the attack. The four men were in their 30s and were big, athletic men, used to taking charge and reacting quickly. It is probable that Louis Nacke, a weightlifter, also had a significant role in the plan. Since he never contacted his family, Nacke's actions have not been as well documented as those of the others.

Lisa Jefferson, the GTC Airfone operator who was still on Todd Beamer's open line, heard him say "Jesus, help me" before saying to the others, "Are you ready? OK, let's roll!" Using a food cart as a battering

---

Tragic Ironies

RUTH CLIFFORD McCourt, 45, and Paige Farley Hackel were inseparable in life. On September 11, in a fluke of airline ticketing, they became inseparable in death. The best friends, along with McCourt's 4-year-old daughter, Juliana Valentine McCourt, planned to fly from Boston to Los Angeles together but could not get tickets on the same flight. Hackel boarded AMERICAN AIRLINES FLIGHT 11. McCourt and her daughter boarded United Airlines Flight 175. Barely an hour later, both jets crashed into the Twin Towers.

Ruth McCourt's brother, Ronnie Clifford, was in one of the towers and escaped before it crumbled to the ground. Their brother John Clifford, of Cork, Ireland, told Irish television "tragically, my sister hit the tower building as my brother was on the ground floor. He phoned to say he made it, he was okay, traumatized that he was within an inch of his life."

ram, the group lined up single file at the rear near the galley and began to push the cart the more than 100 feet to the cockpit with the force of their combined weights and strengths for momentum. For weapons, they carried whatever they could find—containers of boiling water, knives, forks, and fire extinguishers. The plane's voice recorder taped the hijackers shouting, "Get out of here! Get out of here!" Holding the phone that his daughter had handed him, Richard Makely, Glick's father-in-law, heard screams, and then total silence.

On the ground in Somerset County, Terry Butler noted the plane overhead was moving abnormally. Kelly Leverknight also observed United Airlines Flight 93 as it flew in the direction of the Shanksville-Stonycreek School, which her three children

Chronology of Events

8:01 A.M. Passengers board United Airlines Flight 93, but takeoff is delayed.

8:42 A.M. Flight 93 leaves Newark and heads for San Francisco, California.

9:24 A.M. Air traffic controllers alert the pilot to the possibility of hijackings. Dahl asks copilot Leroy Homer to confirm the validity of the report. He learns that bomb threats have been received in Cleveland and Boston.

9:27 A.M. The first news of the HIJACKING is passed on when Tom Burnett (see THOMAS E. BURNETT) calls his wife Deena in San Ramon, California, and asks her to call authorities.

9:28 A.M. Through the transmitter the hijackers have inadvertently left open, ground flight controllers hear screaming and scuffling as the hijackers enter the cockpit. At this time, Flight 93 is 35,000 feet over eastern Ohio.

9:28:40 A.M. Dahl and Homer are heard telling the hijackers to get out of the cockpit. It is later revealed that they were thrown out of the cockpit after being killed by the hijackers. Over the intercom, one of the hijackers orders the passengers to remain seated.

9:29 A.M. Tom Burnett calls his wife a second time. From her descriptions of events taking place in New York and Washington, Burnett recognizes the hijacking as a suicide mission.

9:36 A.M. Just above Cleveland, Ohio, Flight 93 turns left and is redirected toward Washington, D.C. A flight attendant reports the hijacking. Herndon Command Center alerts the Federal Aviation Administration (FAA) that Flight 93 is in the hands of hijackers. The plane does not respond to further communication from the ground.

9:37 A.M. JEREMY GLICK learns of events at the Twin Towers in New York City and passes the news to others on the plane.

9:41 A.M. The hijackers turn off the plane's transponders, disabling the tracking of Flight 93's movements.

9:54 A.M. Tom Burnett admits to his wife that he does not believe they will survive the hijacking but informs her that they have a plan to rush the hijackers as soon as they reach a rural area.

9:57 A.M. The voice recorder tape indicates that the revolt begins, and passengers are heard scuffling with the guard outside the cockpit. Someone says, "Let's get them." On the ground, the caddie master at the Laurel Valley Country Club in Ligonier, Pennsylvania, sees the plane wobble as it moves toward Shanksville.

9:58 A.M. TODD BEAMER tells GTC Airfone operator Lisa Jefferson that they are ready to carry out the attack.

attended. A biking couple, Michael and Amy Merringer, saw the plane and heard its motor gunning, followed by a loud explosion. The only witness to Flight 93's impact was Lee Purbaugh, who saw the plane pass overhead as he was working on a car. At 10:10 A.M., Flight 93 crashed into the ground near the small town of Shanksville, PENNSYLVANIA, approximately 20 flight-minutes from Washington, D.C. The field where the plane went down was an abandoned strip mine, so no buildings were in the immediate area. The Shanksville-Stonycreek Elementary School was only two miles away.

AFTER THE CRASH

When witnesses arrived at the scene, they found a crater 8 to 10 feet deep and 15 to 20 feet long. Some

The last thing she hears him say is "Let's roll." This rallying cry was picked up by the news media and used in a number of songs and MEMORIALS. The voice of Jarrah, the hijacker assumed to be piloting the plane, is heard telling a cohort to block the door. When the passengers continue their battering, Jarrah begins rolling the plane to throw them off balance.

10:00:03 A.M. Again, Jarrah stabilizes the airplane.

10:00:05 A.M. Now convinced that they will not be able to reach their target, the hijackers discuss whether they should "finish it off." As the sound of fighting continues to be heard outside the cockpit, Jarrah manipulates the nose of the plane up and down.

10:00:26 A.M. An unidentified passenger is heard saying, "In the cockpit. If we don't, we'll die."

10:00:42 A.M. A passenger, possibly Todd Beamer, is recorded saying, "Roll it!"

10:01 A.M. Jarrah restabilizes the plane. The hijackers agree to put it down and shout "Allah is the greatest."

10:03 A.M. Waiting on the phone, Robert Makely, Jeremy Glick's father-in-law, hears a silence, followed by a mechanical sound and screams. He listens to the ensuing silence for an hour before hanging up the phone. After recording loud thumps, crashes, shouts, screams, the sound of breaking glass, and finally the sound of wind, nothing more is heard on Flight 93's voice box recorder. On its way downward, Flight 93 rolls over on its back.

10:07 A.M. The Cleveland Center reports the hijacking of Flight 93 to the Northeast Air Defense Sector (NEADS).

10:10 A.M. United Flight 93 is driven into the ground near Shanksville, PENNSYLVANIA, at a speed of 580 miles per hour. There are no survivors.

10:15 A.M. Word reaches United Airlines and NEADS that Flight 93 crashed in rural Pennsylvania.

FAR LEFT *A United Airlines Boeing 757, the same model as Flight 93, prepares for takeoff.* BELOW *Evidence submitted in the Zacarias Moussaoui trial included this photo of the crash site. Recovery workers can be seen at the top of the photo, standing above the gaping hole.*

ABOVE *A U.S. Air Force B-52G Stratofortress with "Let's Roll" nose art, immortalizing the words of Todd Beamer as he and passengers foiled terrorist hijackers, bringing down the aircraft in a Pennsylvania field that fatal morning.*

trees had fallen, others were on fire. The smell of jet fuel was strong. Fragments of debris littered the ground and stuck to trees. Although hospitals in the tri-county area evacuated visitors and canceled elective surgeries to prepare for survivors, not one arrived. Both Newark and San Francisco International airports were evacuated, and a counseling team was assembled in San Francisco to meet with the families and friends of the passengers and crew of United Airlines Flight 93. Despite the loss of everyone on board, Flight 93 was the only plane hijacked on September 11 that did not incur casualties except those aboard the plane.

On Sunday, September 16, families and friends arrived in Shanksville. They drove through the area on chartered buses, saluted by officers and crowds lining the streets. Afterward, they visited a temporary altar made of hay bales and American flags where they were able to leave personal notes and other items of significance to loved ones. They could not get close to the crash site because hazardous materials experts were still combing the area. Lisa Beamer, the wife of TODD BEAMER, thought that the crater made by Flight 93 resembled a "large, bloated cross." A memorial service followed at a separate location and was attended by national and state dignitaries; First Lady Laura Bush spoke to the mourners.

Rumors persist that United Airlines Flight 93 was shot down, but the Air Force did not receive permission to shoot down unauthorized planes that refused to identify themselves until after Flight 93 crashed. In the days following the attack, it became clear that the passengers and crew had sacrificed their own lives so that Flight 93 would not be used as a fourth weapon on September 11.

MEMORIALS have included monuments and internet sites, foundations, scholarships, programs, books, songs, poems, movies, television shows, and documentaries (see FILMS OF SEPTEMBER 11). In April 2006, a controversial dramatization of the events of September 11 was released in cooperation with some family members. *United 93* was written and directed by Paul Greengrass. The name of Newark airport was changed to Newark Liberty International Airport.

On September 19, 2001, Senator Arlen Specter (R-PA) introduced a bill to posthumously award the passengers and crew of United Airlines Flight 93 the Congressional Gold Medal.

The True American Heroes Act received some bipartisan support before being referred to a House Committee, where it remained. Congress passed the Aviation and Transportation Security Act, which tightened AIRPORT SECURITY and required all baggage to be searched for explosives before it could be loaded onto planes. The act also created the Transportation Security Administration (TSA) in the Treasury Department and charged it with protection of all transportation systems. The TSA was moved to the DEPARTMENT OF HOMELAND SECURITY in March 2003.

Survivors of Flight 93's passengers and crew have received monetary compensation to ease the financial burdens of losing their loved ones. Many voluntary contributions went directly to surviving relatives, and United Airlines's insurance company paid $1.5 billion to be divided among the families of the victims. The federal VICTIM COMPENSATION FUND combined funds from government, corporate, and individual sources to allot payments to survivors based on potential earnings of lost family members. Twenty-five families of United Airlines Flight 93 victims accepted these funds, but others retained their right to sue.

Further Reading: Jon Barrett, *Hero of Flight 93: Mark Bingham: A Man Who Fought Back on September 11* (Alyson Publications, 2002); Lisa Beamer, *Let's Roll: Ordinary People, Extraordinary Courage* (Tyndale House, 2002); Steven Brill, *After: How America Confronted the September 12 Era* (Simon and Schuster, 2003); Tonya Buell, *The Crash of United Flight 93 on September 11, 2001* (Rosen, 2005); Lyz Glick and Dan Zegart, *Your Father's Voice: Letters for Emmy about Life with Jeremy— And without him after 9/11* (St. Martin's Press, 2005); Jerre Longman, *Among the Heroes: United Flight 93 And the Passengers and Crew Who Fought Back* (HarperCollins, 2002).

— **ELIZABETH PURDY, PH.D.**

United Airlines Flight 175

United Airlines Flight 175 departed Boston's Logan International Airport at 8:14 A.M. As Flight 175 took off, hijackers had already taken over AMERICAN AIRLINES FLIGHT 11, which had departed earlier. Captain Victor Saracini and First Officer Michael Horrocks piloted Flight 175, a Boeing 767 carrying seven flight attendants and 56 passengers, five of them hijackers. Marwan Alshehri, Fayez Ahmed Banihammad, Mohand Alshehri, Ahmed Alghamdi, and Hamza Alghamdi were prepared to take over the plane.

Pilot Saracini, 51, had been a Navy fighter pilot in Vietnam, and routinely flown Boeing 767s during his 16 years as a commercial pilot. Saracini and his wife Ellen and children Kirsten and Brielle had moved to Lower Makefield, Pennsylvania, in the mid 1990s. Copilot Horrocks, 38, a retired Marine, had been a pilot instructor in a Fixed Wing Instructor Training Unit. Residents of Glen Mills, Pennsylvania, Michael and Miriam Horrocks had two children, a son in first grade and daughter in fourth grade. Miriam was a physical education teacher at a nearby grade school.

Seven flight attendants were on Flight 175. Robert John Fangman had been a salesman for Verizon Wireless. His favorite part of that job was the travel, so he took a pay cut to join United Airlines as a flight attendant, and often took last minute assignments to Europe.

Amy Jarrett, 28, of North Smithfield, Rhode Island, was the third of four children. Her father, attorney Aram Jarret, said, "I don't know what happened up there, but she would have been one of those people trying to do the right thing."

Kathryn LaBorie, 42, worked only two routes, one to Los Angeles and one to San Francisco. She attended the University of Colorado at Colorado Springs, and later won a scholarship to the University of Denver. Her family included her husband of two years, Eric, her parents, and two brothers, Mark and Kevin. She had worked for United Airlines for almost seven years.

Alfred G. "Al" Marchand, 44, had been a police officer in Alamogordo, New Mexico, for over 20 years when he retired and started a new career with United Airlines. He planned to become a pilot. He had a wife, Rebecca; his mother Irene died on December 12, 2001 of what her priest called "a broken heart."

Michael Tarrou, 38, and Amy King, 29, were together as flight attendants and as a couple. Michael grew up in Wantagh, New York, and Amy in Jamestown, New York. Both moved to Stafford Springs where they met as flight attendants. His ex-wife and 11-year-old daughter Gina had recently moved to Florida, and his mother lived in Clearwater. Michael and Amy had hoped to move to Florida to be near his family.

Alicia Titus, 28, earned a B.A. in international marketing from Miami University, then left her job at Netcentives in 2000 to become a flight attendant. She had been working for United Airlines for just nine months, but had already visited Paris, Hawaii, Morocco, and Spain.

There were 56 passengers aboard Flight 175 (see APPENDIX for a complete list of passengers and crew). Alona Abraham, 30, had stayed with a college friend in Boston on her first trip to the United States. The oldest of three children of Israeli immigrants from Bombay, Alona worked as an industrial engineer. Traveling to America had been a dream, and she had remarked that for a few weeks, she would escape the bombings in Israel.

Garnet Bailey, his wife, Katherine, and their son Todd, 23, lived in Lynnfield, Massachusetts. Bailey played eleven seasons in the National Hockey League and scouted for 20 years, garnering seven Stanley Cup rings. Since 1994, he had directed pro scouting for the Los Angeles Kings.

Mark Bavis, 32, a hockey scout, was flying to the Los Angeles Kings training camp to check on players he had advised the team to draft. Mark had starred for the Boston University Terriers from 1990 to 1993.

Graham Berkeley, 37, was director of e-commerce solutions for the Compuware Corporation and a classical violinist. A Briton, he had lived in the United States for 10 years. The green card that would secure him resident status came in June 2001, and Graham had started making plans to move to New York City from Boston.

Dorothy DeAraujo nurtured an artistic yearning from her childhood in Depression-era Chicago, where she studied nights at the Art Institute of Chicago. After 20 years as an executive administrative assistant at California State University, Long Beach, at age 69, Dorothy earned a B.A. in Fine Art. At age 80, she drew pen and ink postcards of Naples' Italian-style canals and had a budding art business in a studio above her garage.

A sonar expert on a Navy destroyer during World War II, the Rev. Francis E. Grogan, 76, spent the rest of his life as a chaplain, teacher, and a parish priest. Father Grogan was the head of the Holy Cross Residence in North Dartmouth, Massachusetts. On September 11, he was off to visit his sister in California.

THE HIJACKERS ATTACK

By 8:33, the jet had reached its cruising altitude of 31,000 feet. At 8:37, the crew received a call from a controller asking whether the pilots could see the earlier American Airlines flight. One of the pilots said that they did see AMERICAN AIRLINES FLIGHT 11, at about 28,000 feet. The controller told the crew to make a right turn to avoid the American Airlines plane.

At 8:41, just four minutes before American Airlines Flight 11 slammed into the North Tower of the World Trade Center, one of the United Airlines Flight 175 pilots reported a suspicious transmission:

ABOVE *United Airlines Flight 175 is caught a moment before impacting the South Tower of the World Trade Center. The airliner was traveling at nearly 500 miles per hour when it hit the building.*

"B-O-S. Sounds like someone keyed the mike and said, 'Everyone, stay in your seats.'" This was Flight 175's last communication with the ground.

The hijackers attacked the crew and passengers between 8:42 and 8:46. Two passengers and a flight attendant reported that the hijackers used knives. Another passenger said they used mace and the threat of a bomb, and a second flight attendant said that both pilots had been killed. Flight 175 veered from its course and made a U-turn north, heading for New York City.

At 8:47, Flight 175 changed its beacon codes twice within a minute, an indication that something irregular was happening. At 8:51, it deviated from its assigned altitude, and New York air traffic controllers were unable to contact the crew after 8:52 A.M.

At 8:52, in Easton, Connecticut, Lee Hanson received a phone call from his son Peter, a passenger on United Airlines Flight 175. Peter said, "I think they've taken over the cockpit...an attendant has been stabbed and someone else up front may have been killed. The plane is making strange moves. Call United Airlines. Tell them it's Flight 175, Boston to LA." Lee Hanson called the Easton Police Department.

At 8:59, passenger Brian David Sweeney left a message for his wife Julie that the plane had been hijacked, and then called his mother, Louise Sweeney. He told her the passengers were thinking about storming the cockpit to take control of the plane.

At 9:00, Lee Hanson received a second call from Peter: "It's getting bad, Dad...A stewardess was stabbed...They seem to have knives and mace— They said they have a bomb—It's getting very bad on the plane—Passengers are throwing up and getting sick—The plane is making jerky movements—I don't think the pilot is flying the plane—I think we are going down—I think they intend to go to Chicago or someplace and fly into a building—Don't worry, Dad—If it happens, it'll be very fast—My God, my God."

The call ended abruptly. Just before it cut off, Lee Hanson heard a woman scream. He turned on the television, and in her home, so did Louise Sweeney. Both saw the airplane hit the South Tower of the World Trade Center at 9:03:11.

Further Reading: David Ray Griffin, *The 9/11 Commission Report: Omissions and Distortions* (Interlink Publishing Group, 2005); Roland

Jacquard, *In the Name of Osama Bin Laden* (Duke University Press, 2002); *Life* Magazine, *One Nation: America Remembers September 11, 2001* (Little, Brown, 2001); "Pentagon Crash Eyewitness Comforted Victims," MDW News Service (September 28, 2001).

— **KATHY WARNES**

U.S. Reaction

Americanairspace remained closed to all commercial air traffic for four days. Landmark buildings like the Seattle Space Needle were temporarily closed. Schools canceled classes. All major sporting events were canceled. All Hollywood studios ceased production, as did filming on most television shows. The Emmy Awards were postponed for the first time in their 52-year history. The stock market did not reopen until September 17.

Americans flocked to houses of worship, joined in candlelight vigils, wrote messages of condolence, gave donations to the Red Cross, and tried to figure out what to tell their children. Most of all, they watched television. There was little escape from the MEDIA COVERAGE; all major broadcast and cable news networks stayed on the story for almost four days without a break, and expanded coverage continued for months longer. Home shopping networks and some entertainment channels went dark in those first days; several sports channels turned over to news. Networks had to make choices about what images to show. ABC and MSNBC, for example, quickly decided not to show any footage of people jumping or falling from the towers.

POWERFUL IMAGES

But Americans saw the dramatic video of AMERICAN AIRLINES FLIGHT 11 slamming into the World Trade Center, over and over, for days. On September 19, ABC News president David Westin announced that ABC would use the video only in rare circumstances. "I was concerned that it was becoming almost like wallpaper," Westin said of his decision. "There's a temptation in television to always go to the most powerful image. But it was playing a lot. I was concerned not only for adults but for children."

Newspapers had to make similar decisions about photographs. The New York *Daily News* ran a close-up of a severed hand, and made no apologies. "You can't do the story without doing the story," said one of the editors. "It's no time to be squeamish." Nevertheless, there was an increasing restraint over the use of graphic images. Associated Press photographer Richard Drew began September 11 with an assignment to photograph a maternity fashion show in Bryant Park. Instead, at 9:41 A.M., he snapped a picture of a man falling from the upper floors of the North Tower. In that instant, the man appeared to be flying, his body vertical to the Trade Center's walls, arms held back against his body, one leg slightly bent at the knee. It was an eerily beautiful photograph that inspired thoughts about the nature of human life and death, and it ran in hundreds of newspapers in the first few days. Then it all but vanished, suddenly deemed exploitative and voyeuristic.

Drew's photo and hundreds like it moved to the internet. So many people were seeking information in the first hours after the attacks that most major news sites crashed. CNN.com, averaging 14 million hits a day, zoomed up to 9 million hits per hour. It took the better part of the day for Web sites and internet service providers to bring extra servers online to handle the increased traffic. Hastily created "survivor bulletin boards" were quickly overwhelmed by people looking for names of missing friends and loved ones. The popular auction site eBay quickly announced that it would not allow anyone to sell "memorabilia" from the attacks.

Internet chat rooms and talk-radio programs filled with people who wanted to share their grief and sorrow—and, more often, their rage and their suspicions. A caller to a Denver radio program said: "It's time for a little schoolyard justice…Put the geographers on notice. We need to rearrange the map." He was typical of thousands of Americans who believed that the best thing to do was to retaliate with overwhelming force. Some Americans believed that the government either had prior warning or was somehow complicit in the attacks. CONSPIRACY THEORIES became so prevalent that President GEORGE W. BUSH mentioned them in his November 2001 address to the United Nations, calling them "outrageous" and denouncing them as an "attempt to shift the blame away from the terrorists."

OUT OF CONTROL

The rage, in a few cases, was directed at U.S. Muslims. The Federal Bureau of Investigation later announced that hate crimes against Muslims rose 34 percent in the months following September 11. Human Rights Watch said the figure was closer to a 1,700 percent increase. Arab-Americans reported being harassed, spat on, and threatened. Molotov cocktails were tossed at several mosques, and Arab-owned stores experienced an increase in vandalism.

There were even some fatalities. On September 15, a Sikh man named Balbir Singh Sodhi was killed outside a gas station in Mesa, Arizona, by a man who had spent the previous night in a Phoenix bar

AT LEFT *Shock and fear expressed in the faces of New Yorkers near the scene of the World Trade Center attack.* **ABOVE** *A woman in tears among the ambulances and rescue workers on the scene.*

ABOVE *Citizens of Hoboken, New Jersey, face the scene of the terrorist attack across the Hudson River. They hold American flags in a memorial service for the victims of the attacks.*

talking about how he was going to "kill the ragheads responsible for September 11." Mark Stroman, a Texan who killed Pakistani Waqar Hasan in Dallas and another man named Vasudev Patel in Mesquite, Texas, announced after his arrest: "I did what every American wanted to do after September 11th but didn't have the nerve." As many as five others may have died in similar hate crimes across the country.

Americans began to look for ways to show their PATRIOTISM when, in October 2001, the United States announced that it would begin military action against the Taliban in Afghanistan. Wal-Mart announced that sales of American flags rose 1,800 percent in the first few days after the attacks. People put bumper stickers on their cars, flags on their mailboxes, caps, sweatshirts, and front porches. Store owners put flags in their windows and made shopping a patriotic activity. Country star Alan Jackson and rock star Bruce Springsteen were among the recording artists who put their feelings to music.

The popular view was that the world changed on September 11 and nothing would ever be the same. However, some aspects of life continued as before. While the economy did not flourish, neither did it collapse. The borders were not closed. Air travel resumed with increased security (see AIRPORT SECURITY).

Other things did change, mostly in the relationship between the Bush administration and U.S. citizens. In the post–September 11 political environment, it was easy to pass laws that could later appear to violate civil liberties. Repeated statements by the new DEPARTMENT OF HOMELAND SECURITY regarding potential attacks frequently seemed to coincide with criticism of the Bush administration.

After a time, when further attacks failed to materialize, some people began to feel that the government was using the terror issue to push its own political agenda. Perhaps because of this, a Scripps Howard-Ohio University poll taken in August 2006 found that 36 percent of Americans believed it "very likely" or "somewhat likely" that federal officials allowed the attacks to occur because "they wanted the United States to go to war in the Middle East."

One of the biggest fears in the days following September 11 was of widespread mental health problems. In the fall of 2006, as the nation prepared for the five-year anniversary of the attacks, researchers announced that while there was an initial spike in reports of post-traumatic stress disorder (PTSD) in the first few weeks, the emotional fallout peaked after the first six months.

End of Illusion

BY ROBERT J. Samuelson, *Washington Post*, September 12, 2001: "What was destroyed yesterday was not just the World Trade Center and part of the Pentagon but also Americans' serenity and sense of security. Watching the horror on television, anyone will find it hard to go about everyday routines without being haunted by the fear that something awful could happen at any time and in almost any place. This was, in a symbolic and psychological sense, the end of the 1990s. Ever since the close of the Cold War, Americans have lived in an almost dreamlike condition, gloating over our global triumph, relishing our role as the world's 'sole surviving superpower,' savoring an ever-improving prosperity and feeling insulated from the rest of the world's hatreds, feuds and conflicts.

"It will no longer be possible to maintain the illusion of invulnerability, and the change in attitudes and assumptions will have profound effects—just what, no one can possibly yet say—on our politics, foreign policy and our concept of who we are as a people. For much of the past decade, Americans have heard and read warnings about the dangers of terrorism and about how many global threats are no longer easily deterred by conventional military might. But these cautions have always had a seductively abstract quality. When we watched the rest of the world's ethnic, religious and national struggles disintegrate into unending violence—in the Balkans, the Middle East and Africa—we consoled ourselves with how far away and un-American they were. Our minds may have told us how easily comparable threats might travel to New York, Washington, Dallas or Los Angeles. But in our hearts, we felt removed and protected.... How we respond to this new fear will take our measure as a people."

Further Reading: Marjorie Agosin and Betty Jean Craige, eds., *To Mend the World: Women Reflect on 9/11* (White Pine Press, 2002); Noam Chomsky and David Barsamian, *Imperial Ambitions: Conversations with Noam Chomsky on the Post-9/11 World* (Henry Holt, 2005); Congressional Research Service Library, *Economic Effects of 9/11: A Retrospective Assessment* (University Press of the Pacific, 2005); Mary L. Dudziak, *September 11 in History: A Watershed Moment?* (Duke University Press, 2003).

— HEATHER K. MICHON

USA Patriot Act

After September 11, the GEORGE W. BUSH administration demanded and received sweeping changes that allowed federal officials to have a free rein in investigating, arresting, and holding individuals identified as possible threats to the United States. A mere 45 days after the attacks, Congress passed the USA Patriot Act by a vote of 98–1 in the Senate and 357–66 in the House of Representatives. The following day, October 26, 2001, Bush signed the bill into law, giving the executive branch the right to put aside Constitutional protections for those suspected of committing crimes ranging from terrorist activity to giving money—even unwittingly–to charities suspected of funding terrorists.

Supporters of the antiterrorism bill gave it a name that silenced protest before it began. The "Uniting and Strengthening America by Providing Appropriate Tools Required to Intercept and Obstruct Terrorism" (USA Patriot) Act was designed to prevent such tragedies as September 11 from ever happening again.

The act defined terrorism as activities designed to affect government policy through threats to human life, including intimidation, coercion, mass destruction, assassination, and kidnapping. Of the more than 1,000 measures included in the act, 16 provisions deemed the most controversial were classified as "sunset provisions" and set to expire on December 31, 2005. Congress was to have the option of removing or revising the provisions or, as the Bush administration hoped, making them permanent.

Under the USA Patriot Act, the federal government was given the right to wiretap all telephone lines of a suspect and to extend the tap to the telephone lines of any individual, group, or business with which the suspect maintained regular contact. Officials were also allowed to intercept e-mails, tap into computers, and search homes and offices without individuals being informed of such actions until after the fact. Search warrants could be obtained from a special federal court, bypassing judges who traditionally handled such procedures. In cases when judges were used, federal agents were allowed to choose members of the bench who were sympathetic to such actions. Discarding traditional requirements that a warrant be obtained for each telephone tapped, the new search warrants allowed for nationwide roving wiretaps.

In general, both the media and the grieving nation assumed that the provisions of the USA Patriot Act were necessary tools for fighting terrorism. Over time, however, protests surfaced as the enormity of the powers granted in the USA Patriot Act became evident. By the beginning of 2006, the U.S. government had admittedly detained over 1,200 people for extended periods. Only four of the detainees were officially charged, and two were acquitted. Georgetown University law professor and civil rights lawyer David Cole has insisted that a close examination of government records indicates that the number detained is closer to 5,000.

Amid the protests, the states of Alaska, Hawaii, and Vermont passed resolutions against compliance with the USA Patriot Act. 140 cities and

ABOVE *Protests were heard from the American public, including this protester seen at an anarchist rally on the final day of the Democratic National Convention, July 29, 2004, in Boston, Massachusetts. The demonstrators were protesing against both President Bush and presidential candidate John Kerry.*

counties that run the gamut from liberal Ann Arbor, Michigan, to conservative Oklahoma City, have joined them. Librarians in Berkeley, California, have begun regularly erasing internet histories and lists of books checked out to avoid their being subpoenaed by the government. The business community has also issued substantial protest to the USA Patriot Act, objecting to violations of privacy and arguing that the cost of complying with the act has created massive problems that could become even more extensive if individuals affected by the act sue in other countries, where the right to privacy is more stringently protected.

The American Medical Association (AMA) has resolved to protect patients' rights to privacy by refusing to release medical records. Protests against the USA Patriot Act have risen from both sides of the political spectrum, with groups such as the left-wing American Civil Liberties Union (ACLU) join-ing arch-conservatives such as Georgia Republican Bob Barr, a former member of Congress and the en-gineer of the movement to impeach Bill Clinton, and the Eagle Forum, founded by antifeminist Phyl-lis Schlafly, in calling for major revisions in the act.

Many have also voiced concern about the lack of Congressional and judicial oversight of executive activities. Even Congressman James Sensenbrenner (R-WI), a strong Bush supporter, has accused offi-cials of withholding details about how often and under what circumstances provisions of the USA Patriot Act have been implemented. By applying to a special court created under the Federal Intelli-gence Surveillance Act (FISA), the government can expedite intelligence-gathering procedures. Crit-ics charge that the FISA court has become a rubber stamp for the Bush administration.

In February 2006, Attorney General Alberto Gonzales admitted that between 2004 and 2005 the number of foreign intelligence warrants rose 18 per-cent. That same month, Senator Arlen Specter (R-PA) announced plans to introduce a bill that would establish strict guidelines for FISA to use in approv-ing intelligence operations.

In November 2005, a three-judge panel of the U. S. Court of Appeals for the Second Circuit in Man-hattan heard the case *Doe v. Gonzales* in which the American Civil Liberties Union and a Connecti-cut library consortium challenged provisions of the USA Patriot Act that allowed the government to sub-poena library and internet records and prohibited the groups from notifying those named in the sub-poena. While the court ruled that the gag order vi-olated the First Amendment and that such searches were unreasonable under the Fourth Amendment, the Bush administration won the right to stay im-plementation while appealing the decision.

With the extension of the USA Patriot Act set to run out in March 2006, Republicans began work-ing to derail the controversy and to comply with Bush's desire to make the sunset provisions of the act permanent. The controversy led Republican op-ponents of the measure to join Democratic oppo-nents in filibustering the bill in late 2005. After a meeting with key administrative officials on Feb-ruary 9, 2006, the four Republicans and two Dem-ocrats most opposed to the changes agreed to sup-port a compromised version.

On March 2, the Senate passed a revised version of the USA Patriot Act 89–10, with 34 Democrats joining the 55 Republicans in supporting the move to make all but two of the 16 provisions of the act permanent. The House followed suit on March 7, passing the bill 280–138 and rushing it to the presi-dent for signing.

The compromises gave subpoena recipients the right to challenge judicial gag orders after a year and prevented the government from forcing them to re-veal the names of lawyers consulted in such cases. However, the compromises did not prevent the gov-ernment from continuing to demand that internet service providers furnish internet histories for pa-trons targeted by the government. Critics of the USA Patriot Act continued to object to the disregard of civil liberties and began writing legislation to amend controversial portions of the compromise bill.

Further Reading: Steven Brill, *After: How America Confronted the Sep-tember 12 Era* (Simon and Schuster, 2003); Ann Fagan Ginger, *Challeng-ing United States Human Rights Violations Since September 11* (Pro-metheus Books, 2005); Eric Lichtblau and James Risen, "Top Aide De-fends Domestic Spying," *New York Times* (February 6, 2006); Declan McCullagh, "White House Discloses Details on Surveillance," *New York Times* (February 9, 2006); Christian Parenti, *The Soft Cage: Surveillance in America from Slavery to the War on Terror* (Basic Books, 2003).

— ELIZABETH PURDY, PH.D.

V

Victim Compensation Fund

The September 11 Victim Compensation Fund (VCF) was created by the Air Transportation Safety and System Stabilization Act, signed into law by President GEORGE W. BUSH on September 22, 2001. The urgency for the bill was the financial difficulties of the airline industry, which was in poor economic condition before September 11 and suffered significant financial losses from the suspension of air travel immediately following the attacks. Airline executives claimed that unless they were protected from the threat of LAWSUITS they would be unable to obtain insurance and their companies would be forced to cease operation. The VCF sought to forestall lawsuits against the airlines by offering compensation for the victims and their families, while requiring them in return to give up their right to sue the airlines.

There were many controversies in the administration of the VCF, probably inevitable given the unprecedented nature of both the events of September 11 and of the fund itself. On the whole, however, the VCF was a success. Ninety-seven percent of the victims received compensation from the fund, and only 70 chose to pursue individual lawsuits. The VCF distributed over $7 billion to victims; the average award was more than $2 million for deceased victims and $400,000 for injured victims. The VCF's operations withstood legal challenges also: a lawsuit filed by some victims' families in January 2003, claiming that the disbursement rulings were improper in

Memorials filled the streets, as victims' families struggled to deal with tragic loss. **ABOVE LEFT** A photo of the World Trade Center in its former glory amid candles and a teddy bear. **ABOVE RIGHT** A section of the Ground Zero memorial in New York City, dedicated to the victims of United Airlines Flight 93. **AT RIGHT** A display for victims at the University of California San Diego's student center.

a number of ways and discriminated against those at the highest income levels, was rejected by both district and appellate courts.

Because the VCF was intended to replace the tort system in which a citizen may sue for damages based on projected future earnings, awards to individual victims varied widely depending on current income and age and individual circumstances such as number of children. This was probably the most controversial aspect of the VCF. Special Master Kenneth R. Feinberg, who administered the fund, has stated that if he were faced with the same situation again he might recommend that an equal amount be paid

to every victim. However, the law that created the VCF required that projected earnings be a factor in determining compensation amounts—establishing a uniform level of award still requires that someone set a dollar amount as the value of a human life or injury. Another controversial factor was the requirement that any collateral awards received by an individual or his heirs, such as the benefit from a life insurance policy, be deducted from the amount paid by the VCF.

Feinberg made two decisions that allowed the benefits of the VCF to reach several classes of people often excluded from the protection of the law. The first were undocumented workers: he extracted an agreement from the Immigration and Naturalization Service that any information collected in processing VCF claims would not be used against the people providing it. The second were domestic partners of victims, including gay and lesbian partners: they were granted the same right to apply for compensation as married partners, and if the claim was disputed by the victim's family Feinberg decided each case on its individual merits.

The VCF was the first time the U.S. government made payments to American victims of terrorist acts, although similar payments had been made, for instance, to the Chinese citizens who were killed when the United States mistakenly bombed the Chinese embassy in Serbia. In the wake of the VCF, families of some American victims of other terrorist acts such as the 1993 World Trade Center bombing, the Oklahoma City bombing, and the bombing of the U.S. embassy in Nairobi in 1998 (see EMBASSY BOMBINGS) have stated that they should be compensated in a similar manner. This is a legal and philosophical issue that ignores the historical and economic context in which the VCF was created: its primary purpose was to keep the U.S. airline industry in operation. Feinberg has argued against establishing a fund to compensate victims of other terrorist acts, not because the victims of one attack are more or less worthy than those of another but because the effects of the events of September 11 were unprecedented.

Further Reading: Lisa Belkin, "Just Money," *New York Times* (December 8, 2002); Kenneth R. Feinberg, "Final Report of the Special Master for the September 11 Victim Compensation Fund of 2001," www.usdoj. gov/final_report.pdf (cited April 2006); Kenneth R. Feinberg, *What is Life Worth? The Unprecedented Effort to Compensate the Victims of 9/11* (Public Affairs, 2005).

— SARAH BOSLAUGH, PH.D.

Kenneth R. Feinberg

ON NOVEMBER 26, 2001, Kenneth R. Feinberg was appointed by Attorney General John Ashcroft as the special master of the September 11 Victim Compensation Fund. In this capacity Feinberg assumed the unprecedented task of administering all aspects of a program in which unlimited U.S. government funds were available to compensate American victims of a terrorist act, and very few guidelines were provided for deciding how much money an individual should receive.

Feinberg served 33 months in this capacity without pay, administering all aspects of the program, including developing regulations governing the program, evaluating applications, determining compensation, and disbursing awards. He was uniquely qualified to serve as special master, as he pioneered this aspect of legal practice. Feinberg's first experience as special master was in the 1984 Agent Orange trial, and he subsequently acted in a similar capacity in other high-profile cases including those involving the fair market value of the Zapruder film of the John F. Kennedy assassination, the legal fees in the Holocaust slave labor litigation, and liability lawsuits for a number of products including asbestos, DES, and the Dalkon Shield.

W

War on Terror

Shortly after the September 11 attacks, the United States declared the Global War on Terror, with the objective of fighting terrorist groups worldwide. The focus was and continues to be on jihadist groups, particularly AL-QAEDA. The U.S. national strategy for combating terrorism and related documents were released in October 2003.

The key conclusion of the strategy is that the United States and its allies will "not triumph solely or even primarily through military might. We must fight terrorist networks and all those who support their efforts to spread fear around the world using every instrument of national power—diplomatic, economic, law enforcement, financial, information, intelligence, and military."

The strategy has become known as the 4D plan: defeat terrorist groups; deny terrorists sanctuary; diminish support for terrorist groups; defend the United States from terrorist attacks.

The goals define victory as the creation of a world in which "our children can live free from fear and where the threat of terrorist attacks does not define our daily lives." The strategy aims to reduce the scope and capability of terrorist organizations to the criminal domain, in which terrorist groups are localized, unorganized, non-state-sponsored, and rare.

The strategy emphasizes working with willing and able states against terrorist groups; enabling weak states to improve their capabilities against terrorism; persuading reluctant states to support a COUNTER-

FIGHTING BACK *U.S. Army soldiers search for terrorists and weapons caches in the Al Jazeera Desert area of Iraq.*

TERRORISM coalition; and compelling unwilling governments to stop their support for terrorism.

Once the United States labeled its campaign against terrorism as a "war," it was inevitable that the most critical components would be led by the Defense Department. Many of the activities called for in the Defense Department strategy for the War on Terror are far removed from normal military operations, including specialized INTELLIGENCE activities and what is officially called "countering ideological support for terrorism." This involves trying to separate the most radical terrorist group members from potential supporters by using propaganda, psychological operations, humanitarian assistance projects, and information operations. Specialized National Guard units are responsible for the response to weapons of mass destruction. Most of these nontraditional missions require close cooperation between the military and civilian agencies. Given earlier interagency coordination problems within the U.S. government, how well these difficulties are resolved is critical in determining how well the strategy works.

Considerable emphasis has been placed on military-to-military contacts through joint training exercises, training of other countries' armed forces, and joint operations. In part, this emphasis on multinational training and operations has been to help other countries improve their security situation. More importantly, the United States does not have enough troops or resources to achieve all the missions required, and there is the consideration of the internal impact of stationing U.S. troops in foreign countries.

U.S. strategy also calls for American troops to conduct unilateral operations when necessary or operationally useful. Many of the military missions required by counterterrorism activities are best suited for Special Operations Forces such as Special Forces, Delta, or SEALs. These specialized forces are in short supply, and major increases both difficult and time-consuming. As a result, conventional forces must become more proficient at these roles. Much of the underlying rationale for multilateral and unilateral efforts is to keep terrorist groups off balance and deny them sanctuary in particular areas. To do this effectively with finite forces, accurate and fast intelligence is critical. For the War on Terror to succeed in the long term, intelligence, security forces, and the military require unparalleled cooperation.

The best-known campaign in the U.S. War on Terror has been AFGHANISTAN. Although the U.S. government has included the ongoing operations in IRAQ as a component of the War on Terror, there has been considerable controversy over whether the Iraq War is an integral part of the campaign. The United States has been actively engaged in several

ABOVE *U.S. Army soldiers offload from a CH-47 Chinook helicopter to secure the landing zone located in the mountains of Afghanistan, the best-known campaign in the U.S. War on Terror.*

United Nations and Counterterrorism

THERE HAVE been problems in gaining an international consensus on terrorism within the UN, given the multiplicity of political views and diplomatic crosscurrents. At the same time, the UN has made progress in providing legal tools for counterterrorism.

The UN has adopted 12 international legal instruments for responding to terrorism and related criminal activities. Sixty-three countries have adopted all 12 instruments, with more adopting at least some of them. All these instruments provide specific criminal offense descriptions; require the countries that accept them to incorporate these offenses into domestic laws; and provide for extradition for these crimes.

The protocols are: Offenses and Certain Other Acts Committed on Board an Aircraft (1963); Unlawful Seizure of Aircraft (1970); Unlawful Acts Against the Safety of Civil Aviation (1971); Unlawful Acts of Violence at Airports Serving International Civil Aviation (1988); Physical Protection of Nuclear Material (1979); Marking of Plastic Explosives for the Purpose of Detection (1991); Suppression of Terrorist Bombings (1997); Prevention and Punishment of Crimes against International Persons, Including Diplomatic Agents (1973); Taking of Hostages (1979); Suppression of Unlawful Acts against the Safety of Maritime Navigation (1988); Unlawful Acts against the Safety of Fixed Platforms Located on the Continental Shelf (1988); and Suppression of the Financing of Terrorism (1999).

The UN Security Council also passed declarations and resolutions concerning terrorism, and the UN Secretariat has established a Counterterrorism Committee. What has not been successfully resolved, however, is an agreed-upon definition of terrorism. The secretary-general proposed the following definition two years ago: in addition to those already proscribed, acts "intended to cause death or serious bodily harm to civilians or non-combatants with the purpose of intimidating a population or compelling a Government or an international organization to do or abstain from doing any act." As of 2006, this definition has not been formally adopted by the UN member states.

other areas, including the Horn of Africa, the Sahel region of Africa, and the Philippines.

In the Horn of Africa—including Djibouti, Somalia, Ethiopia, Eritrea, and bordering Kenya—Joint Task Force Horn of Africa (JTF-HOA) has been conducting operations since December 2002. JTF-HOA, headquartered in Djibouti, has various civil affairs and civic action missions as primary goals. The underlying rationale is to address some of the critical problems in the region before they escalate into extremism or violence. Since their area of operations includes Somalia, which many experts consider a failed state, prevention of further regional unrest remains a critical mission.

In the Sahel region—Algeria, Mali, Niger, and Chad—the United States has deployed forces as trainers and advisors to local armies in an effort to preclude the growth of small terrorist groups and to improve counterterrorism coordination. These training programs started on a small scale with the Pan Sahel Initiative, but significantly greater resources were being devoted in the mid-2000s to the Trans Sahara Counterterrorism Initiative. Likewise, in the Philippines, the United States has been involved in regular COUNTERTERRORISM training and advising exercises with the Philippine military.

U.S. forces continue to be deployed globally to assist other countries and in some cases to conduct unilateral operations.

Further Reading: Richard A. Clarke, *Against All Enemies: Inside America's War on Terror* (Free Press, 2004); Mary Habeck, *Knowing the Enemy: Jihadist Ideology and the War on Terror* (Yale University Press, 2006); Ronald Kessler, *The CIA at War: Inside the Secret Campaign Against Terror* (St. Martin's, 2004); Gary Schroen, *First In: An Insider's Account of How the CIA Spearheaded the War on Terror in Afghanistan* (Presidio Press, 2005).

— LAWRENCE E. CLINE, PH.D.

Washington, D.C.

When AMERICAN AIRLINES FLIGHT 77 hit the Pentagon, members of Congress reported hearing an explosion and some believed that a helicopter had blown up. Witnesses stated that it became eerily quiet as onlookers reacted with shock. Around the city, various officials, including Vice President RICHARD B. CHENEY, were already glued to television sets watching events unfold in New York.

As word of the crash at the PENTAGON spread, security forces took action. Government offices were evacuated, and First Lady Laura Bush, the vice president and his wife, and the national security staff were taken to bunkers beneath the White House designed to withstand nuclear attacks. The president's daughters were removed to safe locations at their schools. Other high-ranking government officials, including those in the line of presidential succession–Speaker of the House Dennis Hastert and President Pro Tempore of the Senate Robert Byrd–were relocated to safe

Rescuers

LIEUTENANT GENERAL Paul K. Carlton, Jr., the surgeon general of the Air Force, was in the PENTAGON on the morning of September 11 for a meeting with the Air Force chief of staff. When Carlton arrived outside the crash site, he saw the landing gear of AMERICAN AIRLINES FLIGHT 77 on the ground and realized there would be a large number of casualties. He organized an assembly line of rescuers with the intention of reaching those trapped inside the building and sending those in need of medical attention to the triage area that had been set up outside the Pentagon.

When Carlton realized that rescuers were having trouble breathing, he commandeered T-shirts to be soaked in water and used as respiratory filters. The heat was so intense that some rescuers became dehydrated and had to be sent to local hospitals for treatment. About 70 rescuers required emergency treatment, including an injured Virginia state trooper who was taken to Inova Alexandria Hospital in serious condition. Whenever rescuers were overcome, others moved up the line to take their places; rescuers of all ranks and services worked together to carry out rescue activities.

houses equipped with secure telephone lines, under the protection of the Secret Service.

Expecting additional attacks, the Situation Room at the White House swung into full operation. Fort Detrick, Maryland, where the army's germ warfare defense laboratory is located, immediately tightened security. All military personnel were placed on full alert, appearing on the streets of Washington carrying M-16s. Secret Service officers with automatic weapons patrolled Lafayette Park. As government employees and visitors left buildings, they were instructed to run as far and as fast as they could. Women in high heels were advised to remove them to speed progress.

Some day care workers forced to evacuate stood on street corners with frightened toddlers. Others gathered in grassy areas where children played, oblivious to the events. Government officials instructed their families not to drink city water for the next 36 hours because of possible contamination by terrorists.

As cell phone systems overloaded and failed, Washington's residents lined up at pay phones to let families and friends know they were unhurt but unable to leave the city. Wherever transistor radios were available, crowds gathered to listen to the news. Over the next hour, the streets of Washington became gridlocked with outgoing vehicles. The Fourteenth Street and Arlington Memorial bridges were closed, along with Union Station, shutting down rail transit. At the naval complex on Hampton Roads in Virginia, security was increased, and the governor instituted a lockdown of all state government offices. By nightfall, about 100 people congregated on Arlington Hill with cameras and tripods to document a city in crisis.

GOVERNMENT REACTION

Rumors abounded. Rescue workers were withdrawn from the Pentagon on three occasions in response to announcements that incoming hijacked planes had been spotted. False reports circulated that the State Department had been bombed, the Capitol Building attacked, and the Mall set aflame. In an unprecedented move, the Federal Aviation Administration grounded planes across the country, and all incoming international flights were rerouted The only planes arriving in Washington were military aircraft, and concern spread about the possibility of the military being forced to shoot down rogue passenger planes. When Attorney General John Ashcroft's plane returned to Washington from

BELOW *The U.S. Capitol building in Washington, D.C.*

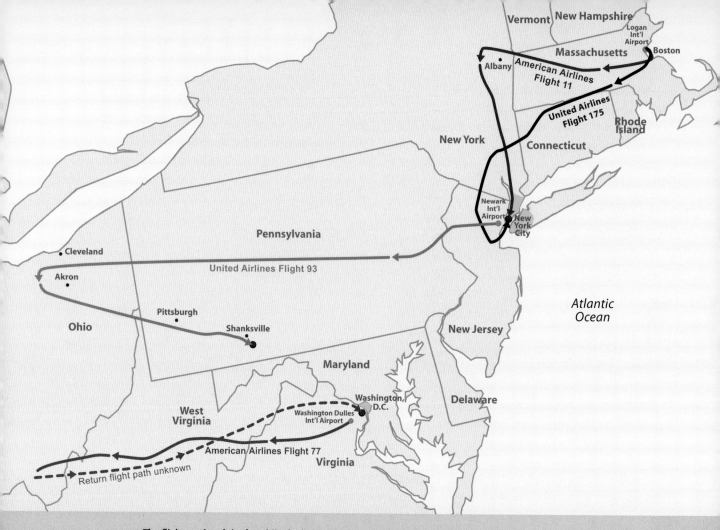

Vermont · New Hampshire · Logan Int'l Airport · Massachusetts · Boston · Albany · American Airlines Flight 11 · United Airlines Flight 175 · Rhode Island · New York · Connecticut · Newark Int'l Airport · New York City · Atlantic Ocean · Pennsylvania · Cleveland · United Airlines Flight 93 · Akron · Pittsburgh · Shanksville · Ohio · New Jersey · Maryland · Washington, D.C. · West Virginia · Washington Dulles Int'l Airport · Delaware · American Airlines Flight 77 · Virginia · Return flight path unknown

ABOVE *The flight paths of the four hijacked planes on September 11, 2001. All four airliners were hijacked shortly after takeoff and commandeered to head for their targets.*

the Midwest where he had been scheduled to speak, the military ordered the plane to land immediately or risk being shot down.

Secretary of State Colin Powell, in South America attending a conference of the Organization of American States, cut his visit short and returned to Washington. Federal Reserve Chairman Alan Greenspan was unable to fly back from Switzerland; he instead depended on his second in command, Roger Ferguson, to carry out telephoned instructions to avert financial disaster and assure the nation that banks would continue normal operations.

President GEORGE W. BUSH was in Sarasota, Florida speaking at an elementary school. After the attacks, Bush was routed from Florida to Barksdale Air Force Base near Shreveport, Louisiana, before being taken to the headquarters of the Strategic Air Command near Omaha, Nebraska. He returned to the White House that evening and addressed the nation at 8:30 P.M., declaring America was at war.

On Friday, September 14, government officials, including President Bush and four former presidents—Bill Clinton, George H.W. Bush, Jimmy Carter, and Gerald Ford—members of Congress, and military officials gathered at the Washington National Cathedral for a Day of Remembrance to honor those who lost their lives on September 11 (see MEMORIALS). Congress appropriated $40 billion dollars for activities related to recovery.

Because debris from AMERICAN AIRLINES FLIGHT 77 had fallen for miles around the Pentagon crash site, the president subsequently declared a state of emergency in Arlington, Virginia, guaranteeing federal aid to supplement local and state funds for recovery efforts.

Over the following days, Washington, D.C., resembled an armed camp. The military remained on high alert. The Federal Bureau of Investigation (FBI) and the Central Intelligence Agency temporarily suspended their territorial differences to begin hunting down terrorists. By September 12, members of Congress had returned to their offices for a joint meeting to address issues relating to the attacks. Congressional offices and buildings were closed to the public, and traffic backed up around the Capitol as police prevented visitors from entering the area.

The PENTAGON and other federal buildings reopened with reduced staffs. Plans were made to increase security in all government offices, although details of the plans were not immediately released. National Guard troops were brought in to patrol city streets, but military police remained at street corners. Although trains were back in operation September 12, all schools and some museums remained closed. Reagan National Airport reopened at 3 P.M. A citywide prayer vigil was held the evening of September 12.

Security and Training

A STUDY conducted by AT&T in September 2006 revealed that less than half of Washington area businesses responded to alerts from the Department of Homeland Security by implementing emergency protocol after September 11. While 45 percent of companies in the area revised emergency contingency plans, less than one-third tested them through training exercises. Some companies, however, responded to September 11 by intensifying emergency preparedness. For instance, the Washington Metropolitan Transit Authority used federal funds to set up a comprehensive emergency system designed to protect more than a million riders and 10,000 employees affected by the city's regular operations.

Post–September 11 measures included increased security involving the use of explosive and chemical detection equipment; increased transit staffing; educating the public and employees about terrorism; and procedures for reporting and investigating any suspicious activities that occur. Canine teams and chemical sensors now are regularly used to check for biochemical elements, and Automatic Vehicle Locators and cameras have been installed on all buses. More than 1,500 first responders have received specific training in evacuation, crashes, terrorism, and fires, and 200 area citizens have received specialized training to prepare them for dealing with possible disasters in local communities. Emergency preparedness drills involving regional first responders are conducted regularly in the Washington, D.C., area.

RESCUE EFFORTS

The 9/11 Commission identified three factors that led to the coordinated emergency response in Washington: efficient professional relationships among emergency responders, implementation of the Incident Command System, and a strong regional response, involving trained first responders who were accustomed to working together. Unlike New York City, no first responders were killed in Washington.

Able to draw on federal, regional, state, and local agencies, the capital city relied on the assistance of local fire, police, and sheriff's departments. The services of the Metropolitan Washington Airports Authority, Ronald Reagan Washington National Airport Fire Department, Fort Myer Fire Department, Virginia State Police, Virginia Department of Emergency Management, FBI, Federal Emergency Management Agency, National Medical Response Team, Bureau of Alcohol, Tobacco, and Firearms, and military forces stationed in the Washington area were also involved in rescue and recovery efforts. The Arlington County Emergency Communications Center coordinated rescue efforts among local fire departments from Washington and from Fairfax and Alexandria in Virginia.

Critics accused government officials, local police and security forces in Washington of being too slow to react to the crisis. Communication problems that included useless cell phones and an overworked radio system complicated rescue efforts and blurred the chain of command. Protocol called for designated disaster plans to be implemented, but some disorganization was apparent immediately after the attack. A *Time* magazine reporter talked to one security guard who sat on a park bench, unsure of his next move because he had been locked out of his office. He expressed concern over the fate of senior officials who might still be in the building. Senate mi-

nority leader Trent Lott noted as he left his office building with his staff that visitors were still roaming the halls of the building. The military was also criticized because air force fighter planes were slow to arrive on the scene to protect the capital.

Further Reading: Steven Brill, *After: How America Confronted the September 12 Era* (Simon and Schuster, 2003); Aseem Inam, *Planning for the Unplanned: Recovering from Crises in Megacities* (Routledge, 2005); Dana Milbank, "Cheney Authorized Shooting Down Planes," *Washington Post* (June 18, 2004); Dean E. Murphy, *September 11: An Oral History* (Doubleday, 2002); *Newsweek Special Report: After the Terror* (September 24, 2001); Gail Stewart, *America under Attack: September 11, 2001* (Lucent, 2002).

— **ELIZABETH PURDY, PH.D.**

Windows on the World

Windows on the World, on the 107th floor of the South Tower, was already open for business when the first plane hit the North Tower at 8:45 A.M. Eighteen minutes later, UNITED AIRLINES FLIGHT 175 crashed into the South Tower, trapping workers and guests inside. Windows on the World, established in 1976, was an ensemble of restaurants that included the Cellar in the Sky, an upscale wine cellar, and Hors D'Oeuvrerie, a lounge that served a Danish smorgasbord during the day and sushi at night. Windows on the World was known for a breathtaking 55-mile view of the city and the region.

At 10:03, the South Tower fell, and at 10:28, the North Tower followed. In August 2003, the Port Authority (see PORT AUTHORITY OF NEW YORK AND NEW JERSEY) released transcripts of telephone and radio conversations between trapped office workers and emergency operators. Four calls from Christine Olender, 39, an assistant manager

Family Benefits

SOME FAMILIES of those who died at Windows on the World have expressed frustration because the majority of charitable donations has been allotted to families of firefighters, police officers, and other rescue workers killed on September 11. Providing financial assistance to survivors of foreign citizens working at Windows on the World has proved to be especially daunting, partly because a number of workers were in the country illegally, and a number of charities stipulated that recipients of donations must be legal residents of the United States.

A number of families who lost loved ones reside abroad; compensating them has proved difficult due to varying tax laws and cultures. Distributing the $350,000 allotted to each surviving spouse and child has been further complicated because of complex family relationships that range from polygamous families to common law marriages with numerous offspring. Kenneth R. Fein-

ABOVE *The view from the restaurant Windows on the World. Every employee at work that day lost his or her life.*

berg, the government official in charge of international compensation, dealt with more than 50 foreign consulates and embassies in his efforts to distribute benefits (see VICTIM COMPENSATION FUND).

at Windows on the World, revealed that 170 employees and guests had gathered on the 106th floor of the South Tower. Olender asked for assistance because all three emergency exits were filled with smoke. During her last call, she informed authorities that air was running out fast and asked if she could break a window. She was told to do anything possible to survive. Her efforts were to no avail, and the entire group perished.

It is believed that 73 employees were at work when the South Tower collapsed. One employee's family created an altar to honor the father of four who had left his life as a Mexican peasant farmer to provide his children with college educations. Eighty-one international guests were attending a conference at the restaurant, hosted by Simon Turner from London. He and his wife were renovating their dream

home as they awaited the birth of a son. William was born two months after his father's death.

The 377 restaurant employees who were not working that morning lost their jobs when the towers fell, and many were unable to find jobs with equal pay. They welcomed the $2,500 checks paid from the September 11 Fund designed to help meet short-term obligations. One group of employees banded together to open a new restaurant, Colors, located a few blocks from Ground Zero.

Further Reading: David Barstow, "Those Who Lost Homes or Jobs Are to Get $2,500 Grants," *New York Times* (December 12, 2001); David W. Chen, "Struggling to Sort out 9/11 Aid to Foreigners," *New York Times* (June 27, 2002); Jim Dwyer and Kevin Flynn, *102 Minutes: The Untold Story of the Fight to Survive Inside the Twin Towers* (Times Books, 2005).

— ELIZABETH PURDY, PH.D.

AT LEFT *World Trade Center employees are evacuated during the 1993 explosion. The ceiling in the underground Port Authority-Trans-Hudson line station collapsed onto commuters, and fires at the base of the building sent heavy smoke through the complex.*

World Trade Center 1993

On February 26, 1993, an explosion in the underground parking garage beneath the North Tower of the World Trade Center resulted in six deaths, over 1,000 injuries, and the evacuation of both towers. The parking garage suffered extensive damage, but the tower remained structurally sound and was reopened after minor repairs. The source of the explosion was a bomb inside a rental van parked in the garage.

The van was large enough to hold a ton of explosives, but the bombers did not completely fill it. The bombers added sodium cyanide to the explosives, hoping to poison people who were not immediately killed, but the resultant cyanide gas apparently burned up in the explosion.

To throw investigators off their trail, friends of the bombers reported the van stolen. Nevertheless, the Federal Bureau of Investigation (FBI) tracked down all involved in the attack. On March 4, FBI officials announced that they had captured Moham-

mad Salameh, one of the conspirators. A search of his apartment led them to co-conspirators. RAMZI AHMED YOUSEF, the principal constructor of the bomb, had already escaped abroad, but was apprehended and brought to trial in the United States. He said that his only regret was failing to use enough explosives to destroy the towers.

In May 1994 four of the principal conspirators—Mohammad Salameh, Nidal Ayyad, Mahmud Abouhalima, and Ahmad Aja—were convicted and sentenced to life imprisonment. In October 1995, radical Muslim cleric Sheikh Omar Abdel-Rahman was convicted of masterminding the bombing and sentenced to life imprisonment. There have been persistent questions about whether he had ties to AL-QAEDA.

Further Reading: Peter Caram, *The 1993 World Trade Center Bombing: Foresight and Warning* (Janus Publishing, 2001); CBS News, "1st Trade Center Attack: 10 Years Ago," www.cbsnews.com/stories/2003/02/12/attack/main540376.shtml (cited September 2006); Steve Coll, *Ghost Wars* (Penguin, 2004); Barry Davies, *Terrorism: Inside a World Phenomenon* (Virgin, 2003).

— **LEIGH KIMMEL**

World Trade Center Plans

The WTC's story began not long after the World Fair in New York in 1939, when ideas for a center for global trade were discussed in professional circles. David Rockefeller became convinced that a world trade center was necessary for Manhattan. He gave the idea to his brother Nelson, who was then governor of New York. Nelson Rockefeller embraced the concept and delegated the responsibility for the project to the PORT AUTHORITY OF NEW YORK AND NEW JERSEY.

A site was identified near the Hudson River tunnel, an old railroad that the Port Authority had recently acquired connecting northern New Jersey with lower Manhattan. The site was a neighborhood known as Radio Row, a small working-class community distinguishable by its dozens of radio and electronics stores in a relatively small area. The shop owners fought the Port Authority for several years, but in the end, the power of the Port Authority, banks, and other big businesses that wanted a World Trade Center won out.

The Port Authority named Japanese architect Minoru Yamasaki as the design architect for the World Trade Center. Yamasaki was asked to develop a plan that would accommodate 12 million square feet of office space on a 16-acre site, all within a budget of around $500 million.

Yamasaki's solution was to develop a complex of several low-rise commercial spaces to supplement the bold decision to build two identical towers that would be the world's highest structures. These Twin Towers would be about 1,353 feet tall, a height requiring a few engineering marvels to accomplish in a functional manner. Typical nonsupporting wall skyscrapers had massive building cores to resist both gravity loads and lateral loads, such as high winds. But with Yamasaki's towers, the exterior walls would resist the lateral forces. A giant steel lattice

ABOVE *The future of Ground Zero, the vision of Studio Daniel Libeskind. The new World Trade Center is meant to be a symbol of the nation's unity and strength, but due to development and design arguments, it has instead been mostly divisive.*

pre-assembled in 10-by-24-foot sections, the walls transmitted force through the floor slabs to the perpendicular walls, which then transferred the force down to the foundation—where it was counterbalanced. Workers bored 70 feet into the soil in order to reach bedrock solid enough for support.

Getting people to the top floors in a reasonable amount of time was an issue. Elevators rising 110 floors would take too long to reach the top floor. Providing enough elevators for each to travel without stopping on every floor would require too much space. To speed travel times and save space, express elevators were designed to carry passengers to intermediate lobbies on higher levels. From these sky lobbies passengers could transfer to local elevators that went to individual floors in the zone. The local elevators could occupy the same space vertically, leaving enough space for offices.

While impressive in its technical solutions to practical problems, The World Trade Center was not aesthetically progressive. The design was several monolithic glass and steel boxes surrounding an immense paved plaza, and the Twin Towers two massive, extruded squares that dominated the skyline. The base modernist style, combined with the colossal scale, generated criticism to match its bold statement.

Once established as part of the city, focus shifted from the visual appeal of the buildings to what went on inside. The Center became a hub for exhibitionists: one man went back and forth between the two towers on a tightrope, eight times. Another constructed braces that could be clamped to the façade, enabling him to climb up, almost reaching the top. A restaurant, WINDOWS ON THE WORLD, was opened on the 107th floor of the North Tower and became a trendy hotspot.

In 1993, the World Trade Center became the target of a terrorist attack. In the underground parking garage, a truck bomb exploded, killing 6 people and injuring hundreds more. That event was only to foreshadow what was to come later.

On September 11, 2001, at 8:45 A.M. a hijacked Boeing 767 airliner struck the North Tower. At 9:03 A.M. the South Tower was struck in the same fashion. As smoke and flames enveloped the upper floors of both towers, the heat from the fires caused the floors, and then the towers, to collapse. the South Tower fell at 10:03 A.M., the North Tower at 10:28 A.M. In less than two hours, nearly 3,000 people were killed.

THE DECISION TO REBUILD

After the September 11 attacks, the question arose regarding what to do with the remains of the Twin Towers and the site, known as Ground Zero. Some suggested leaving it in ruins as a memorial to the victims (see MEMORIALS). Others argued that the towers should be rebuilt, but even higher, as an act of defiance. Real Estate developer Larry Silverstein, who just six weeks before the attacks had signed a lease on the site, declared that it was his intention to rebuild.

The Port Authority, which owned the site, had come to the same conclusion. A special group was formed to oversee the redevelopment efforts, the LMDC, or Lower Manhattan Development Corporation. Silverstein, the Port Authority, and the LMDC determined that rebuilding the office space along with a memorial would be the proper way to honor the victims of the attacks as well as satisfy the commercial and public interests.

A call was issued for architects and urban designers to submit proposals for the redevelopment. Six were invited for formal presentation: Lord Norman Foster; Daniel Libeskind; the firm of Skidmore, Owings, and Merrill; a team led by Rafael Vinoly that called itself THINK; a collaboration

Architectural rendering of the planned Freedom Tower (L), and the surrounding buildings of the new financial center. The fountain memorials can be seen on the footprints of the former twin towers, at the bottom of rendering.

of prominent New York architects Richard Meier, Stephen Holl, Charles Gwathmey, and Peter Eisenman working together; and a team of young computer-based architects called United Architects. A seventh group, the urban design firm Peterson/Littenberg, asked to present their design and were allowed to do so.

The teams presented their designs in the Winter Garden of the World Financial Center on December 18, 2002. The event was televised live, a measure of how much the public had become interested in what would become of Ground Zero.

Studio Daniel Libeskind's plan called for a 1,776-foot-tall tower to be the summit of a spiral of glass shardlike towers surrounding a memorial space. These sharp, angular towers were aligned so that on September 11 each year, an unimpeded wedge of sunlight would penetrate the site from precisely 8:45 to 10:28 A.M., the time between the first plane striking and the second tower collapsing. Libeskind envisioned the memorial space 70 feet below ground, where the slurry wall of the foundation, which held back the waters of the Hudson River, was located. Had the slurry wall given way when the towers collapsed, much of New York's subway system would have been flooded.

Lord Norman Foster, a high-tech British architect who has become world renowned for his innovative and sustainable designs, conceived a colossal tower. It appeared as two separate towers, but was really one, separated from itself as it rose and bent in and outward, "kissing" in three points that were to become public observation decks. The original footprints of the Twin Towers would be encompassed by a stone wall, and a void would remain in their place.

Peter Eisenman made the New York architects' presentation. His consortium's idea was to create a skyscraper modeled after the very regular street grid of Manhattan. They designed five vertical towers interconnected by two horizontal bands, making one large grid of a building. The footprints of the original towers would become reflecting pools, and the last shadows cast by the towers would become tree-lined piers extending into New York Harbor.

ABOVE LEFT *The design submitted by Richard Meier.* ABOVE CENTER *The Peterson/Littenberg proposal, an aerial view.* ABOVE RIGHT *Studio Daniel Libeskind, model view.*

The THINK team under Rafael Vinoly presented three proposals. One called Great Hall was an enclosed 13-acre public room that covered most of the site and the original footprints, which would be encased in glass cylinders. Another, called Sky Park, was a 16-acre park covering most of the site, raised 10 stories above street level and surrounded by high-rise office buildings. Their final design, World Cultural Center, was to have nine office towers arranged on the site, along with two open-framed steel-lattice towers that would be built around the original footprints.

Greg Lynn represented United Architects. Their proposal was for five individual towers that rose and twisted into one another, forming one superstructure, or city in the sky, 800 feet above the street.

The husband-wife firm of Petersen/Littenberg proposal was the least radical. Citing the importance of New York's streets and building traditions as an important factor in their design, they called for a conservative urbanism in which five mid-rise and two high-rise towers flanked memorial gardens; one of the original footprints would become a the-ater, the other would be a reflecting pool. They also included a school in their plan.

Skidmore, Owings, and Merrill's proposal was presented by senior partner David Childs, an expert on corporate high-rise design who had already begun work for developer Larry Silverstein on a tower on an unrelated site. Their design called for nine massive office towers, each 940 feet tall, topped with gardens and connected by ramps and escalators. One of the footprints would be made into a reflecting pool. A unique aspect of the design was that one of the towers would function as a heat exchanger and contribute electrical power to the city.

THE DESIGN CHOICE

Studio Daniel Libeskind was chosen by the LMDC to be the master planner. Libeskind's parents were Holocaust survivors who brought him to New York as a young boy, where he grew up in Brooklyn and watched the rise of the original World Trade Center.

Even though Libeskind won the competition to design the master plan, he was not Silverstein's first choice to design the individual buildings, and according to his lease, Silverstein had the right to hire his own architect. He did just that. Silverstein hired David Childs to design the individual buildings in Libeskind's master plan, and Libeskind was to work with Childs as a design consultant.

Both critics and the public disliked the first attempt at a collaborative design effort, called the Freedom Tower by New York Governor George Pataki. It was essentially a boxier version of what Libeskind had intended. Neither architect seemed pleased with the outcome of their forced union.

Meanwhile, the NEW YORK POLICE DEPARTMENT (NYPD) mandated security codes that would place severe restrictions on the design of the Freedom Tower. The NYPD thought the building might be vulnerable to another car-bomb attack and ordered the base moved as far away from the street as possible and the first 15 stories to be heavily fortified. Although construction had already begun, it had to be abandoned so that the tower could be redesigned to meet these new security requirements.

These changes brought even harsher criticism. Making the Freedom Tower into a fortress seemed a contradiction to many. Some rejected fear as the motivation for the design, believing that this would be the wrong message and counterproductive to promoting democracy and capitalism.

The new World Trade Center was supposed to be a symbol of the nation's unity and strength, yet, like its predecessor, it has been mostly divisive. The architects have argued over design issues, and the Port Authority and the developer have been at odds over who has the rights to redevelop. Politicians have used the project to further their own political careers.

Further Reading: Sarah Boxer, "Debating Ground Zero Architecture and the Value of the Void," *New York Times* (September 20, 2002); James Glanz and Eric Lipton, *City in the Sky: The Rise and Fall of the World Trade Center* (Times Books, 2003); Paul Goldberger, *Up from Zero: Politics, Architecture, and the Rebuilding of New York* (Random House, 2004); Daniel Libeskind, *Breaking Ground: Adventures in Life and Architecture* (Riverhead Books, 2004); Max Protetch, *A New World Trade Center: Design Proposals* (HarperCollins, 2002).

— CHRIS DOCHNEY
MOHAMMAD GHARIPOUR

World Trade Towers

Minoru Yamasaki, chief architect of the World Trade Center, died of cancer in 1986. The rebuilding of the World Trade Center complex gives his words special meaning in the aftermath of September 11, 2001: "World trade means world peace and consequently the World Trade Center buildings in New York…had a bigger purpose than just to provide room for tenants. The World Trade Center is a living symbol of man's dedication to world peace… the World Trade Center should, because of its importance, become a representation of man's belief in humanity, his need for individual dignity, his beliefs in the cooperation of men, and through cooperation, his ability to find greatness."

The World Trade Center had been a dream of New York bankers, businessmen, and community leaders since the end of World War II. In the late 1950s the PORT AUTHORITY OF NEW YORK AND NEW JERSEY embraced the project and in 1962 selected a site on the west side of lower Manhattan on a large block bounded by Vesey, Liberty, Church, and West Streets. The Port Authority planned a 10 million-square-foot complex consisting of seven buildings and two 110-story towers on 16 acres. The complex would cost $525 million and the Twin Towers would be the tallest buildings on earth, each 100 feet higher than the

ABOVE *The World Trade Center towers, nearly completed here, were finished in 1973.*

Empire State Building. The Port Authority chose architect Minoru Yamasaki to design the project and architects Emery Roth & Sons to handle the production work. Yamasaki asked the firm of Worthington, Skilling, Helle and Jackson to serve as engineers. Minoru Yamasaki and Associates considered over 100 different designs before deciding on the concept of the two towers and three lower-rise structures.

Yamasaki worked closely with engineers John Skilling and Les Robertson to develop the relationship between the design and the structure of the towers. The engineers designed the buildings to utilize tube construction, an innovation for skyscrapers popular in the 1970s. The Twin Towers were constructed of lightweight steel and glass supported by exterior columns. To meet the challenge of constructing to such heights, the engineers created an unprecedented structural model, a rigid hollow tube of closely spaced steel columns with floor trusses extended across a central core. Finished with a silver-colored aluminum alloy, the columns measured 18 and three-quarters inches wide and were set only 22 inches apart, causing the towers to appear windowless from a distance.

The Twin Towers were the first ultra-tall buildings designed without any masonry. The Empire State Building, built in the early 1930s, was constructed using heavy internal supports and thick masonry. A ten-ton B-25 bomber crashed into the Empire State Building in 1945, putting a 20-foot hole in its side, but leaving the building standing.

To allay concerns that the intense air pressure created by the buildings' high speed elevators might buckle conventional shafts, engineers designed a drywall system fixed to the reinforced steel core. Otis Elevators developed an express and local system where passengers could change elevators at "sky lobbies" on the 44th and 78th floors, cutting the number of elevator shafts in half.

Groundbreaking was on August 6, 1966, and in late 1970 One World Trade Center– the North Tower–was ready for tenants, although the upper stories were not completed until 1972. Two World Trade Center–the South Tower–was finished in 1973. The towers soared skyward at the center of the complex, Tower One rising to 1,368 feet and Tower Two rising 1,362 feet, and each containing 110 stories.

On September 11, 2001, the towers stood for about one hour after the terrorist strikes, and engineers later told *New York Times* reporters that the jet fuel fire caused their demise. Temperatures ranging from 1,000 to 2,000 degrees caused the steel columns around the tower facades to buckle, and with their supports weakened, the concrete-slab floors collapsed. Because the jets hit the towers near the top, the buildings became the instruments of their own destruction as the weight of many floors crushed downward. Later, falling debris and more fires led to the collapse of the smaller SEVEN WORLD TRADE CENTER building adjacent to the towers.

On September 12, 2001, Leon Harris, a CNN anchor interviewed architect Aaron Swirsky of Jerusalem, one of a team of 14 architects that chief architect Yamasaki led in designing the World Trade Center. He told Harris "We had heard so many times over the years that the buildings have been built to withstand an impact from the crash of a plane," he said. The belief was that if a plane hit, it would go through the building. The tower was supposedly protected in such a way that the damage would be limited to one story, and would not affect other stories. But Swirsky also pointed out that at the time that the World Trade Center towers were built, planes did not have the passenger or fuel capacity of 21st-century jumbo jet airplanes.

Further Reading: Leon Harris, "Interview with Aaron Swirsky, Architect, September 12, 2001," http://CNN.com/2001/US/09/20/vic.personal.account (cited September 2006); Karl Koch with Richard Firstman, *Men of Steel: The Story of the Family that Built the World Trade Center* (Crown Publishing Group, 2003); John Seabrook, "The Tower Builder," *New Yorker* (November 19, 2001).

— KATHY WARNES

Structural Engineer

HIS OFFICE is located on the top two floors of 30 Broad Street, a 48-story building standing a few blocks from Ground Zero. From his conference room he can look directly down into the space where the South Tower once stood. Leslie E. Robertson and his one-time partner John Skilling were the structural engineers who designed the major elements of the Twin Towers, and for Robertson, surviving his creation has been traumatic. He said to a *New Yorker* reporter, "The World Trade Center was a team effort, but the collapse of the World Trade Center is my responsibility, and that's the way I feel about it."

Robertson designed the towers to absorb the impact of a jet airliner. He designed the towers for the impact of such an airplane but did not expand his study and designs to include explosion of fuel loads, presuming that the architect was the one who designed for fire safety.

On September 11, each of the Twin Towers absorbed the impact of a Boeing 767 jumbo jet. Each tower stood long enough for most people below the crash points to escape.

In his *New Yorker* interview, Robertson said, as his eyes filled with tears, "There are all kinds of terrible things that take place on this planet, that nature brings on us. But this event...Not only was it man against man, but it was live on television, and we watched it, and you could reach out and touch it." He stretched out his hand toward the windows where the towers had once stood. "But there was nothing you could do."

BELOW *A panoramic photo looking up at the 110-story World Trade Center towers.*

Y

Yemen

Questions have arisen about Yemen, a country bordering SAUDI ARABIA and Oman in the Middle East, and the September 11 plot. AL-QAEDA maintained an active presence in Yemen for more than a decade. In addition to receiving money from commercial enterprises in the country, al-Qaeda cells in other countries have received shipments of weapons and resources from elements within Yemen, and in some cases reportedly from within the Yemeni government. The Yemeni government has been accused of being slow to respond to its domestic Islamic extremist threat. Observers have noted that this is because Islamists joined government troops to help President Ali Abdullah Saleh win Yemen's civil war in 1994. Even before the USS *Cole* attack on October 12, 2000, the al-Qaeda network within Yemen had been large and active.

The Yemen Central Bank investigated the accounts of several enterprises after September 11. They included the Al-Hamati Sweets Bakeries, Al-Nur Honey Press Shops, and the Al-Shifa Honey Press for Industry and Commerce. These companies were known or believed to be financial conduits for al-Qaeda prior to September 11 and directly associated with the finances of OSAMA BIN LADEN and his brother-in-law Jamal Khalifa. Besides financial interests, al-Qaeda had various training camps throughout the country and some experts suspect that it maintained a large presence of Afghan-Arab SLEEPER CELLS in Yemen.

MINARETS OVER YEMEN *Cityscape of Sana'a, Yemen. The Yemeni government has been criticized for not responding quickly to the threat of Islamic extremism in the country.*

AT LEFT *Yemenis in Sana'a, Yemen, raise stones and copies of the Koran as they protest the killing of Hamas founder and spiritual leader Sheikh Ahmed Yassin in March 2004. Thousands of students called for jihad, or holy war.*

The Yemeni government chose to fight Islamist elements and has been targeted by a group close to al-Qaeda. The Supporters of Sharia (SOS) organization, led by radical preacher Abu Hamza al-Masri, was responsible for a number of attacks and for assassination attempts on the president of Yemen. It is known that al-Masri and his organization, through the Finsbury Park Mosque in London, have had multiple connections with al-Qaeda—both before and after September 11. That organization also was responsible for the recruitment and financing of elements of the Islamic Army of Aden (see ADEN, ISLAMIC ARMY OF) and contributed to their fight against both the Yemeni government and Western interests in that country.

Further Reading: Peter L. Bergen, *Holy War, Inc.: Inside the Secret War of Osama Bin Laden* (Simon and Schuster, 2002); Jonathan Schanzer, *Al-Qaeda's Armies: Middle East Affiliate Groups and the Next Generation of Terror* (SPI Books, 2004); Shaul Shay, *The Red Sea Terror Triangle: Sudan, Somalia, Yemen, and Islamic Terror* (Transaction Publishers, 2006).

— **WADE K. EWING**

Yemen Islamic Jihad

The Yemen Islamic Jihad was founded by Tariq al-Fadhli, a Southern Yemen aristocrat and veteran of the Afghan resistance, after the Soviet Union pulled out of AFGHANISTAN. It is believed that there are bases of operation in Afghanistan, Libya, the United Kingdom, and the United States. It is also believed that the group has militant wings in Palestine. Tariq al-Fadhli is associated with OSAMA BIN LADEN, and the Yemen Islamic Jihad is thought to be funded by AL-QAEDA. In addition, they obtain money by kidnapping victims for ransom and through support networks overseas. The group is believed to have more than 200 members.

The Yemen Islamic Jihad originally helped the president of Yemen defeat the socialists of South Yemen in 1994. Unable to recruit a large number of people into the party, the group left the government and pursued militant Islamic goals on its own. The group does, however, have some de facto support from the political elite at various levels of the Yemen government, and are able to enforce their own idea of Sharia law in South Yemen.

The Yemen Islamic Jihad's goals (see ISLAMIC FUNDAMENTALISM) include the establishment of Sharia law in all of YEMEN, and opposition to non-believers. The group strives to fight the "enemies" of Islam, primarily Israel, the United States, and the West in general. To advance this goal, they want to end Western intervention in the Middle East, including the removal of foreign military, commercial, and civilian presences in Yemen, Saudi Arabia, and other areas of the Middle East.

The Yemen Islamic Jihad, along with AL-QAEDA and the Islamic Army of Aden Abyan, were implicated in the bombing of the USS *Cole* in October 2000. In this attack, 17 American sailors were killed and 39 were injured.

Further Reading: "In the Spotlight: The Islamic Army of Aden Abyan (IAA)," http://news.bbc.co.uk (November 23, 2004); "Yemen Islamic Jihad," "Tariq al-Fadhli," "Abu al-Migdad," "Selah Haidara al-Atwi," MIPT Terrorism Knowledge Base, www.tkb.org (cited July 2006).

— **MARGARET H. WILLIAMSON**

Yousef, Ramzi Ahmed (1968–)

Ramzi Ahmed Yousef led the terrorist cell that executed the 1993 bombing at the World Trade Center. He is currently serving 240 years in the Supermax security prison in Florence, Colorado. A world traveler with at least 40 aliases, Yousef is fluent in English, Urdu, and Arabic, and is called "the evil genius" in Pakistani security circles.

Yousef was born April 27, 1968, in Kuwait of Kuwaiti, Pakistani, and Palestinian descent. His mother is the sister of Khalid Sheikh Mohammed, formerly AL-QAEDA's chief of operations. He has lived in the Middle East, England, the Philippines, and the United States. In England, he received a degree in electrical engineering from the West Glamorgan Institute in Swansea, Wales. Yousef executed terrorist operations around the world.

Yousef organized the terrorist cell (see SLEEPER CELLS) in Jersey City, New Jersey. The plan was to place a 1,310-pound bomb made of urea nitrate and fuel oil in a rented van and park it in the basement parking garage beneath the North Tower of the World Trade Center. The intention was to cause the North Tower to fall into the South Tower. Although the outcome was not as planned, six people were killed and more than 1,000 were injured. Yousef escaped, for a time.

He went to the Philippines, where he planned Operation Bojinka, a day of rage, which was intended to take down 11 jets over the Pacific in a 48-hour period. When smoke and gas escaped his Manila apartment, summoning the police and fire departments, his plan was exposed. Yousef escaped from the Philippines to Pakistan via Thailand, but was eventually arrested by special agents of the U.S. Diplomatic Security Service.

Further Reading: Rohan Gunaratna, *Inside al-Qaeda* (Penguin, 2003); The Institute for Counter-Terrorism, www.ict.org.il (cited September 2006); Simon Reeve, *The New Jackals: Ramzi Yousef, Osama bin Laden and the Future of Terrorism* (Northeastern University Press, 1999).

— **RAY BROWN**

AT RIGHT *Ramzi Ahmed Yousef, leader and organizer of the terrorist cell that planted a bomb in the parking garage of the World Trade Center in 1993.*

APPENDIX: VICTIMS LIST

Compiled by Alex Spector at www.September11victims.com
As of most recent database update, September 9, 2006:

Confirmed Dead: 2,948
Reported Dead: 24
Reported Missing: 24
Total: 2,996

CONFIRMED DEAD. Includes those who have been confirmed dead by a coroner's office or the Defense Department. It also includes those for whom death certificates have been issued, even if no body has been recovered.

REPORTED DEAD. Includes those whose deaths have been reported by family, employers, mortuaries, places of worship or by the airlines that listed them as aboard one of the four flights. Includes people for whom memorial services have been held, even if their bodies have not been recovered or positively identified. (Those identified by federal authorities as the hijackers are not included in the database.)

REPORTED MISSING. People identified by family, official agencies or employers as missing.

AMERICAN AIRLINES FLIGHT 11
CREW
Barbara Arestegui, 38, Marstons Mills, Massachusetts
Jeffrey Collman, 41, Novato, California
Sara Low, 28, Batesville, Arkansas
Karen A. Martin, 40, Danvers, Massachusetts
First Officer Thomas McGuinness, 42, Portsmouth, New Hampshire
Kathleen Nicosia, 54, Winthrop, Massachusetts
John Ogonowski, 52, Dracut, Massachusetts
Betty Ong, 45, Andover, Massachusetts
Jean Roger, 24, Longmeadow, Massachusetts
Dianne Snyder, 42, Westport, Massachusetts
Madeline Sweeney, 35, Acton, Massachusetts

PASSENGERS
Anna Williams Allison, 48, Stoneham, Massachusetts
David Angell, 54, Pasadena, California
Lynn Angell, 45, Pasadena, California
Seima Aoyama, 48, Culver City, California
Myra Aronson, 52, Charlestown, Massachusetts
Christine Barbuto, 32, Brookline, Massachusetts
Carolyn Beug, 48, Los Angeles, California
Kelly Ann Booms, 24, Brookline, Massachusetts
Carol Bouchard, 43, Warwick, Rhode Island
Neilie Anne Heffernan Casey, 32, Wellesley, Massachusetts
Jeffrey Coombs, 42, Abington, Massachusetts
Tara Creamer, 30, Worcester, Massachusetts
Thelma Cuccinello, 71, Wilmot, New Hampshire
Patrick Currivan, 52, Winchester, Massachusetts
Brian Dale, 43, Warren, New Jersey
David DiMeglio, 22, Wakefield, Massachusetts
Donald Americo DiTullio, 49, Peabody, Massachusetts

Albert Dominguez, 66, Sydney, Australia
Paige Farley-Hackel, 46, Newton, Massachusetts
Alex Filipov, 70, Concord, Massachusetts
Carol Flyzik, 40, Plaistow, New Hampshire
Paul Friedman, 45, Belmont, Massachusetts
Karleton D.B. Fyfe, 31, Brookline, Massachusetts
Peter Gay, 54, Tewksbury, Massachusetts
Linda George, 27, Westboro, Massachusetts
Edmund Glazer, 41, Los Angeles, California
Lisa Fenn Gordenstein, 41, Needham, Massachusetts
Andrew Peter Charles Curry Green, 34, Santa Monica, California
Peter Hashem, 40, Tewksbury, Massachusetts
Robert Hayes, 37, from Amesbury, Massachusetts
Edward (Ted) R. Hennessy, 35, Belmont, Massachusetts
John A. Hofer, 45, Los Angeles, California
Cora Hidalgo Holland, 52, of Sudbury, Massachusetts
Nicholas Humber, 60, of Newton, Massachusetts,
Waleed Iskandar, 34, London, England
John Charles Jenkins, 45, Cambridge, Massachusetts
Charles Edward Jones, 48, Bedford, Massachusetts
Robin Kaplan, 33, Westboro, Massachusetts
Barbara Keating, 72, Palm Springs, California
David P. Kovalcin, 42, Hudson, New Hampshire
Judy Larocque, 50, Framingham, Massachusetts
Natalie Janis Lasden, 46, Peabody, Massachusetts
Daniel John Lee, 34, Van Nuys, California
Daniel C. Lewin, 31, Charlestown, Massachusetts
Susan A. MacKay, 44, Westford, Massachusetts
Christopher D. Mello, 25, Boston, Massachusetts
Jeff Mladenik, 43, Hinsdale, Illinois
Antonio Jesus Montoya Valdes, 46, East Boston, Massachusetts
Carlos Alberto Montoya, 36, Bellmont, Massachusetts
Laura Lee Morabito, 34, Framingham, Massachusetts
Mildred Rose Naiman, 81, Andover, Massachusetts
Laurie Ann Neira, 48, Los Angeles, California
Renee Newell, 37, of Cranston, Rhode Island
Jacqueline J. Norton, 61, Lubec, Maine
Robert Grant Norton, 85, Lubec, Maine
Jane M. Orth, 49, Haverhill, Massachusetts
Thomas Pecorelli, 31, of Los Angeles, California
Berinthia Berenson Perkins, 53, Los Angeles, California
Sonia Morales Puopolo, 58, of Dover, Massachusetts
David E. Retik, 33, Needham, Massachusetts
Philip M. Rosenzweig, 47, Acton, Massachusetts
Richard Ross, 58, Newton, Massachusetts
Jessica Sachs, 22, Billerica, Massachusetts
Rahma Salie, 28, Boston, Massachusetts
Heather Lee Smith, 30, Boston, Massachusetts
Douglas J. Stone, 54, Dover, New Hampshire
Xavier Suarez, 41, Chino Hills, California
Michael Theodoridis, 32, Boston, Massachusetts
James Trentini, 65, Everett, Massachusetts
Mary Trentini, 67, Everett, Massachusetts
Pendyala Vamsikrishna, 30, Los Angeles, California
Mary Wahlstrom, 78, Kaysville, Utah
Kenneth Waldie, 46, Methuen, Massachusetts
John Wenckus, 46, Torrance, California
Candace Lee Williams, 20, Danbury, Connecticut
Christopher Zarba, 47, Hopkinton, Massachusetts

AMERICAN AIRLINES FLIGHT 77
CREW
Charles Burlingame, 51, Herndon, Virginia
David M. Charlebois, 39, Washington, D.C.
Michele Heidenberger, 57, Chevy Chase, Maryland
Jennifer Lewis, 38, Culpeper, Virginia
Kenneth Lewis, 49, Culpeper, Virginia
Renee A. May, 39, Baltimore, Md

PASSENGERS
Paul Ambrose, 32, Washington, D.C.
Yeneneh Betru, 35, Burbank, California
Mary Jane (MJ) Booth, 64, Falls Church, Virginia
Bernard Curtis Brown, 11, Washington, D.C.
Suzanne Calley, 42, San Martin, California
William Caswell, 54, Silver Spring, Maryland
Sarah Clark, 65, Columbia, Maryland
Zandra Cooper, Annandale, Virginia
Asia Cottom, 11, Washington, D.C.
James Debeuneure, 58, Upper Marlboro, Maryland
Rodney Dickens, 11, Washington, D.C.
Eddie Dillard, Alexandria, Virginia
Charles Droz, 52, Springfield, Virginia
Barbara G. Edwards, 58, Las Vegas, Nevada
Charles S. Falkenberg, 45, University Park, Maryland
Zoe Falkenberg, 8, University Park, Maryland
Dana Falkenberg, 3, of University Park, Maryland
James Joe Ferguson, 39, Washington, D.C.
Wilson "Bud" Flagg, 63, Millwood, Virginia
Darlene Flagg, 63, Millwood, Virginia
Richard Gabriel, 54, Great Falls, Virginia
Ian J. Gray, 55, Columbia, Maryland
Stanley Hall, 68, Rancho Palos Verdes, California
Bryan Jack, 48, Alexandria, Virginia
Steven D. Jacoby, 43, Alexandria, Virginia
Ann Judge, 49, Great Falls, Virginia
Chandler Keller, 29, El Segundo, California
Yvonne Kennedy, 62, Sydney, New South Wales, Australia
Norma Khan, 45, Reston, Virginia
Karen A. Kincaid, 40, Washington, D.C.
Dong Lee, 48, Leesburg, Virginia
Dora Menchaca, 45, of Santa Monica, California
Christopher Newton, 38, Anaheim, California
Barbara Olson, 45, Great Falls, Virginia
Ruben Ornedo, 39, Los Angeles, California
Robert Penniger, 63, of Poway, California
Robert R. Ploger, 59, Annandale, Virginia
Lisa J. Raines, 42, Great Falls, Virginia
Todd Reuben, 40, Potomac, Maryland
John Sammartino, 37, Annandale, Virginia
Diane Simmons, Great Falls, Virginia
George Simmons, Great Falls, Virginia
Mari-Rae Sopper, 35, Santa Barbara, California
Robert Speisman, 47, Irvington, New York
Norma Lang Steuerle, 54, Alexandria, Virginia
Hilda E. Taylor, 62, Forestville, Maryland
Leonard Taylor, 44, Reston, Virginia
Sandra Teague, 31, Fairfax, Virginia
Leslie A. Whittington, 45, University Park, Maryland.
John D. Yamnicky, 71, Waldorf, Maryland
Vicki Yancey, 43, Springfield, Virginia

Shuyin Yang, 61, Beijing, China
Yuguag Zheng, 65, Beijing, China

UNITED AIRLINES FLIGHT 175
CREW
Robert Fangman, 33, Claymont, Delaware
Michael R. Horrocks, 38, Glen Mills, Pennsylvania
Amy N. Jarret, 28, North Smithfield, Rhode Island
Amy R. King, 29, Stafford Springs, Connecticut
Kathryn L. LaBorie, 44, Providence, Rhode Island
Alfred Gilles Padre Joseph Marchand, 44, Alamogordo, New Mexico
Capt. Victor Saracini, 51, Lower Makefield Township, Pennsylvania
Michael C. Tarrou, 38, Stafford Springs, Connecticut
Alicia Nicole Titus, 28, San Francisco, California

PASSENGERS
Alona Avraham, 30, Asdod, Israel
Garnet Edward (Ace) Bailey, 54, Lynnfield, Massachusetts
Mark Bavis, 31, West Newton, Massachusetts
Graham Andrew Berkeley, 37, Boston, Massachusetts
Touri Bolourchi, 69, Beverly Hills, California
Klaus Bothe, 31, Linkenheim, Baden-Wurttemberg, Germany
Daniel R. Brandhorst, 41, Los Angeles, California
David Reed Gamboa Brandhorst, 3, Los Angeles, California
John Brett Cahill, 56, Wellesley, Massachusetts
Christoffer Carstanjen, 33, Turner Falls, Massachusetts
John (Jay) J. Corcoran, 43, Norwell, Mass
Dorothy Alma DeAraujo, 80, Long Beach, California
Ana Gloria Pocasangre de Barrera, 49, San Salvador, El Salvador
Lisa Frost, 22, Rancho Santa Margarita, California
Ronald Gamboa, 33, Los Angeles, California
Lynn Catherine Goodchild, 25, Attleboro, Massachusetts
Peter Morgan Goodrich, 33, Sudbury, Massachusetts
Douglas A. Gowell, 52, Methuen, Massachusetts
The Rev. Francis E. Grogan, 76, of Easton, Massachusetts
Carl Max Hammond, 37, Derry, New Hampshire
Peter Hanson, 32, Groton, Massachusetts
Sue Kim Hanson, 35, Groton, Massachusetts
Christine Lee Hanson, 2, Groton, Massachusetts
Gerald F. Hardacre, 61, Carlsbad, California
Eric Samadikan Hartono, 20, Boston, Massachusetts
James E. Hayden, 47, Westford, Massachusetts
Herbert W. Homer, 48, Milford, Massachusetts
Robert Adrien Jalbert, 61, Swampscott, Massachusetts
Ralph Francis Kershaw, 52, Manchester-by-the-Sea, Massachusetts
Heinrich Kimmig, 43, Willstaett, Germany
Brian Kinney, 29, Lowell, Massachusetts
Robert George LeBlanc, 70, Lee, New Hampshire
Maclovio Lopez, Jr., 41, Norwalk, California
Marianne MacFarlane, MacFarlane, 34, Revere, Massachusetts
Louis Neil Mariani, 59, Derry, New Hampshire
Juliana Valentine McCourt, 4, New London, Connecticut
Ruth Magdaline McCourt, 45, New London, Connecticut
Wolfgang Peter Menzel, 59, Wilhelmshaven, Germany
Shawn M. Nassaney, 25, Pawtucket, Rhode Island
Marie Pappalardo, 53, Paramount, California
Patrick Quigley, 40, of Wellesley, Massachusetts
Frederick Charles Rimmele, 32, Marblehead, Massachusetts
James M. Roux, 43, Portland, Maine
Jesus Sanchez, 45, Hudson, Massachusetts
Mary Kathleen Shearer, 61, Dover, New Hampshire
Robert Michael Shearer, 63, Dover, New Hampshire

Jane Louise Simpkin, 36, Wayland, Massachusetts
Brian D. Sweeney, 38, Barnstable, Massachusetts
Timothy Ward, 38, San Diego, California
William M. Weems, 46, Marblehead, Massachusetts

UNITED AIRLINES FLIGHT 93
CREW
Lorraine G. Bay, 58, East Windsor, New Jersey
Sandra W. Bradshaw, 38, Greensboro, North Carolina
Jason Dahl, 43, Denver, Colo.
Wanda Anita Green, 49, Linden, New Jersey
Leroy Homer, 36, Marlton, New Jersey
CeeCee Lyles, 33, Fort Myers, Florida
Deborah Welsh, 49, New York, New York

PASSENGERS
Christian Adams, 37, Biebelsheim, Germany
Todd Beamer, 32, Cranbury, New Jersey
Alan Beaven, 48, Oakland, California
Mark K. Bingham, 31, San Francisco, California
Deora Frances Bodley, 20, San Diego, California
Marion Britton, 53, New York, New York
Thomas E. Burnett Jr., 38, San Ramon, California
William Cashman, 57, North Bergen, New Jersey
Georgine Rose Corrigan, 56, Honolulu, Hawaii
Patricia Cushing, 69, Bayonne, New Jersey
Joseph Deluca, 52, Ledgewood, New Jersey
Patrick Joseph Driscoll, 70, Manalapan, New Jersey
Edward P. Felt, 41, Matawan, New Jersey
Jane C. Folger, 73, Bayonne, New Jersey
Colleen Laura Fraser, 51, Elizabeth, New Jersey
Andrew Garcia, 62, Portola Valley, California
Jeremy Glick, 31, Hewlett, New Jersey
Lauren Grandcolas, 38, San Rafael, California
Donald F. Greene, 52, Greenwich, Connecticut
Linda Gronlund, 46, Warwick, New York
Richard Guadagno, 38, of Eureka, California
Toshiya Kuge, 20, Nishimidoriguoska, Japan
Hilda Marcin, 79, Budd Lake, New Jersey
Nicole Miller, 21, San Jose, California
Louis J. Nacke, 42, New Hope, Pennsylvania
Donald Arthur Peterson, 66, Spring Lake, New Jersey
Jean Hoadley Peterson, 55, Spring Lake, New Jersey
Waleska Martinez Rivera, 37, Jersey City, New Jersey
Mark Rothenberg, 52, Scotch Plains, New Jersey
Christine Snyder, 32, Kailua, Hawaii
John Talignani, 72, New York, New York
Honor Elizabeth Wainio, 27, Watchung, New Jersey
Olga Kristin Gould White, 65, New York, New York

PENTAGON
Spc. Craig Amundson, 28, Fort Belvoir, Virginia
Melissa Rose Barnes, 27, Redlands, California
(Retired) Master Sgt. Max Beilke, 69, Laurel, Maryland
Kris Romeo Bishundat, 23, Waldorf, Maryland
Carrie Blagburn, 48, Temple Hills, Maryland
Lt. Col. Canfield D. Boone, 54, Clifton, Virginia
Donna Bowen, 42, Waldorf, Maryland
Allen Boyle, 30, Fredericksburg, Virginia
Christopher Lee Burford, 23, Hubert, North Carolina
Daniel Martin Caballero, 21, Houston, Texas
Sgt. 1st Class Jose Orlando Calderon-Olmedo, 44, Annandale, Virginia

Angelene C. Carter, 51, Forrestville, Maryland
Sharon Carver, 38, Waldorf, Maryland
John J. Chada, 55, Manassas, Virginia
Rosa Maria (Rosemary) Chapa, 64, Springfield, Virginia
Julian Cooper, 39, Springdale, Maryland
Lt. Cmdr. Eric Allen Cranford, 32, Drexel, North Carolina
Ada M. Davis, 57, Camp Springs, Maryland
Capt. Gerald Francis Deconto, 44, Sandwich, Massachusetts
Lt. Col. Jerry Don Dickerson, 41, Durant, Miss.
Johnnie Doctor, 32, Jacksonville, Florida
Capt. Robert Edward Dolan, 43, Alexandria, Virginia
Cmdr. William Howard Donovan, 37, Nunda, New York
Cmdr. Patrick S. Dunn, 39, Springfield, Virginia
Edward Thomas Earhart, 26, Salt Lick, Kentucky
Lt. Cmdr. Robert Randolph Elseth, 37, Vestal, New York
Jamie Lynn Fallon, 23, Woodbridge, Virginia
Amelia V. Fields, 36, Dumfries, Virginia
Gerald P. Fisher, 57, Potomac, Maryland
Matthew Michael Flocco, 21, Newark, Delaware
Sandra N. Foster, 41, Clinton, Maryland
Capt. Lawrence Daniel Getzfred, 57, Elgin, Nebraska
Cortz Ghee, 54, Reisterstown, Maryland
Brenda C. Gibson, 59, Falls Church, Virginia
Ron Golinski, 60, Columbia, Maryland
Diane M. Hale-McKinzy, 38, Alexandria, Virginia
Carolyn B. Halmon, 49, Washington, D.C.
Sheila Hein, 51, University Park, Maryland
Ronald John Hemenway, 37, Shawnee, Kan.
Maj. Wallace Cole Hogan, 40, Florida
Jimmie Ira Holley, 54, Lanham, Maryland
Angela Houtz, 27, La Plata, Maryland
Brady K. Howell, 26, Arlington, Virginia
Peggie Hurt, 36, Crewe, Virginia
Lt. Col. Stephen Neil Hyland, 45, Burke, Virginia
Robert J. Hymel, 55, Woodbridge, Virginia
Sgt. Maj. Lacey B. Ivory, 43, Woodbridge, Virginia
Lt. Col. Dennis M. Johnson, 48, Port Edwards, Wisconsin
Judith Jones, 53, Woodbridge, Virginia
Brenda Kegler, 49, Washington, D.C.
Lt. Michael Scott Lamana, 31, Baton Rouge, Louisiana
David W. Laychak, 40, Manassas, Virginia
Samantha Lightbourn-Allen, 36, Hillside, Maryland
Maj. Steve Long, 39, Georgia
James Lynch, 55, Manassas, Virginia
Terence M. Lynch, 49, Alexandria, Virginia
Nehamon Lyons, 30, Mobile, Alabama
Shelley A. Marshall, 37, Marbury, Maryland
Teresa Martin, 45, Stafford, Virginia
Ada L. Mason, 50, Springfield, Virginia
Lt. Col. Dean E. Mattson, 57, California
Lt. Gen. Timothy J. Maude, 53, Fort Myer, Virginia
Robert J. Maxwell, 53, Manassas, Virginia
Molly McKenzie, 38, Dale City, Virginia
Patricia E. (Patti) Mickley, 41, Springfield, Virginia
Maj. Ronald D. Milam, 33, Washington, D.C.
Gerard (Jerry) P. Moran, 39, Upper Marlboro, Maryland
Odessa V. Morris, 54, Upper Marlboro, Maryland
Brian Anthony Moss, 34, Sperry, Oklahoma
Ted Moy, 48, Silver Spring, Maryland
Lt. Cmdr. Patrick Jude Murphy, 38, Flossmoor, Illinois
Khang Nguyen, 41, Fairfax, Virginia
Michael Allen Noeth, 30, New York, New York

Diana Borrero de Padro, 55, Woodbridge, Virginia
Spc. Chin Sun Pak, 25, Lawton, Oklahoma
Lt. Jonas Martin Panik, 26, Mingoville, Pennsylvania
Maj. Clifford L. Patterson, 33, Alexandria, Virginia
Lt. J.G. Darin Howard Pontell, 26, Columbia, Maryland
Scott Powell, 35, Silver Spring, Maryland
(Retired) Capt. Jack Punches, 51, Clifton, Virginia
Joseph John Pycior, 39, Carlstadt, New Jersey
Deborah Ramsaur, 45, Annandale, Virginia
Rhonda Rasmussen, 44, Woodbridge, Virginia
Marsha Dianah Ratchford, 34, Prichard, Alabama
Martha Reszke, 36, Stafford, Virginia
Cecelia E. Richard, 41, Fort Washington, Maryland
Edward V. Rowenhorst, 32, Lake Ridge, Virginia
Judy Rowlett, 44, Woodbridge, Virginia
Robert E. Russell, 52, Oxon Hill, Maryland
William R. Ruth, 57, Mount Airy, Maryland
Charles E. Sabin, 54, Burke, Virginia
Marjorie C. Salamone, 53, Springfield, Virginia
Lt. Col. David M. Scales, 44, Cleveland, Ohio
Cmdr. Robert Allan Schlegel, 38, Alexandria, Virginia
Janice Scott, 46, Springfield, Virginia
Michael L. Selves, 53, Fairfax, Virginia
Marian Serva, 47, Stafford, Virginia
Cmdr. Dan Frederic Shanower, 40, Naperville, Illinois
Antoinette Sherman, 35, Forest Heights, Maryland
Don Simmons, 58, Dumfries, Virginia
Cheryle D. Sincock, 53, Dale City, Virginia
Gregg Harold Smallwood, 44, Overland Park, Kan.
(Retired) Lt. Col. Gary F. Smith, 55, Alexandria, Virginia
Patricia J. Statz, 41, Takoma Park, Maryland
Edna L. Stephens, 53, Washington, D.C.
Sgt. Maj. Larry Strickland, 52, Woodbridge, Virginia
Maj. Kip P. Taylor, 38, McLean, Virginia
Sandra C. Taylor, 50, Alexandria, Virginia
Karl W. Teepe, 57, Centreville, Virginia
Sgt. Tamara Thurman, 25, Brewton, Alabama
Lt. Cmdr. Otis Vincent Tolbert, 38, Lemoore, California
Willie Q. Troy, 51, Aberdeen, Maryland
Lt. Cmdr. Ronald James Vauk, 37, Nampa, Idaho
Lt. Col. Karen Wagner, 40, Houston, Texas
Meta L. Waller, 60, Alexandria, Virginia
Staff Sgt. Maudlyn A. White, 38, St. Croix, Virgin Islands
Sandra L. White, 44, Dumfries, Virginia
Ernest M. Willcher, 62, North Potomac, Maryland
Lt. Cmdr. David Lucian Williams, 32, Newport, Oregon
Maj. Dwayne Williams, 40, Jacksonville, Alabama
Marvin R. Woods, 57, Great Mills, Maryland
Kevin Wayne Yokum, 27, Lake Charles, Louisiana
Donald McArthur Young, 41, Roanoke, Virginia
Lisa L. Young, 36, Germantown, Maryland
Edmond Young, 22, Owings, Maryland

WORLD TRADE CENTER

Gordon McCannel Aamoth, 32, New York, New York
Maria Rose Abad, 49, Syosset, New York
Edelmiro (Ed) Abad, 54, New York, New York
Andrew Anthony Abate, 37, Melville, New York
Vincent Abate, 40, New York, New York
Laurence Christopher Abel, 37
William F. Abrahamson, 58, Cortland Manor, New York
Richard Anthony Aceto, 42, Wantagh, New York

Erica Van Acker, 62, New York, New York
Heinrich B. Ackermann, 38, New York, New York
Paul Andrew Acquaviva, 29, Glen Rock, New Jersey
Donald L. Adams, 28, Chatham, New Jersey
Shannon Lewis Adams, 25, New York, New York
Stephen Adams, 51, New York, New York
Patrick Adams, 60, New York, New York
Ignatius Adanga, 62, New York, New York
Christy A. Addamo, 28, New Hyde Park, New York
Terence E. Adderley, 22, Bloomfield Hills, Michigan
Sophia B. Addo, 36, New York, New York
Lee Adler, 48, Springfield, New Jersey
Daniel Thomas Afflitto, 32, Manalapan, New Jersey
Emmanuel Afuakwah, 37, New York, New York
Alok Agarwal, 36, Jersey City, New Jersey
Mukul Agarwala, 37, New York, New York
Joseph Agnello, 35, New York, New York
David Scott Agnes, 46, New York, New York
Joao A. Aguiar Jr., 30, Red Bank, New Jersey
Lt. Brian G. Ahearn, 43, Huntington, New York
Jeremiah J. Ahern, 74, Cliffside Park, New Jersey
Joanne Ahladiotis, 27, New York, New York
Shabbir Ahmed, 47, New York, New York
Terrance Andre Aiken, 30, New York, New York
Godwin Ajala, 33, New York, New York
Gertrude M. Alagero, 37, New York, New York
Andrew Alameno, 37, Westfield, New Jersey
Margaret Ann (Peggy) Jezycki Alario, 41, New York, New York
Gary Albero, 39, Emerson, New Jersey
Jon L. Albert, 46, Upper Nyack, New York
Peter Craig Alderman, 25, New York, New York
Jacquelyn Delaine Aldridge, 46, New York, New York
Grace Alegre-Cua, 40, Glen Rock, New Jersey
David D. Alger, 57, New York, New York
Ernest Alikakos, 43, New York, New York
Edward L. Allegretto, 51, Colonia, New Jersey
Eric Allen, 44, New York, New York
Joseph Ryan Allen, 39, New York, New York
Richard Lanard Allen, 30, New York, New York
Richard Dennis Allen, 31, New York, New York
Christopher Edward Allingham, 36, River Edge, New Jersey
Janet M. Alonso, 41, Stony Point, New York
Anthony Alvarado, 31, New York, New York
Antonio Javier Alvarez, 23, New York, New York
Telmo Alvear, 25, New York, New York
Cesar A. Alviar, 60, Bloomfield, New Jersey
Tariq Amanullah, 40, Metuchen, New Jersey
Angelo Amaranto, 60, New York, New York
James Amato, 43, Ronkonkoma, New York
Joseph Amatuccio, 41, New York, New York
Christopher Charles Amoroso, 29, New York, New York
Kazuhiro Anai, 42, Scarsdale, New York
Calixto Anaya, 35, Suffern, New York
Jorge Octavio Santos Anaya, 25, Aguascalientes, Aguascalientes, Mexico
Joseph Peter Anchundia, 26, New York, New York
Kermit Charles Anderson, 57, Green Brook, New Jersey
Yvette Anderson, 53, New York, New York
John Andreacchio, 52, New York, New York
Michael Rourke Andrews, 34, Belle Harbor, New York
Jean A. Andrucki, 42, Hoboken, New Jersey
Siew-Nya Ang, 37, East Brunswick, New Jersey
Joseph Angelini, 38, Lindenhurst, New York

Joseph Angelini, 63, Lindenhurst, New York
Laura Angilletta, 23, New York, New York
Doreen J. Angrisani, 44, New York, New York
Lorraine D. Antigua, 32, Middletown, New Jersey
Peter Paul Apollo, 26, Hoboken, New Jersey
Faustino Apostol, 55, New York, New York
Frank Thomas Aquilino, 26, New York, New York
Patrick Michael Aranyos, 26, New York, New York
David Gregory Arce, 36, New York, New York
Michael G. Arczynski, 45, Little Silver, New Jersey
Louis Arena, 32, New York, New York
Adam Arias, 37, Staten Island, New York
Michael J. Armstrong, 34, New York, New York
Jack Charles Aron, 52, Bergenfield, New Jersey
Joshua Aron, 29, New York, New York
Richard Avery Aronow, 48, Mahwah, New Jersey
Japhet J. Aryee, 49, Spring Valley, New York
Carl Asaro, 39, Middletown, New York
Michael A. Asciak, 47, Ridgefield, New Jersey
Michael Edward Asher, 53, Monroe, New York
Janice Ashley, 25, Rockville Centre, New York
Thomas J. Ashton, 21, New York, New York
Manuel O. Asitimbay, 36, New York, New York
Lt. Gregg Arthur Atlas, 45, Howells, New York
Gerald Atwood, 38, New York, New York
James Audiffred, 38, New York, New York
Kenneth W. Van Auken, 47, East Brunswick, New Jersey
Louis F. Aversano, Jr, 58, Manalapan, New Jersey
Ezra Aviles, 41, Commack, New York
Ayodeji Awe, 42, New York, New York
Samuel (Sandy) Ayala, 36, New York, New York
Arlene T. Babakitis, 47, Secaucus, New Jersey
Eustace (Rudy) Bacchus, 48, Metuchen, New Jersey
John James Badagliacca, 35, New York, New York
Jane Ellen Baeszler, 43, New York, New York
Robert J. Baierwalter, 44, Albertson, New York
Andrew J. Bailey, 29, New York, New York
Brett T. Bailey, 28, Bricktown, New Jersey
Tatyana Bakalinskaya, 43, New York, New York
Michael S. Baksh, 36, Englewood, New Jersey
Sharon Balkcom, 43, White Plains, New York
Michael Andrew Bane, 33, Yardley, Pennsylvania
Kathy Bantis, 44, Chicago, Illinois
Gerard Jean Baptiste, 35, New York, New York
Walter Baran, 42, New York, New York
Gerard A. Barbara, 53, New York, New York
Paul V. Barbaro, 35, Holmdel, New Jersey
James W. Barbella, 53, Oceanside, New York
Ivan Kyrillos Fairbanks Barbosa, 30, Jersey City, New Jersey
Victor Daniel Barbosa, 23, New York, New York
Colleen Ann Barkow, 26, East Windsor, New Jersey
David Michael Barkway, 34, Toronto, Ontario, Canada
Matthew Barnes, 37, Monroe, New York
Sheila Patricia Barnes, 55, Bay Shore, New York
Evan J. Baron, 38, Bridgewater, New Jersey
Renee Barrett-Arjune, 41, Irvington, New Jersey
Arthur T. Barry, 35, New York, New York
Diane G. Barry, 60, New York, New York
Maurice Vincent Barry, 49, Rutherford, New Jersey
Scott D. Bart, 28, Malverne, New York
Carlton W. Bartels, 44, New York, New York
Guy Barzvi, 29, New York, New York

Inna Basina, 43, New York, New York
Alysia Basmajian, 23, Bayonne, New Jersey
Kenneth William Basnicki, 48, Etobicoke, Ontario, Canada
Lt. Steven J. Bates, 42, New York, New York
Paul James Battaglia, 22, New York, New York
W. David Bauer, 45, Rumson, New Jersey
Ivhan Luis Carpio Bautista, 24, New York, New York
Marlyn C. Bautista, 46, Iselin, New Jersey
Jasper Baxter, 45, Philadelphia, Pennsylvania
Michele (Du Berry) Beale, 37, Essex, Britain
Paul F. Beatini, 40, Park Ridge, New Jersey
Jane S. Beatty, 53, Belford, New Jersey
Larry I. Beck, 38, Baldwin, New York
Manette Marie Beckles, 43, Rahway, New Jersey
Carl John Bedigian, 35, New York, New York
Michael Beekman, 39, New York, New York
Maria Behr, 41, Milford, New Jersey
Yelena Belilovsky, 38, Mamaroneck, New York
Nina Patrice Bell, 39, New York, New York
Andrea Della Bella, 59, Jersey City, New Jersey
Debbie S. Bellows, 30, East Windsor, New Jersey
Stephen Elliot Belson, 51, New York, New York
Paul Michael Benedetti, 32, New York, New York
Denise Lenore Benedetto, 40, New York, New York
Bryan Craig Bennett, 25, New York, New York
Oliver Duncan Bennett, 29, London, England
Eric L. Bennett, 29, New York, New York
Margaret L. Benson, 52, Rockaway, New Jersey
Dominick J. Berardi, 25, New York, New York
James Patrick Berger, 44, Lower Makefield, Pennsylvania
Steven Howard Berger, 45, Manalapan, New Jersey
John P. Bergin, 39, New York, New York
Alvin Bergsohn, 48, Baldwin Harbor, New York
Daniel D. Bergstein, 38, Teaneck, New Jersey
Michael J. Berkeley, 38, New York, New York
Donna Bernaerts-Kearns, 44, Hoboken, New Jersey
David W. Bernard, 57, Chelmsford, Massachusetts
William Bernstein, 44, New York, New York
David M. Berray, 39, New York, New York
David S. Berry, 43, New York, New York
Joseph J. Berry, 55, Saddle River, New Jersey
William Reed Bethke, 36, Hamilton, New Jersey
Timothy D. Betterly, 42, Little Silver, New Jersey
Edward F. Beyea, 42, New York, New York
Paul Michael Beyer, 37, New York, New York
Anil T. Bharvaney, 41, East Windsor, New Jersey
Bella Bhukhan, 24, Union, New Jersey
Shimmy D. Biegeleisen, 42, New York, New York
Peter Alexander Bielfeld, 44, New York, New York
William Biggart, 54, New York, New York
Brian Bilcher, 36, New York, New York
Carl Vincent Bini, 44, New York, New York
Gary Bird, 51, Tempe, Arizona
Joshua David Birnbaum, 24, New York, New York
George Bishop, 52, Granite Springs, New York
Jeffrey D. Bittner, 27, New York, New York
Balewa Albert Blackman, 26, New York, New York
Christopher Joseph Blackwell, 42, Patterson, New York
Susan L. Blair, 35, East Brunswick, New Jersey
Harry Blanding, 38, Blakeslee, Pennsylvania
Janice L. Blaney, 55, Williston Park, New York
Craig Michael Blass, 27, Greenlawn, New York

Rita Blau, 52, New York, New York
Richard M. Blood, 38, Ridgewood, New Jersey
Michael A. Boccardi, 30, Bronxville, New York
John Paul Bocchi, 38, New Vernon, New Jersey
Michael L. Bocchino, 45, New York, New York
Susan Mary Bochino, 36, New York, New York
Bruce Douglas (Chappy) Boehm, 49, West Hempstead, New York
Mary Katherine Boffa, 45, New York, New York
Nicholas A. Bogdan, 34, Browns Mills, New Jersey
Darren C. Bohan, 34, New York, New York
Lawrence Francis Boisseau, 36, Freehold, New Jersey
Vincent M. Boland, 25, Ringwood, New Jersey
Alan Bondarenko, 53, Flemington, New Jersey
Andre Bonheur, 40, New York, New York
Colin Arthur Bonnett, 39, New York, New York
Frank Bonomo, 42, Port Jefferson, New York
Yvonne L. Bonomo, 30, New York, New York
Sean Booker, 35, Irvington, New Jersey
Sherry Ann Bordeaux, 38, Jersey City, New Jersey
Krystine C. Bordenabe, 33, Old Bridge, New Jersey
Martin Boryczewski, 29, Parsippany, New Jersey
Richard E. Bosco, 34, Suffern, New York
John Howard Boulton, 29, New York, New York
Francisco Bourdier, 41, New York, New York
Thomas H. Bowden, 36, Wyckoff, New Jersey
Kimberly S. Bowers, 31, Islip, New York
Veronique (Bonnie) Nicole Bowers, 28, New York, New York
Larry Bowman, 46, New York, New York
Shawn Edward Bowman, 28, New York, New York
Kevin L. Bowser, 45, Philadelphia, Pennsylvania
Gary R. Box, 37, North Bellmore, New York
Gennady Boyarsky, 34, New York, New York
Pamela Boyce, 43, New York, New York
Michael Boyle, 37, Westbury, New York
Alfred Braca, 54, Leonardo, New Jersey
Sandra Conaty Brace, 60, New York, New York
Kevin H. Bracken, 37, New York, New York
David Brian Brady, 41, Summit, New Jersey
Alexander Braginsky, 38, Stamford, Connecticut
Nicholas W. Brandemarti, 21, Mantua, New Jersey
Michelle Renee Bratton, 23, Yonkers, New York
Patrice Braut, 31, New York, New York
Lydia Estelle Bravo, 50, Dunellen, New Jersey
Ronald Michael Breitweiser, 39, Middletown Township, New Jersey
Edward A. Brennan, 37, New York, New York
Frank H. Brennan, 50, New York, New York
Michael Emmett Brennan, 27, New York, New York
Peter Brennan, 30, Ronkonkoma, New York
Thomas M. Brennan, 32, Scarsdale, New York
Capt. Daniel Brethel, 43, Farmingdale, New York
Gary L. Bright, 36, Union City, New Jersey
Jonathan Eric Briley, 43, Mount Vernon, New York
Mark A. Brisman, 34, Armonk, New York
Paul Gary Bristow, 27, New York, New York
Victoria Alvarez Brito, 38, New York, New York
Mark Francis Broderick, 42, Old Bridge, New Jersey
Herman C. Broghammer, 58, North Merrick, New York
Keith Broomfield, 49, New York, New York
Janice J. Brown, 35, New York, New York
Lloyd Brown, 28, Bronxville, New York
Capt. Patrick J. Brown, 48, New York, New York
Bettina Browne, 49, Atlantic Beach, New York

Mark Bruce, 40, Summit, New Jersey
Richard Bruehert, 38, Westbury, New York
Andrew Brunn, 28
Capt. Vincent Brunton, 43, New York, New York
Ronald Paul Bucca, 47, Tuckahoe, New York
Brandon J. Buchanan, 24, New York, New York
Greg Joseph Buck, 37, New York, New York
Dennis Buckley, 38, Chatham, New Jersey
Nancy Bueche, 43, Hicksville, New York
Patrick Joseph Buhse, 36, Lincroft, New Jersey
John E. Bulaga, 35, Paterson, New Jersey
Stephen Bunin, 45, New York, New York
Thomas Daniel Burke, 38, Bedford Hills, New York
Capt. William F. Burke, 46, New York, New York
Matthew J. Burke, 28, New York, New York
Donald James Burns, 61, Nissequogue, New York
Kathleen A. Burns, 49, New York, New York
Keith James Burns, 39, East Rutherford, New Jersey
John Patrick Burnside, 36, New York, New York
Irina Buslo, 32, New York, New York
Milton Bustillo, 37, New York, New York
Thomas M. Butler, 37, Kings Park, New York
Patrick Byrne, 39, New York, New York
Timothy G. Byrne, 36, Manhattan, New York
Jesus Cabezas, 66, New York, New York
Lillian Caceres, 48, New York, New York
Brian Joseph Cachia, 26, New York, New York
Steven Cafiero, 31, New York, New York
Richard M. Caggiano, 25, New York, New York
Cecile M. Caguicla, 55, Boonton, New Jersey
Michael John Cahill, 37, East Williston, New York
Scott W. Cahill, 30, West Caldwell, New Jersey
Thomas J. Cahill, 36, Franklin Lakes, New Jersey
George Cain, 35, Massapequa, New York
Salvatore B. Calabro, 38, New York, New York
Joseph Calandrillo, 49, Hawley, Pennsylvania
Philip V. Calcagno, 57, New York, New York
Edward Calderon, 44, Jersey City, New Jersey
Kenneth Marcus Caldwell, 30, New York, New York
Dominick E. Calia, 40, Manalapan, New Jersey
Felix (Bobby) Calixte, 38, New York, New York
Capt. Frank Callahan, 51, New York, New York
Liam Callahan, 44, Rockaway, New York
Luigi Calvi, 34, East Rutherford, New Jersey
Roko Camaj, 60, Manhasset, New York
Michael Cammarata, 22, Huguenot, New York
David Otey Campbell, 51, Basking Ridge, New Jersey
Geoffrey Thomas Campbell, 31, New York, New York
Sandra Patricia Campbell, 45, New York, New York
Jill Marie Campbell, 31, New York, New York
Robert Arthur Campbell, 25, New York, New York
Juan Ortega Campos, 32, New York, New York
Sean Canavan, 39, New York, New York
John A. Candela, 42, Glen Ridge, New Jersey
Vincent Cangelosi, 30, New York, New York
Stephen J. Cangialosi, 40, Middletown, New Jersey
Lisa B. Cannava, 30, New York, New York
Brian Cannizzaro, 30, New York, New York
Michael R. Canty, 30, Schenectady, New York
Louis A. Caporicci, 35, New York, New York
Jonathan N. Cappello, 23, Garden City, New York
James Christopher Cappers, 33, Wading River, New York

Richard M. Caproni, 34, Lynbrook, New York
Jose Cardona, 32, New York, New York
Dennis M Carey, 51, Wantagh, New York
Edward Carlino, 46, New York, New York
Michael Scott Carlo, 34, New York, New York
David G. Carlone, 46, Randolph, New Jersey
Rosemarie C. Carlson, 40, New York, New York
Mark Stephen Carney, 41, Rahway, New Jersey
Joyce Ann Carpeneto, 40, New York, New York
Alicia Acevedo Carranza, Teziutlan, Puebla, Mexico
Jeremy M. Carrington, 34, New York, New York
Michael T. Carroll, 39, New York, New York
Peter Carroll, 42, New York, New York
James J. Carson, 32, Massapequa, New York
James Marcel Cartier, 26, New York, New York
Vivian Casalduc, 45, New York, New York
John F. Casazza, 38, Colts Neck, New Jersey
Paul Cascio, 23, Manhasset, New York
Kathleen Hunt Casey, 43, Middletown, New Jersey
Margarito Casillas, 54, Guadalajara, Jalisco, Mexico
Thomas Anthony Casoria, 29, New York, New York
William Otto Caspar, 57, Eatontown, New Jersey
Alejandro Castano, 35, Englewood, New Jersey
Arcelia Castillo, 49, Elizabeth, New Jersey
Leonard M. Castrianno, 30, New York, New York
Jose Ramon Castro, 37, New York, New York
Richard G. Catarelli, 47, New York, New York
Christopher Sean Caton, 34, New York, New York
Robert J. Caufield, 48, Valley Stream, New York
Mary Teresa Caulfield, 58, New York, New York
Judson Cavalier, 26, Huntington, New York
Michael Joseph Cawley, 32, Bellmore, New York
Jason D. Cayne, 32, Morganville, New Jersey
Juan Armando Ceballos, 47, New York, New York
Marcia G. Cecil-Carter, 34, New York, New York
Jason Cefalu, 30, West Hempstead, New York
Thomas J. Celic, 43, New York, New York
Ana M. Centeno, 38, Bayonne, New Jersey
Joni Cesta, 37, Bellmore, New York
Jeffrey M. Chairnoff, 35, West Windsor, New Jersey
Swarna Chalasani, 33, Jersey City, New Jersey
William Chalcoff, 41, Roslyn, New York
Eli Chalouh, 23, New York, New York
Charles Lawrence (Chip) Chan, 23, New York, New York
Mandy Chang, 40, New York, New York
Mark L. Charette, 38, Millburn, New Jersey
Gregorio Manuel Chavez, 48, New York, New York
Jayceryll M. de Chavez, 24, Carteret, New Jersey
Pedro Francisco Checo, 35, New York, New York
Douglas MacMillan Cherry, 38, Maplewood, New Jersey
Stephen Patrick Cherry, 41, Stamford, Connecticut
Vernon Paul Cherry, 49, New York, New York
Nestor Chevalier, 30, New York, New York
Swede Joseph Chevalier, 26, Locust, New Jersey
Alexander H. Chiang, 51, New City, New York
Dorothy J. Chiarchiaro, 61, Glenwood, New Jersey
Luis Alfonso Chimbo, 39, New York, New York
Robert Chin, 33, New York, New York
Wing Wai (Eddie) Ching, 29, Union, New Jersey
Nicholas P. Chiofalo, 39, Selden, New York
John Chipura, 39, New York, New York
Peter A. Chirchirillo, 47, Langhorne, Pennsylvania

Catherine E. Chirls, 47, Princeton, New Jersey
Kyung (Kaccy) Cho, 30, Clifton, New Jersey
Abul K. Chowdhury, 30, New York, New York
Mohammed Salahuddin Chowdhury, 38, New York, New York
Kirsten L. Christophe, 39, Maplewood, New Jersey
Pamela Chu, 31, New York, New York
Steven Paul Chucknick, 44, Cliffwood Beach, New Jersey
Wai-ching Chung, 36, New York, New York
Christopher Ciafardini, 30, New York, New York
Alex F. Ciccone, 38, New Rochelle, New York
Frances Ann Cilente, 26, New York, New York
Elaine Cillo, 40, New York, New York
Edna Cintron, 46, New York, New York
Nestor Andre Cintron, 26, New York, New York
Lt. Robert Dominick Cirri, 39, Nutley, New Jersey
Juan Pablo Alvarez Cisneros, 23, Weehawken, New Jersey
Gregory Alan Clark, 40, Teaneck, New Jersey
Mannie Leroy Clark, 54, New York, New York
Thomas R. Clark, 37, Summit, New Jersey
Eugene Clark, 47, New York, New York
Benjamin Keefe Clark, 39, New York, New York
Christopher Robert Clarke, 34, Philadelphia, Pennsylvania
Donna Clarke, 39, New York, New York
Michael Clarke, 27, Prince's Bay, New York
Suria R.E. Clarke, 30, New York, New York
Kevin Francis Cleary, 38, New York, New York
James D. Cleere, 55, Newton, Iowa
Geoffrey W. Cloud, 36, Stamford, Connecticut
Susan M. Clyne, 42, Lindenhurst, New York
Steven Coakley, 36, Deer Park, New York
Jeffrey Coale, 31, Souderton, Pennsylvania
Patricia A. Cody, 46, Brigantine, New Jersey
Daniel Michael Coffey, 54, Newburgh, New York
Jason Matthew Coffey, 25, Newburgh, New York
Florence Cohen, 62, New York, New York
Kevin Sanford Cohen, 28, Edison, New Jersey
Anthony Joseph Coladonato, 47, New York, New York
Mark J. Colaio, 34, New York, New York
Stephen J. Colaio, 32, Montauk, New York
Christopher M. Colasanti, 33, Hoboken, New Jersey
Michel Paris Colbert, 39, West New York, New Jersey
Kevin Nathaniel Colbert, 25, New York, New York
Keith Eugene Coleman, 34, Warren, New Jersey
Scott Thomas Coleman, 31, New York, New York
Tarel Coleman, 32
Liam Joseph Colhoun, 34, Flushing,, New York
Robert D. Colin, 49, West Babylon, New York
Robert J. Coll, 35, Glen Ridge, New Jersey
Jean Marie Collin, 42, New York, New York
John Michael Collins, 42, New York, New York
Michael L. Collins, 38, Montclair, New Jersey
Thomas J. Collins, 36, New York, New York
Joseph Collison, 50, New York, New York
Patricia Malia Colodner, 39, New York, New York
Linda M. Colon, 46, Perrineville, New Jersey
Soledi Colon, 39, New York, New York
Ronald Comer, 56, Northport, New York
Jaime Concepcion, 46, New York, New York
Albert Conde, 62, Englishtown, New Jersey
Denease Conley, 44, New York, New York
Susan Clancy Conlon, 41, New York, New York
Margaret Mary Conner, 57, New York, New York

John E. Connolly, 46, Allenwood, New Jersey
Cynthia L. Connolly, 40, Metuchen, New Jersey
James Lee Connor, 38, Summit, New Jersey
Jonathan (J.C.) Connors, 55, Old Brookville, New York
Kevin P. Connors, 55, Greenwich, Connecticut
Kevin Francis Conroy, 47, New York, New York
Brenda E. Conway, 40, New York, New York
Dennis Michael Cook, 33, Colts Neck, New Jersey
Helen D. Cook, 24, New York, New York
John A. Cooper, 40, Bayonne, New Jersey
Joseph J. Coppo, 47, New Canaan, Connecticut
Gerard J. Coppola, 46, New Providence, New Jersey
Joseph Albert Corbett, 28, Islip, New York
Alejandro Cordero, 23, New York, New York
Robert Cordice, 28, New York, New York
Ruben D. Correa, 44, New York, New York
Danny A. Correa-Gutierrez, 25, Fairview, New Jersey
James Corrigan, 60, New York, New York
Carlos Cortes, 57, New York, New York
Kevin M. Cosgrove, 46, West Islip, New York
Dolores Marie Costa, 53, Middletown, New Jersey
Digna Alexandra Rivera Costanza, 25, New York, New York
Charles Gregory Costello, 46, Old Bridge, New Jersey
Michael S. Costello, 27, Hoboken, New Jersey
Conrod K.H. Cottoy, 51, New York, New York
Martin Coughlan, 54, New York, New York
Sgt. John Gerard Coughlin, 43, Pomona, New York
Timothy John Coughlin, 42, New York, New York
James E. Cove, 48, Rockville Centre, New York
Andre Cox, 29, New York, New York
Frederick John Cox, 27, New York, New York
James Raymond Coyle, 26, New York, New York
Michelle Coyle-Eulau, 38, Garden City, New York
Anne M. Cramer, 47, New York, New York
Christopher Seton Cramer, 34, Manahawkin, New Jersey
Denise Crant, 46, Hackensack, New Jersey
Robert James Crawford, 62, New York, New York
James L. Crawford, 33, Madison, New Jersey
Joanne Mary Cregan, 32, New York, New York
Lucia Crifasi, 51, Glendale, New York
Lt. John Crisci, 48, Holbrook, New York
Daniel Hal Crisman, 25, New York, New York
Dennis A. Cross, 60, Islip Terrace, New York
Helen Crossin-Kittle, 34, Larchmont, New York
Kevin Raymond Crotty, 43, Summit, New Jersey
Thomas G. Crotty, 42, Rockville Centre, New York
John Crowe, 57, Rutherford, New Jersey
Welles Remy Crowther, 24, Upper Nyack, New York
Robert L. Cruikshank, 64, New York, New York
Francisco Cruz, 47, New York, New York
John Robert Cruz, 32, Jersey City, New Jersey
Kenneth John Cubas, 48, Woodstock, New York
Richard Joseph Cudina, 46, Glen Gardner, New Jersey
Neil James Cudmore, 38, Port Washington, New York
Thomas Patrick Cullen, 31, New York, New York
Joan McConnell Cullinan, 47, Scarsdale, New York
Joyce Cummings, 65
Brian Thomas Cummins, 38, Manasquan, New Jersey
Nilton Albuquerque Fernao Cunha, 41
Michael Joseph Cunningham, 39, Princeton Junction, New Jersey
Robert Curatolo, 31, New York, New York
Laurence Curia, 41, Garden City, New York

Paul Dario Curioli, 53, Norwalk, Connecticut
Beverly Curry, 41, New York, New York
Sgt. Michael Curtin, 45, Medford, New York
Gavin Cushny, 47, Hoboken, New Jersey
Caleb Arron Dack, 39, Montclair, New Jersey
Carlos S. DaCosta, 41, Elizabeth, New Jersey
John D'Allara, 47, Pearl River, New York
Vincent D'Amadeo, 36, East Patchoque, New York
Thomas A. Damaskinos, 33, Matawan, New Jersey
Jack L. D'Ambrosi, 45, Woodcliff Lake, New Jersey
Jeannine Marie Damiani-Jones, 28, New York, New York
Patrick W. Danahy, 35, Yorktown Heights, New York
Nana Kwuku Danso, 47, New York, New York
Mary D'Antonio, 55, New York, New York
Vincent G. Danz, 38, Farmingdale, New York
Dwight Donald Darcy, 55, Bronxville, New York
Elizabeth Ann Darling, 28, Newark, New Jersey
Annette Andrea Dataram, 25, New York, New York
Lt. Edward Alexander D'Atri, 38, New York, New York
Michael D. D'Auria, 25, New York, New York
Lawrence Davidson, 51, New York, New York
Michael Allen Davidson, 27, Westfield, New Jersey
Scott Matthew Davidson, 33, New York, New York
Titus Davidson, 55, New York, New York
Niurka Davila, 47, New York, New York
Clinton Davis, 38, New York, New York
Wayne Terrial Davis, 29, Fort Meade, Maryland
Calvin Dawson, 46, New York, New York
Anthony Richard Dawson, 32, Southampton, Hampshire, England
Edward James Day, 45, New York, New York
Emerita (Emy) De La Pena, 32, New York, New York
Melanie Louise De Vere, 30, London, England
William T. Dean, 35, Floral Park, New York
Robert J. DeAngelis, 48, West Hempstead, New York
Thomas P. Deangelis, 51, Westbury, New York
Tara Debek, 35, Babylon, New York
Anna Debin, 30, East Farmingdale, New York
James V. DeBlase, 45, Manalapan, New Jersey
Paul DeCola, 39, Ridgewood, New York
Simon Dedvukaj, 26, Mohegan Lake, New York
Jason Christopher DeFazio, 29, New York, New York
David A. Defeo, 37, New York, New York
Jennifer DeJesus, 23, New York, New York
Monique E. DeJesus, 28, New York, New York
Nereida DeJesus, 30, New York, New York
Donald A. Delapenha, 37, Allendale, New Jersey
Vito Joseph Deleo, 41, New York, New York
Danielle Delie, 47, New York, New York
Colleen Ann Deloughery, 41, Bayonne, New Jersey
Francis (Frank) Albert DeMartini, 49, New York, New York
Anthony Demas, 61, New York, New York
Martin DeMeo, 47, Farmingville, New York
Francis X. Deming, 47, Franklin Lakes, New Jersey
Carol K. Demitz, 49, New York, New York
Kevin Dennis, 43, Peapack, New Jersey
Thomas F. Dennis, 43, Setauket, New York
Jean C. DePalma, 42, Newfoundland, New Jersey
Jose Nicolas Depena, 42, New York, New York
Robert J. Deraney, 43, New York, New York
Michael DeRienzo, 37, Hoboken, New Jersey
David Paul Derubbio, 38, New York, New York
Jemal Legesse DeSantis, 28, Jersey City, New Jersey

Christian L. DeSimone, 23, Ringwood, New Jersey
Edward DeSimone, 36, Atlantic Highlands, New Jersey
Lt. Andrew Desperito, 44, Patchogue, New York
Michael Jude D'Esposito, 32, Morganville, New Jersey
Cindy Ann Deuel, 28, New York, New York
Jerry DeVito, 66, New York, New York
Robert P. Devitt, 36, Plainsboro, New Jersey
Dennis Lawrence Devlin, 51, Washingtonville, New York
Gerard Dewan, 35, New York, New York
Simon Suleman Ali Kassamali Dhanani, 62, Hartsdale, New York
Michael L. DiAgostino, 41, Garden City, New York
Matthew Diaz, 33, New York, New York
Nancy Diaz, 28, New York, New York
Obdulio Ruiz Diaz, 44, New York, New York
Lourdes Galletti Diaz, 32, New York, New York
Michael Diaz-Piedra, 49
Judith Belguese Diaz-Sierra, 32, Bay Shore, New York
Patricia F. DiChiaro, 63, New York, New York
Joseph Dermot Dickey, 50, Manhasset, New York
Lawrence Patrick Dickinson, 35, Morganville, New Jersey
Michael David Diehl, 48, Brick, New Jersey
John DiFato, 39, New York, New York
Vincent F. DiFazio, 43, Hampton, New Jersey
Carl DiFranco, 27, New York, New York
Donald J. DiFranco, 43, New York, New York
Debra Ann DiMartino, 36, New York, New York
Stephen P. Dimino, 48, Basking Ridge, New Jersey
William J. Dimmling, 47, Garden City, New York
Christopher Dincuff, 31, Jersey City, New Jersey
Jeffrey M. Dingle, 32, New York, New York
Anthony DiOnisio, 38, Glen Rock, New Jersey
George DiPasquale, 33, New York, New York
Joseph DiPilato, 57, New York, New York
Douglas Frank DiStefano, 24, Hoboken, New Jersey
Ramzi A. Doany, 35, Bayonne, New Jersey, Jordanian
John J. Doherty, 58, Hartsdale, New York
Melissa C. Doi, 32, New York, New York
Brendan Dolan, 37, Glen Rock, New Jersey
Neil Dollard, 28, Hoboken, New Jersey
James Joseph Domanico, 56, New York, New York
Benilda Pascua Domingo, 37, New York, New York
Charles (Carlos) Dominguez, 34, East Meadow, New York
Geronimo (Jerome) Mark Patrick Dominguez, 37, Holtsville, New York
Lt. Kevin W. Donnelly, 43, New York, New York
Jacqueline Donovan, 34, New York, New York
Stephen Dorf, 39, New Milford, New Jersey
Thomas Dowd, 37, Monroe, New York
Lt. Kevin Christopher Dowdell, 46, New York, New York
Mary Yolanda Dowling, 46, New York, New York
Raymond M. Downey, 63, Deer Park, New York
Joseph M. Doyle, 25, New York, New York
Frank Joseph Doyle, 39, Englewood, New Jersey
Randy Drake, 37, Lee's Summit, Mo.
Stephen Patrick Driscoll, 38, Lake Carmel, New York
Mirna A. Duarte, 31, New York, New York
Luke A. Dudek, 50, Livingston, New Jersey
Christopher Michael Duffy, 23, New York, New York
Gerard Duffy, 53, Manorville, New York
Michael Joseph Duffy, 29, Northport, New York
Thomas W. Duffy, 52, Pittsford, New York
Antoinette Duger, 44, Belleville, New Jersey
Jackie Sayegh Duggan, 34

Sareve Dukat, 53, New York, New York
Christopher Joseph Dunne, 28, Mineola, New York
Richard A. Dunstan, 54, New Providence, New Jersey
Patrick Thomas Dwyer, 37, Nissequogue, New York
Joseph Anthony Eacobacci, 26, New York, New York
John Bruce Eagleson, 53, Middlefield, Connecticut
Robert D. Eaton, 37, Manhasset, New York
Dean P. Eberling, 44, Cranford, New Jersey
Margaret Ruth Echtermann, 33, Hoboken, New Jersey
Paul Robert Eckna, 28, West New York, New Jersey
Constantine (Gus) Economos, 41, New York, New York
Dennis Michael Edwards, 35, Huntington, New York
Michael Hardy Edwards, 33, New York, New York
Lisa Egan, 31, Cliffside Park, New Jersey
Capt. Martin Egan, 36, New York, New York
Michael Egan, 51, Middletown, New Jersey
Christine Egan, 55, Winnipeg, Manitoba, Canada
Samantha Egan, 24, Jersey City, New Jersey
Carole Eggert, 60, New York, New York
Lisa Caren Weinstein Ehrlich, 36, New York, New York
John Ernst (Jack) Eichler, 69, Cedar Grove, New Jersey
Eric Adam Eisenberg, 32, Commack, New York
Daphne F. Elder, 36, Newark, New Jersey
Michael J. Elferis, 27, College Point, New York
Mark J. Ellis, 26, South Huntington, New York
Valerie Silver Ellis, 46, New York, New York
Albert Alfy William Elmarry, 30, North Brunswick, New Jersey
Edgar H. Emery, 45, Clifton, New Jersey
Doris Suk-Yuen Eng, 30, New York, New York
Christopher S. Epps, 29, New York, New York
Ulf Ramm Ericson, 79, Greenwich, Connecticut
Erwin L. Erker, 41, Farmingdale, New York
William J. Erwin, 30, Verona, New Jersey
Sarah (Ali) Escarcega, 35, New York, New York
Jose Espinal, 31
Fanny M. Espinoza, 29, Teaneck, New Jersey
Francis Esposito, 32, New York, New York
Lt. Michael Esposito, 41, New York, New York
William Esposito, 51, Bellmore, New York
Brigette Ann Esposito, 34, New York, New York
Ruben Esquilin, 35, New York, New York
Sadie Ette, 36, New York, New York
Barbara G. Etzold, 43, Jersey City, New Jersey
Eric Brian Evans, 31, Weehawken, New Jersey
Robert Edward Evans, 36, Franklin Square, New York
Meredith Emily June Ewart, 29, Hoboken, New Jersey
Catherine K. Fagan, 58, New York, New York
Patricia M. Fagan, 55, Toms River, New Jersey
Keith G. Fairben, 24, Floral Park, New York
William Fallon, 38, Coram, New York
William F. Fallon, 53, Rocky Hill, New Jersey
Anthony J. Fallone, 39, New York, New York
Dolores B. Fanelli, 38, Farmingville, New York
John Joseph Fanning, 54, West Hempstead, New York
Kathleen (Kit) Faragher, 33, Denver, Colo.
Capt. Thomas Farino, 37, Bohemia, New York
Nancy Carole Farley, 45, Jersey City, New Jersey
Elizabeth Ann (Betty) Farmer, 62, New York, New York
Douglas Farnum, 33, New York, New York
John W. Farrell, 41, Basking Ridge, New Jersey
Terrence Patrick Farrell, 45, Huntington, New York
John G. Farrell, 32, New York, New York

Capt. Joseph Farrelly, 47, New York, New York
Thomas P. Farrelly, 54, East Northport, New York
Syed Abdul Fatha, 54, Newark, New Jersey
Christopher Faughnan, 37, South Orange, New Jersey
Wendy R. Faulkner, 47, Mason, Ohio
Shannon M. Fava, 30, New York, New York
Bernard D. Favuzza, 52, Suffern, New York
Robert Fazio, 41, Freeport, New York
Ronald C. Fazio, 57, Closter, New Jersey
William Feehan, 72, New York, New York
Francis J. (Frank) Feely, 41, Middletown, New York
Garth E. Feeney, 28, New York, New York
Sean B. Fegan, 34, New York, New York
Lee S. Fehling, 28, Wantagh, New York
Peter Feidelberg, 34, Hoboken, New Jersey
Alan D. Feinberg, 48, New York, New York
Rosa Maria Feliciano, 30, New York, New York
Edward T. Fergus, 40, Wilton, Connecticut
George Ferguson, 54, Teaneck, New Jersey
Henry Fernandez, 23, New York, New York
Judy H. Fernandez, 27, Parlin, New Jersey
Jose Manuel Contreras Fernandez, El Aguacate, Jalisco, Mexico
Elisa Giselle Ferraina, 27, London, England
Anne Marie Sallerin Ferreira, 29, Jersey City, New Jersey
Robert John Ferris, 63, Garden City, New York
David Francis Ferrugio, 46, Middletown, New Jersey
Louis V. Fersini, 38, Basking Ridge, New Jersey
Michael David Ferugio, 37, New York, New York
Bradley James Fetchet, 24, New York, New York
Jennifer Louise Fialko, 29, Teaneck, New Jersey
Kristen Fiedel, 27, New York, New York
Samuel Fields, 36, New York, New York
Michael Bradley Finnegan, 37, Basking Ridge, New Jersey
Timothy J. Finnerty, 33, Glen Rock, New Jersey
Michael Curtis Fiore, 46, New York, New York
Stephen J. Fiorelli, 43, Aberdeen, New Jersey
Paul M. Fiori, 31, Yorktown Heights, New York
John Fiorito, 40, Stamford, Connecticut
Lt. John R. Fischer, 46, New York, New York
Andrew Fisher, 42, New York, New York
Thomas J. Fisher, 36, Union, New Jersey
Bennett Lawson Fisher, 58, Stamford, Connecticut
John Roger Fisher, 46, Bayonne, New Jersey
Lucy Fishman, 37, New York, New York
Ryan D. Fitzgerald, 26, New York, New York
Thomas Fitzpatrick, 35, Tuckahoe, New York
Richard P. Fitzsimons, 57, Lynbrook, New York
Salvatore A. Fiumefreddo, 47, Manalapan, New Jersey
Christina Donovan Flannery, 26, New York, New York
Eileen Flecha, 33, New York, New York
Andre G. Fletcher, 37, North Babylon, New York
Carl Flickinger, 38, Conyers, New York
John Joseph Florio, 33, Oceanside, New York
Joseph W. Flounders, 46, East Stroudsburg, Pennsylvania
David Fodor, 38, Garrison, New York
Lt. Michael N. Fodor, 53, Warwick, New York
Steven Mark Fogel, 40, Westfield, New York
Thomas Foley, 32, West Nyack, New York
David Fontana, 37, New York, New York
Chih Min (Dennis) Foo, 40, Holmdel, New Jersey
Del Rose Forbes-Cheatham, 48, New York, New York
Godwin Forde, 39, New York, New York

Donald A. Foreman, 53, New York, New York
Christopher Hugh Forsythe, 44, Basking Ridge, New Jersey
Claudia Alicia Martinez Foster, 26, New York, New York
Noel J. Foster, 40, Bridgewater, New Jersey
Ana Fosteris, 58, Coram, New York
Robert J. Foti, 42, Albertson, New York
Jeffrey L. Fox, 40, Cranbury, New Jersey
Virginia Fox, 58, New York, New York
Virgin (Lucy) Francis, 62, New York, New York
Pauline Francis, 57, New York, New York
Joan Francis
Gary J. Frank, 35, South Amboy, New Jersey
Morton Frank, 31, New York, New York
Peter Christopher Frank, 29, New York, New York
Richard K. Fraser, 32, New York, New York
Kevin Joseph Frawley, 34, Bronxville, New York
Clyde Frazier, 41, New York, New York
Lillian I. Frederick, 46, Teaneck, New Jersey
Andrew Fredericks, 40, Suffern, New York
Tamitha Freemen, 35, New York, New York
Brett O. Freiman, 29, Roslyn, New York
Lt. Peter L. Freund, 45, Westtown, New York
Arlene E. Fried, 49, Roslyn Heights, New York
Alan Wayne Friedlander, 52, Yorktown Heights, New York
Andrew K. Friedman, 44, Woodbury, New York
Gregg J. Froehner, 46, Chester, New Jersey
Peter Christian Fry, 36, Wilton, Connecticut
Clement Fumando, 59, New York, New York
Steven Elliot Furman, 40, Wesley Hills, New York
Paul James Furmato, 37, Colts Neck, New Jersey
Fredric Gabler, 30, New York, New York
Richard S. Gabrielle, 50, West Haven, Connecticut
James Andrew Gadiel, 23, New York, New York
Pamela Gaff, 51, Robinsville, New Jersey
Ervin Vincent Gailliard, 42, New York, New York
Deanna L. Galante, 32, New York, New York
Grace Galante, 29, New York, New York
Anthony Edward Gallagher, 41, New York, New York
Daniel James Gallagher, 23, Red Bank, New Jersey
John Patrick Gallagher, 31, Yonkers, New York
Cono E. Gallo, 30, New York, New York
Vincenzo Gallucci, 36, Monroe Township, New Jersey
Thomas Edward Galvin, 32, New York, New York
Giovanna (Genni) Gambale, 27, New York, New York
Thomas Gambino, 48, Babylon, New York
Giann F. Gamboa, 26, New York, New York
Peter J. Ganci, 55, North Massapequa, New York
Claude Michael Gann, 41, Roswell, Georgia
Lt. Charles William Garbarini, 44, Pleasantville, New York
Cesar Garcia, 36, New York, New York
David Garcia, 40, Freeport, New York
Jorge Luis Morron Garcia, 38, New York, New York
Juan Garcia, 50, New York, New York
Marlyn C. Garcia, 21, New York, New York
Christopher Gardner, 36, Darien, Connecticut
Douglas B. Gardner, 39, New York, New York
Harvey J. Gardner, 35, Lakewood, New Jersey
Thomas A. Gardner, 39, Oceanside, New York
Jeffrey B. Gardner, 36, Hoboken, New Jersey
William Arthur Gardner, 45, Lynbrook, New York
Francesco Garfi, 29, New York, New York
Rocco Gargano, 28, Bayside, New York

James M. Gartenberg, 36, New York, New York
Matthew David Garvey, 37
Bruce Gary, 51, Bellmore, New York
Palmina Delli Gatti, 33, New York, New York
Boyd A. Gatton, 38, Jersey City, New Jersey
Donald Richard Gavagan, 35, New York, New York
Terence D. Gazzani, 24, New York, New York
Gary Geidel, 44, New York, New York
Paul Hamilton Geier, 36, Farmingdale, New York
Julie M. Geis, 44, Lees Summit, Mo.
Peter Gelinas, 34, New York, New York
Steven Paul Geller, 52, New York, New York
Howard G. Gelling, 28, New York, New York
Peter Victor Genco, 36, Rockville Centre, New York
Steven Gregory Genovese, 37, Basking Ridge, New Jersey
Alayne F. Gentul, 44, Mountain Lakes, New Jersey
Edward F. Geraghty, 45, Rockville Centre, New York
Suzanne Geraty, 30, New York, New York
Ralph Gerhardt, 33, New York, New York
Robert J. Gerlich, 56, Monroe, Connecticut
Denis P. Germain, 33, Tuxedo Park, New York
Marina R. Gertsberg, 25, New York, New York
Susan M. Getzendanner, 57, New York, New York
James Gerard Geyer, 41, Rockville Centre, New York
Joseph M. Giaccone, 43, Monroe, New Jersey
Lt. Vincent Francis Giammona, 40, Valley Stream, New York
Debra L. Gibbon, 43, Hackettstown, New Jersey
James A. Giberson, 43, New York, New York
Craig Neil Gibson, 37, New York, New York
Ronnie Gies, 43, Merrick, New York
Laura A. Giglio, 35, Oceanside, New York
Andrew Clive Gilbert, 39, Califon, New Jersey
Timothy Paul Gilbert, 35, Lebanon, New Jersey
Paul Stuart Gilbey, 39, Chatham, New Jersey
Paul John Gill, 34, New York, New York
Mark Y. Gilles, 33, New York, New York
Evan H. Gillette, 40, New York, New York
Ronald Gilligan, 43, Norwalk, Connecticut
Sgt. Rodney C. Gillis, 34, New York, New York
Laura Gilly, 32, New York, New York
Lt. John F. Ginley, 37, Warwick, New York
Jeffrey Giordano, 46, New York, New York
John Giordano, 46, Newburgh, New York
Donna Marie Giordano, 44, Parlin, New Jersey
Steven A. Giorgetti, 43, Manhasset, New York
Martin Giovinazzo, 34, New York, New York
Kum-Kum Girolamo, 41, New York, New York
Salvatore Gitto, 44, Manalapan, New Jersey
Cynthia Giugliano, 46, Nesconset, New York
Mon Gjonbalaj, 65, New York, New York
Dianne Gladstone, 55, New York, New York
Keith Alexander Glascoe, 38, New York, New York
Thomas I. Glasser, 40, Summit, New Jersey
Harry Glenn, 38, Piscataway, New Jersey
Barry H. Glick, 55, Wayne, New Jersey
Steven Lawrence Glick, 42, Greenwich, Connecticut
John T. Gnazzo, 32, New York, New York
William (Bill) Robert Godshalk, 35, New York, New York
Michael Gogliormella, 43, New Providence, New Jersey
Brian Fredric Goldberg, 26, Union, New Jersey
Jeffrey Grant Goldflam, 48, Melville, New York
Michelle Herman Goldstein, 31, New York, New York

Monica Goldstein, 25, New York, New York
Steven Goldstein, 35, Princeton, New Jersey
Andrew H. Golkin, 30, New York, New York
Dennis James Gomes, 40, New York, New York
Enrique Antonio Gomez, 42, New York, New York
Jose Bienvenido Gomez, 45, New York, New York
Manuel Gomez, 42, New York, New York
Wilder Gomez, 38, New York, New York
Jenine Gonzalez, 27, New York, New York
Joel Guevara Gonzalez. 23, Aguascalientes, Aguascalientes, Mexico
Rosa J. Gonzalez, 32, Jersey City, New Jersey
Mauricio Gonzalez, 27, New York, New York
Calvin J. Gooding, 38, Riverside, New York
Harry Goody, 50, New York, New York
Kiran Reddy Gopu, 24, Bridgeport, Connecticut
Catherine Carmen Gorayeb, 41, New York, New York
Kerene Gordon, 43, New York, New York
Sebastian Gorki, 27, New York, New York
Thomas E. Gorman, 41, Middlesex, New Jersey
Kieran Gorman, 35, Yonkers, New York
Michael Edward Gould, 29, Hoboken, New Jersey
Yugi Goya, 42, Rye, New York
Jon Richard Grabowski, 33, New York, New York
Christopher Michael Grady, 39, Cranford, New Jersey
Edwin John Graf, 48, Rowayton, Connecticut
David M. Graifman, 40, New York, New York
Gilbert Granados, 51, Hicksville, New York
Elvira Granitto, 43, New York, New York
Winston Arthur Grant, 59, West Hempstead, New York
Christopher Stewart Gray, 32, Weehawken, New Jersey
James Michael Gray, 34, New York, New York
Linda Mair Grayling, 44, New York, New York
John Michael Grazioso, 41, Middletown, New Jersey
Timothy Grazioso, 42, Gulf Stream, Florida
Derrick Arthur Green, 44, New York, New York
Wade Brian Green, 42, Westbury, New York
Elaine Myra Greenberg, 56, New York, New York
Gayle R. Greene, 51, Montville, New Jersey
James Arthur Greenleaf, 32, New York, New York
Eileen Marsha Greenstein, 52, Morris Plains, New Jersey
Elizabeth (Lisa) Martin Gregg, 52, New York, New York
Donald H. Gregory, 62, Ramsey, New Jersey
Florence M. Gregory, 38, New York, New York
Denise Gregory, 39, New York, New York
Pedro (David) Grehan, 35, Hoboken, New Jersey
John M. Griffin, 38, Waldwick, New Jersey
Tawanna Griffin, 30, New York, New York
Joan D. Griffith, 39, Willingboro, New Jersey
Warren Grifka, 54, New York, New York
Ramon Grijalvo, 58
Joseph F. Grillo, 46, New York, New York
David Grimner, 51, Merrick, New York
Kenneth Grouzalis, 56, Lyndhurst, New Jersey
Joseph Grzelak, 52, New York, New York
Matthew J. Grzymalski, 34, New Hyde Park, New York
Robert Joseph Gschaar, 55, Spring Valley, New York
Liming (Michael) Gu, 34, Piscataway, New Jersey
Jose A. Guadalupe, 37, New York, New York
Yan Zhu (Cindy) Guan, 25, New York, New York
Geoffrey E. Guja, 47, Lindenhurst, New York
Lt. Joseph Gullickson, 37, New York, New York
Babita Guman, 33, New York, New York

Douglas B. Gurian, 38, Tenafly, New Jersey
Philip T. Guza, 54, Sea Bright, New Jersey
Barbara Guzzardo, 49, Glendale, New York
Peter Gyulavary, 44, Warwick, New York
Gary Robert Haag, 36, Ossining, New York
Andrea Lyn Haberman, 25, Chicago, Illinois
Barbara M. Habib, 49, New York, New York
Philip Haentzler, 49, New York, New York
Nizam A. Hafiz, 32, New York, New York
Karen Hagerty, 34, New York, New York
Steven Hagis, 31, New York, New York
Mary Lou Hague, 26, New York, New York
David Halderman, 40, New York, New York
Maile Rachel Hale, 26, Cambridge, Massachusetts
Richard Hall, 49, Purchase, New York
Vaswald George Hall, 50, New York, New York
Robert John Halligan, 59, Basking Ridge, New Jersey
Lt. Vincent Gerard Halloran, 43, North Salem, New York
James D. Halvorson, 56, Greenwich, Connecticut
Mohammad Salman Hamdani, 23, New York, New York
Felicia Hamilton, 62, New York, New York
Robert Hamilton, 43, Washingtonville, New York
Frederic Kim Han, 45, Marlboro, New Jersey
Christopher James Hanley, 34, New York, New York
Sean Hanley, 35, New York, New York
Valerie Joan Hanna, 57, Freeville, New York
Thomas Hannafin, 36, New York, New York
Kevin James Hannaford, 32, Basking Ridge, New Jersey
Michael L. Hannan, 34, Lynbrook, New York
Dana Hannon, 29, Suffern, New York
Vassilios G. Haramis, 56, New York, New York
James A. Haran, 41, Malverne, New York
Jeffrey P. Hardy, 46, New York, New York
Timothy John Hargrave, 38, Readington, New Jersey
Daniel Harlin, 41, Kent, New York
Frances Haros, 76, New York, New York
Lt. Harvey L. Harrell, 49, New York, New York
Lt. Stephen Gary Harrell, 44, Warwick, New York
Stewart D. Harris, 52, Marlboro, New Jersey
Aisha Harris, 22, New York, New York
John Patrick Hart, 38, Danville, California
John Clinton Hartz, 64, Basking Ridge, New Jersey
Emeric J. Harvey, 56, Montclair, New Jersey
Capt. Thomas Theodore Haskell, 37, Massapequa, New York
Timothy Haskell, 34, Seaford, New York
Joseph John Hasson, 34, New York, New York
Capt. Terence S. Hatton, 41, New York, New York
Leonard William Hatton, 45, Ridgefield Park, New Jersey
Michael Helmut Haub, 34, Roslyn Heights, New York
Timothy Aaron Haviland, 41, Oceanside, New York
Donald G. Havlish, 53, Yardley, Pennsylvania
Anthony Hawkins, 30, New York, New York
Nobuhiro Hayatsu, 36, Scarsdale, New York
Philip Hayes, 67, Northport, New York
William Ward Haynes, 35, Rye, New York
Scott Hazelcorn, 29, Hoboken, New Jersey
Lt. Michael K. Healey, 42, East Patchogue, New York
Roberta Bernstein Heber, 60, New York, New York
Charles Francis Xavier Heeran, 23, Belle Harbor, New York
John Heffernan, 37, New York, New York
Howard Joseph Heller, 37, Ridgefield, Connecticut
JoAnn L. Heltibridle, 46, Springfield, New Jersey

Mark F. Hemschoot, 45, Red Bank, New Jersey
Ronnie Lee Henderson, 52, Newburgh, New York
Janet Hendricks, 48, New York, New York
Brian Hennessey, 35, Ringoes, New Jersey
Michelle Marie Henrique, 27, New York, New York
Joseph P. Henry, 25, New York, New York
William Henry, 49, New York, New York
John Henwood, 35, New York, New York
Robert Allan Hepburn, 39, Union, New Jersey
Mary (Molly) Herencia, 47, New York, New York
Lindsay Coates Herkness, 58, New York, New York
Harvey Robert Hermer, 59, New York, New York
Claribel Hernandez, 31, New York, New York
Norberto Hernandez, 42, New York, New York
Raul Hernandez, 51, New York, New York
Gary Herold, 44, Farmingdale, New York
Jeffrey A. Hersch, 53, New York, New York
Thomas Hetzel, 33, Elmont, New York
Capt. Brian Hickey, 47, New York, New York
Ysidro Hidalgo-Tejada, 47, New York, New York, Dominican Republic
Lt. Timothy Higgins, 43, Farmingville, New York
Robert D. Higley, 29, New Fairfield, Connecticut
Todd Russell Hill, 34, Boston, Massachusetts
Clara Victorine Hinds, 52, New York, New York
Neal Hinds, 28, New York, New York
Mark D. Hindy, 28, New York, New York
Richard Bruce Van Hine, 48, Greenwood Lake, New York
Katsuyuki Hirai, 32, Hartsdale, New York
Heather Malia Ho, 32, New York, New York
Tara Yvette Hobbs, 31, New York, New York
Thomas A. Hobbs, 41, Baldwin, New York
James L. Hobin, 47, Marlborough, Connecticut
Robert Wayne Hobson, 36, New Providence, New Jersey
DaJuan Hodges, 29, New York, New York
Ronald George Hoerner, 58, Massapequa Park, New York
Patrick Aloysius Hoey, 53, Middletown, New Jersey
Stephen G. Hoffman, 36, Long Beach, New York
Marcia Hoffman, 52, New York, New York
Frederick J. Hoffmann, 53, Freehold, New Jersey
Michele L. Hoffmann, 27, Freehold, New Jersey
Judith Florence Hofmiller, 53, Brookfield, Connecticut
Thomas Warren Hohlweck, 57, Harrison, New York
Jonathan R. Hohmann, 48, New York, New York
Joseph Francis Holland, 32, Glen Rock, New Jersey
John Holland, 30
Elizabeth Holmes, 42, New York, New York
Thomas P. Holohan, 36, Chester, New York
Bradley Hoorn, 22, New York, New York
James P. Hopper, 51, Farmingdale, New York
Montgomery McCullough Hord, 46, Pelham, New York
Michael Horn, 27, Lynbrook, New York
Matthew D. Horning, 26, Hoboken, New Jersey
Robert L. Horohoe, 31, New York, New York
Aaron Horwitz, 24, New York, New York
Charles J. Houston, 42, New York, New York
Uhuru G. Houston, 32, Englewood, New Jersey
George Howard, 45, Hicksville, New York
Steven L. Howell, 36, New York, New York
Michael C. Howell, 60, New York, New York
Jennifer L. Howley, 34, New Hyde Park, New York
Milagros "Millie" Hromada, 35, New York, New York
Marian Hrycak, 56, New York, New York

Stephen Huczko, 44, Bethlehem, New Jersey

Kris R. Hughes, 30, Nesconset, New York

Melissa Harrington Hughes, 31, San Francisco, California

Thomas F. Hughes, 46, Spring Lake Heights, New Jersey

Timothy Robert Hughes, 43, Madison, New Jersey

Paul R. Hughes, 38, Stamford, Connecticut

Robert T. "Bobby" Hughes, 23, Sayreville, New Jersey

Susan Huie, 43, Fair Lawn, New Jersey

Mychal Lamar Hulse, 30, New York, New York

William C. Hunt, 32, Norwalk, Connecticut

Joseph G. Hunter, 31, South Hempstead, New York

Robert Hussa, 51, Roslyn, New York

Capt. Walter Hynes, 46, Belle Harbor, New York

Thomas E. Hynes, 28, Norwalk, Connecticut

Joseph Anthony Ianelli, 28, Hoboken, New Jersey

Zuhtu Ibis, 25, Clifton, New Jersey

Jonathan Lee Ielpi, 29, Great Neck, New York

Michael Patrick Iken, 37, New York, New York

Daniel Ilkanayev, 36, New York, New York

Capt. Frederick Ill, 49, Pearl River, New York

Abraham Nethanel Ilowitz, 51, New York, New York

Anthony P. Infante, 47, Chatham, New Jersey

Louis S. Inghilterra, 45, New Castle, New York

Christopher N. Ingrassia, 28, Watchung, New Jersey

Paul Innella, 33, East Brunswick, New Jersey

Stephanie V. Irby, 38, New York, New York

Douglas Irgang, 32, New York, New York

Todd A. Isaac, 29, New York, New York

Erik Hans Isbrandtsen, 30, New York, New York

Taizo Ishikawa, 50

Aram Iskenderian, 41, Merrick, New York

John Iskyan, 41, Wilton, Connecticut

Kazushige Ito, 35, New York, New York

Aleksandr Valeryerich Ivantsov, 23, New York, New York

Virginia Jablonski, 49, Matawan, New Jersey

Brooke Alexandra Jackman, 23, New York, New York

Aaron Jacobs, 27, New York, New York

Jason Kyle Jacobs, 32, Mendham, New Jersey

Michael Grady Jacobs, 54, Danbury, Connecticut

Ariel Louis Jacobs, 29, Briarcliff Manor, New York

Steven A. Jacobson, 53, New York, New York

Ricknauth Jaggernauth, 58, New York, New York

Jake Denis Jagoda, 24, Huntington, New York

Yudh V.S. Jain, 54, New City, New York

Maria Jakubiak, 41, Ridgewood, New York

Gricelda E. James, 44, Willingboro, New Jersey

Ernest James, 40, New York, New York

Mark Jardim, 39, New York, New York

Mohammed Jawara, 30, New York, New York

Francois Jean-Pierre, 58, New York, New York

Maxima Jean-Pierre, 40, Bellport, New York

Paul E. Jeffers, 39, New York, New York

Joseph Jenkins, 47, New York, New York

Alan K. Jensen, 49, Wyckoff, New Jersey

Prem N. Jerath, 57, Edison, New Jersey

Farah Jeudy, 32, Spring Valley, New York

Hweidar Jian, 42, East Brunswick, New Jersey

Eliezer Jimenez, 38, New York, New York

Luis Jimenez, 25, New York, New York

Charles Gregory John, 44, New York, New York

Nicholas John, 42, New York, New York

Scott M. Johnson, 26, New York, New York

LaShawana Johnson, 27, New York, New York

William Johnston, 31, North Babylon, New York

Arthur Joseph Jones, 37, Ossining, New York

Allison Horstmann Jones, 31, New York, New York

Brian L. Jones, 44, New York, New York

Christopher D. Jones, 53, Huntington, New York

Donald T. Jones, 39, Livingston, New Jersey

Donald W. Jones, 43, Fairless Hills, Pennsylvania

Linda Jones, 50, New York, New York

Mary S. Jones, 72, New York, New York

Andrew Jordan, 35, Remsenburg, New York

Robert Thomas Jordan, 34, Williston, New York

Ingeborg Joseph, 60, Germany

Karl Henri Joseph, 25, New York, New York

Stephen Joseph, 39, Franklin Park, New Jersey

Albert Joseph, 79

Jane Eileen Josiah, 47, Bellmore, New York

Lt. Anthony Jovic, 39, Massapequa, New York

Angel Luis Juarbe, 35, New York, New York

Karen Susan Juday, 52, New York, New York

The Rev. Mychal Judge, 68, New York, New York

Paul W. Jurgens, 47, Levittown, New York

Thomas Edward Jurgens, 26, Lawrence, New York

Kacinga Kabeya, 63, McKinney, Texas

Shashi Kiran Lakshmikantha Kadaba, 25, Hackensack, New Jersey

Gavkharoy Mukhometovna Kamardinova, 26, New York, New York

Shari Kandell, 27, Wyckoff, New Jersey

Howard Lee Kane, 40, Hazlet, New Jersey

Jennifer Lynn Kane, 26, Fair Lawn, New Jersey

Vincent D. Kane, 37, New York, New York

Joon Koo Kang, 34, Riverdale, New Jersey

Sheldon R. Kanter, 53, Edison, New Jersey

Deborah H. Kaplan, 45, Paramus, New Jersey

Alvin Peter Kappelmann, 57, Green Brook, New Jersey

Charles Karczewski, 34, Union, New Jersey

William A. Karnes, 37, New York, New York

Douglas G. Karpiloff, 53, Mamaroneck, New York

Charles L. Kasper, 54, New York, New York

Andrew Kates, 37, New York, New York

John Katsimatides, 31, East Marion, New York

Sgt. Robert Kaulfers, 49, Kenilworth, New Jersey

Don Jerome Kauth, 51, Saratoga Springs, New York

Hideya Kawauchi, 36, Fort Lee, New Jersey

Edward T. Keane, 66, West Caldwell, New Jersey

Richard M. Keane, 54, Wethersfield, Connecticut

Lisa Kearney-Griffin, 35, Jamaica, New York

Karol Ann Keasler, 42, New York, New York

Paul Hanlon Keating, 38, New York, New York

Leo Russell Keene, 33, Westfield, New Jersey

Joseph J. Keller, 31, Park Ridge, New Jersey

Peter Rodney Kellerman, 35, New York, New York

Joseph P. Kellett, 37, Riverdale, New York

Frederick H. Kelley, 57, Huntington, New York

James Joseph Kelly, 39, Oceanside, New York

Joseph A. Kelly, 40, Oyster Bay, New York

Maurice Patrick Kelly, 41, New York, New York

Richard John Kelly, 50, New York, New York

Thomas Michael Kelly, 41, Wyckoff, New Jersey

Thomas Richard Kelly, 38, Riverhead, New York

Thomas W. Kelly, 51, New York, New York

Timothy C. Kelly, 37, Port Washington, New York

William Hill Kelly, 30, New York, New York

Robert C. Kennedy, 55, Toms River, New Jersey
Thomas J. Kennedy, 36, Islip Terrace, New York
John Keohane, 41, Jersey City, New Jersey
Lt. Ronald T. Kerwin, 42, Levittown, New York
Howard L. Kestenbaum, 56, Montclair, New Jersey
Douglas D. Ketcham, 27, New York, New York
Ruth E. Ketler, 42, New York, New York
Boris Khalif, 30, New York, New York
Sarah Khan, 32, New York, New York
Taimour Firaz Khan, 29, New York, New York
Rajesh Khandelwal, 33, South Plainfield, New Jersey
SeiLai Khoo, 38, Jersey City, New Jersey
Michael Kiefer, 25, Hempstead, New York
Satoshi Kikuchihara, 43, Scarsdale, New York
Andrew Jay-Hoon Kim, 26, Leonia, New Jersey
Lawrence Don Kim, 31, Blue Bell, Pennsylvania
Mary Jo Kimelman, 34, New York, New York
Andrew Marshall King, 42, Princeton, New Jersey
Lucille T. King, 59, Ridgewood, New Jersey
Robert King, 36, Bellerose Terrace, New York
Lisa M. King-Johnson, 34, New York, New York
Takashi Kinoshita, 46, Rye, New York
Chris Michael Kirby, 21, New York, New York
Howard (Barry) Kirschbaum, 53, New York, New York
Glenn Davis Kirwin, 40, Scarsdale, New York
Richard J. Klares, 59, Somers, New York
Peter A. Klein, 35, Weehawken, New Jersey
Alan D. Kleinberg, 39, East Brunswick, New Jersey
Karen J. Klitzman, 38, New York, New York
Ronald Philip Kloepfer, 39, Franklin Square, New York
Yevgeny Kniazev, 46, New York, New York
Thomas Patrick Knox, 31, Hoboken, New Jersey
Andrew Knox, 30, Adelaide, Australia
Rebecca Lee Koborie, 48, Guttenberg, New Jersey
Deborah Kobus, 36, New York, New York
Gary Edward Koecheler, 57, Harrison, New York
Frank J. Koestner, 48, New York, New York
Ryan Kohart, 26, New York, New York
Vanessa Lynn Kolpak, 21, New York, New York
Irina Kolpakova, 37, New York, New York
Suzanne Kondratenko, 27, Chicago, Illinois
Abdoulaye Kone, 37, New York, New York
Bon-seok Koo, 42, River Edge, New Jersey
Dorota Kopiczko, 26, Nutley, New Jersey
Scott Kopytko, 32, New York, New York
Bojan Kostic, 34, New York, New York
Danielle Kousoulis, 29, New York, New York
John J. Kren, 52
William Krukowski, 36, New York, New York
Lyudmila Ksido, 46, New York, New York
Shekhar Kumar, 30, New York, New York
Kenneth Kumpel, 42, Cornwall, New York
Frederick Kuo, 53, Great Neck, New York
Patricia Kuras, 42, New York, New York
Nauka Kushitani, 44, New York, New York
Thomas Joseph Kuveikis, 48, Carmel, New York
Victor Kwarkye, 35, New York, New York
Kui Fai Kwok, 31, New York, New York
Angela R. Kyte, 49, Boonton, New Jersey
Amarnauth Lachhman, 42, Valley Stream, New York
Andrew LaCorte, 61, Jersey City, New Jersey
Ganesh Ladkat, 27, Somerset, New Jersey

James P. Ladley, 41, Colts Neck, New Jersey
Daniel M. Van Laere, 46, Glen Rock, New Jersey
Joseph A. Lafalce, 54, New York, New York
Jeanette LaFond-Menichino, 49, New York, New York
David LaForge, 50, Port Richmond, New York
Michael Patrick LaForte, 39, Holmdel, New Jersey
Alan Lafrance, 43
Juan Lafuente, 61, Poughkeepsie, New York
Neil K. Lai, 59, East Windsor, New Jersey
Vincent A. Laieta, 31, Edison, New Jersey
William David Lake, 44, New York, New York
Franco Lalama, 45, Nutley, New Jersey
Chow Kwan Lam, 48, Maywood, New Jersey
Stephen LaMantia, 38, Darien, Connecticut
Amy Hope Lamonsoff, 29, New York, New York
Robert T. Lane, 28, New York, New York
Brendan M. Lang, 30, Red Bank, New Jersey
Rosanne P. Lang, 42, Middletown, New Jersey
Vanessa Langer, 29, Yonkers, New York
Mary Lou Langley, 53, New York, New York
Peter J. Langone, 41, Roslyn Heights, New York
Thomas Langone, 39, Williston Park, New York
Michele B. Lanza, 36, New York, New York
Ruth Sheila Lapin, 53, East Windsor, New Jersey
Carol Ann LaPlante, 59, New York, New York
Ingeborg Astrid Desiree Lariby, 42, New York, New York
Robin Larkey, 48, Chatham, New Jersey
Christopher Randall Larrabee, 26, New York, New York
Hamidou S. Larry, 37, New York, New York
Scott Larsen, 35, New York, New York
John Adam Larson, 37, Colonia, New Jersey
Gary E. Lasko, 49, Memphis, Tenn.
Nicholas C. Lassman, 28, Cliffside Park, New Jersey
Paul Laszczynski, 49, Paramus, New Jersey
Jeffrey Latouche, 49, New York, New York
Cristina de Laura
Oscar de Laura
Charles Laurencin, 61, New York, New York
Stephen James Lauria, 39, New York, New York
Maria Lavache, 60, New York, New York
Denis F. Lavelle, 42, Yonkers, New York
Jeannine M. LaVerde, 36, New York, New York
Anna A. Laverty, 52, Middletown, New Jersey
Steven Lawn, 28, West Windsor, New Jersey
Robert A. Lawrence, 41, Summit, New Jersey
Nathaniel Lawson, 61, New York, New York
Eugen Lazar, 27, New York, New York
James Patrick Leahy, 38, New York, New York
Lt. Joseph Gerard Leavey, 45, Pelham, New York
Neil Leavy, 34, New York, New York
Leon Lebor, 51, Jersey City, New Jersey
Kenneth Charles Ledee, 38, Monmouth, New Jersey
Alan J. Lederman, 43, New York, New York
Elena Ledesma, 36, New York, New York
Alexis Leduc, 45, New York, New York
Myung-woo Lee, 41, Lyndhurst, New Jersey
David S. Lee, 37, West Orange, New Jersey
Gary H. Lee, 62, Lindenhurst, New York
Hyun-joon (Paul) Lee, 32, New York, New York
Jong-min Lee, 24, New York, New York
Juanita Lee, 44, New York, New York
Lorraine Lee, 37, New York, New York

Richard Y.C. Lee, 34, Great Neck, New York
Yang Der Lee, 63, New York, New York
Kathryn Blair Lee, 55, New York, New York
Stuart (Soo-Jin) Lee, 30, New York, New York
Linda C. Lee, 34, New York, New York
Stephen Lefkowitz, 50, Belle Harbor, New York
Adriana Legro, 32, New York, New York
Edward J. Lehman, 41, Glen Cove, New York
Eric Andrew Lehrfeld, 32, New York, New York
David Ralph Leistman, 43, Garden City, New York
David Prudencio LeMagne, 27, North Bergen, New Jersey
Joseph A. Lenihan, 41, Greenwich, Connecticut
John J. Lennon, 44, Howell, New Jersey
John Robinson Lenoir, 38, Locust Valley, New York
Jorge Luis Leon, 43, Union City, New Jersey
Matthew Gerard Leonard, 38, New York, New York
Michael Lepore, 39, New York, New York
Charles Antoine Lesperance, 55
Jeffrey Earle LeVeen, 55, Manhasset, New York
John D. Levi, 50, New York, New York
Alisha Caren Levin, 33, New York, New York
Neil D. Levin, 47, New York, New York
Robert Levine, 56, West Babylon, New York
Robert M. Levine, 66, Edgewater, New Jersey
Shai Levinhar, 29, New York, New York
Adam J. Lewis, 36, Fairfield, Connecticut
Margaret Susan Lewis, 49, Elizabeth, New Jersey
Ye Wei Liang, 27, New York, New York
Orasri Liangthanasarn, 26, Bayonne, New Jersey
Daniel F. Libretti, 43, New York, New York
Ralph M. Licciardi, 30, West Hempstead, New York
Edward Lichtschein, 35, New York, New York
Steven B. Lillianthal, 38, Millburn, New Jersey
Carlos R. Lillo, 37, Babylon, New York
Craig Damian Lilore, 30, Lyndhurst, New Jersey
Arnold A. Lim, 28, New York, New York
Darya Lin, 32, Chicago, Illinois
Wei Rong Lin, 31, Jersey City, New Jersey
Nickie L. Lindo, 31, New York, New York
Thomas V. Linehan, 39, Montville, New Jersey
Robert Thomas Linnane, 33, West Hempstead, New York
Alan Linton, 26, Jersey City, New Jersey
Diane Theresa Lipari, 42, New York, New York
Kenneth P. Lira, 28, Paterson, New Jersey
Francisco Alberto Liriano, 33, New York, New York
Lorraine Lisi, 44, New York, New York
Paul Lisson, 45, New York, New York
Vincent Litto, 52, New York, New York
Ming-Hao Liu, 41, Livingston, New Jersey
Nancy Liz, 39, New York, New York
Harold Lizcano, 31, East Elmhurst, New York
Martin Lizzul, 31, New York, New York
George A. Llanes, 33, New York, New York
Elizabeth Claire Logler, 31, Rockville Centre, New York
Catherine Lisa Loguidice, 30, New York, New York
Jerome Robert Lohez, 30, Jersey City, New Jersey
Michael W. Lomax, 37, New York, New York
Laura M. Longing, 35, Pearl River, New York
Salvatore P. Lopes, 40, Franklin Square, New York
Daniel Lopez, 39, New York, New York
Luis Lopez, 38, New York, New York
Manuel L. Lopez, 54, Jersey City, New Jersey

George Lopez, 40, Stroudsburg, Pennsylvania
Joseph Lostrangio, 48, Langhorne, Pennsylvania
Chet Louie, 45, New York, New York
Stuart Seid Louis, 43, East Brunswick, New Jersey
Joseph Lovero, 60, Jersey City, New Jersey
Michael W. Lowe, 48, New York, New York
Garry Lozier, 47, Darien, Connecticut
John Peter Lozowsky, 45, New York, New York
Charles Peter Lucania, 34, East Atlantic Beach, New York
Edward (Ted) H. Luckett, 40, Fair Haven, New Jersey
Mark G. Ludvigsen, 32, New York, New York
Lee Charles Ludwig, 49, New York, New York
Sean Thomas Lugano, 28, New York, New York
Daniel Lugo, 45, New York, New York
Marie Lukas, 32, New York, New York
William Lum, 45, New York, New York
Michael P. Lunden, 37, New York, New York
Christopher Lunder, 34, Wall, New Jersey
Anthony Luparello, 62, New York, New York
Gary Lutnick, 36, New York, New York
Linda Luzzicone, 33, New York, New York
Alexander Lygin, 28, New York, New York
Farrell Peter Lynch, 39, Centerport, New York
James Francis Lynch, 47, Woodbridge, New Jersey
Louise A. Lynch, 58, Amityville, New York
Michael Lynch, 34, New York, New York
Michael F. Lynch, 33, New Hyde Park, New York
Michael Francis Lynch, 30, New York, New York
Richard Dennis Lynch, 30, Bedford Hills, New York
Robert H. Lynch, 44, Cranford, New Jersey
Sean Patrick Lynch, 36, Morristown, New Jersey
Sean Lynch, 34, New York, New York
Michael J. Lyons, 32, Hawthorne, New York
Patrick Lyons, 34, South Setauket, New York
Monica Lyons, 53, New York, New York
Robert Francis Mace, 43, New York, New York
Jan Maciejewski, 37, New York, New York
Catherine Fairfax MacRae, 23, New York, New York
Richard B. Madden, 35, Westfield, New Jersey
Simon Maddison, 40, Florham Park, New Jersey
Noell Maerz, 29, Long Beach, New York
Jeannieann Maffeo, 40, New York, New York
Joseph Maffeo, 30, New York, New York
Jay Robert Magazine, 48, New York, New York
Charles Wilson Magee, 51, Wantagh, New York
Brian Magee, 52, Floral Park, New York
Joseph Maggitti, 47, Abingdon, Maryland
Ronald E. Magnuson, 57, Park Ridge, New Jersey
Daniel L. Maher, 50, Hamilton, New Jersey
Thomas Anthony Mahon, 37, East Norwich, New York
William Mahoney, 38, Bohemia, New York
Joseph Maio, 32, Roslyn Harbor, New York
Takashi Makimoto, 49, New York, New York
Abdu Malahi, 37, New York, New York
Debora Maldonado, 47, New York, New York
Myrna T. Maldonado-Agosto, 49, New York, New York
Alfred R. Maler, 39, Convent Station, New Jersey
Gregory James Malone, 42, Hoboken, New Jersey
Edward Francis (Teddy) Maloney, 32, Darien, Connecticut
Joseph E. Maloney, 46, Farmingville, New York
Gene E. Maloy, 41, New York, New York
Christian Maltby, 37, Chatham, New Jersey

Francisco Miguel (Frank) Mancini, 26, New York, New York
Joseph Mangano, 53, Jackson, New Jersey
Sara Elizabeth Manley, 31, New York, New York
Debra M. Mannetta, 31, Islip, New York
Terence J. Manning, 36, Rockville Centre, New York
Marion Victoria (vickie) Manning, 27, Rochdale, New York
James Maounis, 42, New York, New York
Joseph Ross Marchbanks, 47, Nanuet, New York
Peter Edward Mardikian, 29, New York, New York
Edward Joseph Mardovich, 42, Lloyd Harbor, New York
Lt. Charles Joseph Margiotta, 44, New York, New York
Kenneth Joseph Marino, 40, Monroe, New York
Lester Vincent Marino, 57, Massapequa, New York
Vita Marino, 49, New York, New York
Kevin D. Marlo, 28, New York, New York
Jose J. Marrero, 32, Old Bridge, New Jersey
John Marshall, 35, Congers, New York
James Martello, 41, Rumson, New Jersey
Michael A. Marti, 26, Glendale, New York
Lt. Peter Martin, 43, Miller Place, New York
William J. Martin, 35, Rockaway, New Jersey
Brian E. Martineau, 37, Edison, New Jersey
Betsy Martinez, 33, New York, New York
Edward J. Martinez, 60, New York, New York
Jose Angel Martinez, 49, Hauppauge, New York
Robert Gabriel Martinez, 24, New York, New York
Lizie Martinez-Calderon, 32, New York, New York
Lt. Paul Richard Martini, 37, New York, New York
Joseph A. Mascali, 44, New York, New York
Bernard Mascarenhas, 54, Newmarket, Ontario, Canada
Stephen F. Masi, 55, New York, New York
Nicholas G. Massa, 65, New York, New York
Patricia A. Massari, 25, Glendale, New York
Michael Massaroli, 38, New York, New York
Philip W. Mastrandrea, 42, Chatham, New Jersey
Rudolph Mastrocinque, 43, Kings Park, New York
Joseph Mathai, 49, Arlington, Massachusetts
Charles William Mathers, 61, Sea Girt, New Jersey
William A. Mathesen, 40, Morristown, New Jersey
Marcello Matricciano, 31, New York, New York
Margaret Elaine Mattic, 51, New York, New York
Robert D. Mattson, 54, Green Pond, New Jersey
Walter Matuza, 39, New York, New York
Charles A. (Chuck) Mauro, 65, New York, New York
Charles J. Mauro, 38, New York, New York
Dorothy Mauro, 55, New York, New York
Nancy T. Mauro, 51, New York, New York
Tyrone May, 44, Rahway, New Jersey
Keithroy Maynard, 30, New York, New York
Robert J. Mayo, 46, Morganville, New Jersey
Kathy Nancy Mazza-Delosh, 46, Farmingdale, New York
Edward Mazzella, 62, Monroe, New York
Jennifer Mazzotta, 23, New York, New York
Kaaria Mbaya, 39, Edison, New Jersey
James J. McAlary, 42, Spring Lake Heights, New Jersey
Brian McAleese, 36, Baldwin, New York
Patricia A. McAneney, 50, Pomona, New York
Colin Richard McArthur, 52, Howell, New Jersey
John McAvoy, 47, New York, New York
Kenneth M. McBrayer, 49, New York, New York
Brendan McCabe, 40, Sayville, New York
Michael J. McCabe, 42, Rumson, New Jersey

Thomas McCann, 46, Manalapan, New Jersey
Justin McCarthy, 30, Port Washington, New York
Kevin M. McCarthy, 42, Fairfield, Connecticut
Michael Desmond McCarthy, 33, Huntington, New York
Robert Garvin McCarthy, 33, Stony Point, New York
Stanley McCaskill, 47, New York, New York
Katie Marie McCloskey, 25, Mount Vernon, New York
Tara McCloud-Gray, 30, New York, New York
Charles Austin McCrann, 55, New York, New York
Tonyell McDay, 25, Colonia, New Jersey
Matthew T. McDermott, 34, Basking Ridge, New Jersey
Joseph P. McDonald, 43, Livingston, New Jersey
Brian G. McDonnell, 38, Wantagh, New York
Michael McDonnell, 34, Red Bank, New Jersey
John F. McDowell, 33, New York, New York
Eamon J. McEneaney, 46, New Canaan, Connecticut
John Thomas McErlean, 39, Larchmont, New York
Daniel F. McGinley, 40, Ridgewood, New Jersey
Mark Ryan McGinly, 26, New York, New York
Lt. William E. McGinn, 43, New York, New York
Thomas H. McGinnis, 41, Oakland, New Jersey
Michael Gregory McGinty, 42, Foxboro, Massachusetts
Ann McGovern, 68, East Meadow, New York
Scott Martin McGovern, 35, Wyckoff, New Jersey
William J. McGovern, 49, Smithtown, New York
Stacey S. McGowan, 38, Basking Ridge, New Jersey
Francis Noel McGuinn, 48, Rye, New York
Patrick J. McGuire, 40, Madison, New Jersey
Thomas M. McHale, 33, Huntington, New York
Keith McHeffey, 31, Monmouth Beach, New Jersey
Denis J. McHugh, 36, New York, New York
Dennis P. McHugh, 34, Sparkill, New York
Michael Edward McHugh, 35, Tuckahoe, New York
Ann M. McHugh, 35, New York, New York
Robert G. McIlvaine, 26, New York, New York
Donald James McIntyre, 38, New City, New York
Stephanie McKenna, 45, New York, New York
Barry J. McKeon, 47, Yorktown Heights, New York
Evelyn C. McKinnedy, 60, New York, New York
Darryl Leron McKinney, 26, New York, New York
Robert C. McLaughlin, 29, Westchester, New York
George Patrick McLaughlin, 36, Hoboken, New Jersey
Gavin McMahon, 35, Bayonne, New Jersey
Robert Dismas McMahon, 35, New York, New York
Edmund M. McNally, 41, Fair Haven, New Jersey
Daniel McNeal, 29, Towson, Maryland
Walter Arthur McNeil, 53, Stroudsburg, Pennsylvania
Sean Peter McNulty, 30, New York, New York
Christine Sheila McNulty, 42, Peterborough, England
Robert William McPadden, 30, Pearl River, New York
Terence A. McShane, 37, West Islip, New York
Timothy Patrick McSweeney, 37, New York, New York
Martin E. McWilliams, 35, Kings Park, New York
Rocco A. Medaglia, 49, Melville, New York
Abigail Cales Medina, 46, New York, New York
Ana Iris Medina, 39, New York, New York
Deborah Medwig, 46, Dedham, Massachusetts
William J. Meehan, 49, Darien, Connecticut
Damian Meehan, 32, Glen Rock, New Jersey
Alok Kumar Mehta, 23, Hempstead, New York
Raymond Meisenheimer, 46, West Babylon, New York
Manuel Emilio Mejia, 54, New York, New York

Eskedar Melaku, 31, New York, New York
Antonio Melendez, 30, New York, New York
Mary Melendez, 44, Stroudsburg, Pennsylvania
Yelena Melnichenko, 28, Brooklyn, New York
Stuart Todd Meltzer, 32, Syosset, New York
Diarelia Jovannah Mena, 30, New York, New York
Charles Mendez, 38, Floral Park, New York
Lizette Mendoza, 33, North Bergen, New Jersey
Shevonne Mentis, 25, New York, New York
Steve Mercado, 38, New York, New York
Wesley Mercer, 70, New York, New York
Ralph Joseph Mercurio, 47, Rockville Centre, New York
Alan H. Merdinger, 47, Allentown, Pennsylvania
George C. Merino, 39, New York, New York
Yamel Merino, 24, Yonkers, New York
George Merkouris, 35, Levittown, New York
Deborah Merrick, 45
Raymond J. Metz, 37, Trumbull, Connecticut
Jill A. Metzler, 32, Franklin Square, New York
David Robert Meyer, 57, Glen Rock, New Jersey
Nurul Huq Miah, 35, New York, New York
William Edward Micciulli, 30, Matawan, New Jersey
Martin Paul Michelstein, 57, Morristown, New Jersey
Luis Clodoaldo Revilla Mier, 54
Peter T. Milano, 43, Middletown, New Jersey
Gregory Milanowycz, 25, Cranford, New Jersey
Lukasz T. Milewski, 21, New York, New York
Craig James Miller, 29, Virginia
Corey Peter Miller, 34, New York, New York
Douglas C. Miller, 34, Port Jervis, New York
Henry Miller, 52, Massapequa, New York
Michael Matthew Miller, 39, Englewood, New Jersey
Phillip D. Miller, 53, New York, New York
Robert C. Miller, 55, Hasbrouck Heights, New Jersey
Robert Alan Miller, 46, Matawan, New Jersey
Joel Miller, 55, Baldwin, New York
Benjamin Millman, 40, New York, New York
Charles M. Mills, 61, Brentwood, New York
Ronald Keith Milstein, 54, New York, New York
Robert Minara, 54, Carmel, New York
William G. Minardi, 46, Bedford, New York
Louis Joseph Minervino, 54, Middletown, New Jersey
Thomas Mingione, 34, West Islip, New York
Wilbert Miraille, 29, New York, New York
Domenick Mircovich, 40, Closter, New Jersey
Rajesh A. Mirpuri, 30, Englewood Cliffs, New Jersey
Joseph Mistrulli, 47, Wantagh, New York
Susan Miszkowicz, 37, New York, New York
Lt. Paul Thomas Mitchell, 46, New York, New York
Richard Miuccio, 55, New York, New York
Frank V. Moccia, 57, Hauppauge, New York
Capt. Louis Joseph Modafferi, 45, New York, New York
Boyie Mohammed, 50, New York, New York
Lt. Dennis Mojica, 50, New York, New York
Manuel Mojica, 37, Bellmore, New York
Manuel Dejesus Molina, 31, New York, New York
Kleber Rolando Molina, 44, New York, New York
Fernando Jimenez Molinar, 21, Oaxaca, Mexico
Carl Molinaro, 32, New York, New York
Justin J. Molisani, 42, Middletown Township, New Jersey
Brian Patrick Monaghan, 21, New York, New York
Franklin Monahan, 45, Roxbury, New York

John Gerard Monahan, 47, Wanamassa, New Jersey
Kristen Montanaro, 34, New York, New York
Craig D. Montano, 38, Glen Ridge, New Jersey
Michael Montesi, 39, Highland Mills, New York
Cheryl Ann Monyak, 43, Greenwich, Connecticut
Capt. Thomas Moody, 45, Stony Brook, New York
Sharon Moore, 37, New York, New York
Krishna Moorthy, 59, Briarcliff Manor, New York
Abner Morales, 37, New York, New York
Carlos Morales, 29, New York, New York
Paula Morales, 42, New York, New York
Luis Morales, 46, New York, New York
John Moran, 43, Rockaway, New York
John Christopher Moran, 38, Haslemere, Surrey, England
Kathleen Moran, 42, New York, New York
Lindsay S. Morehouse, 24, New York, New York
George Morell, 47, Mount. Kisco, New York
Steven P. Morello, 52, Bayonne, New Jersey
Vincent S. Morello, 34, New York, New York
Arturo Alva Moreno, 47, Mexico City, Mexico
Yvette Nicole Moreno, 25, New York, New York
Dorothy Morgan, 47, Hempstead, New York
Richard Morgan, 66, Glen Rock, New Jersey
Nancy Morgenstern, 32, New York, New York
Sanae Mori, 27, Tokyo, Japan
Blanca Morocho, 26, New York, New York
Leonel Morocho, 36, New York, New York
Dennis G. Moroney, 39, Eastchester, New York
Lynne Irene Morris, 22, Monroe, New York
Seth A. Morris, 35, Kinnelon, New Jersey
Stephen Philip Morris, 31, Ormond Beach, Florida
Christopher M. Morrison, 34, Charlestown, Massachusetts
Ferdinand V. Morrone, 63, Lakewood, New Jersey
William David Moskal, 50, Brecksville, Ohio
Manuel Da Mota, 43, Valley Stream, New York
Marco Motroni, 57, Fort Lee, New Jersey
Iouri A. Mouchinski, 55, New York, New York
Jude J. Moussa, 35, New York, New York
Peter C. Moutos, 44, Chatham, New Jersey
Damion Mowatt, 21, New York, New York
Christopher Mozzillo, 27, New York, New York
Stephen V. Mulderry, 33, New York, New York
Richard Muldowney, 40, Babylon, New York
Michael D. Mullan, 34, New York, New York
Dennis Michael Mulligan, 32, New York, New York
Peter James Mulligan, 28, New York, New York
Michael Joseph Mullin, 27, Hoboken, New Jersey
James Donald Munhall, 45, Ridgewood, New Jersey
Nancy Muniz, 45, New York, New York
Carlos Mario Munoz, 43
Francisco Munoz, 29, New York, New York
Theresa (Terry) Munson, 54, New York, New York
Robert M. Murach, 45, Montclair, New Jersey
Cesar Augusto Murillo, 32, New York, New York
Marc A. Murolo, 28, Maywood, New Jersey
Robert Eddie Murphy, 56, New York, New York
Brian Joseph Murphy, 41, New York, New York
Christopher W. Murphy, 35, Easton, Maryland
Edward C. Murphy, 42, Clifton, New Jersey
James F. Murphy, 30, Garden City, New York
James Thomas Murphy, 35, Middletown, New Jersey
Kevin James Murphy, 40, Northport, New York

Patrick Sean Murphy, 36, Millburn, New Jersey
Lt. Raymond E. Murphy, 46, New York, New York
Charles Murphy, 38, New York, New York
John Joseph Murray, 32, Hoboken, New Jersey
John Joseph Murray, 52, Colts Neck, New Jersey
Susan D. Murray, 54, Summit, New Jersey
Valerie Victoria Murray, 65, New York, New York
Richard Todd Myhre, 37, New York, New York
Lt. Robert B. Nagel, 55, New York, New York
Takuya Nakamura, 30, Tuckahoe, New York
Alexander J.R. Napier, 38, Morris Township, New Jersey
Frank Joseph Naples, 29, Cliffside Park, New Jersey
John Napolitano, 33, Ronkonkoma, New York
Catherine A. Nardella, 40, Bloomfield, New Jersey
Mario Nardone, 32, New York, New York
Manika Narula, 22, Kings Park, New York
Narender Nath, 33, Colonia, New Jersey
Karen S. Navarro, 30, New York, New York
Joseph M. Navas, 44, Paramus, New Jersey
Francis J. Nazario, 28, Jersey City, New Jersey
Glenroy Neblett, 42, New York, New York
Marcus R. Neblett, 31, Roslyn Heights, New York
Jerome O. Nedd, 39, New York, New York
Laurence Nedell, 51, Lindenhurst, New York
Luke G. Nee, 44, Stony Point, New York
Pete Negron, 34, Bergenfield, New Jersey
Ann Nicole Nelson, 30, New York, New York
David William Nelson, 50, New York, New York
James Nelson, 40, Clark, New Jersey
Michele Ann Nelson, 27, Valley Stream, New York
Peter Allen Nelson, 42, Huntington Station, New York
Oscar Nesbitt, 58, New York, New York
Gerard Terence Nevins, 46, Campbell Hall, New York
Christopher Newton-Carter, 51, Middletown, New Jersey
Kapinga Ngalula, 58, McKinney, Texas
Nancy Yuen Ngo, 36, Harrington Park, New Jersey
Jody Tepedino Nichilo, 39, New York, New York
Martin Niederer, 23, Hoboken, New Jersey
Alfonse J. Niedermeyer, 40, Manasquan, New Jersey
Frank John Niestadt, 55, Ronkonkoma, New York
Gloria Nieves, 48, New York, New York
Juan Nieves, 56, New York, New York
Troy Edward Nilsen, 33, New York, New York
Paul R. Nimbley, 42, Middletown, New Jersey
John Ballantine Niven, 44, Oyster Bay, New York
Katherine (Katie) McGarry Noack, 30, Hoboken, New Jersey
Curtis Terrence Noel, 22, Poughkeepsie, New York
Daniel R. Nolan, 44, Hopatcong, New Jersey
Robert Walter Noonan, 36, Norwalk, Connecticut
Daniela R. Notaro, 25, New York, New York
Brian Novotny, 33, Hoboken, New Jersey
Soichi Numata, 45, Irvington, New York
Brian Felix Nunez, 29, New York, New York
Jose R. Nunez, 42, New York, New York
Jeffrey Nussbaum, 37, Oceanside, New York
James A. Oakley, 52, Cortlandt Manor, New York
Dennis O'Berg, 28, Babylon, New York
James P. O'Brien, 33, New York, New York
Scott J. O'Brien, 40, New York, New York
Timothy Michael O'Brien, 40, Brookville, New York
Michael O'Brien, 42, Cedar Knolls, New Jersey
Captain Daniel O'Callaghan, 42, Smithtown, New York

Richard J. O'Connor, 49, Poughkeepsie, New York
Dennis J. O'Connor, 34, New York, New York
Diana J. O'Connor, 38, Eastchester, New York
Keith K. O'Connor, 28, Hoboken, New Jersey
Amy O'Doherty, 23, New York, New York
Marni Pont O'Doherty, 31, Armonk, New York
Douglas Oelschlager, 36, New York, New York
Takashi Ogawa, 37, Tokyo, Japan
Albert Ogletree, 49, New York, New York
Philip Paul Ognibene, 39, New York, New York
James Andrew O'Grady, 32, Harrington Park, New Jersey
Joseph J. Ogren, 30, New York, New York
Lt. Thomas O'Hagan, 43, New York, New York
Samuel Oitice, 45, Peekskill, New York
Patrick O'Keefe, 44, Oakdale, New York
Capt. William O'Keefe, 49, New York, New York
Gerald Michael Olcott, 55, New Hyde Park, New York
Gerald O'Leary, 34, Stony Point, New York
Christine Anne Olender, 39, New York, New York
Elsy Carolina Osorio Oliva, 27, New York, New York
Linda Mary Oliva, 44, New York, New York
Edward K. Oliver, 31, Jackson, New Jersey
Leah E. Oliver, 24, New York, New York
Eric T. Olsen, 41, New York, New York
Jeffrey James Olsen, 31, New York, New York
Maureen L. Olson, 50, Rockville Centre, New York
Steven John Olson, 38, New York, New York
Matthew Timothy O'Mahony, 39, New York, New York
Toshihiro Onda, 39, New York, New York
Seamus L. Oneal, 52, New York, New York
John P. O'Neill, 49, New York, New York
Sean Gordon Corbett O'Neill, 34, Rye, New York
Peter J. O'Neill, 21, Amityville, New York
Michael C. Opperman, 45, Selden, New York
Christopher Orgielewicz, 35, Larchmont, New York
Margaret Orloske, 50, Windsor, Connecticut
Virginia A. Ormiston, 42, New York, New York
Kevin O'Rourke, 44, Hewlett, New York
Juan Romero Orozco, Acatlan de Osorio, Puebla, Mexico
Ronald Orsini, 59, Hillsdale, New Jersey
Peter K. Ortale, 37, New York, New York
Emilio (Peter) Ortiz, 38, New York, New York
David Ortiz, 37, Nanuet, New York
Paul Ortiz, 21, New York, New York
Sonia Ortiz, 58, New York, New York
Alexander Ortiz, 36, Ridgewood, New York
Pablo Ortiz, 49, New York, New York
Masaru Ose, 36, Fort Lee, New Jersey
Robert W. O'Shea, 47, Wall, New Jersey
Patrick J. O'Shea, 45, Farmingdale, New York
James Robert Ostrowski, 37, Garden City, New York
Timothy O'Sullivan, 68, Albrightsville, Pennsylvania
Jason Douglas Oswald, 28, New York, New York
Michael Otten, 42, East Islip, New York
Isidro Ottenwalder, 35, New York, New York
Michael Chung Ou, 53, New York, New York
Todd Joseph Ouida, 25, River Edge, New Jersey
Jesus Ovalles, 60, New York, New York
Peter J. Owens, 42, Williston Park, New York
Adianes Oyola, 23, New York, New York
Angel M. Pabon, 54, New York, New York
Israel Pabon, 31, New York, New York

Roland Pacheco, 25, New York, New York
Michael Benjamin Packer, 45, New York, New York
Deepa K. Pakkala, 31, Stewartsville, New Jersey
Jeffrey Matthew Palazzo, 33, New York, New York
Thomas Anthony Palazzo, 44, Armonk, New York
Richard (Rico) Palazzolo, 39, New York, New York
Orio Joseph Palmer, 45, Valley Stream, New York
Frank A. Palombo, 46, New York, New York
Alan N. Palumbo, 42, New York, New York
Christopher M. Panatier, 36, Rockville Centre, New York
Dominique Pandolfo, 27, Hoboken, New Jersey
Paul Pansini, 34, New York, New York
John M. Paolillo, 51, Glen Head, New York
Edward J. Papa, 47, Oyster Bay, New York
Salvatore Papasso, 34, New York, New York
James N. Pappageorge, 29, Yonkers, New York
Vinod K. Parakat, 34, Sayreville, New Jersey
Vijayashanker Paramsothy, 23, New York, New York
Nitin Ramesh Parandkar, 28, Waltham, Massachusetts
Hardai (Casey) Parbhu, 42, New York, New York
James Wendell Parham, 32, New York, New York
Debra (Debbie) Paris, 48, New York, New York
George Paris, 33, New York, New York
Gye-Hyong Park, 28, New York, New York
Philip L. Parker, 53, Skillman, New Jersey
Michael A. Parkes, 27, New York, New York
Robert Emmett Parks, 47, Middletown, New Jersey
Hasmukhrai Chuckulal Parmar, 48, Warren, New Jersey
Robert Parro, 35, Levittown, New York
Diane Marie Moore Parsons, 58, Malta, New York
Leobardo Lopez Pascual, 41, New York, New York
Michael J. Pascuma, 50, Massapequa Park, New York
Jerrold H. Paskins, 56, Anaheim Hills, California
Horace Robert Passananti, 55, New York, New York
Suzanne H. Passaro, 38, East Brunswick, New Jersey
Victor Antonio Martinez Pastrana, 38, Tlachichuca, Puebla, Mexico
Manish K. Patel, 29, Edison, New Jersey
Avnish Ramanbhai Patel, 28, New York, New York
Dipti Patel, 38, New Hyde Park, New York
Steven B. Paterson, 40, Ridgewood, New Jersey
James Matthew Patrick, 30, Norwalk, Connecticut
Manuel Patrocino, 34
Bernard E. Patterson, 46, Upper Brookville, New York
Cira Marie Patti, 40, New York, New York
Robert Edward Pattison, 40, New York, New York
James R. Paul, 58, New York, New York
Sharon Cristina Millan Paz, 31, New York, New York
Patrice Paz, 52, New York, New York
Victor Paz-Gutierrez, 43, New York, New York
Stacey L. Peak, 36, New York, New York
Richard Allen Pearlman, 18, New York, New York
Durrell Pearsall, 34, Hempstead, New York
Thomas E. Pedicini, 30, Hicksville, New York
Todd D. Pelino, 34, Fair Haven, New Jersey
Michel Adrian Pelletier, 36, Greenwich, Connecticut
Anthony Peluso, 46, New York, New York
Angel Ramon Pena, 45, River Vale, New Jersey
Richard Al Penny, 53, New York, New York
Salvatore F. Pepe, 45, New York, New York
Carl Allen Peralta, 37, New York, New York
Robert David Peraza, 30, New York, New York
Jon A. Perconti, 32, Brick, New Jersey

Alejo Perez, 66, Union City, New Jersey
Angel Perez, 43, Jersey City, New Jersey
Angela Susan Perez, 35, New York, New York
Ivan Perez, 37, New York, New York
Nancy E. Perez, 36, Secaucus, New Jersey
Anthony Perez, 33, Locust Valley, New York
Joseph John Perroncino, 33, Smithtown, New York
Edward J. Perrotta, 43, Mount Sinai, New York
Lt. Glenn C. Perry, 41, Monroe, New York
Emelda Perry, 52, Elmont, New York
John William Perry, 38, New York, New York
Franklin Allan Pershep, 59, New York, New York
Daniel Pesce, 34, New York, New York
Michael J. Pescherine, 32, New York, New York
Davin Peterson, 25, New York, New York
William Russel Peterson, 46, New York, New York
Mark Petrocelli, 28, New York, New York
Lt. Philip S. Petti, 43, New York, New York
Glen Kerrin Pettit, 30, Oakdale, New York
Dominick Pezzulo, 36, New York, New York
Kaleen E. Pezzuti, 28, Fair Haven, New Jersey
Lt. Kevin Pfeifer, 42, New York, New York
Tu-Anh Pham, 42, Princeton, New Jersey
Lt. Kenneth John Phelan, 41, New York, New York
Michael V. San Phillip, 55, Ridgewood, New Jersey
Eugenia Piantieri, 55, New York, New York
Ludwig John Picarro, 44, Basking Ridge, New Jersey
Matthew Picerno, 44, Holmdel, New Jersey
Joseph O. Pick, 40, Hoboken, New Jersey
Christopher Pickford, 32, New York, New York
Dennis J. Pierce, 54, New York, New York
Joseph A. Della Pietra, 24, New York, New York
Bernard T. Pietronico, 39, Matawan, New Jersey
Nicholas P. Pietrunti, 38, Belford, New Jersey
Theodoros Pigis, 60, New York, New York
Susan Elizabeth Ancona Pinto, 44, New York, New York
Joseph Piskadlo, 48, North Arlington, New Jersey
Christopher Todd Pitman, 30, New York, New York
Josh Michael Piver, 23, New York, New York
Joseph Plumitallo, 45, Manalapan, New Jersey
John M. Pocher, 36, Middletown, New Jersey
William Howard Pohlmann, 56, Ardsley, New York
Laurence M. Polatsch, 32, New York, New York
Thomas H. Polhemus, 39, Morris Plains, New Jersey
Steve Pollicino, 48, Plainview, New York
Susan M. Pollio, 45, Long Beach Township, New Jersey
Joshua Poptean, 37, New York, New York
Giovanna Porras, 24, New York, New York
Anthony Portillo, 48, New York, New York
James Edward Potorti, 52, Princeton, New Jersey
Daphne Pouletsos, 47, Westwood, New Jersey
Richard Poulos, 55, Levittown, New York
Stephen E. Poulos, 45, Basking Ridge, New Jersey
Brandon Jerome Powell, 26, New York, New York
Shawn Edward Powell, 32, New York, New York
Tony Pratt, 43, New York, New York
Gregory M. Preziose, 34, Holmdel, New Jersey
Wanda Ivelisse Prince, 30, New York, New York
Vincent Princiotta, 39, Orangeburg, New York
Kevin Prior, 28, Bellmore, New York
Everett Martin (Marty) Proctor, 44, New York, New York
Carrie B. Progen, 25, New York, New York

David Lee Pruim, 53, Upper Montclair, New Jersey
Richard Prunty, 57, Sayville, New York
John F. Puckett, 47, Glen Cove, New York
Robert D. Pugliese, 47, East Fishkill, New York
Edward F. Pullis, 34, Hazlet, New Jersey
Patricia Ann Puma, 33, New York, New York
Hemanth Kumar Puttur, 26, White Plains, New York
Edward R. Pykon, 33, Princeton, New Jersey
Christopher Quackenbush, 44, Manhasset, New York
Lars Peter Qualben, 49, New York, New York
Lincoln Quappe, 38, Sayville, New York
Beth Ann Quigley, 25, New York, New York
Lt. Michael Quilty, 42, New York, New York
Ricardo Quinn, 40, New York, New York
James Francis Quinn, 23, New York, New York
Carol Rabalais, 38, New York, New York
Christopher Peter A. Racaniello, 30, New York, New York
Leonard Ragaglia, 36, New York, New York
Eugene J. Raggio, 55, New York, New York
Laura Marie Ragonese-Snik, 41, Bangor, Pennsylvania
Michael Ragusa, 29, New York, New York
Peter F. Raimondi, 46, New York, New York
Harry A. Raines, 37, New York, New York
Ehtesham U. Raja, 28, Clifton, New Jersey
Valsa Raju, 39, Yonkers, New York
Edward Rall, 44, Holbrook, New York
Lukas (Luke) Rambousek, 27, New York, New York
Julio Fernandez Ramirez, 51, New York, New York
Maria Isabel Ramirez, 25, New York, New York
Harry Ramos, 41, Newark, New Jersey
Vishnoo Ramsaroop, 44, New York, New York
Lorenzo Ramzey, 48, East Northport, New York
A. Todd Rancke, 42, Summit, New Jersey
Adam David Rand, 30, Bellmore, New York
Jonathan C. Randall, 42, New York, New York
Srinivasa Shreyas Ranganath, 26, Hackensack, New Jersey
Anne Rose T. Ransom, 45, Edgewater, New Jersey
Faina Rapoport, 45, New York, New York
Robert Arthur Rasmussen, 42, Hinsdale, Illinois
Amenia Rasool, 33, New York, New York
Roger Mark Rasweiler, 53, Flemington, New Jersey
David Alan James Rathkey, 47, Mountain Lakes, New Jersey
William Ralph Raub, 38, Saddle River, New Jersey
Gerard Rauzi, 42, New York, New York
Alexey Razuvaev, 40, New York, New York
Gregory Reda, 33, New Hyde Park, New York
Sarah Prothero Redheffer, 35, London, England
Michele Reed, 26, Ringoes, New York
Judith A. Reese, 56, Kearny, New Jersey
Donald J. Regan, 47, Wallkill, New York
Lt. Robert M. Regan, 48, Floral Park, New York
Thomas M. Regan, 43, Cranford, New Jersey
Christian Michael Otto Regenhard, 28, New York, New York
Howard Reich, 59, New York, New York
Gregg Reidy, 26, Holmdel, New Jersey
Kevin O. Reilly, 28, New York, New York
James Brian Reilly, 25, New York, New York
Timothy E. Reilly, 40, New York, New York
Joseph Reina, 32, New York, New York
Thomas Barnes Reinig, 48, Bernardsville, New Jersey
Frank B. Reisman, 41, Princeton, New Jersey
Joshua Scott Reiss, 23, New York, New York

Karen Renda, 52, New York, New York
John Armand Reo, 28, Larchmont, New York
Richard Rescorla, 62, Morristown, New Jersey
John Thomas Resta, 40, New York, New York
Sylvia San Pio Resta, 26, New York, New York
Eduvigis (Eddie) Reyes, 37, New York, New York
Bruce A. Reynolds, 41, Columbia, New Jersey
John Frederick Rhodes, 57, Howell, New Jersey
Francis S. Riccardelli, 40, Westwood, New Jersey
Rudolph N. Riccio, 50, New York, New York
AnnMarie (Davi) Riccoboni, 58, New York, New York
Eileen Mary Rice, 57, New York, New York
David Rice, 31, New York, New York
Kenneth F. Rice, 34, Hicksville, New York
Lt. Vernon Allan Richard, 53, Nanuet, New York
Claude D. Richards, 46, New York, New York
Gregory Richards, 30, New York, New York
Michael Richards, 38, New York, New York
Venesha O. Richards, 26, North Brunswick, New Jersey
James C. Riches, 29, New York, New York
Alan Jay Richman, 44, New York, New York
John M. Rigo, 48, New York, New York
Theresa (Ginger) Risco, 48, New York, New York
Rose Mary Riso, 55, New York, New York
Moises N. Rivas, 29, New York, New York
Joseph Rivelli, 43, New York, New York
Isaias Rivera, 51, Perth Amboy, New Jersey
Linda Rivera, 26, New York, New York
Juan William Rivera, 27, New York, New York
Carmen A. Rivera, 33, Westtown, New York
David E. Rivers, 40, New York, New York
Joseph R. Riverso, 34, White Plains, New York
Paul Rizza, 34, Park Ridge, New Jersey
John Frank Rizzo, 50, New York, New York
Stephen Louis Roach, 36, Verona, New Jersey
Joseph Roberto, 37, Midland Park, New Jersey
Leo A. Roberts, 44, Wayne, New Jersey
Michael Roberts, 30, New York, New York
Michael Edward Roberts, 31, New York, New York
Donald Walter Robertson, 35, Rumson, New Jersey
Catherina Robinson, 45, New York, New York
Jeffrey Robinson, 38, Monmouth Junction, New Jersey
Michell Lee Robotham, 32, Kearny, New Jersey
Donald Robson, 52, Manhasset, New York
Antonio Augusto Tome Rocha, 34, East Hanover, New Jersey
Raymond J. Rocha, 29, Malden, Massachusetts
Laura Rockefeller, 41, New York, New York
John M. Rodak, 39, Mantua, New Jersey
Antonio Jose Carrusca Rodrigues, 35, Port Washington, New York
Anthony Rodriguez, 36, New York, New York
Carmen Milagros Rodriguez, 46, Freehold, New Jersey
Marsha A. Rodriguez, 41, West Paterson, New Jersey
Richard Rodriguez, 31, Cliffwood, New Jersey
Gregory E. Rodriguez, 31, White Plains, New York
David B. Rodriguez-Vargas, 44, New York, New York
Matthew Rogan, 37, West Islip, New York
Karlie Barbara Rogers, 25, London, England
Scott Rohner, 22, Hoboken, New Jersey
Keith Roma, 27, New York, New York
Joseph M. Romagnolo, 37, Coram, New York
Elvin Santiago Romero, 34, Matawan, New Jersey
Efrain Franco Romero, 57, Hazleton, Pennsylvania

James A. Romito, 51, Westwood, New Jersey
Sean Rooney, 50, Stamford, Connecticut
Eric Thomas Ropiteau, 24, New York, New York
Aida Rosario, 42, Jersey City, New Jersey
Angela Rosario, 27, New York, New York
Fitzroy St. Rose, 40, New York, New York
Mark H. Rosen, 45, West Islip, New York
Linda Rosenbaum, 41, Little Falls, New Jersey
Brooke David Rosenbaum, 31, Franklin Square, New York
Sheryl Lynn Rosenbaum, 33, Warren, New Jersey
Lloyd D. Rosenberg, 31, Morganville, New Jersey
Mark Louis Rosenberg, 26, Teaneck, New Jersey
Andrew I. Rosenblum, 45, Rockville Centre, New York
Joshua M. Rosenblum, 28, Hoboken, New Jersey
Joshua A. Rosenthal, 44, New York, New York
Richard David Rosenthal, 50, Fair Lawn, New Jersey
Daniel Rossetti, 32, Bloomfield, New Jersey
Norman Rossinow, 39, Cedar Grove, New Jersey
Nicholas P. Rossomando, 35, New York, New York
Michael Craig Rothberg, 39, Greenwich, Connecticut
Donna Marie Rothenberg, 53, New York, New York
Nick Rowe, 29, Hoboken, New Jersey
Timothy A. Roy, 36, Massapequa Park, New York
Paul G. Ruback, 50, Newburgh, New York
Ronald J. Ruben, 36, Hoboken, New Jersey
Joanne Rubino, 45, New York, New York
David Michael Ruddle, 31, New York, New York
Bart Joseph Ruggiere, 32, New York, New York
Susan Ann Ruggiero, 30, Plainview, New York
Adam K. Ruhalter, 40, Plainview, New York
Gilbert Ruiz, 57, New York, New York
Stephen P. Russell, 40, Rockaway Beach, New York
Steven Harris Russin, 32, Mendham, New Jersey
Lt. Michael Thomas Russo, 44, Nesconset, New York
Wayne Alan Russo, 37, Union, New Jersey
John J. Ryan, 45, West Windsor, New Jersey
Edward Ryan, 42, Scarsdale, New York
Jonathan Stephan Ryan, 32, Bayville, New York
Matthew Lancelot Ryan, 54, Seaford, New York
Kristin A. Irvine Ryan, 30, New York, New York
Tatiana Ryjova, 36, South Salem, New York
Christina Sunga Ryook, 25, New York, New York
Thierry Saada, 27, New York, New York
Jason E. Sabbag, 26, New York, New York
Thomas E. Sabella, 44, New York, New York
Scott Saber, 36, New York, New York
Joseph Sacerdote, 48, Freehold, New Jersey
Mohammad Ali Sadeque, 62, New York, New York
Francis J. Sadocha, 41, Huntington, New York
Jude Elias Safi, 24, New York, New York
Brock Joel Safronoff, 26, New York, New York
Edward Saiya, 49, New York, New York
John Patrick Salamone, 37, North Caldwell, New Jersey
Hernando R. Salas, 71, New York, New York
Juan Salas, 35, New York, New York
Esmerlin Salcedo, 36, New York, New York
John Salvatore Salerno, 31, Westfield, New Jersey
Richard L. Salinardi, 32, Hoboken, New Jersey
Wayne John Saloman, 43, Seaford, New York
Nolbert Salomon, 33, New York, New York
Catherine Patricia Salter, 37, New York, New York
Frank Salvaterra, 41, Manhasset, New York

Paul R. Salvio, 27, New York, New York
Samuel R. Salvo, 59, Yonkers, New York
Carlos Samaniego, 29, New York, New York
Rena Sam-Dinnoo, 28, New York, New York
James Kenneth Samuel, 29, Hoboken, New Jersey
Hugo Sanay-Perafiel, 41, New York, New York
Alva Jeffries Sanchez, 41, Hempstead, New York
Jacquelyn P. Sanchez, 23, New York, New York
Erick Sanchez, 43, New York, New York
Eric Sand, 36, Westchester, New York
Stacey Leigh Sanders, 25, New York, New York
Herman Sandler, 57, New York, New York
James Sands, 39, Bricktown, New Jersey
Ayleen J. Santiago, 40, New York, New York
Kirsten Santiago, 26, New York, New York
Maria Theresa Santillan, 27, Morris Plains, New Jersey
Susan G. Santo, 24, New York, New York
Christopher Santora, 23, New York, New York
John Santore, 49, New York, New York
Mario L. Santoro, 28, New York, New York
Rafael Humberto Santos, 42, New York, New York
Rufino Conrado F. (Roy) Santos, 37, New York, New York
Kalyan K. Sarkar, 53, Westwood, New Jersey
Chapelle Sarker, 37, New York, New York
Paul F. Sarle, 38, Babylon, New York
Deepika Kumar Sattaluri, 33, Edison, New Jersey
Gregory Thomas Saucedo, 31, New York, New York
Susan Sauer, 48, Chicago, Illinois
Anthony Savas, 72, New York, New York
Vladimir Savinkin, 21, New York, New York
John Sbarbaro, 45, New York, New York
Robert L. Scandole, 36, Pelham Manor, New York
Michelle Scarpitta, 26, New York, New York
Dennis Scauso, 46, Dix Hills, New York
John A. Schardt, 34, New York, New York
John G. Scharf, 29, Manorville, New York
Fred Claude Scheffold, 57, Piermont, New York
Angela Susan Scheinberg, 46, New York, New York
Scott M. Schertzer, 28, Edison, New Jersey
Sean Schielke, 27, New York, New York
Steven Francis Schlag, 41, Franklin Lakes, New Jersey
Jon S. Schlissel, 51, Jersey City, New Jersey
Karen Helene Schmidt, 42, Bellmore, New York
Ian Schneider, 45, Short Hills, New Jersey
Thomas G. Schoales, 27, Stony Point, New York
Marisa Di Nardo Schorpp, 38, White Plains, New York
Frank G. Schott, 39, Massapequa Park, New York
Gerard P. Schrang, 45, Holbrook, New York
Jeffrey Schreier, 48, New York, New York
John T. Schroeder, 31, Hoboken, New Jersey
Susan Lee Kennedy Schuler, 55, Allentown, New Jersey
Edward W. Schunk, 54, Baldwin, New York
Mark E. Schurmeier, 44, McLean, Virginia
Clarin Shellie Schwartz, 51, New York, New York
John Schwartz, 49, Goshen, Connecticut
Mark Schwartz, 50, West Hempstead, New York
Adriane Victoria Scibetta, 31, New York, New York
Raphael Scorca, 61, Beachwood, New Jersey
Randolph Scott, 48, Stamford, Connecticut
Christopher J. Scudder, 34, Monsey, New York
Arthur Warren Scullin, 57, New York, New York
Michael Seaman, 41, Manhasset, New York

Margaret Seeliger, 34, New York, New York
Carlos Segarra, 54, New York, New York
Anthony Segarra, 52, New York, New York
Jason Sekzer, 31, New York, New York
Matthew Carmen Sellitto, 23, Morristown, New Jersey
Howard Selwyn, 47, Hewlett, New York
Larry John Senko, 34, Yardley, Pennsylvania
Arturo Angelo Sereno, 29, New York, New York
Frankie Serrano, 23, Elizabeth, New Jersey
Alena Sesinova, 57, New York, New York
Adele Sessa, 36, New York, New York
Sita Nermalla Sewnarine, 37, New York, New York
Karen Lynn Seymour-Dietrich, 40, Millington, New Jersey
Davis (Deeg) Sezna, 22, New York, New York
Thomas Joseph Sgroi, 45, New York, New York
Jayesh Shah, 38, Edgewater, New Jersey
Khalid M. Shahid, 25, Union, New Jersey
Mohammed Shajahan, 41, Spring Valley, New York
Gary Shamay, 23, New York, New York
Earl Richard Shanahan, 50, New York, New York
Shiv Shankar, New York, New York
Neil G. Shastri, 25, New York, New York
Kathryn Anne Shatzoff, 37, New York, New York
Barbara A. Shaw, 57, Morris Township, New Jersey
Jeffrey J. Shaw, 42, Levittown, New York
Robert J. Shay, 27, New York, New York
Daniel James Shea, 37, Pelham Manor, New York
Joseph Patrick Shea, 47, Pelham, New York
Linda Sheehan, 40, New York, New York
Hagay Shefi, 34, Tenafly, New Jersey
John Anthony Sherry, 34, Rockville Centre, New York
Atsushi Shiratori, 36, New York, New York
Thomas Shubert, 43, New York, New York
Mark Shulman, 47, Old Bridge, New Jersey
See-Wong Shum, 44, Westfield, New Jersey
Allan Shwartzstein, 37, Chappaqua, New York
Johanna Sigmund, 25, Wyndmoor, Pennsylvania
Dianne T. Signer, 32, New York, New York
Gregory Sikorsky, 34, Spring Valley, New York
Stephen Gerard Siller, 34, West Brighton, New York
David Silver, 35, New Rochelle, New York
Craig A. Silverstein, 41, Wyckoff, New Jersey
Nasima H. Simjee, 38, New York, New York
Bruce Edward Simmons, 41, Ridgewood, New Jersey
Arthur Simon, 57, Thiells, New York
Kenneth Alan Simon, 34, Secaucus, New Jersey
Michael John Simon, 40, Harrington Park, New Jersey
Paul Joseph Simon, 54, New York, New York
Marianne Simone, 62, New York, New York
Barry Simowitz, 64, New York, New York
Jeff Simpson, 38, Lake Ridge, Virginia
Roshan R. (Sean) Singh, 21, New York, New York
Khamladai K. (Khami) Singh, 25, New York, New York
Thomas E. Sinton, 44, Croton-on-hudson, New York
Peter A. Siracuse, 29, New York, New York
Muriel F. Siskopoulos, 60, New York, New York
Joseph M. Sisolak, 35, New York, New York
John P. Skala, 31, Clifton, New Jersey
Francis J. Skidmore, 58, Mendham, New Jersey
Toyena Corliss Skinner, 27, Kingston, New Jersey
Paul A. Skrzypek, 37, New York, New York
Christopher Paul Slattery, 31, New York, New York

Vincent R. Slavin, 41, Belle Harbor, New York
Robert Sliwak, 42, Wantagh, New York
Paul K. Sloan, 26, New York, New York
Stanley S. Smagala, 36, Holbrook, New York
Wendy L. Small, 26, New York, New York
Catherine T. Smith, 44, West Haverstraw, New York
Daniel Laurence Smith, 47, Northport, New York
George Eric Smith, 38, West Chester, Pennsylvania
James G. Smith, 43, Garden City, New York
Joyce Smith, 55, New York, New York
Karl Trumbull Smith, 44, Little Silver, New Jersey
Kevin Smith, 47, Mastic, New York
Leon Smith, 48, New York, New York
Moira Smith, 38, New York, New York
Rosemary A. Smith, 61, New York, New York
Sandra Fajardo Smith, 37, New York, New York
Jeffrey Randall Smith, 36, New York, New York
Bonnie S. Smithwick, 54, Quogue, New York
Rochelle Monique Snell, 24, Mount Vernon, New York
Leonard J. Snyder, 35, Cranford, New Jersey
Astrid Elizabeth Sohan, 32, Freehold, New Jersey
Sushil Solanki, 35, New York, New York
Ruben Solares, 51, New York, New York
Naomi Leah Solomon, 52, New York, New York
Daniel W. Song, 34, New York, New York
Michael C. Sorresse, 34, Morris Plains, New Jersey
Fabian Soto, 31, Harrison, New Jersey
Timothy P. Soulas, 35, Basking Ridge, New Jersey
Gregory T. Spagnoletti, 32, New York, New York
Donald F. Spampinato, 39, Manhasset, New York
Thomas Sparacio, 35, New York, New York
John Anthony Spataro, 32, Mineola, New York
Robert W. Spear, 30, Valley Cottage, New York
Maynard S. Spence, 42, Douglasville, Georgia
George E. Spencer, 50, West Norwalk, Connecticut
Robert Andrew Spencer, 35, Red Bank, New Jersey
Mary Rubina Sperando, 39, New York, New York
Frank J. Spinelli, 44, Short Hills, New Jersey
William E. Spitz, 49, Oceanside, New York
Joseph P. Spor, 35, Yorktown Heights, New York
Klaus Johannes Sprockamp, 42, Muhltal, Germany
Saranya Srinuan, 23, New York, New York
Michael F. Stabile, 50, New York, New York
Lawrence T. Stack, 58, Lake Ronkonkoma, New York
Capt. Timothy Stackpole, 42, New York, New York
Richard James Stadelberger, 55, Middletown, New Jersey
Eric A. Stahlman, 43, Holmdel Township, New Jersey
Gregory M. Stajk, 46, Long Beach, New York
Corina Stan, 31, Middle Village, New York
Alexandru Liviu Stan, 34, New York, New York
Mary D. Stanley, 53, New York, New York
Joyce Stanton
Patricia Stanton
Anthony M. Starita, 35, Westfield, New Jersey
Jeffrey Stark, 30, New York, New York
Derek James Statkevicus, 30, Norwalk, Connecticut
Craig William Staub, 30, Basking Ridge, New Jersey
William V. Steckman, 56, West Hempstead, New York
Eric Thomas Steen, 32, New York, New York
William R. Steiner, 56, New Hope, Pennsylvania
Alexander Robbins Steinman, 32, Hoboken, New Jersey
Andrew Stergiopoulos, 23, New York, New York

Andrew Stern, 41, Bellmore, New York
Martha Jane Stevens, 55, New York, New York
Richard H. Stewart, 35, New York, New York
Michael James Stewart, 42, New York, New York
Sanford M. Stoller, 54, New York, New York
Lonny J. Stone, 43, Bellmore, New York
Jimmy Nevill Storey, 58, Katy, Texas
Timothy Stout, 42, Dobbs Ferry, New York
Thomas S. Strada, 41, Chatham, New Jersey
James J. Straine, 36, Oceanport, New Jersey
Edward W. Straub, 48, Morris Township, New Jersey
George Strauch, 53, Avon-by-the-Sea, New Jersey
Edward T. Strauss, 44, Edison, New Jersey
Steven R. Strauss, 51, Fresh Meadows, New York
Steven F. Strobert, 33, Ridgewood, New Jersey
Walwyn W. Stuart, 28, Valley Stream, New York
Benjamin Suarez, 36, New York, New York
David S. Suarez, 24, Princeton, New Jersey
Ramon Suarez, 45, New York, New York
Yoichi Sugiyama, 34, Fort Lee, New Jersey
William Christopher Sugra, 30, New York, New York
Daniel Suhr, 37, Nesconset, New York
David Marc Sullins, 30, New York, New York
Lt. Christopher P. Sullivan, 38, Massapequa, New York
Patrick Sullivan, 32, New York, New York
Thomas Sullivan, 38, Kearney, New Jersey
Hilario Soriano (Larry) Sumaya, 42, New York, New York
James Joseph Suozzo, 47, Hauppauge, New York
Colleen Supinski, 27, New York, New York
Robert Sutcliffe, 39, Huntington, New York
Selina Sutter, 63, New York, New York
Claudia Suzette Sutton, 34, New York, New York
John F. Swaine, 36, Larchmont, New York
Kristine M. Swearson, 34, New York, New York
Brian Edward Sweeney, 29, Merrick, New York
Kenneth J. Swensen, 40, Chatham, New Jersey
Thomas F. Swift, 30, Jersey City, New Jersey
Derek O. Sword, 29, New York, New York
Kevin T. Szocik, 27, Garden City, New York
Gina Sztejnberg, 52, Ridgewood, New Jersey
Norbert P. Szurkowski, 31, New York, New York
Harry Taback, 56, New York, New York
Joann Tabeek, 41, New York, New York
Norma C. Taddei, 64, New York, New York
Michael Taddonio, 39, Huntington, New York
Keiji Takahashi, 42, Tenafly, New Jersey
Keiichiro Takahashi, 53, Port Washington, New York
Phyllis Gail Talbot, 53, New York, New York
Robert R. Talhami, 40, Shrewsbury, New Jersey
Sean Patrick Tallon, 26, Yonkers, New York
Paul Talty, 40, Wantagh, New York
Maurita Tam, 22, New York, New York
Rachel Tamares, 30, New York, New York
Hector Tamayo, 51, New York, New York
Michael Andrew Tamuccio, 37, Pelham Manor, New York
Kenichiro Tanaka, 52, Rye Brook, New York
Rhondelle Cherie Tankard, 31, Devonshire, Bermuda
Michael Anthony Tanner, 44, Secaucus, New Jersey
Dennis Gerard Taormina, 36, Montville, New Jersey
Kenneth Joseph Tarantino, 39, Bayonne, New Jersey
Allan Tarasiewicz, 45, New York, New York
Ronald Tartaro, 39, Bridgewater, New Jersey

Darryl Taylor, 52, New York, New York
Donnie Brooks Taylor, 40, New York, New York
Lorisa Ceylon Taylor, 31, New York, New York
Michael M. Taylor, 42, New York, New York
Paul A. Tegtmeier, 41, Hyde Park, New York
Yeshavant Moreshwar Tembe, 59, Piscataway, New Jersey
Anthony Tempesta, 38, Elizabeth, New Jersey
Dorothy Temple, 52, New York, New York
Stanley L. Temple, 77, New York, New York
David Tengelin, 25, New York, New York
Brian J. Terrenzi, 29, Hicksville, New York
Lisa Marie Terry, 42, Rochester, Michigan
Goumatie T. Thackurdeen, 35, New York, New York
Harshad Sham Thatte, 30, Norcross, Georgia
Thomas F. Theurkauf, 44, Stamford, Connecticut
Lesley Anne Thomas, 40, Hoboken, New Jersey
Brian T. Thompson, 49, Dix Hills, New York
Clive Thompson, 43, Summit, New Jersey
Glenn Thompson, 44, New York, New York
Perry Anthony Thompson, 36, Mount Laurel, New Jersey
Vanavah Alexi Thompson, 26, New York, New York
Capt. William Harry Thompson, 51, New York, New York
Nigel Bruce Thompson, 33, New York, New York
Eric Raymond Thorpe, 35, New York, New York
Nichola A. Thorpe, 22, New York, New York
Sal Tieri, 40, Shrewsbury, New Jersey
John Patrick Tierney, 27, New York, New York
Mary Ellen Tiesi, 38, Jersey City, New Jersey
William R. Tieste, 54, Basking Ridge, New Jersey
Kenneth F. Tietjen, 31, Matawan, New Jersey
Stephen Edward Tighe, 41, Rockville Centre, New York
Scott C. Timmes, 28, Ridgewood, New York
Michael E. Tinley, 56, Dallas, Texas
Jennifer M. Tino, 29, Livingston, New Jersey
Robert Frank Tipaldi, 25, New York, New York
John J. Tipping, 33, Port Jefferson, New York
David Tirado, 26, New York, New York
Hector Luis Tirado, 30, New York, New York
Michelle Titolo, 34, Copiague, New York
John J. Tobin, 47, Kenilworth, New Jersey
Richard J. Todisco, 61, Wyckoff, New Jersey
Vladimir Tomasevic, 36, Etobicoke, Ontario, Canada
Stephen K. Tompsett, 39, Garden City, New York
Thomas Tong, 31, New York, New York
Azucena de la Torre, 50, New York, New York
Doris Torres, 32, New York, New York
Luis Eduardo Torres, 31, New York, New York
Amy E. Toyen, 24, Newton, Massachusetts
Christopher M. Traina, 25, Bricktown, New Jersey
Daniel Patrick Trant, 40, Northport, New York
Abdoul Karim Traore, 41, New York, New York
Glenn J. Travers, 53, Tenafly, New Jersey
Walter (Wally) P. Travers, 44, Upper Saddle River, New Jersey
Felicia Traylor-Bass, 38, New York, New York
Lisa L. Trerotola, 38, Hazlet, New Jersey
Karamo Trerra, 40, New York, New York
Michael Trinidad, 33, New York, New York
Francis Joseph Trombino, 68, Clifton, New Jersey
Gregory J. Trost, 26, New York, New York
William Tselepis, 33, New Providence, New Jersey
Zhanetta Tsoy, 32, Jersey City, New Jersey
Michael Patrick Tucker, 40, Rumson, New Jersey

Lance Richard Tumulty, 32, Bridgewater, New Jersey
Ching Ping Tung, 44, New York, New York
Simon James Turner, 39, London, England
Donald Joseph Tuzio, 51, Goshen, New York
Robert T. Twomey, 48, New York, New York
Jennifer Tzemis, 26, New York, New York
John G. Ueltzhoeffer, 36, Roselle Park, New Jersey
Tyler V. Ugolyn, 23, New York, New York
Michael A. Uliano, 42, Aberdeen, New Jersey
Jonathan J. Uman, 33, Westport, Connecticut
Anil Shivhari Umarkar, 34, Hackensack, New Jersey
Allen V. Upton, 44, New York, New York
Diane Maria Urban, 50, Malverne, New York
John Damien Vaccacio, 30, New York, New York
Bradley H. Vadas, 37, Westport, Connecticut
William Valcarcel, 54, New York, New York
Mayra Valdes-Rodriguez, 39, New York, New York
Felix Antonio Vale, 29, New York, New York
Ivan Vale, 27, New York, New York
Santos Valentin, 39, New York, New York
Benito Valentin, 33, New York, New York
Manuel Del Valle, 32, New York, New York
Carlton Francis Valvo, 38, New York, New York
Edward Raymond Vanacore, 29, Jersey City, New Jersey
Jon C. Vandevander, 44, Ridgewood, New Jersey
Frederick T. Varacchi, 35, Greenwich, Connecticut
Gopalakrishnan Varadhan, 32, New York, New York
David Vargas, 46, New York, New York
Scott C. Vasel, 32, Park Ridge, New Jersey
Santos Vasquez, 55, New York, New York
Azael Ismael Vasquez, 21, New York, New York
Arcangel Vazquez, 47, New York, New York
Peter Anthony Vega, 36, New York, New York
Sankara S. Velamuri, 63, Avenel, New Jersey
Jorge Velazquez, 47, Passaic, New Jersey
Lawrence Veling, 44, New York, New York
Anthony M. Ventura, 41, Middletown, New Jersey
David Vera, 41, New York, New York
Loretta A, Vero, 51, Nanuet, New York
Christopher Vialonga, 30, Demarest, New Jersey
Matthew Gilbert Vianna, 23, Manhasset, New York
Robert A. Vicario, 40, Weehawken, New Jersey
Celeste Torres Victoria, 41, New York, New York
Joanna Vidal, 26, Yonkers, New York
John T. Vigiano, 36, West Islip, New York
Joseph Vincent Vigiano, 34, Medford, New York
Frank J. Vignola, 44, Merrick, New York
Joseph B. Vilardo, 44, Stanhope, New Jersey
Sergio Villanueva, 33, New York, New York
Chantal Vincelli, 38, New York, New York
Melissa Vincent, 28, Hoboken, New Jersey
Francine A. Virgilio, 48, New York, New York
Lawrence Virgilio, 38
Joseph G. Visciano, 22, New York, New York
Joshua S. Vitale, 28, Great Neck, New York
Maria Percoco Vola, 37, New York, New York
Lynette D. Vosges, 48, New York, New York
Garo H. Voskerijian, 43, Valley Stream, New York
Alfred Vukosa, 37, New York, New York
Gregory Wachtler, 25, Ramsey, New Jersey
Gabriela Waisman, 33, New York, New York
Wendy Alice Rosario Wakeford, 40, Freehold, New Jersey

Courtney Wainsworth Walcott, 37, New York, New York
Victor Wald, 49, New York, New York
Benjamin Walker, 41, Suffern, New York
Glen J. Wall, 38, Rumson, New Jersey
Mitchel Scott Wallace, 34, Mineola, New York
Lt. Robert F. Wallace, 43, New York, New York
Roy Michael Wallace, 42, Wyckoff, New Jersey
Peter G. Wallace, 66, Lincoln Park, New Jersey
Jean Marie Wallendorf, 23, New York, New York
Matthew Blake Wallens, 31, New York, New York
John Wallice, 43, Huntington, New York
Barbara P. Walsh, 59, New York, New York
James Walsh, 37, Scotch Plains, New Jersey
Jeffrey Patrick Walz, 37, Tuckahoe, New York
Ching H. Wang, 59, New York, New York
Weibin Wang, 41, Orangeburg, New York
Lt. Michael Warchola, 51, Middle Village, New York
Stephen Gordon Ward, 33, Gorham, Maine
James A. Waring, 49, New York, New York
Brian G. Warner, 32, Morganville, New Jersey
Derrick Washington, 33, Calverton, New York
Charles Waters, 44, New York, New York
James Thomas (Muddy) Waters, 39, New York, New York
Capt. Patrick J. Waters, 44, New York, New York
Kenneth Watson, 39, Smithtown, New York
Michael H. Waye, 38, Morganville, New Jersey
Walter E. Weaver, 30, Centereach, New York
Todd C. Weaver, 30, New York, New York
Nathaniel Webb, 56, Jersey City, New Jersey
Dinah Webster, 50, Port Washington, New York
Joanne Flora Weil, 39, New York, New York
Michael Weinberg, 34, New York, New York
Steven Weinberg, 41, New City, New York
Scott Jeffrey Weingard, 29, New York, New York
Steven Weinstein, 50, New York, New York
Simon Weiser, 65, New York, New York
David T. Weiss, 50, New York, New York
David M. Weiss, 41, Maybrook, New York
Vincent Michael Wells, 22, Redbridge, England
Timothy Matthew Welty, 34, Yonkers, New York
Christian Hans Rudolf Wemmers, 43, San Francisco, California
Ssu-Hui (Vanessa) Wen, 23, New York, New York
Oleh D. Wengerchuk, 56, Centerport, New York
Peter M. West, 54, Pottersville, New Jersey
Whitfield West, 41, New York, New York
Meredith Lynn Whalen, 23, Hoboken, New Jersey
Eugene Whelan, 31, Rockaway Beach, New York
John S. White, 48, New York, New York
Edward James White, 30, New York, New York
James Patrick White, 34, Hoboken, New Jersey
Kenneth W. White, 50, New York, New York
Leonard Anthony White, 57, New York, New York
Malissa White, 37, New York, New York
Wayne White, 38, New York, New York
Adam S. White, 26, New York, New York
Leanne Marie Whiteside, 31, New York, New York
Mark Whitford, 31, Salisbury Mills, New York
Michael T. Wholey, 34, Westwood, New Jersey
Mary Lenz Wieman, 43, Rockville Centre, New York
Jeffrey David Wiener, 33, New York, New York
William J. Wik, 44, Crestwood, New York
Alison Marie Wildman, 30, New York, New York

Lt. Glenn Wilkinson, 46, Bayport, New York
John C. Willett, 29, Jersey City, New Jersey
Brian Patrick Williams, 29, New York, New York
Crossley Williams, 28, Uniondale, New York
David Williams, 34, New York, New York
Deborah Lynn Williams, 35, Hoboken, New Jersey
Kevin Michael Williams, 24, New York, New York
Louis Calvin Williams, 53, Mandeville, Louisiana
Louie Anthony Williams, 44, New York, New York
Lt. John Williamson, 46, Warwick, New York
Donna Wilson, 48, Williston Park, New York
William E. Wilson, 58, New York, New York
Cynthia Wilson, 52, New York, New York
David H. Winton, 29, New York, New York
Glenn J. Winuk, 40, New York, New York
Thomas Francis Wise, 43, New York, New York
Alan L. Wisniewski, 47, Howell, New Jersey
Frank T. Wisniewski, 54, Basking Ridge, New Jersey
David Wiswall, 54, North Massapequa, New York
Sigrid Charlotte Wiswe, 41, New York, New York
Michael R. Wittenstein, 34, Hoboken, New Jersey
Christopher W. Wodenshek, 35, Ridgewood, New Jersey
Martin P. Wohlforth, 47, Greenwich, Connecticut
Katherine S. Wolf, 40, New York, New York
Jenny Seu Kueng Low Wong, 25, New York, New York
Jennifer Y. Wong, 26, New York, New York
Siu Cheung Wong, 34, Jersey City, New Jersey
Yin Ping (Steven) Wong, 34, New York, New York
Yuk Ping Wong, 47, New York, New York
Brent James Woodall, 31, Oradell, New Jersey
James J. Woods, 26, New York, New York
Patrick Woods, 36, New York, New York
Richard Herron Woodwell, 44, Ho-Ho-Kus, New Jersey
Capt. David Terence Wooley, 54, Nanuet, New York
John Bentley Works, 36, Darien, Connecticut
Martin Michael Wortley, 29, Park Ridge, New Jersey
Rodney James Wotton, 36, Middletown, New Jersey
William Wren, 61, Lynbrook, New York

John Wright, 33, Rockville Centre, New York
Neil R. Wright, 30, Asbury, New Jersey
Sandra Wright, 57, Langhorne, Pennsylvania
Jupiter Yambem, 41, Beacon, New York
Suresh Yanamadala, 33, Plainsboro, New Jersey
Matthew David Yarnell, 26, Jersey City, New Jersey
Myrna Yaskulka, 59, New York, New York
Shakila Yasmin, 26, New York, New York
Olabisi L. Yee, 38, New York, New York
Edward P. York, 45, Wilton, Connecticut
Kevin Patrick York, 41, Princeton, New Jersey
Raymond York, 45, Valley Stream, New York
Suzanne Youmans, 60, New York, New York
Jacqueline (Jakki) Young, 37, New York, New York
Barrington L. Young, 35, New York, New York
Elkin Yuen, 32, New York, New York
Joseph Zaccoli, 39, Valley Stream, New York
Adel Agayby Zakhary, 50, North Arlington, New Jersey
Arkady Zaltsman, 45, New York, New York
Edwin J. Zambrana, 24, New York, New York
Robert Alan Zampieri, 30, Saddle River, New Jersey
Mark Zangrilli, 36, Pompton Plains, New Jersey
Ira Zaslow, 55, North Woodmere, New York
Kenneth Albert Zelman, 37, Succasunna, New Jersey
Abraham J. Zelmanowitz, 55, New York, New York
Martin Morales Zempoaltecatl, 22, New York, New York
Zhe (Zack) Zeng, 28, New York, New York
Marc Scott Zeplin, 33, Harrison, New York
Jie Yao Justin Zhao, 27, New York, New York
Ivelin Ziminski, 40, Tarrytown, New York
Michael Joseph Zinzi, 37, Newfoundland, New Jersey
Charles A. Zion, 54, Greenwich, Connecticut
Julie Lynne Zipper, 44, Paramus, New Jersey
Salvatore J. Zisa, 45, Hawthorne, New Jersey
Prokopios Paul Zois, 46, Lynbrook, New York
Joseph J. Zuccala, 54, Croton-on-Hudson, New York
Andrew Steven Zucker, 27, New York, New York
Igor Zukelman, 29, New York, New York

INDEX

A

defining victory and success of, 213, 214
strategy and tactics of, 31, 213–216
U.S. declaration of, ix, 213–216
Washington, D.C.,
coordinated emergency protocol of, 216–220
emergency response to terrorist attack on Pentagon, 216–220
Incident Command System of, 220
memorials and vigils held in, 127
as terrorist target, 10
Washington, Rudy, 81
Washington Metropolitan Transit Authority, 219
Washington National Cathedral, 127, 219
Washington Post, 80, 205
Weapons of mass destruction (WMD), ix, 99
Welsh, Debbie, 193
Westin, David, 202
What Went Wrong? (Lewis), 116
Whistleblowers, 164
White House,
President Bush's return after 9/11 attacks, 5, 31, 218
Presidential Emergency Operating Center in, 39
Situation Room at, 216
Whitman, Christine Todd, 45, 87
Whitmore, Mena, 151
Whittington, Leslie A., 16
Why Terrorism Works (Dershowitz), 117
Wild Blue, 156
Wilders, Geert, 180
Wilkinson, Paul, 183
Williams, Candace Lee, 13
Williams, Rowan, 118
Windows of Hope Family Relief Fund, 53
Windows on the World, 53, 126, 220–222, 223, 224
Windows on the World (Beigbeder), 117
Wolfowitz, Paul, 99
Woods, James, 172
Woodward, Michael, 14, 36
World Islamic Front for Jihad against Jews and Crusaders, 9
World Markets Research Center, 51
World Trade Center (2006), 70
"World Trade Center Cough," 85
World Trade Center Foundation, 129
World Trade Center Stabile (Calder), 156
World Trade Center (WTC),
aesthetic appeal of, 224
alternate theories on destruction of, 41
"Bathtub" under, 54
calls made from during September 11 attacks, 34
casualties on September 11, 36, 238–259
as center for global trade, 223–224

data storage methods after 1993 attack, 34
design and construction of, 52, 54, 129, 223
digitally eliminated in movies after 9/11, 69
evacuation and exit areas of, 75
FDNY casualties on September 11, 35, 53, 57–60, 70, 71–72, 74, 75
fire code requirements of, 75
lack of "triangles of life" within, 35
memorial and rebuilding plans for, 67–68, 129–130, 223–227
1993 terrorist bombing of, 9, 10, 34, 55, 60, 74, 75, 94, 142, 222
NYPD casualties on September 11, 36, 53, 58–60, 144–145
police force of, 156–157
recovery of remains in debris, of, 38–39, 60, 87
as symbol, x, 10
as terrorist target, 1–2, 223, 224
Tribute in Light memorial of, 127, 128
Twin Towers of, 223–224, 227–229
victims jumping from, 37, 139, 202
See also North Tower; Seven World Trade Center; South Tower
World War II, American involvement in, x
Wright, David, 138
Writing in the Dust: After September 11 (Williams), 118
WTC: The First 24 Hours (2002), 69
WTC Health Registers, 87
WTC Uncut (2002), 69

Y

Yamasaki, Minoru, 223, 227, 228, 229
Yamnicky, John D., Sr., 16
Yasmin (2004), 69
Yemen,
Coast Guard of, 3
terrorist activities in, 2, 231–232
U.S. bases in, 2
Yemen Islamic Jihad, 232–233
Yesterday and Today (2002), 69
Your Father's Voice: Letters for Emmy about Life with Jeremy—And without him after 9/11 (Glick), 83
Yousef, Ramzi Ahmed, 10, 111, 222, 233

Z

Zadroga, James, 86
Zaitsved, Alex, 139
Zakat, 11
Zammar, Mohammad Aydar, 79
Zamora, Fernando, 68
Zapatero, Jose Luis Rodriguez, 121, 181
Zelman, Barry, 41
Zemin, Jiang, 97
Zinni, Anthony, 56–57
Zogby International, 41